JUMP INTO HELL

JUMP INTO HELL

German Paratroopers in World War II

Franz Kurowski

STACKPOLE
BOOKS

English translation © 2010 by Battle Born Books and Consulting

Published in 2010 by
STACKPOLE BOOKS
5067 Ritter Road
Mechanicsburg, PA 17055
www.stackpolebooks.com

Printed in the United States of America

10 9 8 7 6 5 4 3 2 1

Library of Congress Cataloging-in-Publication Data

Kurowski, Franz.
[Deutsche Fallschirm-Jäger, 1939–1945 English.]
Jump into hell : German paratroopers in World War II / Franz Kurowski.
    p. cm.
Includes bibliographical references and index.
  ISBN 978-0-8117-0582-0
1. Germany. Heer—Parachute troops—History—20th century. 2. World War, 1939–1945—Aerial operations, German. I. Title.
D757.63.K87513 2010
940.54'1343—dc22
2009028377

Contents

CHAPTER 1

From Paratroopers to Airborne Forces, the Buildup

When the former commander of the American Air Corps in France during the First World War, Major General William "Billy" Mitchell, published his memoirs in 1930, attentive readers were captivated by one of his chapters. They read about the planning for an offensive from the air against Ypres. Major General Mitchell had proposed the parachuting of the U.S. 1st Infantry Division when the Allies failed to break through the German front at Menin-Roselare.

It was intended to parachute the infantry behind the front. This first airborne force was to be supplied with ammunition, machine-guns and rations from the air by means of giant cargo chutes. All of the aircraft of the Allies—some 2,000 machines—were to support the offensive from the air by bombing and strafing the German front.

Major General Mitchell was firmly convinced that such an attack, which had never before been attempted, would force the breakthrough at Roselare and cause the German front to collapse. But the operation was postponed to February 1919. Thus, the end of the war thwarted the first operation from the "third dimension."

Many declared the general—even twelve years after the war had ended—as crazy. That wasn't the case in the Soviet Union, however. There, the first airborne formations were activated as early as 1928. The Commander-in-Chief of the Red Army at the time, Marshall Tuchatschewskij, was a strong proponent of the new concept. In the process, he was also strongly supported by the Minister of Defense, Woroschilow.

During the maneuvers of 1931, the Soviets attempted the first jump of a group of paratroopers in the area around Woronesch. The group consisted of a lieutenant and six men. They jumped with a heavy machine-gun from an Antonov 14, which had transported them to their jump zone. The group pressed forward to a corps command post and took it prisoner.

At the time, the interwar German military, the *Reichswehr*, was also acquainted with the idea of using paratroopers as an attack force, but it never went beyond the theoretical stage.

The Soviet maneuvers were followed a year later by the first actual operation, when the Soviet military needed to overpower a group of bandits from Basmach, who had heretofore been able to escape capture by the military. A platoon of paratroopers jumped in with a few machine-guns and blocked the area behind the bandits. Once the escape route had been sealed, the ground forces were able to advance and eliminate them.

The Ossawiachim—a club for those interested in aviation and related matters—established parachuting clubs in all of the larger cities of the Soviet Union. All different parachute types throughout the world were brought in and tested. The best of the designs were then copied—without permission, of course.

In the winter of 1931, Marshall Tuchatschewskij ordered that all aviators were to be trained to parachute. The idea of air-transporting forces for landing them in the rear of the enemy seemed to have caught hold in the Soviet Union. That thought was conveyed in France in 1932 when the Soviet air general Schtscherbakow visited. He was guided through the Maginot Line, where Marshall Pètain, full of pride, told him that it was impregnable.

The Soviet general replied: "These facilities and fortresses will be completely superfluous in the future. When an enemy takes to heart the recommendations of General Mitchell, he can simply jump past them. Parachute divisions will land to the rear of these gigantic fortifications and cut them off from their lines of communication."

Marshall Pètain was taken aback momentarily, but he then regained his composure and smiled: "That, my dear general, most assuredly will never happen."

Despite that assurance, the aged French Marshall soon issued a directive that air defenses were to be constructed in the vicinity of the Maginot Line and heavy antiaircraft batteries to be positioned near all fortress facilities.

The training for airborne warfare continued in Moscow. In the Aero-Hydrodynamic Central Institute, aircraft and power plants purchased abroad were taken apart and reverse engineered. By 1932, some 1,500 airframes had been constructed. By 1937, the Soviet Commander-in-Chief wanted to have 8,000 aircraft on hand. In order to man those aircraft, the military branch of the Ossawiachim had all of its members—both male and female—trained as pilots, observers, radio operators and parachutists. The Air Academy and the Training Institute for Navigation—in all, a total of 20 aviation preparatory schools and 32 schools for mechanics, maintenance personnel and meteorologists—provided the ground personnel. In the large amusement park in Moscow, a parachute tower, from which young people could jump with parachutes, was constructed in 1932.

During the Moscow Aviation Days of 1933 and again in 1934, some 400 parachutists jumped from around 5,000 meters, free fell some 4,000 meters and then opened their chutes simultaneously at 1,000 meters.

It was not until 1935, however, that there was a massed jump by a larger parachute formation. This was done during the summer maneuvers in the Ukraine. No fewer than 1,000 parachutists jumped at the same time. They then secured an airfield for the air landing of 5,000 additional forces.

The Soviet demonstration had deeply impressed the military forces of the world. Colonel Archibald P. Wavell, the future senior commander in the Near East and Africa, wrote the following to his government: "If I had not personally witnessed this operation, I would have never believed that such a thing were possible."[1]

The German military attaché in Moscow also reported the massed jump of parachutists to Berlin. Although the formation of an airborne force had already been contemplated in Germany, the attaché's report gave urgency to the matter. It was something like the spark that set off the fire for the development of German airborne forces.

It was intended in 1936 for 1,500 parachutists of the Red Army to force a river crossing during an exercise and then open up an avenue of advance for an attacking corps. That maneuver also succeeded and it appeared as though the Soviet Union would be the first country in the world to have a fully formed and trained airborne force. But with the fall of the Commander-in-Chief of the Red Army (Marshall Tuchatschewskij fell victim to a purge on the part of Stalin), the thought also disappeared—a thought that had almost been transformed into practice—of having an operational airborne force. Even during the Second World War there were few Soviet airborne operations and those were largely unsuccessful.

✠

After the Soviet summer maneuvers of 1935, *Oberstleutnant*[2] Jakoby, the commander of *Luftwaffe* Regiment *"General Göring"*—which had been formed on 1 April from *Landespolizeigruppe "General Göring"*[3]—was summoned to report to the Commander-in-Chief of the *Luftwaffe* at Romintern. Göring told the officer: "My regiment will be transferred into the *Luftwaffe* on 1 October. Jakoby, you need to form a parachute battalion from volunteers from the regiment. The battalion will be used to form the cadre for the future German airborne forces."

---

1. Translator's Note: This quote was reverse-translated back into English from the German from an unknown source. Therefore, the translation may not completely correspond with that what was originally written.

2. Translator's Note: Lieutenant colonel. German ranks will be used throughout the text. For those unfamiliar with them, a table is furnished at the end of the book.

3. Translator's Note: State Police Regiment. Göring was initially also the head of the police in Prussia when the National Socialists took power. The *Landespolizeigruppe* that bore his name as an honorific was essentially a party arm and used initially as a paramilitary force to combat remaining Communist elements. It later evolved into a division with elite status and, by the end of the war, was designated a corps, even though its total end strength barely merited that designation.

Regiment *"General Göring"* was moved to the Altengrabow Training Area in October 1935. The soldiers of the regiment were then witness to a parachute jump at the Döberitz Training Area. When the assembled soldiers saw how the parachutist was injured upon jumping and remained motionless in the jump zone, there were a few long faces in the crowd. Despite that, some 600 men from the regiment volunteered, including almost all of the officers. The 1st Battalion of the regiment was then designated as its airborne battalion. The names found on the list of senior duty positions of the battalion would later become well known during the first operations of the airborne forces in World War II:

Battalion commander: *Major* Bräuer

Adjutant: *Oberleutnant* Vogel

Signals Officer: *Leutnant* Dunz

1st Company: Oberleutnant Walther

2nd Company: Oberleutnant Kroh

3rd Company: Oberleutnant Schulz

4th Company: Hauptmann Reinberger

During the reorganization of the regiment in November 1935, the paratrooper battalion was redesignated as the 4th Battalion. The future *General der Fallschirmtruppe* Bräuer wrote the following about the organization's first few months of existence:

When I was given the mission of establishing the first paratrooper battalion in September 1935, it was a mission that seemed monumental in the scope of it. I did not have the slightest amount of professional abilities in the area of flying. Up to that point, I had never even flown before nor seen a parachute jump. As was the case with me, it was also the case with all of the members of the battalion.

After discussing things with the regimental commander, I was initially under the impression that perhaps 30 or 40 men would volunteer. The regimental commander was no less surprised than I was when the regiment put out the word for volunteering and the reports started to come in from the individual companies. There were between 30 and 60 men from each company who volunteered.

In one fell swoop, the battalion had 24 officers and 800 men.[4]

The first airborne school was established at Stendal and soon the first jumps were being conducted. Two officers from the *Luftwaffe, Hauptmann*

---

4. The regiment's 15th Company of engineers, under the command of *Oberleutnant* Karl-Lothar Schulz, was not initially given the opportunity to volunteer, since no engineers were initially called for. It was not until three months later that an airborne engineer company was formed.

Immans and *Hauptmann* Kuhno, provided the instruction. Technical issues were addressed by *Major* Bassenge. The three-month training session was conducted with guidelines he established.

After the birthing pangs were over, the young airborne force was "baptized" on 29 January 1936. It came in the form of the first order issued by the Commander-in-Chief of the *Luftwaffe*, Hermann Göring:

The *Reich* Minister for Aviation and the Commander-in-Chief of the *Luftwaffe*

Berlin, 29 January 1936

LA No. 262/368 III, 1 A (SECRET)

TO: Military Air District II[5], Berlin.

In order to prepare *Regiment* "General Göring" for parachuting, the following is ordered:

As future instructional personnel, 15 volunteer officers, senior noncommissioned officers and junior noncommissioned officers are to be identified and trained.

To be considered are personnel weighing less than 85 kilograms, who are in physically good shape and must be medically examined for aviation suitability.

Start of the training: Most likely on 1 March 1936. Length: 8 weeks, of which 4 weeks are devoted to parachute maintenance under the tutelage of *Luftwaffe* equipment inspectors and 4 weeks of hands-on training in jumping out of aircraft. The airfield at Neubrandenburg is being considered for these purposes. A Ju 52 will be provided by the *Reich* Air Ministry (LC). The *Reich* Air Ministry (LA III) will provided suitable instructors.

Guidelines for the training will be provided in a timely manner by *Reich* Air Ministry (LA III).

Military District II will report the following by 15 March:

1. Name and rank of the volunteers.
2. The completion of the aviation medical examinations.
3. The suitability of the designated airfield

DRAFT FOR THE COMMANDER:

/signed: Milch/

---

5. Translator's Note: The original German contained a number of abbreviations, which are not repeated here. In order to prevent confusion or remain indecipherable for those not versed in either German or these particular abbreviations, an English equivalent will be presented wherever possible.

In addition to that small group of instructor personnel at Stendal, the parachute battalion was billeted in a rapidly erected barracks camp.

The major issue for the airborne forces at the time was a suitable parachute and sufficient lift capacity to transport the paratroopers to their drop zone.

The Ju 52, which had been in service since 1932, was found to be a suitable machine. Lufthansa had flown it since its inception and had enjoyed terrific experience with it. A military version of the aircraft was produced and entered service in 1934. By the end of 1935, some 450 Ju 52's were part of the *Luftwaffe*'s inventory. The aircraft could carry 18 fully equipped paratroopers. It had a flight radius of 560 kilometers and was capable of taking off from unimproved runways and landing in open fields. The fact that the aircraft was also being mass-produced guaranteed that there would be enough of them for larger-scale parachute and airborne operations.

It proved more difficult to come up with a suitable parachute, however. In 1933, the military parachute came under the auspices of the Technical Office of the General Air Procurement Office within the Air Ministry. The Technical Office had a number of subordinate agencies reporting to it that were responsible for developing, testing and researching all matters related to parachuting, including the world famous Testing Center for Aviation (*Versuchsanstalt für Luftfahrt*) in Berlin, the Testing Center for the *Luftwaffe* at Rechlin and the Aviation Technical Institute of the Technical University in Darmstadt.

The parachute testing center of the Aviation Technical Institute had a surveying station at its disposal that was capable of capturing all phases of the deployment of a parachute on film.

Regular parachutes, known as "lifesavers in the air," were taken out of consideration as the "transport device" for paratroopers. A parachute had to be developed that guaranteed opening and deploying at the intended jump heights of only about 120 meters. That height had been determined so that the paratrooper would only spend as short a time as possible during his jump helpless in the air.

In rapid succession, three different parachutes were developed, the RZ 1, the RZ 16 and the RZ 20. The canopy was rounded with a diameter of 8.5 meters and a central set of risers, ending in ropes. The parachute was of the backpack variety. It connected to a 7-meter-long lead line in the aircraft, which forced open the parachute upon jumping. Back then, there were no reserve parachutes.

✠

During the same time frame, in 1936, the German Army High Command was interested in establishing a paratroop battalion. Initially, there was only a company of Army paratroopers, which were commanded by *Oberleutnant* Zahn. The Executive Officer was *Oberleutnant* Pelz, a well-known pentathlete.

Both of these elements, the company and the battalion, were directed to participate for the first time in the Army Maneuvers of 1937 in Mecklenburg. *Oberstleutnant* Bassenge, who was in charge of the testing center for parachute equipment and had also written the tactical employment doctrine for the new force, had 14 "destroyer" sections dropped. They were directed to "blow up railway facilities and bridges in enemy territory."

The Army's paratrooper company was not employed until the very end of the exercise, however, when it made a demonstration jump. Hitler was impressed by what he saw, and *Oberstleutnant* Bassenge hoped that he would be given even more authority. He turned in a long list of recommendations, in which he also outlined how the airborne forces should be organized and employed. But as was the case with his previous recommendations, he received no answer.

Major Richard Heidrich, who had assumed command of the Army's *Fallschirm-Infanterie-Bataillon*[6] on 1 March 1938, pressed hard to establish his battalion. The former tactics instructor at the military academy in Potsdam moved his battalion to the newly built garrison at Braunschweig-Riddagshausen.

While the *Luftwaffe* trained its parachute forces in "destroyer" tactics and intended to operate deep in the enemy's rear with small sections, the Army sought to use its parachute forces as infantry in a more traditionally tactical role.

Everything changed in a fundamental fashion when the *Fliegerkommandeur 3*[7] in Münster, *Generalmajor* Kurt Student, received orders from Göring in Berlin to "establish an airborne division as quickly as possible."

Correspondingly, Student received command of the fledgling German airborne forces. His division was designated as the *7. Flieger-Division*, which, for operational security reasons, made it appear to be another regular *Luftwaffe* air division.

Generalmajor Student had his own ideas about how best to employ airborne forces. In his memoirs, he wrote:

> I could not accept the "destroyer" tactics. Despite the necessary boldness, I did not see a completely satisfactory mission in it for a soldier and for the force as a whole. The chances of returning [from such employment] also appeared to me to be too slight. In most cases, the only thing left after conducting the operation was being taken prisoner and perhaps even being treated as a saboteur or even a spy. Such a prospect would undermine the morale of even the best

---

6. Translator's Note: Parachute Infantry Battalion.

7. Translator's Note: The *Luftwaffe* divided the *Reich* up into military districts as well, with the *Fliegerkommandeur 3* being the equivalent of a corps headquarters.

troops. Good troops bear losses in battle. But they must also have a realizable chance of coming back in one piece.

The tactically limited employment also appeared to me to not correspond to the nature and meaning of airborne forces. My ideas concerning this new force started to go far beyond that from the very beginning. I saw my mission in gradually developing the parachute and airborne forces into an instrument of operational import, perhaps even decisive in battles.

The operations of airborne forces provided for ground operations, which had hitherto only been executable in two dimensions, the great advantage of the third dimension. Consequently, they brought with them the opportunity for military commands to simply jump over the enemy's front and hit the enemy in the rear, where and when they wanted. As is well known, an attack in the enemy's rear has always been the goal, since it is usually demoralizing and, therefore, the most effective. Airborne forces presented the opportunity to do that and were therefore of immeasurable value for the conduct of warfare.

In addition, there was the moment of surprise with the sudden appearance of an attack from paratroopers, which led to a paralyzing effect. The surprise becomes ever greater as more paratroopers jump into the enemy's territory. But therein also lies the greatest danger for the jump-in force: The danger of landing too close to the enemy, who is prepared to defend, and thereby experience an unpleasant surprise itself.

From the very beginning, I dedicated myself to the important complex of questions that argue for and against these operations.

✠

The decision to establish an airborne division had not materialized out of thin air, of course. It originated against a backdrop of real events. Hitler had decided to solve the Sudeten problem with force. In occupying the Sudetenland, the Czech line of bunkers was to be taken out as quickly as possible. The new airborne division was to be employed to that end. For the attack, the Army's parachute infantry battalion of *Major* Heidrich was also to be attached to the division.

Student received directives from Göring to have the division established and operational by 15 September. Since up to that point he had only had the two parachute battalions at his disposal, he also received an air-landed battalion (*Major* Sydow) and *Infanterie-Regiment 16* (*Oberst* Kreysing). At the behest of Göring, *SA-Regiment "Standarte Feldherrnhalle"* was also added to the ad hoc division. The *7. Flieger-Division* was also augmented with an aviation section, which consisted of reconnaissance assets, 8 transport groups (with Ju 52's) and 12 DFS 230 gliders. Also attached to the division were a ground-support wing with three groups and a fighter wing, also with three groups.

On 1 September 1938, *Generalmajor* Student reported the division as being combat ready. A large-scale air-landed operation had just taken place at Jüterbog, in which the 12 gliders participated under the command of *Leutnant* Kiess.

When *Generalmajor* Student visited the small group, which had been billeted at the Prenzlau Air Base, he climbed into one of the gliders. He understood the importance of just such a silent aircraft and gave Kiess the mission of taking dominant terrain—Hill 698, just south of Freudenthal—in the occupation of the Sudetenland, which was to take place in short order. The hill was to be taken in a surprise attack.

As a result of the Accord in Munich on 29 September 1938, in which England gave into Hitler's demands and the Czechs lost the Sudetenland without a shot being fired, the first planned operation of parachute and air-landed troops had been overcome by events. The operation was then conducted as an exercise, although the jumping-in of paratroopers and the landing of gliders was not exercised in the interest of secrecy. Nevertheless, the 250 jammed Ju 52's that set down on the designated airstrips in the Sudetenland on 7 October 1938 made for a great impression. Later on, when Göring arrived in Freudenthal, Student, who was never shy to engage in some public relations, had a battalion of paratroopers brought in from the air. Göring was enthusiastic.

"This has a great future!" he said. *Oberst* Bassenge, who had been outmaneuvered by *Generalmajor* Student, complained bitterly: "That completely unimportant demonstration had won over the Commander-in-Chief to such an extent that he spontaneously told Student that he wanted to establish an airborne corps and give its command to Student."

But Student would have been content with just the command of a real airborne division, because the forces that he commanded were anything but a homogenous formation. After "Operation Sudetenland" the formations returned to all of their home stations and Student was left standing with a single parachute infantry battalion.

In the meantime, Student had also been designated as the Inspector of Parachute and Air-Landed Forces, where he attempted to transform Göring's promise into action. His Chief-of-Staff became *Oberst* Bassenge, a marriage that was probably not made in heaven.

In January 1939, the entire *22. Infanterie-Division* was reequipped, retrained and redesignated as an air-landed division. In addition, two more parachute infantry battalions were formed to finally create a real regiment, *Fallschirmjäger-Regiment (FJR) 1*. These were commanded as follows: *I./FJR 1 by Oberstleutnant* Herbert Gratzi; *II./FJR 1 by Major* Richard Heydrich; and *III./FJR 1 by Major* Sydow. The regimental commander was *Oberst* Bräuer.

All of the paratroopers were volunteers and this principle was never deviated from until the summer of 1944, when there were some 130,000 of them. From then until the end of the war, an additional 40,000 were impressed into airborne service from other formations and even branches of service, although most of them came from the *Luftwaffe*. Student placed great emphasis on the selection of his volunteers. The treatment of the paratroopers and their training were given strict guidelines by him. He later wrote:

> Treatment must respect the feeling of pride the paratrooper has in belonging to the airborne forces. It must be more generous, more circumspect and more comradely than anywhere else. The culture [of the airborne forces] must rest more on mutual trust to one another than on discipline and obedience. I personally made efforts to give the best example. Whenever I visited the forces, I frequently talked to individual paratroopers and discussed their interests, their personal relationships and concerns. I asked them about their point of view and was happy whenever I received open and honest answers. In that manner, my company and battalion commanders and I brought together the airborne forces to an ever larger family, and it was an exceptionally difficult punishment for a paratrooper whenever he was kicked out of the family and assigned to another arm.

To a large extent, this basic attitude was the secret to success for the airborne forces.

✠

A somewhat strained relationship existed between *Generalmajor* Student and *Oberst* Bassenge. While Bassenge was a proponent of airborne operations of limited scope, Student wanted large-scale operations. He wanted to see operations conducted on a large scale, which, for the most part, were to be independent of Army operations. Tactical mobility on the battlefield was a necessary prerequisite, for him, of a powerful airborne force.

Student was reinforced in his opinions by Hitler, who paid a great deal of attention to the airborne forces as a consequence of impressions gained during the maneuvers of 1937 and the "test runs" of 1938. That said, the enthusiasm the airborne forces received was not matched by an equal amount of resources.

Steps continued to build up the parachute and air-landed forces, however. On 1 January 1939, the Army's parachute infantry battalion was transferred to *FJR 1* as its 2nd Battalion. *Hauptmann* Fritz Prager assumed command of the battalion, while the original commander, *Oberstleutnant* Heidrich, was transferred to the headquarters of the *7. Flieger-Division.*

That division, which reported directly to the *Luftwaffe* High Command, continued to grow as well. Division troops were added—e.g., *Luftlande-Geschütz-Batterie 7*[8]—under the command of *Oberleutnant* Schram.

On 20 April 1939, the airborne forces appeared at Hitler's birthday parade for the first time. Under the command of *Oberst* Bräuer, they marched in review past Hitler.

Airborne forces employed the first large-scale deception maneuver at exercises held at the Bergen Training Area in July 1939. *Oberstleutnant* Heidrich had the idea of attaching life-size dolls to parachutes and then dropping them to deceive the enemy. The dolls landed in the rear of an "enemy" combat formation, which promptly turned about to engage the non-breathing enemy.

While that was happening, the *II./FJR 1*, under the command of *Hauptmann* Prager, jumped into the high ground that was supposed to be defended by the enemy and took it without a fight. *General der Artillerie* von Kluge, who was the director of the exercises, was enthusiastic.

It should be mentioned, however, that the Commander-in-Chief of the Army, *Generaloberst* von Brauchitsch, had uttered a negative opinion about the airborne forces at a similar air-drop exercise held at the Munster Training Area: "On paper and in war games that all looks very nice. But, in practice, this whole business is only suitable on a very small scale."

When *Generalmajor* Student raised some fact-based objections to that observation, von Brauchitsch did not even allow him to finish his train of thought. Von Brauchistch stated: "Everything's still in its baby shoes. It is not useable within a large-scale tactical framework. You are an eternal optimist, Student!"

When the Second World War began, the German airborne forces were still in the process of being established. The *7. Flieger-Division* had only *FJR 1* and the *I./FJR 2*. The latter regiment's 2nd Battalion was still being formed. On the day of mobilization, 26 August 1939, the airborne units and formations were located in their peacetime garrisons. They received the following order: "*7. Flieger-Division*, reinforced by *Infanterie-Regiment 16*, is the operational reserve of the Supreme Command. For that purpose, it marches to the Liegnitz area."

---

8. Translator's Note: 7th Gun Battery (Air-Landed).

Kurt Student, the Commander-in-Chief of the German airborne forces.

The first parade of the recently formed airborne forces in Berlin.

Parachutes are aired out and maintained.

Parachute gathered up for repacking after use.

A practice jump from a *Junkers Ju 52*. Note the characteristic "diving" position that the paratroopers had to adopt in order to successfully exit the aircraft and properly deploy the parachute.

The jumpers float to earth. The design of the German parachute allowed jumping from very low altitudes but the paratrooper had little control over the rate and direction of the descent.

CHAPTER 2

Paratroopers at War

IDLE DURING THE POLISH CAMPAIGN

The *II./FJR 1* experienced the first day of the war—1 September 1939—on the *Autobahn* between Berlin and Breslau. Marching to the southeast, its march objective was the airfields around Breslau, from which the operations would be flown, if they were committed. *Generalmajor* Student had wargamed a number of employment possibilities for his small number of paratroopers. One of them was to be employed at the bridge over the Vistula at Pulawy. The paratroopers would jump into the area around the bridge, eliminate its security, remove the charges and hold open the route for the advancing armored forces.

The soldiers of the battalion were already sitting in their transports when the operation was called off. Cursing, they got off the aircraft. It was later found out that the German armored forces had already taken the bridge in a *coup de main*. It was not until 24 September that the men of that battalion had their first contact with the enemy, albeit employed on the ground initially. They suffered their first casualties at Wola Gulowska, losing eight of their number killed.

The *III./FJR 1* was not employed at all. Instead, it was used to provide security for the command post of *General* von Richthofen.

The waiting game was not something the paratroopers enjoyed. The men were unhappy and, when the formations returned to their garrisons in the middle of October, many men asked to be transferred from an "inactive force" to the infantry. They could not know, after all, that a large-scale operation for the airborne forces was just around the corner.

AN OPERATION IS PLANNED

On 27 October 1939, Student was summoned to see Hitler in the *Reich* Chancellery. He stood face-to-face with Hitler for the first time and discovered why his airborne forces were not employed in Poland.

"The airborne forces are too valuable to me, Student. I will only employ them if there's a payoff. The Army could take care of things by itself in Poland. As a result, I didn't want to reveal the secret of this new branch prematurely."

Following that, Hitler revealed to the general officer his intentions for the airborne forces, whose employment he had held back for the campaign in the west. Since the Western Campaign was scheduled to begin on 12 November, it appeared that all matters had to assume extreme urgency. According to Hitler's plan, as Student discovered, a specially equipped assault detachment was to take the strongly fortified and exceptionally modern Belgian fortifications at Eben Emael on the Belgian Albert Canal by means of glider insertion. The three bridges beyond the canal were also to be taken by gliderborne troops, thus preventing them from being blown up by the enemy.

Student later wrote about the encounter with Hitler:

> During my conversation, Hitler developed the theme of the meaning and operational purpose of air-landed forces with extraordinary clarity and in his own uniquely persuasive manner. To my great surprise, he demonstrated great professional knowledge of the material, even including the area of gliders. He initially placed great stress on the fact that one should not lose sight of the fact that parachute and air-landed forces were a completely new and, for the time being, secret weapon.
>
> That meant that their first employment had to be at a place of decisive importance, with no holding back and boldness.
>
> I then told him about the large disappointment on the part of the paratroopers and the psychological consequences that had to result. Hitler listened to me attentively and then said: "You will most certainly be employed in the west!" Smiling, he added: "And it will be a *big* deal."
>
> He then informed me of the missions he wanted to give the air-landed forces during the upcoming offensive in the west:
>
> 1. The *7. Flieger-Division* and the *22. Luftlande-Division* were intended to take the *Reduit National* from the air and hold that important line of fortifications until the arrival of the Army.
>
> 2. An additional parachute battalion was to take the blocking redoubt of Eben Emael near Lüttich [Liege] by a surprise attack with gliders, as well as the bridges to the north over the Albert Canal and the bridges over the Meuse at Maastricht, which would allow the rapid crossing of the *6. Armee* (*General* von Reichenau) over the Meuse and the Albert Canal.

✠

Generalmajor Student, when queried as to the possibility of success for both of the operations, replied that the first part was certainly within the realm of possibilities but that the second part, the taking of Eben Emael from the air, was too fantastic to achieve.

"Sleep on it, Student. Report back to me tomorrow and tell me your decision then."

That night, there was no sleep for Student, however. He weighed all of the options from every angle and finally came to the conclusion that a surprise attack on Eben Emael was possible if all the preparations for the assault could be kept secret. He reported back to Hitler and told him of his conclusions.

Together with *Oberst* Bräuer, Student selected the units that were to be employed for the surprise assault on the three bridges over the Albert Canal and the elimination of Eben Emael.

Hauptmann Koch, the commander of the *1./FJR 1* was charged with forming *Sturmabteilung Koch*[1], which was then responsible for carrying out the operation. Joining Koch's detachment was the engineer platoon from the *II./FJR 1*, which was led by *Oberleutnant* Witzig. The glider element was under the command of *Oberleutnant* Kiess. Using replacements from the airborne school, the detachment was brought up to a total strength of 500 men.

The start of the Campaign in the West was delayed, one week at a time, by bad weather. When it was finally decided to launch the offensive on 17 January 1940, the entire operational plans for the offensive fell into enemy hands. An airborne *Major*, who was being sent to *Luftflotte 2*[2] at Münster as a liaison officer, had copies of all of the operations orders with him in a briefcase. The pilot who was flying him there, a *Major* in the *Luftwaffe*, was flying an *Me 108 "Taifun"*[3] for the first time. Not only did he get lost, he also had to make an emergency landing when the engine gave out. The aircraft went down in the vicinity of the Belgian city of Mechelen-sur-Meuse.

Major Reinberger, the liaison officer, attempted to burn all of the plans, but he did not completely succeed before he was captured. Since the Germans did not know how much of the operational plan had fallen into enemy hands, the start of the Offensive in the West was postponed until the spring.

The missions of the airborne forces were then modified, adding as follows:

1. Taking the bridges at Moerdijk, Dordrecht and Rotterdam for the *18. Armee*, since it would operate with its main effort south of the river area.
2. Simultaneous occupation of the Dutch capital, Den Haag, thus taking the Dutch leadership out of the picture.

The preparations for the air-landed operations were given under unified command to *Generalleutnant* Student.

✠

To the surprise of all involved, Hitler decided on 3 March 1940 to conduct operations against Norway prior to the start of the Campaign in the West. To that end, he directed the use of a parachute battalion. Student recommended against that, but his objections were overruled. In order not to tear apart *Sturmabteilung Koch*, which was still training for its original mission, Student placed the *I./FJR 1* at the disposal of the High Command. *Hauptmann* Walther's battalion received the following missions:

1. Half of the battalion was to be employed to occupy and secure the

1. Translator's Note: Assault Battalion "Koch." Standard German practice was to name ad hoc formations after their commanders.

2. Translator's Note: 2nd Tactical Air Force.

3. Translator's Note: "Typhoon."

Oslo-Fornebu airport for subsequent landings. The half-battalion was to remain under the command of Walther.

2. The *3./FJR 1*, under the command of *Oberleutnant* von Brandis, was to take the Stavanger-Sola airport.

3. The *4./FJR 1* of *Hauptmann* Gericke was to take the most important bridges and airports of Denmark.

THE FIRST AIR-LANDED AND JUMP OPERATIONS IN DENMARK AND NORWAY

When the *Ju 52's* carrying *Hauptmann* Walther's half battalion of men neared the Norwegian coast, there was such a "pea soup" of a fog that visibility was reduced to barely 20 meters. The pilot commanding Walther's machine reported the minimal visibility, and Walther ordered him to go lower. But no matter how low they went, the fog seemed to extend all the way to the ocean surface.

Seconds after the order to continue flying at the lowest level possible, a loud crash shook the men in the fourth machine. Two *Ju 52's* that had been following closely behind had crashed into one another and dropped to the sea below.

"Climb!" *Oberstleutnant* Drewes, the group commander of the *II./Kampfgeschwader z.b.V. 1*[4], ordered as visibility dropped to zero over the islands that made up Oslo.

"What's going on?" *Hauptmann* Walther asked.

"A safe drop of the two companies is impossible, Walther. We have to head for Aalborg."

"If we don't take the airfield, the transports following us can't land with their forces," he retorted.

But, in the end, the major had to bend to the insight of the transport commander. The entire formation turned and flew to Aalborg, where it landed.

The group that was following was also ordered back. But *Hauptmann* Wagner, the flight leader of the second group, thought the radio transmission was an enemy trick and continued the flight on to Oslo-Fornebu by himself.

The eight *Me 110's* of the *I./Zerstörergeschwader 76*[5] of *Hauptmann* Ingenhoven had also arrived in the meantime. The aircraft had been detailed to support the airborne forces. Once over the air space of the airport, they started preparations to land, convinced that the paratroopers had already jumped and had the airfield under their control.

Once they started receiving defensive fires, they knew otherwise. But the aircraft had to land there. They didn't have enough fuel to return to their home base.

---

4. Translator's Note: 1st Special-Purpose Ground-Support Wing.

5. Translator's Note: The *Me 110* was a twin-engined aircraft that could be configured for fighter, night fighter and fighter-bomber roles. Ingenhoven's men were from the 76th Destroyer Wing.

Ingenhoven: "Attack and engage the enemy defenses with machine-gun fire."

The twin-engined aircraft dove and aimed their weapons in the direction of the muzzle flashes they could see. Two English "Gladiator" fighters were set ablaze before they could take off to intercept the German destroyers.

While that was happening, the aircraft with *Hauptmann* Wagner arrived on scene. The *Ju 52* also started to turn to land and suddenly received heavy machine-gun fire. A machine-gun salvo went through the aircraft. *Hauptmann* Wagner, who was at the stick, was shot in the head and killed. The assistant pilot caught the machine in time, although rounds continued their deadly arc through the aircraft and hit men cried out in surprise and pain. Although the aircraft swung wildly from side to side, it climbed up out of the deathtrap over the airfield as the *Me 110's* made another run.

The stricken *Ju 52* also managed to reach Aalborg, where the rest of the second group had already arrived. The eight *Me 110's* remained behind. They had a choice: Take the airfield or go down at sea somewhere.

Once again, the *Me 110's* returned fire on the enemy and then attempted to land. The first aircraft touched down but ran out of runway. When it came to a stop, it was slightly damaged. But the rest landed without incident. Once on the ground, they all turned so that the rear of the aircraft faced the airport facilities. That way, the rear gunners had an opportunity to return fire. But the fires had ceased. The enemy had given up and abandoned his positions.

Hauptmann Ingenhoven reported: "Fornebu airfield in our hands! Airfield free for follow-on landings by paratroopers!" The airborne forces turned around, occupied the airfield and held it until *Infanterie-Regiment 324*, which had been designated to relieve the airborne forces, arrived. When the sixth company finished landing around noon on 9 April, they moved out on Oslo. The mission of the main group had been accomplished.

✠

Hauptmann Gericke sat in the lead machine of the *4./FJR 1*. He was waiting for the signal to jump. When the red lamp lit up, the doors of the *Ju 52* were opened, and the lead jumper stood with spread legs in the open door, holding on to the framework with both hands.

The jump horn blasted, signaling it was clear to jump. The first men to jump sprang out, with the remainders of their sticks following closely behind. They knew that only a rapid jump meant the company would remain cohesive.

The paratroopers landed without being engaged. Three minutes later, they had assembled. They headed for the bridge that connected the islands of Falster and Fünen. The road there led to Copenhagen. The completely surprised Danes were disarmed, and the bridge was secured by the paratroopers. They had not even waited for the drop of the containers with their heavy weapons. Instead, they had assaulted with their small-arms. They had cleared the route to Copenhagen, and *Hauptmann* Gericke reported that the bridge was in German hands. A few hours later, *Infanterie-Regiment 305* marched across the bridge and headed for Copenhagen, taking the Danish capital.

At the same time, the *3./FJR 1* of *Oberleutnant Freiherr* [6] von Brandis flew in the direction of Stavanger-Sola. But there was thick fog along their route as well. The machines flew barely 10 meters above the sea's surface. Suddenly, the fog lifted and they saw Sola in front of them. Clear weather.

"Climb to a jump height of 140 meters!" The *Oberleutnant* ordered. As they were climbing, they started to receive fire from the ground. Parachutes started floating to earth. The antiaircraft guns at the airfield picked up their fires, but the paratroopers were already on the ground and were advancing in leaps and bounds. They received fire, but the first pocket of resistance was eliminated. The bounding started towards the second one. At the same time, two long-range *Bf 109's* thundered over the airfield and strafed the enemy with their cannon. Because of the weather, they were the only two fighters that had made it to the objective.

The remaining two pockets of resistance at the edge of the airfield were then attacked. They were silenced with hand grenades and submachine-gun fire.

Exactly 31 minutes after landing, *Oberleutnant* von Brandis was able to report another airfield in German hands.

The tarmac was cleared, and the transport aircraft with the air-landed soldiers followed a short while later. Destroyers (Me 110s) and fighters also landed, so that they might be able to engage the English fleet from there.

The three main missions for the airborne forces in Norway had been accomplished. Another mission developed when English forces landed at Namsos on 14 April and on both sides of Drontheim three days later. When the mountain forces positioned there ran into trouble, the *1./FJR 1* of *Oberleutnant* Herbert Schmidt was ordered to help them. It was intended for them to be dropped in the area of Dombas and block Gudbrans Valley, thus preventing the Norwegian forces fighting north of Oslo from linking up with the English forces that had landed.

During the afternoon of 14 April, *Kompanie Schmidt* started on its way to Dombas, 150 kilometers north of the German lines, in 15 *Ju 52's*. It was already turning dark, when the transport group, led by *Oberstleutnant* Drewes, approached the deeply snowed-over area of operations in the broad valley. Once again, the *Ju 52's* had to fly through a low-lying fog. The enemy antiaircraft defenses opened up when they saw the aircraft. One of the *Ju 52's* received a direct hit, bursting apart in a brilliant ball of flame before the paratroopers had even left it. Machine-gun fire raced through the oncoming night, identifiable by the tracer elements. In some cases, the paratroopers were forced to jump at an altitude of only 60 to 80 meters. A few of the chutes had not even deployed when the hapless paratroopers struck the ground.

---

6. Translator's Note: Baron (nobility).

A portion of the company landed safely and gathered around the company commander. A short while later, Schmidt ordered his 61 men to move to the road. As they ran in that direction, they fired against enemy positions they had identified and which were firing machine-guns at them. Finally, they reached the road.

"Over there, *Herr Oberleutnant*! Good terrain for defending!" The headquarters section leader called out to his commanding officer. He was pointing to some cliffs on the other side of the road.

"Everyone at once . . . let's go!" The men jumped up and ran, bent over, across the road. Machine-gun fire commenced to hammer away. The sounds of carbines firing could be heard in between bursts.

Oberleutnant Schmidt ran right in the midst of a burst of machine-gun fire. He felt a heavy blow against his right leg and started to topple. Then there was a biting pain in his lower body. Unconscious, he collapsed to the ground.

"Take out the enemy machine-gun!" *Feldwebel* Meinka ordered, while he hit the ground along with two messengers and crawled over to his wounded company commander.

The enemy machine-gun was silenced. The company commander was carried by four men into the cover afforded by the cliffs. His wounds were dressed. In addition to being shot in the leg, he was also hit in the hip and the stomach.

The paratroopers set up defensive positions in the cold night. Of the 15 *Ju 52's*, 8 had crashed or been shot down by Norwegian antiaircraft fires.

Over the next few days, the paratroopers defended bitterly against their Norwegian opponents, who were attempting to break through that bottleneck in the valley to link up with the English.

Demolition parties headed out on the second and third nights and blew up a bridge. Despite his bad wounds, *Oberleutnant* Schmidt continued to lead his company from a stretcher. For five nights and four days, the paratroopers held firm against an attacking enemy. In the end, the remaining Germans had to surrender. They had blocked the important road for four days, thus allowing the Germans the opportunity to reinforce themselves.

On 29 May, *Oberleutnant* Schmidt was awarded the Knight's Cross for his decisive actions. He did not survive the war, however. He was killed in action as a *Major* on 16 June 1944 in the Bretagne by a sniper.

✠

The northern theater of operations saw one more operation by paratroopers. This occurred when the situation for the mountain troops around Narvik became critical. The specter of surrender was not far removed from those forces. Because both land and sea routes for logistics had been cut off, the *I./FJR 1* of *Hauptmann* Walther landed in the far north. In addition to the trained paratroopers, a few mountain infantry units also jumped in after they had received a fast course in parachuting. Among them was *Oberst*

Meindl, an artillery officer, who later went on to become one of the leading airborne commanders.

The *Ju 52's*, which had been filled with as much fuel as was possible, were able to make it that far, whereupon they allowed their sticks to jump in smaller groups. All the more remarkable was the fact that the airfield from which the *Ju 52's* started was not fully operational. It took 12 days to send in the entire battalion. For *General* Dietl and his mountain troops, however, these paratroopers and "mountain paratroopers" were a decisive help.

Hauptmann Walther led his battalion into Narvik on 8 June 1940. At the same time, the *II./FJR 1* rolled north on trains from Oslo towards Narvik to also be employed. But the enemy gave up before that happened, and the battalion was sent back to Germany.

With their employment from the air in Norway, the airborne forces received their baptism of fire. Great possibilities were demonstrated; at the same time, however, the grave danger that these forces were exposed to came to light. Student, who was promoted to *Generalleutnant* on 1 January 1940, drew conclusions from these smaller actions that were of importance for the coming large-scale operations in the west. Despite the successes enjoyed by the airborne forces, many of the opponents to them were still not convinced of their potential.

While the Campaign in Norway was taking place, *Oberst* Bassenge was able to coordinate the necessary amount of *Ju 52's* for the upcoming operations in France and the Low Countries.

In the waiting period that was forced upon him, Student used the time to convince his chain-of-command and, more importantly, Hitler as well that the cautious plans created by *General der Artillerie* von Küchler for his *18. Armee* to break through the Grebbe Line at Soesterberg during the attack on Holland would not suffice. Student recommended a jump into the middle of Holland. The recommendation was made more palatable to the General Staff by casting it as a support operation for the *18. Armee*.

Generalleutnant Student's proposal—open the southern approach routes to Rotterdam, occupy the airfields at Den Haag and capture the royal family, the government and the headquarters of the Dutch forces—was *the* way to end the war in Holland quickly, almost as a *coup de main*. Both Hitler and Göring were more than a little bit taken by this recommendation.

According to the plan, an insertion group from the *22. Luftlande-Division* of *Generalmajor Graf* Sponeck, with its *Infanterie-Regiment 47* and *Infanterie-Regiment 65*, along with a battalion of paratroopers, was to take the airfields at Den Haag, Ockenburg, Ypenburg and Valkenburg, after which the main body of the division was to be brought in. Once on the ground, it would march on Den Haag.

For the *7. Flieger-Division*, Student wanted the paratroopers to jump into the bridges over the Deep at Moerdijk, the Old Maas at Dordrecht, at the Waalhaven airfield and the bridges over the Nieuwe Maas.

As was to be expected, there was a beehive of activity in the *Führer* Headquarters in Berlin just prior to the start of the Campaign in the West. On 2 May 1940, Student and von Sponeck were summoned to see Hitler. Hitler told them that the start of the operation was planned for 6 May. Hitler then informed Student:

> I believe that the Queen of the Netherlands, Wilhelmina, will remain in her country. She can stay in her palace in the city or at her place in the country, the *Huis ten Bosch*. It's her choice. Both of you, Student and Sponeck, have to guarantee me that nothing will happen to the royal house in the course of the fighting.
>
> I can accept responsibility for almost everything, except if something happens to Queen Wilhelmina. She is popular in her nation and around the world.

But the 6th of May passed without the slightest thing happening. It was not until noon on 9 May that the telephone rang in Student's office. On the other end of the line was *Major* von Bulow, who gave him Hitler's orders: "D-Day is 10 May."

The attack against Fortress Holland, Eben Emael and the bridges over the Albert Canal could commence.

Generalleutnant Student (middle) and *Major i.G.* Trettner in Rotterdam.

Kurt Student and wounded paratroopers in a military hospital.

Paratroopers land in Rotterdam.

The harbor of Rotterdam. A Fokker G1 is parked beside a road that was used as an expedient runway

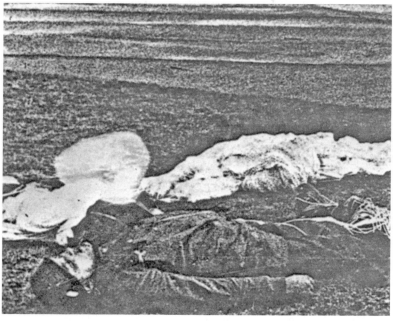

Casualty of war: A dead German paratrooper

CHAPTER 3

Put to the Test

STURMABTEILUNG KOCH ASSAULTS EBEN EMAEL

Sturmabteilung Koch was alerted during the evening of 9 May. Eleven officers and 427 men were transported from the areas Hilden and Düsseldorf to the Ostheim and Butzweilerhof airfields around Cologne. Four assault groups had been formed, which were to be taken to the landing zone in four detachments with a total of 42 gliders in tow.

Sturmgruppe "Stahl"[1], commanded by *Oberleutnant* Altmann, had orders to take the bridge over the Albert Canal at Veldwezelt by surprise and prevent it from being blown up.

Sturmgruppe "Beton", under *Leutnant* Schacht, was directed to take the bridge at Vroenhoven and hold it open for the crossing of the *4. Panzer-Division*.

Sturmgruppe "Eisen", led by *Leutnant* Schächter, was to hold the bridge at Canne. That bridge was directly observable from the fortress of Eben Emael. The bridge was important because *Infanterie-Regiment 151*, which would be advancing from Maastricht, was intended to cross it and then assault Eben Emael. This was to be the toughest mission of all.

Sturmgruppe "Granit", under *Oberleutnant* Witzig, was given the mission of attacking Eben Emael proper. The fort, which dominated the adjacent Albert Canal, consisted of 64 individual redoubts and was considered to be impregnable.

The fortress had dimensions of 900 meters by 700 meters. When one considers a squad of paratroopers jumping out of a *Ju 52* will separate 300 meters in the course of the seven seconds required for the group to jump and, at the same time, the parachutist will hang helplessly for about 15 seconds in his chute before landing, then that ruled out a parachute operation because the objective was too small.

Consequently, *Sturmgruppe "Granit"* practiced on gliders. Practiced glider pilots could bring down the *DFS 320* to within 15 to 20 meters of their target. That ensured a powerful massed attack that was coupled with surprise. Towed at an altitude of 2,000 meters, the gliders could be released some 20 kilometers before the objective on a descending glide path of 1:12. They could then glide to the objective without making a sound.

Sturmgruppe "Granit" headed out for its mission early on 10 May. A firsthand account of the operation by *Oberjäger* Peter Arent survived the war:

---

1. Translator's Note: The various assault groups were named *Stahl* (steel), *Beton* (concrete), *Eisen* (iron) and *Granit* (granite).

We were alerted on 9 May at the *Flak* barracks in Hilden, near Düsseldorf. That was where our entire assault group had been moved. The group consisted of an airborne engineer platoon under *Oberleutnant* Witzig and 11 *DFS 230* gliders with their pilots.

I gathered together my 3rd Section. We moved rapidly to Cologne-Ostheim, where the gliders were to be boarded. The gliders were transported there in furniture vans. At 2100 hours, we reported that we were ready to go to *Oberleutnant* Witzig.

"Comrades!" the *Oberleutnant* said to us. "We're going into action tomorrow. We need to prove that we haven't been wasting our time and that everything we had to learn has really been learned."

We were awakened at 0245 hours and formed up in full gear at 0330 hours. After reporting in, we headed for our glider when *Oberleutnant* Witzig ordered, "Get on the gliders!"

Right at 0430 hours, the 11 tow aircraft rolled up. One after the other, the 11 small gliders were lifted up and towed into the morning skies. When we linked up with *Sturmgruppe "Eisen"*, whose gliders and aircraft had taken off at Cologne-Butzweilerhof, there was an unexpected incident. Of all the gliders, it was the one with the 11th Section and the assault group leader, *Oberleutnant* Witzig, which had to make a sharp evasive maneuver to avoid hitting another glider. The tow cable snapped in the process, and the glider with the assault-group leader just made it back across the Rhine. Later on, the 2nd Section also had to abort, landing near Düren.

"Merz," I said to my second-in-command. "You know what to do if something happens to me."

"You bet, Peter. I got it all up here," the *Obergefreiter* answered.

There were seven paratroopers sitting with me in the glider, which was being piloted by *Oberjäger* Sapper. I checked out my equipment. Today would be the test of whether the 50-kilogram charges, of which we had three, could crack open the cupolas of the Belgian fortifications. We had been given Fortress Complex 12 as our target. In addition to the heavy charge, we also had 12.5-kilogram ones, a couple of Bangalore torpedoes, a crate of igniters, a flare gun, one machine-gun and submachine-guns.

When the towing *Ju 52* radioed that it had reached the release point, from which we would glide on on our own, *Oberjäger* Sapper released the cable. A jerk went through the glider, whereupon it sailed through the air only to dive in tight spirals on the target a little later, which was already plainly visible in the early light of 10 May. Sapper steered in to "our" casemate. He pushed the machine down even more steeply so as to land right in the middle of the target. The ground raced toward us. Bringing it under control, Sapper put the glider down about 50 meters south of our target.

"Get out . . . let's go!" Arent ordered his men. The seven paratroopers dashed out into the open. *Oberjäger* Arent saw another three or four gliders land. Farther off to his right, one of them crashed into the ground. Two gliders landed at the northern end of the complex. Machine-gun fires were starting to whip across the plateau of the fortress. Guns fired.

Peter Arent ran in long strides towards his objective. He could hear Merz struggling for air as he ran behind with his 12.5-kilogram charge. The charge was paced at exactly the point that had been rehearsed in the sandtable exercises. Once the igniter was charged, everyone threw themselves under cover. A powerful, sharp blow echoed through the morning. A hole had been created in the casemate.

The antiaircraft position was taken in the first assault. Then men from another section attacked Barracks 25, which was destroyed with shaped charges.

Seven of the total of nine sections that had been landed there were in action. After *Oberleutnant* Witzig's glider had had to abort, *Feldwebel* Teddy Wenzel had assumed command on the top of the fortress complex. The remaining sections had landed at the northern extreme of the complex, but they had only found deception measures consisting of dummy cupolas there.

The 50-kilogram charge on Redoubt 25, with its flat-topped armored cupola with a diameter of 6 meters, under which were twin 12-centimeter guns, failed. Two paratroopers then succeeded in placing 1-kilogram charges in the barrels of the guns, which then jammed the breeches when they went off, rendering the guns useless.

The machine-gun, which was firing from Redoubt 13, was taken out of action with a flamethrower, after the wire obstacle had been breached. Demolitions were then set off, silencing another redoubt.

Ever since 0520 hours, the battle was raging on the roof of the "invincible" fortress of Eben Emael, conducted by 55 paratroopers and coordinated by *Feldwebel* Wenzel. At 0540 hours, Wenzel had the first message radioed to *Sturmabteilung Koch*: "*Sturmgruppe Granit*: Object reached; everything in order!"

After taking out Redoubt 12, *Oberjäger* Arent received instructions from *Feldwebel* Wenzel to knock out Redoubt 4, which had two antitank guns. Arent ordered his men to attack the redoubt's observer in a cupola: "He was spotting for the two machine-guns that are firing at us."

Three minutes later, they had reached the observation cupola. The powerful detonation burst it asunder. The 50-kilogram charges were capable of boring right through 25 centimeters of steel.

"Recon forward as far as the entrance redoubt!" Wenzel ordered, after the designated targets had been eliminated. During the conduct of that reconnaissance, the paratroopers suffered their first casualties. A short while later, Belgian forces attacked from the underbrush along the northwest slope of the adjacent high ground. The paratroopers had to defend: 55 against some 1,200 Belgians.

At 0835 hours, Wenzel had another message sent: "Eben Emael: Enemy driven farther back. High ground occupied!"

Just before the radio message from Wenzel was sent, a single glider appeared over Eben Emael and then descended steeply. The word spread quickly from mouth to mouth: "Our *Oberleutnant* has come!"

Oberleutnant Witzig had succeeded in calling in a *Ju 52* after he had landed in a pasture. By the time the aircraft appeared, Witzig's men had torn down the fences and the *Ju 52* was able to land. With Glider 11 in tow, the *Ju 52* brought it to its objective area. In broad daylight, the glider then set down so that *Oberleutnant* Witzig could resume command of the operation.

The patrol, which had been sent out against Redoubt 3, was wiped out. At that point, Belgian artillery also opened fire after slowly registering on the roof of the fortress. In a dense carpet, the impacting rounds forced the paratroopers to seek cover.

Despite that, the paratroopers succeeded in the course of the afternoon and then the early evening to blow open the passages to Redoubts 12, 13 and 19, some of which were 40 meters deep, with bundled charges, one of which weighed 90 kilograms. The obstacles that had been emplaced in front of the casemate doors—metal rails and sandbags—were pushed aside. The concussion from the detonations reverberated through the underground passageways and caused the defenders to believe that the Germans had already entered the connecting passageways.

That night, Arent's section reported Belgians feeling their way forward in the vicinity of Redoubt 12. *Oberleutnant* Witzig had the redoubt evacuated, since he believed there might be a night attack. Before the redoubt was left for good, the entryway was sealed with a 50-kilogram demolition.

Peter Arent collected his men and took up covered positions on the fortress roof. Despite the initial fears, the Belgians did not attack that night. The death-defying landing of the paratroopers and their subsequent dramatic and lightning-fast operations had completely paralyzed the men manning the redoubts.

Early in the morning of 11 May, an assault detachment from *Pionier-Bataillon 51*[2] under *Oberfeldwebel* Portsteffen crossed the water-filled ditch in front of Redoubt 4 in an inflatable boat and silenced the firing points facing the waterway. By doing so, Portsteffen opened the way for his battalion into Eben Emael. In addition to the engineer battalion, elements of *Infanterie-Regiment 151* and *Artillerie-Regiment 161*—all of the *61. Infanterie-Division*—were being employed to take the fortress and relieve the paratroopers.

It was noon before the assault groups of the relieving infantry regiment were able to cross to the west bank and attack Redoubt 4. The defenders surrendered. Redoubts 17, 23 and 35, which had continued to fire, also gave up the fight. Major Jottrand, the commander of the fortress, marched into captivity along with the remaining personnel of his command.

2. Translator's Note: 51st Engineer Battalion.

The previously untried paratroopers had proven themselves. Of the 85 soldiers assigned to *Kampfgruppe "Granit"*, 6 had been killed and 15 wounded. Four paratroopers had been injured during the landing.

"VELDWEZELT BRIDGE TAKEN"

The nine gliders of *Sturmgruppe "Stahl"* reached the release point for their assault on the bridge over the canal at Veldwezelt at 0520 hours. *Oberleutnant* Altmann issued the orders to land. Moving at high speed, the nine fully loaded gliders raced towards earth.

"Brace!" the pilot called out, as he literally shot forward toward the landing area. He pulled back on the stick and the barbed-wire wrapped skids of the glider screeched across the ground. A mighty jerk threw the men forward.

The first one to climb out of his glider was *Oberleutnant* Altmann. He saw the glider with Ellersiek's section land just in front of the bunker at the bridge, which was their target. Machine-gun fire rattled into the morning stillness. Fires whipped toward *Oberjäger* Ellersiek as he stormed toward the bunker, from which there was also defensive fires coming from the ports. As he ran, Ellersiek tossed several hand grenades. His men assaulted behind him. When one of the men reached the door to the bunker and ignited a bundled charge, all the men sought cover, waiting to jump up again after the charge went off. They charged into the bunker. While the firefight was still ongoing, a few paratroopers climbed over the framework of the bridge and removed the igniter lines that led to the explosive-filled chambers.

Oberleutnant Altmann set up his command post about 150 meters south of the bridge. He directed the individual sections from there and had a message sent to the command post of *Sturmabteilung Koch*. It was a message all had been waiting for: "*Sturmgruppe Stahl:* Object taken!"

But the enemy had not yet been defeated, however. He tried to take back the bridge so as to be able to blow it up. A short while later, *Ju 52's* appeared on the horizon, grew larger and larger, and then tightly dropped the men of the machine-gun section of *Leutnant* Ringler out of the aircraft. Once landed, they helped secure the bridge. The Belgians pulled back into the village of Veldwezelt. The only fire they were still receiving came from a slope some 500 meters away, where automatic cannon were barking.

The location of that pocket of resistance was radioed in. A *Stuka* attack was promised, and *Oberleutnant* Altmann had aerial recognition panels laid out.

When the *Stukas* arrived over the Albert Canal, the paratroopers stared up at them. They hoped the pilots saw the panels. The first element of two tipped its wings, promptly followed by the others. With their sirens turned on, they shrieked towards earth.

The bombs landed exactly on target. The village of Veldwezelt was also hit by the *Stukas*. A few houses went up in flames.

Despite that, the Belgians did not give up. They attacked again and again. Reinforcements were slow to arrive for *Kampfgruppe "Stahl"*, which had to defend the bridge all by itself to almost 2130 hours. The group was then relieved and moved back towards Maastricht. In all, 8 paratroopers had been killed. There were 14 badly wounded soldiers and 16 slightly wounded ones, all pointing to the intensity of the fighting there.

STURMGRUPPE "BETON" AT VROENHOVEN

With *Sturmgruppe "Beton"*, which also started from Cologne-Ostheim at 0430, was the entire headquarters of *Sturmabteilung Koch*. As a result, this flight carried 5 officers and 129 men. The first abort was at Hottdorf when the tow line of the glider of the engineer section of *Oberjäger* Kempa tore loose. The glider had to make an emergency landing. The remaining 10 gliders were released from their tow aircraft between the border and Maastricht and glided towards the Albert Canal over the brightly lit Dutch villages.

Leutnant Schach's assault group started to receive fire as it made its approach. Antiaircraft cannon and machine-gun fires hammered away at it as early as Maastricht, with the glider pilots attempting to maneuver through it as best they could. They then dove through a curtain of *Flak* and turned into their targets.

The glider with Stolzewaski's section was hit and went down from an altitude of 15 meters. It landed with a crashing sound on the ground; three badly wounded men had to be recovered from the wreck of the glider. The glider of *Oberjäger* Bading, which also had a *Feldwebel* from the detachment staff on board, put down only 150 meters from the main bunker. The wiring for blowing up the bridge was to be found in that bunker. Shots rang out as the men assaulted the bunker. *Gefreiter* Stenzel was the first one to the firing trench. When two Belgians fired at him, *Oberjäger* Bading provided suppressive fire. Stenzel jumped into the trench, shot down an enemy who was waiting for him there and then ran the last 40 meters to the bunker. When the bunker door was thrown open, Stenzel saw a rifle barrel pointing at him. He quickly tossed in a hand grenade and then took cover.

Right after the detonation, he jumped back up, ran into the bunker and tore the wiring from its connections. That meant that the bridge had been prevented from being blown up for the time being. The Belgians in the bunker surrendered; some of them were wounded.

The fighting for the two flanking canal bunkers turned intense, however. The paratroopers had to fend off Belgian attacks repeatedly from the Belgians' former positions on the bridge. Sprengert's section of heavy machine-guns jumped in at 0615 hours, providing considerable reinforcement for *Sturmgruppe "Beton"*. Even then, however, everything was razor close. Belgian artillery registered on the positions of the paratroopers, and the assault detachment took heavy casualties. In all, there were 7 killed and 24 wounded. Despite the losses, the men held fast and turned back the enemy. Around 2140 hours, the relief force arrived, and *Leutnant* Schacht was able to hand over the intact bridge to the infantry battalion commander.

"THE BRIDGE AT CANNE IS BLOWN UP"

Starting from Cologne-Butzweilerhof was *Sturmgruppe "Eisen"* with 10 *Ju 52's* and attendant gliders. The detachment's target was the bridge at Canne. The flight flew over the beacon lights that were intended to provide the proper direction and approached the border. But the gliders were not released on time and, in fact, were not decoupled until well over Dutch territory. Despite that, 9 of the 10 gliders were able to reach their objective, even though they had started to receive fire after crossing the German border at Aachen.

When the group started to descend for the bridge at Canne, it was exactly 0535 hours. Ever since the landing of *Sturmgruppe "Beton"* at 0515, the Belgian defenders knew they might be attacked.

While the gliders were still descending in tight spirals towards the bridge, four columns of flame shot up from demolition charges placed at four locations on the bridge. The charges had been ignited remotely from the fortress of Eben Emael.

Despite that, the men still had to try to carry out their mission, which was to clear a path at that location for the *61. Infanterie-Division*, advancing from the German frontier, across the canal.

The glider with the third section was shot down by a direct hit from an antiaircraft weapon only 30 meters above the ground. Burning, it dove vertically into the ground. The fact that six soldiers—most of them wounded—were able to be saved from the burning wreckage bordered on a miracle. A few of the nine gliders landed right in the middle of the Belgian positions. Some of the men had to engage in close combat from the very beginning.

Leutnant Martin Schächter, the commander of this detachment, moved to the front of his men and charged through an enemy trench line before a bullet to the head toppled him. A previous round to the leg had not been able to stop him. *Leutnant* Meissner assumed command. The men entered the village of Canne, firing, and smoked out pockets of resistance. They pressed on to the bridge and took the bunkers. At 0550 hours, *Leutnant* Meissner reported: "*Sturmgruppe Eisen:* Object reached. Bridge blown up by the enemy while landing. Can be made passable with engineer preparation."

When the enemy moved out to launch an immediate counterattack, 12 *Stukas* roared in. They dipped their wings and screamed earthwards, dropping their bombs in the middle of the attack groups before they climbed into the heavens again with howling motors.

Later on, after it had become afternoon, Belgian forces attacked from the west and then from the southwest. But the paratroopers had crawled their way into the earth and defended the ground they had taken bitterly. The enemy was thrown back again and again.

It was a half hour before midnight when the first reinforcements arrived—men of *Pionier-Bataillon 51* and *Infanterie-Regiment 151* of the *51. Infanterie-Division*—and helped support the paratroopers against what had been the heaviest Belgian attacks mounted against the airborne insertions. It was not until 11 May that *Sturmgruppe "Eisen"* was able to march back towards

Maastricht. It had suffered the heaviest casualties of the four airborne groups: 22 dead and 26 wounded.

✠

Sturmabteilung Koch had achieved decisive success and Student had this to say about it after the war:

> It accomplished its mission in a magnificent manner . . . [and with regard to *Sturmgruppe Granit*] It was an accomplishment of unique boldness and decisive importance. A handful of paratroopers, strongly supported by the *Luftwaffe*, was able to force a breakthrough for a field army. I have studied the history of the last war on all fronts. Among the many brilliant feats of arms by both friend and foe, I have not been able to find a single example that could compare with the great success of *Sturmabteilung Koch*.

THE ATTACK ON WAALHAVEN

The *III./FJR 1* of *Hauptmann* Karl-Lothar Schulz had received orders to jump into the airfield at Waalhaven. *Oberst* Bräuer had raised the bar for the captain the night before the operation: "Schulz, your mission is the most important of the entire regiment. You have to take Waalhaven so that the air-landed forces of the *22. Infanterie-Division* can follow."

✠

After receiving the go-ahead signal, the battalion was ready to jump. *Hauptmann* Schulz stood prepared to jump in the door of the lead machine. The wind pressure was pushing him back into the cabin, forcing him to grip even tighter to the door frame. Then he heard the jump horn.

With a leap, Schulz found himself in the open. He felt the weight of the equipment bag and the weapon, which were rushing him to earth. The wind resistance tore at him. Then he felt the heavy thud of the deployment. The white bell of silk above him spread out and he sank, floating, the remaining 80 to 90 meters to earth.

Floating all around him were the broad, bright chutes with paratroopers hanging underneath them. The men of the battalion had jumped in clusters. Gray clouds of antiaircraft fire greeted them from Rotterdam's airport at Waalhaven. Then there was a burst near Schulz. Machine-gun salvoes arched up towards the parachutes, but they were already starting to touch down. Schulz pressed his leather gloves to his face. He drew up his legs and executed a landing fall. The chute collapsed quickly. With a quick, well-practiced grip he dropped the harness. He was on the ground in one piece.

He ran forward in long strides and jumped into the cover offered by a shallow ditch, as machine-gun fire started swinging his way. He raised his flare gun and fired the pre-arranged signal: "Assemble around the commander!"

Leutnant Schuller was the first one to reach him. A machine-gun squad followed.

The companies reassembled, one after the other.

"Over there, *Herr Hauptmann!*" Schuller called out. Three Dutch personnel carriers were racing towards them. The burst of fire from the first machine-gun hit the wheeled vehicle in the front. It spun around sharply, turned over and landed on its roof. The two other vehicles closed up to their stricken comrade, braked sharply and spewed their human cargo, a handful of men. Their rifle fires were stopped by bursts of machine-gun fire.

Oberleutnant Becker, the commander of the 10th Company, worked his way over to the battalion commander by leaps and bounds.

Schulz then issued orders: "Becker, take your company to the antiaircraft position at the northern end of the runway. The 9th goes to the bunkers at the southern end. Kerfin, take the 11th to the islands in the Meuse. Knock out the antiaircraft batteries there. Schuller, you and the machine-gun section come with me! We're going for the admin buildings!"

The companies worked their way forward to their separate objectives. *Hauptmann* Schulz thrust his arm three times into the air and then took off with his group. They had barely gotten 10 meters, when machine-gun fire forced them to take cover in a drainage ditch. One of his squads put down covering fire, while the two remaining squads ran in one bound to the two abandoned Dutch trucks, jumped in and then raced towards the airfield admin buildings in a zigzag fashion.

All of the companies were receiving fire. Two rapid-fire weapons were firing salvoes in the direction of the approaching trucks. Luckily, none hit before the vehicles reached the dead zone around the buildings. While still coming to a stop, Schulz and his men jumped out and assaulted the offices of the airfield administrator. The machine-gun squad helped keep the Dutch officers assembled there in check.

"Gentlemen!" Schulz addressed the officers. "The airfield is in German hands. You are my prisoners."

"You've attacked a neutral country," the senior officer, a lieutenant colonel, yelled, enraged. On his desk was a silver wreath with the number 40 in it. It turned out that he was going to celebrate his 40th year of military service that day.

"Is the airfield mined?" Schulz asked. The lieutenant colonel answered no. But Schulz had to ascertain that the area was clear for the follow-on forces. He intended to drive over the entire area, and he asked the lieutenant colonel to accompany him. Not until that had occurred did Schulz have his situation report radioed to the headquarters for the Rotterdam operation: "Airfield in our hands. Antiaircraft batteries taken. Possible to land."

It took barely 10 minutes before the first German transporters appeared on the horizon. They approached at a fairly low altitude, their escort fighters circling above them.

A few seconds later, the paratroopers saw their first enemy fighters. It was a flight of Hurricanes, which dove on the hapless *Ju 52's* from the northwest.

But they were unable to drive home the attack, because the German fighters had spotted their opponents at exactly the right time. From a higher altitude, they dove on the Hurricanes. A wild dogfight ensued, and muzzle flashes from machine-guns and cannon could be seen. The first Hurricane was hit; it burst apart in a huge ball of flame in the middle of the skies. A German fighter then headed straight for the ground. There was a thick plume of smoke behind it. There was a brief flash of flame as it slammed into the ground.

The attackers were knocked out of the sky. The first *Ju 52's* made it through and landed on the conquered airfield. As they taxied in, Schulz was already on his way to greet them in the fast Dutch truck. *Oberstleutnant* von Choltitz was the first to leave the aircraft. He approached the *Hauptmann* rapidly.

"Man alive, Schulz, you did it!" he exclaimed, out of breath.

At that moment, as the *Ju 52's* started to taxi in, a previously unidentified antiaircraft position opened fire. One of the *Ju 52's* making its final approach was hit and burst asunder. Burning pieces of wreckage were scattered to the four winds. A second aircraft was then hit; it came down on fire but was able to land. It taxied to a stop and soldiers spewed out of the fuselage before it went completely up in flames.

Schulz called out: "Becker, report to me with your company!" When the *Oberleutnant* arrived, Schulz told him what to do: "The fire is coming from that finger of land at Waalhaven. We have to silence it!"

The Dutch airfield commander stated that he would attempt to get it to surrender. He jumped into Schulz's vehicle and they approached the battery at speed. They had approached to within 200 meters, when the battery let loose with another salvo. The Dutch officer ran towards it, arms waving. "Stop firing!" he called out. "Stop firing!"

A few seconds later, machine-gun fire bellowed from out of the position. Arms still outstretched, the Dutch officer fell to the ground, mortally wounded.

The paratroopers attacked. They entered the battery's firing positions and silenced the guns. The Rotterdam airfield was then unquestionably in German hands. The remaining *Ju 52's* started to land again.

A short while later, *Generalleutnant* Student landed. He was accompanied by his operations officer, *Major i.G.*[3] Trettner, and the rest of his battle staff. Schulz reported to him, and Student shook his hand: "Thank you, Schulz. You did well!"

Gradually, the *Flak*, artillery and the entire *III./Infanterie-Regiment* were landed. The headquarters of the *7. Flieger-Division* then jumped in.

After the war, Student would write: "Schulz's battalion brought about a terrific feat-of-arms against a prepared defense at that highly important place, which was so important for the continued conduct of the operation."

---

3. Translator's Note: General Staff Major. = *i.G. im General-Stab.* There were generally two general-staff-trained officers in a German division, the operations officer and the logistics officer.

✠

While the *7. Flieger-Division* and other forces were being brought in, *General der Flieger* Kesselring's *Luftflotte 2* continued to fly support sorties. *Stukas* dove on Belgian and Dutch artillery positions, scattered reserve formations that were being brought forward, and took out identified enemy command posts. To the west of the area where the paratroopers of the machine-gun company had jumped to reinforce the personnel who had taken the bridges, feints were launched and dummy equipment dropped. The intent was to confuse the enemy and prevent his forces from concentrating.

Hauptmann Koch, who had set up his command post at the middle bridge in Vroenhaven, was in constant contact with the *61. Infanterie-Division*, especially *Pionier-Bataillon 51*, which had advanced the farthest to the west.

The great concern was a Belgian counterattack, which the paratroopers probably could not have withstood. The advancing *61. Infanterie-Division* was unable to move as rapidly as had been planned, since the bridge at Maastricht had been blown up. Had the Belgians attacked at this moment of German weakness, who knows what the outcome might have been. But everything worked out for the Germans.

THE REMAINING JUMPS

The *II./FJR 1* of *Hauptmann* Prager was employed against the bridges at Moerdijk. Prager, who was suffering from intestinal cancer and who had been in a hospital, reported back for duty despite the advice of physicians. Student gave him command of the battalion, even though he knew Prager's condition. The general was unable to turn down the request of that terrific officer; at the same time, he knew it would be his last military operation.

The battalion jumped into the southeast bulwark of Fortress Holland. The north end of the bridge at Moerdijk was dominated by an enormous concrete bunker. Once on the ground, the paratroopers were receiving heavy fires from the firing ports of the bunker. The *5./FJR 1* of *Oberleutnant* Straeler-Pohl attacked the bunker from two sides. The 1st Platoon was able to approach the bunker under the covering fire of the two other platoons. The bundled charges were placed into position after *Gefreiter* Boehm had fired a long burst from his submachine-gun into one of the firing ports. All the charges were lit at the same time. Everybody threw himself on the ground. After the charges exploded, everyone in the bunker surrendered.

Leutnant Cord Tietjen then ran with his platoon across the bridge to the other bank. The charging men broke the remaining resistance on the other end. The men then stormed into the bunker on the far side with the electrical wiring for the detonations and tore them out from their connections, preventing the bridge from being blown up.

There was an intense fight for the railway bridge as well. There, some of the defenders had to be shot out of the bridgeworks because they would not surrender and fought to the bitter end. Five Dutch engineers held out with their carbines in the village of Moerdijk until three of their own were killed. On the German side, a *Leutnant* was killed who had actually lived in the area some years past. He was shot by rifle fire.

Even more difficult was the operation of the *3./FJR 1* under *Oberleutnant* von Brandis at Dordrecht. It had been directed to take the bridges over the Kill intact. The attacking paratroopers received machine-gun fire, accompanied by small-arms fire, from the Dutch trench and bunker positions. The first few paratroopers collapsed to the ground even before reaching their objective. *Oberleutnant* von Brandis was one of the first to get hit. One of his platoon leaders assumed acting command and rallied the company. The paratroopers combed the trenches, entered the village and advanced as far as the large bunker, which was being defended by a Dutch noncommissioned officer and police units.

The fighting raged back and forth for a long time. The Dutch noncommissioned officer turned down the offer to surrender. He had a 5-centimeter gun and a heavy machine-gun. The bunker was covered with smoke pots and grenades. The Dutch turned down a second and third offer to surrender. In the end, the bunker down was blown open and the barrel of the 5-centimeter gun was damaged by hand grenades and bundled charges. At that point, the Dutch noncommissioned officer was compelled to surrender. Because of his bravery, the Germans allowed the Dutch soldier to retain his sidearm, a Klewang.[4]

As a result of the crisis situation that threatened at the bridge, *Oberst* Bräuer, who had jumped with the *I./FJR 1* at Tweede Tool, ordered the remaining companies of the battalion to attack. During the afternoon of 10 May, they succeeded in taking the road bridge over the Kill after bitter fighting. It was not possible to take the railway bridge, however. The enemy put up a tough and bitter fight, and he succeeded in blowing it up before the majority of the paratroopers could arrive.

At first light on 11 May, the enemy started launching counterattacks at Dordrecht. The airborne invasion of Fortress Holland has always been written up in German histories as some sort of cake walk, a kind of *coup de main*, whereby the enemy was so surprised that he was unable to defend himself. The attacks of that morning proved otherwise.

The 3rd Company of the Dutch 28th Infantry Regiment and two platoons from its sister 2nd Company attempted to take back the artillery positions of the 1st and 3rd Battalions of the 17th Artillery Regiment that had been lost the previous day. Supporting those elements was an artillery battery that had not been run over. It fired at full bore to soften up the German positions

---

4. A Malay ceremonial dagger.

for the attack; its guns also landed some direct hits among the paratroopers. The Dutch then assaulted the positions and took them back, capturing some Germans in the process. When more paratroopers jumped in a short while later, they fired mortars on the Dutch, who then fell back to the Dordrecht-Sliedrecht rail line.

On the southern end of the island of Dordrecht were an additional two platoons of Dutch infantry. They were from the 2nd Company of the 28th Infantry Regiment and led by Officer Candidate Marijs. When a Red Cross vehicle stopped to pick up wounded from him, he asked the wounded men climbing aboard to inform the local military commander in Dordrecht that he needed reinforcements. Marijs was to wait in vain, however.

On the morning of 11 May, those two Dutch platoons collided with the German paratroopers, who had just jumped in. After fighting for several hours, the German forces had to surrender, since they had used up their ammunition. The Dutch officer assembled the Germans in an empty farmyard that evening, where both sides buried their dead. The Germans had lost 4 men, the Dutch 1. There were wounded on both sides. In all, some 33 Germans had been taken prisoner. On the morning of 12 May, as other German paratroopers moved in to attack, Officer Candidate Marijs surrendered, since his situation had become hopeless.

The Dutch marched with their former captives to the German command post. *Oberst* Bräuer was horrified to see that the Dutch still carried all of their weapons. He dressed down the *Oberleutnant,* asking why the enemy forces had not been disarmed. The younger officer explained what had happened and Bräuer, who appreciated bravery on both sides of the lines, allowed the officer candidate to keep his sidearm.

✠

In the suburbs of Rotterdam there had been heavy fighting. For instance, 120 soldiers of the *11./Infanterie-Regiment 16* under *Oberleutnant* Schrader had landed in 12 *He 59* seaplanes right next to the two bridges over the Nieuwe Maas and were able to cut the fuses to the demolition chambers. Then, however, the men ran into problems when the Dutch had collected themselves enough to launch an immediate counterattack. *Oberleutnant* Horst Kerfin's platoon of paratroopers from the *III./FJR 1,* which had jumped into the area south of the bridges, had to race to their help. Kerfin stopped a streetcar, had the passengers dismount and then moved to the location of *Oberleutnant* Schrader's air-landed forces.

During the morning of 11 May, *Oberst* Bräuer summoned the commander of the 3rd Battalion. *Hauptmann* Schulz and his men had Waalhaven firmly under control, and the follow-on forces of the *22. Luftlande-Division* could secure the area from that point forward. The situation at Moerdijk and Dordrecht gave *Oberst* Bräuer an even bigger headache than the situation described above. It was Bräuer's intent to have Schulz's battalion assist those forces.

"Schulz," the regimental commander stated sharply, "take a company and head off to there. Leave one company here so we have a reserve in case a hole should open up somewhere. Go straight to the main bridge at Moerdijk; some of the area is still in Dutch hands. *Hauptmann* Prager is still fighting. They have the bridge but can't expand the bridgehead."

The company took off in confiscated Dutch motorcycles and trucks. At the very front was Schulz, sitting on the passenger seat of a motorcycle. When they reached the area around the bridge, they started to receive machine-gun fire from the Dutch forces that had made their way up to the bridgework and were taking cover behind it.

"Haaalt!!! . . . Dismount and move forward in the ditches left and right of the street . . . put the machine-gun in position here and take the enemy under fire!"

While the German machine-gun went into position and took the muzzle flashes on the bridge under fire, Schulz and his men advanced in leaps and bounds. Just 50 meters from the bridge, Schulz felt a stinging pain in his hand. A round had gone through his clenched fist and taken off a finger. The battalion commander continued to run. He had gotten to within 20 meters of the bridge when he collapsed as the result of a round having gone through his right foot.

He remained where he had fallen, while his paratroopers ran past him and retook the bridge.

Hauptmann Schulz was evacuated to Germany with the other wounded. He had always led is battalion from the front; he had paid the price with two wounds.

But that did not signal the end of the fighting in that sector, however. Dutch artillery opened heavy fire on the paratrooper positions north of the bridge during the morning of 12 May. The Dutch planned a concentric attack with an *ad hoc* division of light infantry advancing on Dordrecht from the southwest, while another attack group from the area around the Kill River was sent east from Wieldrecht. The Dutch leadership hoped to block the Moerdijk—Dordrecht highway by doing so. But there were not enough supporting weapons to execute the plan, however. Above all, the Dutch were lacking in airpower. The only place they had been able to fly sorties had been at Grebbeberg.

When Colonel van der Baijl, the commander of the Dutch light division, received news that the first German tanks were already rolling over the bridge at Moerdijk and he was asked by a German emissary to surrender, he decided to attack anyway. But an aerial bombardment on the assembly areas of his division, prevented the execution of that plan, since the lead elements, the 2nd Regiment, was badly battered in the bombing raid.

When tanks started to appear near the assembly area, it was hoped that they were the French tanks that had been promised to support them. Once again, the Dutch colonel suffered a setback; they were German tanks.

The horse artillery of the Dutch managed to knock out two German tanks with their antitank guns. The remaining German tanks pulled back. Colonel van der Baijl issued orders to pull back behind the Merwede. The Dutch division had to abandon a lot of materiel in its former assembly areas. The attack by the Dutch group around the Kill was also called off.

THE BREAKTHROUGH OF THE *18. ARMEE*

As early as 11 May, the *18. Armee* had forced the Peel with its lead elements. The *9. Panzer-Division* had succeeded in crossing the Meuse at Gennap across the only bridge over that river that had not been blown up. It advanced rapidly towards Breda, pushing the French forces to the side, which were attempting to link up with the Dutch there, and reached the paratroopers at Moerdijk during the afternoon of 12 May with its reconnaissance battalion. The next day, the reconnaissance battalion moved out again, followed by the division's tank regiment following close behind. On 12 May, the Dutch 3rd Frontier Battalion was forced back at Wieldrecht. Since it had no armor-defeating weapons, it suffered 12 killed and the Germans took 40 prisoners.

The German armor then advanced on Dordrecht on 13 May, where a Dutch attack had started in the city center. Krispijn, a portion of the city that had been taken by the Dutch, was regained by the paratroopers with support from the tanks. As the German tanks approached, the Dutch pulled back.

That afternoon, the tanks rolled into Dordrecht proper. They were held up at three bridges by antitank guns. One tank was knocked out at the Vriese Bridge. All of the remaining tanks rolled across the bridges, eliminated the antitank guns and continued the advance. One Dutch antitank gun managed to knock out two German tanks before it was put out of commission.

The Dutch artillery positions, which had continued to engage the paratroopers in their bridgehead and at the bridge at Moerdijk, were put out of operation by an air strike.

A Dutch Fokker T-5 bomber, escorted by two G-1 fighter-bombers, attempted to take out the bridge at Moerdijk, but it was shot down. The entire crew was killed. Among the dead was Lieutenant Swagermann, who had also participated in the bombing of Ockenburg on 10 May.

After the German tanks had crossed the Kill at Gravendeel and reached the Barendrecht Bridge, they were engaged by two antitank guns positioned there that were under Gun Commander van der Boom. His gunner knocked out three German tanks, and the German attack stalled. The Dutch commander in the sector ordered a general withdrawal that night across the Spui, west of the Dordse Kill. That opened the route to the south part of Rotterdam for the tanks of *General* Hubicki's *9. Panzer-Division.*

THE YPENBURG AIRFIELD

The airfield at Ypenburg, which was the closest one to Den Haag, was supposed to be taken by the *I./FJR 2* of *Hauptmann* Noster, as were the other two airfields at Valkenburg and Ockenburg. To that end, the *6./FJR 2* was also attached to his battalion, as well as a platoon of engineers.

The Ypenburg airfield was guarded by a battalion of grenadiers. Forming the backbone of the defense was half a squadron of Hussars with six light tanks and a company with 9 heavy and 11 light machine-guns.

When the *Luftwaffe* ranged in to start its preparatory bombardment, it was greeted by 11 Douglas 8A reconnaissance aircraft that rose to defend the airfield. Eight of them were shot down. Of the Fokker DXXI fighters that took off, the German escort fighters were able to shot down two of them. In the turbulent dogfights, five *Bf 109's* were shot down by Dutch fighters.

After the aerial bombardment, the *Ju 52's* made their final approaches. The first sticks of paratroopers jumped, but they had been given the "green light" in the wrong place in some instances and had to work their way to the airfield later.

The paratroopers who approached the northern end of the runway were turned back by Dutch 1st Lieutenant Warnaars. The *Ju 52's* that came in a short while later with the forces to be air-landed were greeted by a hail of defensive fires. The first three *Ju 52's* landed at the southwest edge of the field, where they were set alight by heavy machine-gun fire. Only some of the soldiers were able to escape the stricken machines. The 3.7-centimeter cannon on the Dutch light tanks also participated in the firing, with the result that 17 of the German transporters were set on fire.

To the north of Delft, southwest of the airfield, the air-dropped paratroopers were held back by a heavy machine-gun. It was not until the machine-gun was eliminated that the paratroopers were able to advance north towards the airfield along the highway. They were able to reach the terminal of the airfield at the northwest corner of the complex. Using hand grenades, the building was stormed. *Oberleutnant* Stiemens was killed, but the airfield commander, Major Ten Taaft, surrendered. Ypenburg was partially under the control of the Germans, but 1st Lieutenant Warnaars refused to give up.

The German advance made it as far as the Hoorn Bridge. *Hauptmann* Nosters attempted in vain to continue the advance with his battalion. He knew that *Generalmajor* von Sponeck, the commander of the *22. Luftlande-Division*, wanted to land at the airfield so as to advance on Den Haag with his assault battalion.

The bridge over the Hoorn was decisive. It controlled the southern approaches to Den Haag. Some paratroopers attempted to cross the bridge with two captured motorcycles. They were shot up. Then, they were followed by a civilian passenger car with six paratroopers in it. Peppered with machine-gun fire, the car careened off to the side, broke through the railing and crashed into the de Vliet Canal. Two *Bf 109's* strafed the bridge with their machine-guns and automatic cannon in an effort to take out the bridge's defenders. Both of them were shot down by the 3.7-centimeter cannon of one of the light tanks that had been summoned from Ypenburg.

The paratrooper groups that were advancing between Rijswijk and Voorburg and were attempting to reach Den Haag from the east and the southeast were turned back at their respective bridges. Forces from Den Haag, even including some recruits, turned back the attacks.

At this difficult moment, the *Ju 52's* started to come on scene that were bringing *Generalmajor* von Sponeck, his battle staff and his fighting forces. In the lead aircraft was the division's artillery commander, *Oberstleutnant* De Boer. As they approached, the pilots realized they would be unable to land on the runway, which was covered with the wrecks of *Ju 52's*. The machines received orders to climb out and head for Rotterdam-Waalhaven, which had been taken and where, in the meantime, a *Flak* battery under *Oberleutnant* Timm had been positioned.

Starting in the afternoon, several Dutch immediate counterattack forces had been moving in on the airfield at Ypenburg. The first Dutch reinforcements arrived from northern Holland. One after the other, the German positions around the edge of the airfield were rolled up. Around 2000 hours of that first day of the offensive, some 240 German paratroopers surrendered. In all, some 425 paratrooper prisoners were taken from Rijswijk to England on the evening of 10 May 1940.

THE FIGHTING FOR OCKENBURG

Around 0400 hours, when the first aerial attacks against Ypenburg had taken place by the bombers and fighters of the *Luftwaffe*, the defenders at Ockenburg were alerted. This auxiliary airfield, which was located south of Den Haag at Kijkduin, was defended by the 22nd Depot Company of Captain Boot. At 0445 hours, a few Dutch fighters landed that had participated in the dogfights over Ypenburg. Five minutes later, the first German machines approached and engaged the airfield. Towards 0520 hours, the first *Ju 52's* arrived and the paratroopers alighted.

Dutch Officer Candidate Gritter opened fire with his platoon against the paratroopers. A Dutch contingent of seven men was taken out by the paratroopers. The Germans approached the airfield, but they were held up again and again by small bands of determined Dutch defenders.

When 18 *Ju 52's* approached to land with elements of the *22. Luftlande-Division*, the airfield was still in Dutch hands. The defenders immediately opened fire and several of the *Ju 52's* were set alight. When eight machines started to approach, that had been turned away from their original objective of Ypenburg, they again saw burning wrecks on the airfield. The Dutch antiaircraft guns were still firing, and the aircraft carrying the division commander was hit. The pilot veered away and then landed in the flat land behind the dunes. Some of the remaining machines landed directly on the dunes or right next to the coast; a few even landed on the Rotterdam–Den Haag Highway.

Out in the open field, *Generalmajor* von Sponeck assembled the forces that could be found. He also established contact with *Luftflotte 2* with a radio that was still functional. Based on Sponeck's reports and those from *Oberstleutnant* De Boer, *General der Flieger* Kesselring, the tactical air force commander, ordered the remaining elements of the *22. Luftlande-Division*, which were still in the air, to head for Rotterdam.

The third wave of the *22. Luftlande-Division* was stopped while it was still in Germany. *Oberst* Fichte, the commander of the division's liaison staff, ordered the operation halted when it was obvious there were no longer any opportunities to take other airfields around Den Haag, since all of the jump battalions had already been employed. The remaining 5,000 soldiers of the division had to wait in Germany.

At the Ockenburg airfield, the paratroopers and the men from *Infanterie-Regiment 65*, who had been air landed, succeeded in breaking the last of the Dutch resistance by 0745 hours. Of the 96 Dutch defenders, 24 had been killed and 14 wounded. The after-action report of *Infanterie-Regiment 65* later stated:

> After two hours of hard fighting, the airfield could be taken after sustaining heavy friendly losses. The rifle and machine-gun fires of the defenders was so strong that the flight crews of the aircraft that had landed were compelled to dismount their aircraft machine-guns and participate in the fighting on the airfield.

Dutch artillery then fired on the airfield when *Ju 52's* were parked there. A series of them went up in flames. The airfield barracks also burned to the ground.

After the success at Ockenburg, it seemed that the way to Den Haag and the imperial palace, despite all of the difficulties that had occurred up to that point, was open to the paratroopers and air-landed forces. The following forces were in the area in and around Ockenburg:

- Elements of the *6./FJR 2* (*Oberleutnant* Schirmer)
- The *3./FJR 2* (*Oberleutnant* von Roon)
- The headquarters of the *22. Luftlande-Division*
- The headquarters of *Infanterie-Regiment 65*
- The headquarters of the *II./Infanterie-Regiment 65*
- The *5./Infanterie-Regiment 65*
- Small elements of *Infanterie-Regiment 47*

This total of between 700 and 900 men then started the assault on Den Haag.

It should be mentioned that the flowers which *Generalmajor* von Sponeck had brought along for presentation to Queen Wilhelmina had been lost when the *Ju 52* he was on had to make its emergency landing. The general hoped he would be able to pick up some more on the way to the palace.

There was still a chance to force the Dutch General Staff, the government and the civil administration to capitulate on this, the first day of the invasion. That would have been better, not only for the German airborne forces but also for Holland, especially the city of Rotterdam. But the continued German advance was held up along the Laan van Meerdevoort–Kijkduinse Road, where any and all Dutch forces to be found around Den Haag were sent. When it appeared that the German airborne forces would force a breakthrough, the 13th Company of Captain van den Putten launched an attack at Loosduinen and threw back the German forces by dint of massed machine-gun fires. For the time being, the threat of a breakthrough by the Germans had been thwarted.

The Dutch then attempted to win back the airfield at Ockenburg. Dutch artillery—it was the 1st Battalion of the 2nd Artillery Regiment—registered on the airfield, aided by observers from Poeldijk, and set 12 more *Ju 52's* alight. The Dutch then attacked and, by the afternoon, had taken back the entire airfield. One hundred and sixty Germans were taken prisoner.

Generalmajor von Sponeck, together with some 300 men, succeeded in escaping to the woods west of Loosduins and digging in there.

With that, the airfield at Ockenburg was also lost. The only remaining airfield of the original three was Valkenburg.

THE ATTACK ON VALKENBURG

At the same time the airfields at Ypenburg and Ockenburg were being attacked, the Germans were also attacking Valkenburg. The airfield had not been completed. The ground was still too soft. As a result, there were neither Dutch military aircraft or heavy antiaircraft defenses there. Even so, there were still 20 light and 4 heavy machine-guns emplaced around the airfield.

Major General Best, the Dutch commander of air defenses for Holland, had all of the airfields under his responsibility beefed up in their defenses after seeing what the German airborne forces had done in Norway. The machine-guns came from a platoon of the 3rd Battalion of the 4th Infantry Regiment. In addition, there were two line companies from the same regiment positioned there.

When the lieutenant on guard duty heard aircraft noises around 0300 hours on 10 May, he sounded the alert. A short while later, the first bombs fell, with their target being the large aircraft hangar. The bombers were followed by the fighters, which dove down to the airfield and strafed it with cannon and machine-guns. The officer-in-charge on duty, 1st Lieutenant Möller, was killed at one of the field positions.

German paratroopers jumped in a short while later at the southeast and northwest ends of the runway. A reinforced platoon had jumped in, and it was engaged while the men were still in the air.

A few minutes later, the *Ju 52* transporters arrived. On board were four companies of *Infanterie-Regiment 47*, the headquarters of the 2nd and 3rd Battalions and the regimental signals platoon. The heavy machine-guns did not open fire until the *Ju 52's* approached. Their rounds peppered the three-engined aircraft, with two of them catching on fire.

Motorcycles were unloaded from the aircraft, manned and then headed off in the direction of the Dutch strongpoints. The first motorcycle was hit by a salvo of fire. The others turned back, but they were also hit and stopped.

Nevertheless, the paratroopers succeeded in advancing on the airfield from three sides and eliminating the pockets of resistance, one after the other. It took until 0730 hours however, before the airfield at Valkenburg could be reported as being in German hands.

A number of *Ju 52's* had sunk up to their axles in the soft ground of the unimproved runway and remained stuck. A portion of the forces intended for Valkenburg—some 320 men—were discharged on the beach at Katwijk.

The paratroopers that had jumped in south of the airfield continued marching south and blocked the important Amsterdam–Den Haag highway. The bridge over the Oude Rijn at Haagse Schouwe was occupied. Another section advanced as far as De Deyl, east of Wassenaar.

The paratroopers had blocked the most important ground transportation artery with their operations. The Dutch forces still in the north of Holland were unable to come to the help of the forces fighting at Den Haag from that point forward.

Dutch assault detachments attempted to win back the airfield during the afternoon of 10 May, but they were unable to accomplish anything against the paratroopers, who had matters in hand.

First Lieutenant Hohendorf, who was in charge of the forces of the 47th Infantry near the airfield, called his battalion headquarters at Katwijk/See on the only remaining telephone line available to him and recommended that the Dutch government surrender, since farther resistance was useless.

He also stressed that the Dutch artillery should not fire on the airfield, since the Dutch prisoners that had been taken were being assembled in the terminal. Despite that request, the commander of the 4th Artillery Regiment had fires commence from his 3rd Battalion from the dunes at Katwijk, after the battalion commander there had provided information. Approximately 20 aircraft on the field were destroyed. The next day, the artillery fired on the airfield another two times before a company under the command of Major Mallinckrodt attacked the airfield and retook it by 1730 hours. Fourteen undamaged *Ju 52's* fell into the hands of the Dutch.

The paratroopers, who had fought their way through to the elements of *Infanterie-Regiment 47*, which had landed in the dunes at Katwijk, were able to encircle the Dutch 1st Battalion of the 1st Infantry Regiment on 11 May. The Dutch commander was killed and half of the battalion's soldiers were taken captive.

The attempted Dutch attack on the village of Valkenburg, which the Germans also held, did not succeed, because the Dutch forces that had penetrated to the middle of the village were taken under fire by their own artillery—a battery of the 1st Battalion of the 6th Artillery Regiment—and had to pull back rapidly.

As the reader will recall, *Generalmajor Graf* von Sponeck, the commander of the air-inserted forces attacking the three airfields around Den Haag, had had to pull back to the woods around Ockenburg and prepared to defend, at least temporarily. The paratroopers and air-landed soldiers dug in. From a nearby hill, the Belvedere, German paratroopers fired on Captain van Eysinga, whose 3rd Company was advancing on the German positions. The Dutch captain was killed while advancing with several machine-guns against this dominant terrain. The woods and a country estate, which had been occupied by the German forces, were surrounded. When the Dutch forces advanced on the estate early in the morning of 12 May, they found the buildings abandoned. Only a few paratroopers, who had served as a rearguard, were captured.

Generalmajor von Sponeck had already had some of his forces advance on Wateringen, where a Dutch headquarters was located. But those forces did not get through. A few tanks rolled up from the direction of Den Haag, and the forces were forced to pull back, only to get caught in the fires of a Dutch battle group at 'T Woud. Those Dutch forces had arrived from Delft in order to assist in cutting off the German forces. The Germans were able to get through that Dutch force and then set up for an all-round defense at Pverschie. They were able to hold out there until 14 May. An attack by some 2,500 Dutch under the command of Lieutenant Colonel Scherpenhuyzen, the commander of a light infantry regiment, was not able to penetrate the defensive positions. The airborne forces were able to hold out.

In the end, the bombing of Rotterdam forced the Dutch to call off their attacks. The ambitious effort to take Holland in a single day by taking the government and queen prisoner had failed. The fighting had cost the Germans considerable casualties and losses in materiel. They were among the hardest fighting that the paratroopers would experience. Up to now, however, they have not been mentioned adequately in any German account, since they did not quite fit in with the outstanding successes enjoyed by the paratroop elements elsewhere.

THE DRAMA OF ROTTERDAM

The command and control headquarters of *Generalleutnant* Student had already started its work in Waalhaven on the evening of 10 May. The next day, *Oberstleutnant* Triebel, from the reconnaissance section of the *Luftflotte 2*, arrived. He had been sent by *General der Flieger* Kesselring, who wanted to get an on-the-ground appraisal from one of his staff officers.

Student was in the process of studying the plans to clean up the situation around Dordrecht, when Triebel, whose *HS 126* light reconnaissance aircraft had been pursued and attacked by enemy fighters on the way back, arrived and reported in. Student gave the liaison officer a handwritten account of the events of the first day and the status of the fighting on 11 May. He informed Kesselring of his farther intentions and ended with the following sentence: "One can already say that the airborne operations will end in complete success."

Kesselring took the report with him to Berlin, where he reported to Hitler and then presented him with the handwritten report from Student after he had finished. Hitler and Goebbels, who was also present, were satisfied. The heavy casualties at the three airfields near Den Haag and the failure of that part of the plan did not cause them any major concern—the basic intent had succeeded.

On 12 May, a *Leutnant* from the *9. Panzer-Division* reported to Student at the bridge at Dordrecht and informed him that he had been sent forward with the armor of his reconnaissance company. Student felt that the planned operations were in the process of being realized.

After the link-up, Student's two divisions were attached to the Commanding General of the *XXXIX Armee-Korps (mot.)*, *Generalleutnant* Rudolf Schmidt. Schmidt had received orders to finish off the fighting in Holland with the capture of Den Haag. That was easier said than done.

On the morning of 13 May, Student and two of his staff liaison officers, conducted a leaders' reconnaissance around Dordrecht. Everything was quiet in the southeast part of the city. A short while later, the commander of the advance guard of the *9. Panzer-Division* reported to Student that the armored attack on the portions of the city still held by the enemy would commence shortly.

Advancing rapidly, the armored forces soon broke the Dutch pockets of resistance. In the afternoon, the Dutch raised a white flag of surrender on the cathedral of Dordrecht. Towards evening, the main body of the *9. Panzer-Division* was at the disposal of Student, so that he could finally put an end to the resistance on the Rotterdam bridges, which were still being held on the north bank. That was intended to be the last mission of the paratroopers. With the help of the *9. Panzer-Division*, they would open the way for the *18. Armee.*

Early on the morning of 14 May, *Generalmajor Dr.* Hubicki, the commander of the armored division appeared at Student's command post at Rijsoord. A short while later, *Generalleutnant* Schmidt, the corps commanders, also appeared. Student then officially turned over command of farther operations to the Commanding General.

Dordrecht had been taken after the tanks had sustained heavy losses. As a result of those losses, Student came to the conclusion that farther operations against the bridgehead of the Dutch north of the Rotterdam bridges could not succeed without support from the air, as long as the Dutch did not capitulate. It was a decision dictated by the situation.

The targets were planned in detail. They were areas where the enemy was still bitterly defending: At the Meuse Train Station and a small section at the northern end of the bridge, no incendiary bombs were to be used.

Generalleutnant Schmidt issued an ultimatum to the local area commander for Rotterdam, after negotiations between *Oberstleutnant* Choltitz, the commander of the fighting forces at the Rotterdam bridges, and an emissary from Colonel Scharroo broke down. After the time for the ultimatum had run out, a captain appeared at the Rotterdam road bridge as an emissary for the Dutch forces and stated that the ultimatum did not have a signature. That was a ploy on the part of the Dutch commander, who was biding for time. In the process, he sealed the fate of Rotterdam. *Generalleutnant* Schmidt initially allowed for a slip of the deadline, at least until a ceasefire could be arranged. At the same time, he sent a radio message that was intended to keep the German bombers at their bases in Germany.

The radio message, which had to be sent through *Luftflotte 2*, did not arrive in time. Where the bottleneck occurred could not be determined after the war.

It is a fact, however, that Kesselring carried on an excited telephone conversation before the bombardment of Rotterdam with Göring. Kesselring insisted that only military targets be bombed; Göring wanted to bomb the entire city.

In the daily logs of *Heeresgruppe B*[5], the radio message of Göring to *Luftflotte 2* is mentioned, in which Göring ordered "breaking through, no matter the cost, to the forces of *Generalmajor* von Sponeck, who were in dire circumstances." In case he did not immediately hear of a breakthrough, he would order a bombing raid by an entire wing on Rotterdam between 1720 and 1820 hours.

On the day before, *Generalleutnant* Schmidt had received orders by radio at 1705 hours from the *18. Armee*: "Resistance in Rotterdam is to be broken by all means available. If necessary, the destruction of the city is to be threatened *and* conducted."

Those reports and transmissions serve today to present the bombing of Rotterdam as an intentional destructive effort, even if that's not really the case.

Early in the afternoon of 14 May, Student and Schmidt were at the circle south of the bridges, waiting for the decision of the Dutch commander. The forces assembled for the attack were waiting under cover along the streets. Suddenly, the general officers heard the sound of aircraft engines.

Those sounds were coming from the 100 German bombers that had taken off from the airfields at Delmenhorst and Gütersloh. Under the leadership of the wing commander, *Oberst* Lackner, they were headed for a surveyed triangle northwest of the Rotterdam bridges. The bombers were only flying at an altitude of 750 meters, in order to be as accurate as possible.

Just before reaching the target area, the bomb group, consisting of elements from all three groups of *Kampfgeschwader 54*, split up. The left-hand group was commanded by *Oberstleutnant* Höhne, while the right-hand group was personally led by *Oberst* Lackner. Time on target was scheduled for 1500 hours.

"For God's sake!" Schmidt exclaimed. "There's going to be hell to pay!"

Both of the generals, who had been indoctrinated in the culture of the old army and were permeated with the dictates of chivalry, were horrified. Right in front of their eye there was about to be a violation of the ceasefire they had arranged. They felt compelled to try to stop it.

"Flare!" Student called out. A man handed him a flare pistol, and he personally fired red signal flares which should have stopped the formation

---

5. Translator's Note: Field Army Group B.

from bombing. Those escorting Schmidt also fired flares into the air.

But it was too late. The bombers crossed the Meuse at 1505 hours. Dutch antiaircraft defenses came to life, and the right-hand group had reached its target area. The bombs fell and howled earthward, hitting the designated targets precisely. A few seconds later, *Oberstleutnant* Höhne's group also reached the target area. He had barely issued the order to drop bombs when he spotted two red flares among the muzzle flashes of the antiaircraft weapons.

"Abort! . . . Abort! . . . Don't drop!" he ordered. But his *He 111* and the other machines of the command group had already dropped their payload. The remaining 43 machines were able to receive the order in time to prevent their bombing. Despite that, 97 tons of bombs had fallen to the earth. They were all high-explosive bombs, not incendiaries, as has often been claimed in other countries. The fact that the old city of Rotterdam burned down was due to the buildings, which went up in flames after one load of bombs missed its target.

The bombing of Rotterdam was a consequence of inadequate communications *and* a chain of unfortunate events. The greater tragedy of the entire affair was that it occurred at a time when it was not really even necessary. Part of the blame can be attributed to the local area commander for Rotterdam. Senseless resistance was occurring, which no longer had any influence at all on the outcome of the fighting in Holland.

Student was put in front of a court in Holland after the war for the bombing—and declared not guilty. His defense team had made the case that the Germans had requested the surrender of the city several times, that the German forces had stopped at the Meuse bridges and that the Dutch had offered resistance there with regular forces. As a result, Article 25 of the Haag Conventions was not applicable. Rotterdam could be considered a defended city and was engaged, as was the case later on with Berlin and other German cities.

According to official Dutch sources, the aerial attack on the city led to the death of 825 civilians.

After the bombing, the city capitulated and the Dutch commander personally appeared at the Wilhelm Bridge leading to the Meuse Island to conduct the negotiations. For him, it was also a tragic experience, for which he blamed himself.

Three and one half hours later, General Winkelmann, the Commander-in-Chief of the Dutch forces, capitulated.

Student received orders to lead the continued negotiations with the Dutch for their disarmament. He then went to northwestern part of the city to the command post of the Dutch, which was located in the upper floor of an apartment building. Accompanied by *Hauptmann* Hübner and *Oberstleutnant* von Choltitz, Student spoke admiring words to the Dutch officers assembled in the meeting room: "In every battle, there will be victors and vanquished. In this case, gentlemen, you were the one who lost. The Dutch forces have proven themselves to be brave and self-sacrificing."

As the talks were going on concerning details of the disarmament, rifle shots were heard outside. Everyone present was aghast. Was the fighting going to flare up again? Student, who was wearing his general officer's overcoat with the white lapels due to the onset of the evening coolness, went up to the window to see what was causing the sounds of fighting. He later wrote:

> Suddenly, I received a monstrous blow to my forehead, as if by a heavy ball peen hammer. Then I perceived an unusual, abhorrent sound in my skull. It was a rubbing, crashing and cracking of bones, which then turned into a vibration and singing throughout my entire head. As was later determined, I had received a tangential shot, which split open by upper skull the width of my hand.
>
> If I had not experienced it myself, I never would have thought it possible to be shot in the head and remain fully conscious and—almost in slow motion—experience such a thing.
>
> I thought I had been mortally wounded. Bu I gathered all my willpower to live. With my last remaining strength, I tried to hold on to the edge of the table. But my knees turned weak and I collapsed under the table. Then deepest night surrounded me.

What had happened?

It turned out that an advance guard of *SS-Regiment "Leibstandarte"* had just reached the area outside of the Dutch military headquarters. When the *SS* men saw the Dutch soldiers still carrying weapons, they immediately opened fire. It is possible that Student was hit by a German bullet, but no convincing evidence has been found of this. The Dutch troops were also firing.

Oberstleutnant von Choltitz ran out into the open to stop the wild firefight.

Generalmajor Richard Putzier, the Chief of the transport formations of the *Luftwaffe*, assumed command of the airborne forces.

Student was taken to the Rotterdam hospital and operated on by a Dutch surgeon. The immediate operation probably saved his life. He gradually regained his speech, which he had also lost for a short while.

A few days later, the famous German brain surgeon, *Professor* Tönnis, went to Rotterdam. It was thanks to his abilities that Student was able to fully recover after nine months.

On 29 May, Student was promoted ahead of his peers to *General der Flieger*. Due to his magnificent leadership, he had been awarded the Knight's Cross on 12 May. A group of other paratroopers who had participated in the operations in Holland were also awarded the Knight's Cross.

✠

To conclude this chapter on operations in the low lands, we turned once again to the pen of Student:

On the German side, the airborne operations against Fortress Holland and the air-landed operations along the Albert Canal bridges and at Eben Emael signaled the final victory against all resistance of the idea of airborne operations. Not only did the entire world pay attention, so did the German Armed Forces.

The paratroopers who had lost faith after Poland also returned to our ranks. The German airborne forces formed the tightest-knit of communities.

The *22. Luftlande-Division* suffered the greatest casualties during these operations. Of the 2,000 soldiers it committed, some 40% of the officers and 28% of the enlisted personnel were killed. One hundred and seventy *Ju 52's* were shot down or lost. Just as many were severely damaged. The objectives of the air-landed forces had not been achieved. Den Haag was not taken by surprise. Nonetheless, the landings at the three nearby airfields had a strongly demoralizing effect on the Dutch leadership.

The paralyzing effect of not knowing what to expect, which negatively influences the ability of the defender to make correct judgments and act decisively, had been achieved by the operations of the division.

The operations of the *7. Flieger-Division* had been crowned with success, even though some of the successes were not achieved in the first round. At Dordrecht, the success teetered on failure. Despite it all, the first massed employment of paratroopers had been a complete success, and the trust that its adherents had placed in it was fully justified.

The paratroopers and air-landed forces returned to their bases in Germany to recover and prepare for future missions. One of them was to be *Operation "Seelöwe"*, the planned invasion of England.

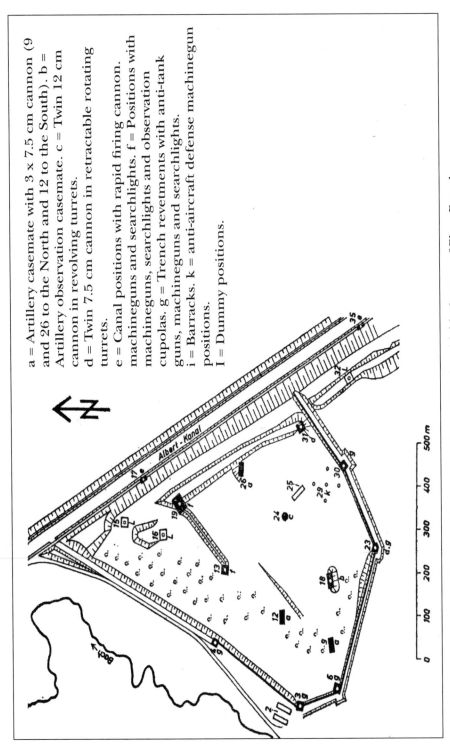

a = Artillery casemate with 3 x 7.5 cm cannon (9 and 26 to the North and 12 to the South). b = Artillery observation casemate. c = Twin 12 cm cannon in revolving turrets.
d = Twin 7.5 cm cannon in retractable rotating turrets.
e = Canal positions with rapid firing cannon. machineguns and searchlights. f = Positions with machineguns, searchlights and observation cupolas. g = Trench revetments with anti-tank guns, machineguns and searchlights.
i = Barracks. k = anti-aircraft defense machinegun positions.
I = Dummy positions.

Details of the gun positions of the formidable fortress of Eben Emael.

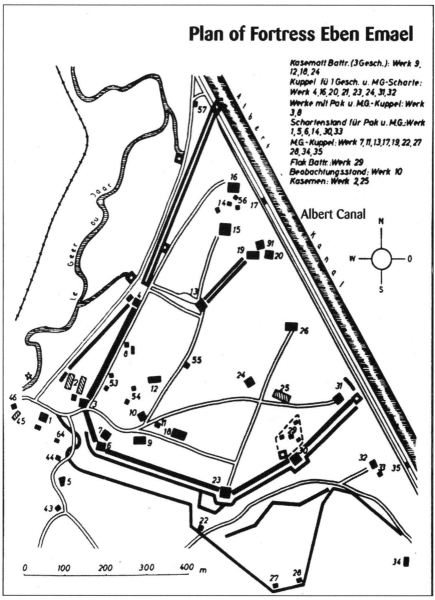

Plan of Fortress Eben Emael

Kasematt Battr. (3 Gesch.): Werk 9, 12, 18, 24
Kuppel fü 1 Gesch. u. MG-Scharte: Werk 4, 16, 20, 21, 23, 24, 31, 32
Werke mit Pak u. MG.-Kuppel: Werk 3, 8
Schartenstand für Pak u. MG.:Werk 1, 5, 6, 14, 30, 33
MG.-Kuppel: Werk 7, 11, 13, 17, 19, 22, 27, 28, 34, 35
Flak Battr.:Werk 29
Beobachtungsstand: Werk 10
Kasernen: Werk 2, 25

Albert Canal

N
W — O
S

Details of the devastating firepower of Eben Emael.
Casemate batteries with 3 guns: numbers 9, 12, 18 and 24.
Cupolas for 1 cannon and a machine-gun: numbers 4, 16, 20, 21, 23, 24, 31 and 32.
Positions with antitank guns and machine-gun cupolas: numbers 3 and 8.
Pillboxes with antitank guns and machine-guns: numbers 1, 5, 6, 14, 30 and 33.
Machine-gun cupolas: numbers 7, 11, 13, 17, 19, 22, 27, 28, 34 and 35.
Antiaircraft battery: number 29.
Artillery observation position: number 10.
Barracks: numbers 2 and 25.

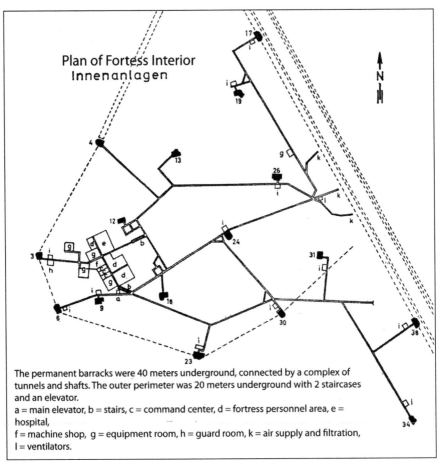

Plan of Fortess Interior
Innenanlagen

N

The permanent barracks were 40 meters underground, connected by a complex of tunnels and shafts. The outer perimeter was 20 meters underground with 2 staircases and an elevator.
a = main elevator, b = stairs, c = command center, d = fortress personnel area, e = hospital,
f = machine shop, g = equipment room, h = guard room, k = air supply and filtration, l = ventilators.

The majority of the fortress was buried deep underground, protected from aerial bombing and artillery. An attack by gliderborne troops was not anticipated.

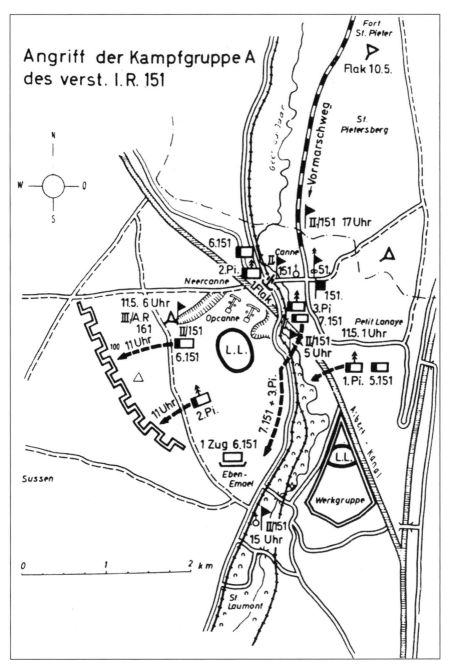

Route of the attack by Battlegroup A of the *Infanterie-Regiment 151*. Eben Emael is at the lower right.

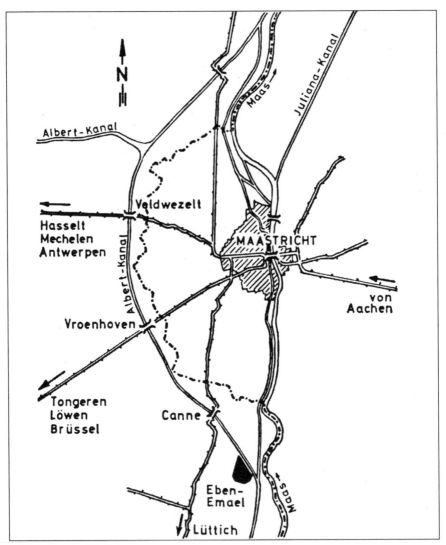

Map indicating the staregic importance of Eben Emael. The guns of the fortress would disrupt both an enemy advance on Maastricht and any attempt to cross the Maas River or the Albert Canal.

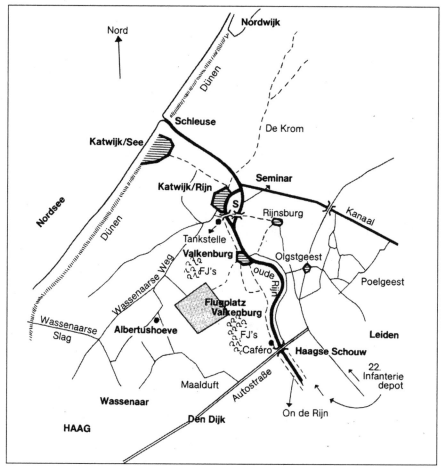

Map showing the location of the strategically important Valkenburg airfield.

Dutch marines surrender at a bridge over the Meuse.

Dutch bunker along the Grebbe Line after taking fire. Direct fires from 88mm antiaircraft guns were particularly effective in penetrating firing ports.

Shot-down *Ju 52* at Valkenburg.

The Paratrooper Assault Badge.

CHAPTER 4

Between the Campaign in the West and Crete

THE 7. *FLIEGER-DIVISION* IS EXPANDED

After a short period of recuperation, the *7. Flieger-Division* started its expansion into a full-fledged airborne division. *Fallschirmjäger-Regiment 3* was established. The new commander was *Oberst* Richard Heidrich. After the Campaign in Poland, he had left the airborne forces due to disagreements on employment modalities and returned to service in the Army. In the middle of the Campaign in the West, however, he was ordered back to Berlin and given the mission of standing up the third regiment, composed partly of soldiers from his former *II./FJR 1* and cadre from the airborne schools.

Heidrich took charge of his new regiment and subjected it to hard training that had nothing to do with the old school of parade ground drills. He was partial to live-fire exercises, camouflage techniques and familiarization with the weapons of the enemy. He once stated:

> Seventy-five percent of success is achieved at the training areas. Consequently, elite forces have to be trained with unflinching toughness. My objective was to create an individual warrior, who fights cleverly and can think independently *and* a cohesive fighting formation that functions like clockwork.

In addition, a *Fallschirmjäger-Sturm-Regiment* was established on 17 July 1940 from what had been *Sturmabteilung Koch*. The commander of the assault regiment was *Oberst* Meindl, who, as commander of *Gebirgs-Artillerie-Regiment 121*, had jumped into action in May 1940 at Narvik without any type of parachute training along with a few sections of mountain troops. This new type of fighting from the third dimension had filled the former mountain officer with such enthusiasm that he transferred to the airborne forces in August 1940. He then completed formal training as a paratrooper and impressed Student so much with his capabilities that he was given command of the assault regiment a few weeks later.

Each of the companies of the former *Sturmabteilung Koch* were distributed among the four new battalions of the regiment, so that each battalion had a cadre of combat-experienced paratroopers. Walther Koch, who was promoted to *Major* after the successful conclusion of operations in the west, was given command of the 1st Battalion.

At the same time that the Parachute Assault Regiment was being formed, a glider wing was also established. It was planned to use paratroopers to jump in from gliders in the future, so as to take advantage of a silent approach, or use the gliders to make precision landings on extremely difficult objectives. *Oberstleutnant* Wilke was the commander of the wing.

Starting in the middle of June 1940, an airborne engineer battalion was established at Dessau-Kochstedt. The first commander was *Hauptmann* Jäckel, who was replaced a short time later by *Hauptmann* Morawetz. He was also replaced a short time later by *Major* Liebach, who would share the fate of the battalion for a long time. The four engineer companies were led by four *Oberleutnants*: Adolff, Tiedjen, Steiner and Gerstner.

Both an artillery battalion and a medical battalion were also established. The cadre of *FJR 2* was beefed up and the regiment also received another battalion.

✠

Operations in the west had demonstrated the problems associated with carried weapons with the soldiers. Initially, even the rifles and machine-pistols that the paratroopers used were carried separately in weapons canisters. Oftentimes, they could not be found, with the result that the soldiers were only armed with pistols and hand grenades and faced opponents who were armed with heavier weapons.

In addition, there was a lack of heavy-support weapons and the lightly armed parachute forces were hopelessly outclassed by any forces that were in permanent positions and armed with heavy weapons.

It became imperative to eliminate those shortfalls. Support weapons had to be developed for the airborne forces. The first step shortly after the Campaign in the West was the development of a "five-fold" parachute, which allowed the air dropping of artillery pieces.[1]

An antitank battalion was established and incorporated into the division. But all of this took time, and time was a precious commodity, since *Operation "Seelöwe"* was imminent, which was the talk of all the airborne forces. The rumor mill conjured up ever more daring operations for the airborne forces.

OPERATION "SEELÖWE"
Even before the Campaign in the West, Student had worked up a plan in which a large-scale airborne operation would serve as the initial blow. He intended to jump into England with all of the then currently available and planned airborne forces and establish a strong airhead. To that end, he intended to have his forces ready within three weeks of the conclusion of the Campaign in the West and to employ well-trained pre-war peacetime infantry regiments, which would be pressed into service as air-landed forces. Student envisioned

---

1. For the landings, a huge glider was also developed, the *Me 321 Gigant*, which had a lift capacity of 21 tons. It was capable of carrying a *Panzer III* or an 8.8-centimeter *Flak* and towing vehicle. However, the *Gigant* was not available until mid 1941.

them landing at the airfields in southern England that his paratroopers had captured. From there, they would launch their attack.

The most important prerequisite for him was having the attack take place during the enemy's weakest period. That would have been the time when the British Expeditionary Force had fled the beaches at Dunkirk.

In an interview with the author after the war, Student stated that "a jump into the harbors and taking them out of service [for the English] would have been a catastrophe. There were no real forces that could have stopped us. But during that time, I was still at home, convalescing."

In his writings, Student also talked about this development:

> If I had been back on duty, I would have recommended to Hitler that the airborne forces fly immediately to England so as to take the ports of debarkation that the British Expeditionary Forces had used. That was to start on the very day that the British forces started to leave the mainland. That would have sealed the fate of England, because the enemy that had escaped from Dunkirk was at the end of his rope. Moreover, most were without weapons. There were not enough forces on the island capable of defeating us.

The British historian, Liddell Hart, has basically confirmed this. He has been quoted as saying that "in the six weeks after Dunkirk the available land forces of England were so weak that even a couple of divisions would have sufficed to sweep them away."[2]

But when Hitler started planning for the invasion at the end of July, the enemy had already recovered. He had hoped in vain to conclude a peace with England. By then it was six weeks too late and almost 400,000 English soldiers had returned to the island from the European mainland.

Hitler's plan envisioned the use of the *22. Luftlande-Division*, which remained attached to the *Luftwaffe*, and the *7. Flieger-Division*. It was intended for both divisions to land at Folkstone and establish a bridgehead there. As a result of that measure, the enemy would be fixed along two fronts and have to split up his forces.

Those two divisions were the only immediately available airborne forces, however. Göring had asked for four airborne divisions before the war, but the request had fallen upon deaf ears within the Army. The failure to do so would extract its pound of flesh for *Operation "Seelöwe"*. At the Nuremberg trials, Göring was asked about that:

> If I had had those four airborne divisions available after the end of the Campaign against France, then I would have immediately gone to England during the time of Dunkirk. With only one division, which, in addition, still did not have any heavy weapons, the prospect seemed hopeless.

---

2. Translator's Note: Not attributed by the author. Reverse-translated from the German text to English.

When Student reported back for light duty on 2 September, he reported to Göring at the latter's estate at *Karinhall*, who received him with the words: "You'll finally be up to your ears in things, Student!"

After a pleasant cup of tea, *Frau* Göring withdrew and Göring lit up one of his famous cigars. The conversation turned to *Operation "Seelöwe"*. When Student started to raise concerns about the proposed employment of his airborne forces, Göring interrupted him with a surprise comment: "The *Führer* doesn't want to go after England, Student!"

"Why not?" the general asked, both surprised and in disbelief. Göring shrugged his shoulders. He didn't know either, but, at least he was relieved that he had avoided the risk. The promised air dominance over England—a prerequisite for the success of an invasion—had not been achieved.

Göring then presented Student with a unique award—the Aviator's Badge in Gold with Diamonds—and took his leave of Student with the words: "It would be better off if you didn't think about those things so much . . . better that you concern yourself with your health."

At the end of September 1940, when Student was in front of Göring again, the latter told him the following: "Hitler is still hoping to be able to talk to England. Perhaps that's the reason for his delaying *'Seelöwe'*." After a long, oppressive pause, he added: "If we lose this war, then so help us God."

✠

On 1 January 1941, Student assumed command of the *XI. Flieger-Korps*, which was in the process of being established. His Chief-of-Staff was *Generalmajor* Schlemm. The corps operations officer was the former operations officer of the *7. Flieger-Division, Oberstleutnant* Trettner. On 25 January 1941, Hitler had a meeting for the senior leadership of the *Luftwaffe* at Berchtesgaden. Göring took Student with him; he wanted to report to Hitler that Student had fully recovered.

Without exception, Hitler talked about England. Student was able to discern that what Göring had said between the two of them was correct: Hitler was terrified of invading England. The threat of an invasion was simply a deception tactic, Student observed. Hitler, he determined, had never had serious intentions of crossing over to the British Isles.

In the farther course of the discussions, Hitler received the directive from Hitler to explore the possibility of conducting airborne operations against Gibraltar. On the trip back on Göring's private train, Göring explored the possibilities with Student of how the struggle against England might be ramped up. He concentrated on the Mediterranean area:

"Something or other keeps holding the *Führer* back from a direct invasion of England. Moreover, the time for such a landing has already gone by. Now, Student, it is of singular importance to cause the British Empire to collapse externally. The Mediterranean and the Middle East are of essential importance for the British Empire. Italy, by itself, cannot accomplish driving the British out of the Mediterranean. Italy is already requiring some assistance just to keep its head above water."

"Then we should explore all of the possibilities available to us in the Mediterranean, *Herr Reichsmarschall*," Student replied. He mentioned the Suez Canal, Crete, Cypress and the British naval base at Malta.

"Good, Student! Don't just limit yourself to the matter of Gibraltar, as ordered by the *Führer*, check out all of the options for airborne operations in the Mediterranean. See whether the objectives you mentioned lay within the realm of the possible."

Student promised to explore the possibilities quickly and thoroughly.

✠

At his headquarters at the Berlin-Tempelhof airfield, Student concentrated on the establishment of his airborne corps in the weeks that followed. He followed events in the Balkans, since there was the possibility of being committed there, as well.

On 20 April 1941, while the Campaign against Yugoslavia was being waged at lightning-like speed and the fighting against the Greek forces in the Balkans was drawing to a close, Student and his operations officer flew to the *Führer* Headquarters at Semmering Mountain Pass in lower Austria.

At the beginning of March, the reinforced *FJR 2* of *Oberst* Sturm was moved to the Plovdiv area in Bulgaria. It was intended for *Kampfgruppe Süßmann*— Süßmann being the commander of the *7. Flieger-Division*, replacing Student— to launch an airborne assault on the island of Lemnos. The Germans feared that General Wilson, the Commander-in-Chief of the British Expeditionary Forces in Greece, would use the island as a strongpoint, as had been the case in the First World War.

During the initial fighting, however, the island was taken by Army ground forces on 6 April, with the result that an airborne operation became unnecessary.

While the fighting in the Balkans continued southward, the planning elements at the Semmering were concerned with how to resume the fight against England after the Balkans had been conquered.

It was there that Student advanced the viewpoint that after the successful conclusion of the Campaign in Greece, Crete, a decisive bastion of the enemy, could not remain under English control. He recommended that Crete be taken from the air. Student had already worked out all of the details of this eventuality. Student was convinced that it was possible to take the island from the air. In fact, he was already thinking beyond that. Crete was just a prerequisite for a second, larger jump on the Suez Canal. After that, he wanted to take Cypress, with Malta also being on the list. One bastion after the other of the British Empire was to be chipped away until the entire structure collapsed.

The operation against Crete was decided upon. But while these discussions were taking place, the possibility of another airborne operation materialized, based on necessity: Jumping along the Corinth Canal.[3]

PARATROOPERS ALONG THE CORINTH CANAL

After the planned operation against Lemnos and, possibly, other islands of that chain, had been retired to the files, *FJR 2* was standing idly by in Plovdiv. The British Expeditionary Force found itself in flight in Greece. All of the Commonwealth forces were aiming for the south Greek ports and the ports on the Peloponnesus.

In order to get to the Peloponnesus, the bridge had to be used that crossed the isthmus at its smallest point and connected the Greek mainland to the south. The canal was only 75 meters wide. It was at that place that the possibility existed of cutting off the retreat route for the English forces. Such a move farthered German goals, since it was obvious that any English forces that escaped to the south would not only head towards Egypt but also to Crete, which was the next major operation for the German airborne forces.

German aerial reconnaissance determined on 24 and 25 April 1941 that two complete Australian brigades and a large number of support elements were crossing the aforementioned bridge.

On 25 April, the paratroopers of *FJR 2*, along with the Parachute Artillery Instructional Battery, airborne engineers, signals personnel and medical elements, headed out on a flight to Larissa. *Oberst* Sturm had been ordered to attack the bridge at the Corinth Canal. Within his own regiment, he had his 1st and 2nd Battalions available for employment.

Once in Larissa, preparations were made to attack the following day. The area would initially be bombed, with the objective of drawing out the fires of the antiaircraft guns positioned around the bridge. The bombers would then be immediately followed by *Stukas*, escorted by *Bf 109's*, which would then attack the antiaircraft positions that had exposed themselves and silence them. This would make it easier for the glider group and the paratroopers that were to follow to approach the target area.

Preceding the main body of the paratroopers was a gliderborne platoon from the *6./FJR 2* under *Leutnant* Teusen and a squad of engineers. They were directed to take the bridge in a *coup de main* and either remove the charges or tear out the fuses. The *II./FJR 2* would then jump south of the canal, while the 1st Battalion would land to the north. Teusen's platoon was given instructions to land on the south side in the vicinity of the antiaircraft batteries, while the engineers, who were increased in size to a platoon at the last minute, were to land on the north side.

The men started out at 0500 hours on 26 April. The towing *Ju 52's* drew the two platoons into the air and headed for the target. The paratroopers who were to follow were able to watch the gliders take off before they climbed into their respective machines.

---

3. Translator's Note: The Isthmus of Corinth joins the Peloponnesus with the mainland of Greece. The canal allows easier transiting through the waters without having to go the long way around.

In the meantime, the bombers had initiated their attack. That was nothing out of the ordinary for the enemy, since bombers had appeared for almost a week by then. The antiaircraft guns opened their fires and their muzzle flashes became the targets for the following *Stukas*. They dove through the curtain of fire and dropped their bombs on the enemy positions. A few of the guns were silenced.

Even before those attacks had ended, the gliders of the engineers and Teusen's paratroopers were approaching their target.

The engineers landed on the north side, where they were not met by any antiaircraft fire. They assaulted the bridge from the north and overwhelmed the guard force. They then tore out the fuses or capped them, if they would not rip loose. The engineers then went around the main defensive positions and the 4-centimeter antiaircraft gun in the vicinity of the crossing point, so as to force them out of their positions before the paratroopers arrived. But the *Ju 52's* were already approaching with their human cargo. The 1st Battalion jumped first, landing on the north side. It was followed by the 2nd Battalion to the south.

Teusen's platoon had landed right next to the antiaircraft guns n the south end of the bridge. One of the gliders was blown apart by a direct hit. The personnel on board dropped to the ground from 14 meters in the air. *Leutnant* Teusen assaulted along with some of the men of his platoon. His submachine-gun hammered, and hand grenades blasted. Rounds went whistling by the ears of the men in the platoon. Teusen and his men were able to make it to the firing position, however, where they eliminated any remaining resistance. After quickly regrouping, they assaulted the second firing battery. *Oberjäger* Helms, who was running behind the *Leutnant*, saw an English soldier rise up to toss a hand grenade. His burst of fire put an end to that thought, and the grenade he had dropped when hit then went off in the English trenches. Three blood-covered figures arose from the ground with raised hands.

"Cease fire!" *Leutnant* Teusen called out when the enemy at the second position gave up. The first squad then ran over the bridge, where the engineers were still ripping out fuses and piling them up on the bridge.

The paratroopers that had landed were engaged in fighting on both sides of the bridge. When firing started up again, the engineers and the gliderborne paratroopers disappeared from the bridge, with *Leutnant* Teusen taking cover behind a pile of rocks near the southern slope. On the far side of the canal, the 4-centimeter antiaircraft gun fired again. Its rounds were hurtling low over the bridge and towards the south, where the paratroopers were engaged in hard fighting.

Hans Teusen was writing a report for his commander when he spied the photographer from the propaganda company, Ernst von der Heyden, who was running across the bridge, camera at the ready and taking pictures.

At the moment when Teusen tore off the report from the pad, he heard the firing of an antiaircraft gun from the north end of the bridge again. He then heard a dull thud, followed by an ear-splitting blast. With a fixed gaze, he watched as the center span of the bridge collapsed, taking with it men of the engineers and paratrooper platoons. The photographer was also killed. Later on, someone found his camera on the banks of the canal. The negatives also had images taken just seconds before the explosion.

The dropping of the center span meant that the two battalions of paratroopers that had landed were now separated.

The *6./FJR 2* had landed south of the bridge in a valley depression, right next to the enemy. The men had fought their way through the English positions in close combat and were in the process of regrouping, when the bridge blew up to their north.

"We've been cut off, *Herr Hauptmann!*" one of the company messengers exclaimed. Schirmer nodded. Then he said, "We'll attack south!"

The company continued its assault. It was engaged a few times by machine-gun nests, which were then attacked and destroyed. By noon, it had reached the Corinth airfield. At that moment, a messenger from the regiment appeared: "*Herr Hauptmann,* report immediately to the regimental commander!"

Schirmer, who had assumed acting command of the battalion after the commander had been wounded, went to *Oberst* Sturm's command post in a captured vehicle. Sturm issued orders that the young company commander had already expected: Schirmer, pursue the enemy farther to the south and hold him at bay so that there can be no more immediate attacks on the bridge. Orient generally towards Argos and Nauplia."

With those orders, the "quest of the Argonauts" started for *Kampfgruppe Schirmer.* The paratroopers advanced, always close on the heels of the enemy and frequently in close combat around buildings and in olive tree orchards. Argos was taken with the first assault. The German battle group followed the enemy at an increasingly fast pace, since the squads had gradually outfitted themselves with captured vehicles.

The company's small advance guard, led by *Leutnant* Teusen, who had rejoined his parent unit, headed in the direction of the port of Nauplia. Everyone thought that was where the enemy wanted to disembark.

"Men, we have to surprise the enemy!" the *Leutnant* said, trying to rally his men. But when the lead motorcycles entered Nauplia and found it clear of the enemy, they turned around and reported back to the company. They then headed in the direction of Tolon, where the enemy was thought to have pulled back.

Just outside of Tolon, Teusen and his men encountered the enemy's rearguard. It was more than 100 men, who opened fire from behind cliffs and from olive tree orchards. The fires from the English twin-barreled machine-guns could be traced, despite the intense brightness of the day. The enemy soon opened up with light antiaircraft weapons as well, and one of the captured vehicles used by the Germans was hit. A few seconds later, it was on fire. Burning figures jumped out and rolled around in the dirt in order to extinguish the flames.

Teusen called for Bose and his squad.

The eight men of *Oberjäger* Bose's squad ran over to their platoon leader. Teusen had taken cover in a drainage ditch, from whose edges weeds jutted skyward.

The squad and the officer then crawled through the dry ditch and reached the bend in the road, from which they could take the double-barreled machine-gun under fire. *Oberjäger* Bose opened fire with a captured machine-gun. After three bursts, the enemy's machine-gun was silenced. The enemy displayed a white rag. "Stop your fires!" Teusen ordered.

The men the continued the assault. The individual squads approached the antiaircraft position from three sides. It was taken after a few hand grenades were thrown. The enemy pulled back abruptly. The Germans captured 40 men.

"Let's go, men! On to Tolon!" Teusen yelled, trying to fire up the exhausted paratroopers. "The closer we stay to them, the less chance they'll have of setting up their defenses."

Teusen's platoon rolled forward. Soon, however, it was held up in broken terrain. From the high ground that was present in a semicircle around Tolon, they received defensive fires.

Despite that, Teusen continued to attack: "Attack the high ground off to the right through the olive tree orchard!"

The men continued their assault, reaching the olive tree orchard, where they advanced by leaps and bounds from one bit of cover to the next. As they had reached the half-way point to the high ground, the fire became so intense that they were unable to advance any farther. To take another meter of ground would have meant high casualties. *Leutnant* Teusen was wounded as he tried to maneuver into a piece of terrain from which he could engage the enemy effectively. He remained motionless, moaning. *Oberjäger* Bose and *Oberfeldwebel* Hencke, the platoon sergeant, asked the officer to call off the attack as they dressed his wounds. Above all, he should personally go back to the rear. A lightly wounded man was tasked to escort him.

But Hans Teusen would hear none of it. He did not want to abandon his platoon in that hour of need. He continued to lead his men.

After making an estimate of the situation, Teusen sent *Feldwebel* Müller II[4], who spoke English, to act as an emissary to the English. He was instructed to inform the English that a division was approaching their positions and that *Stukas* had already been called in to bomb the high ground around Tolon.

4. Translator's Note: Since Müller is such a common name in Germany and the Germans generally only referred to one another by their last names, the second one in a unit was referred to as Müller II.

The men at Tolon surrendered. They left their positions with raised arms and without weapons. More and more of them started coming, and Teusen explained to them that he had ordered a stop to the *Stuka* attack by radio. The English soldiers formed up on the road. By the time the rest of the *6./FJR 2* and the battalion arrived, there were 1,400 captured soldiers along the edge of the road. The *Stuka* trick had worked wonders. *Hauptmann* Schirmer smiled in amusement as his advance guard leader reported to him.

By dint of this relatively small airborne operation, the Corinth Canal was blocked for the English forces. Gone with it was an avenue for retreat. Unfortunately, the operation took place about 24 hours too late, as the main body of the English forces in southern Greece was able to escape to Alexandria and Crete. That almost proved fatal for the next airborne operation, the invasion of Crete from the air.

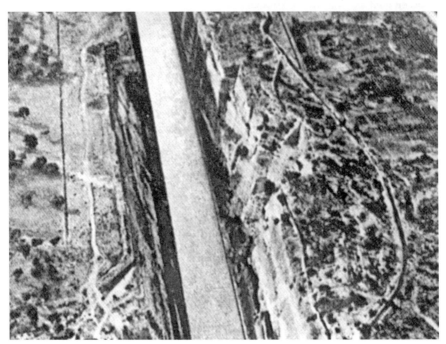

The Corinth Canal.

Oberst Sturm, whose regiment jumped into the area around the canal.

CHAPTER 5

Hell Was a Place Called Crete

PREPARATIONS

On 15 May 1941, Student and his battle staff flew to Athens. On the next day, he assembled all of his senior leaders for a conference at the *Grande Bretagne* Hotel. They discussed the concept of the operation and suggested courses of action. In the process, Student also discussed lessons learned from recent experience, especially the taking of the bridge of Corinth.

The initial planning saw the following division of responsibilities and phases: *Generalmajor* Meindl's *Fallschirmjäger-Sturm-Regiment (FJSR)*, which had been sent by rail to the southern tip of Greece, was to take the western part of the island. The focal point of its operation was to be the airfield at Malemes. The individual battalions had the following missions:

Major Koch's *I./FJSR*, attacking in the first wave, would take the antiaircraft defenses on the high ground north of Chania (Caneá), the airfield proper and the attendant antiaircraft defenses by means of a gliderborne assault. By doing that, he would make it easier for the following forces—air-landed and parachute—to come in. *Major* Koch's primary mission was to create a safe airhead for the invasion force, including the taking of Hill 107 near Malemes.

Major Stentzler's *II./FJSR* formed the second wave. His men would jump west of Malemes (west of Spilia) and assist in taking the airfield.

Hauptmann Scherber's *III./FJSR* would also attack in the second wave, jumping in to the east of Malemes. His men would block to the east, preventing the enemy from bringing any reinforcements. Of vital importance after his men landed was the establishment of contact with the other two battalions. He was also charged with taking a jump-off point for the assault on Chania.

The *IV./FJSR* of *Hauptmann* Gericke would jump in to the west of Malemes at the road bridge over the Tavronitis and block any forces coming from that direction. He was also to clear the area around Castelli Bay.

Oberst Heidrich's *FJR 3* was also employed with its three battalions receiving the following missions:

The *I./FJR 3* of *Hauptmann Freiherr* von der Heydte was to jump into the flat area near the Agya Penitentiary and be committed along the Chania-Suda road.

Major Derpa's *II./FJR 3* was to jump east of the penitentiary and take the high ground at Galatas.

Major Heilmann's *III./FJR 3* was to jump in as the advance guard for the regiment in the area bounded by Galatas-Daratso-Alikianou-Chania Road.

The division's engineer battalion, minus its 3rd Company, under *Major* Liebach had the mission jumping north of the area around Alikianou.

The second wave saw the employment of *Oberst* Sturm's *FJR 2* (minus its 2nd Battalion, which was retained as an operational reserve).

Major Kroh's reinforced *I./FJR 2* was to jump into the airfield at Rethymnon.

The reinforced *III./FJR 2* of *Hauptmann* Wiedemann was to jump into the area between Rethymnon and its airfield.

Also committed with the second wave was *Oberst* Bräuer's *FJR 1*.

Major Walther's *I./FJR 1* would jump into Gournes, to the east of the city and the airfield at Heraklion.

The *II./FJR 1* of *Hauptmann* Burckhardt would jump east of city of Heraklion.

The *III./FJR 1* of *Major* Schulz had the mission of jumping into Heraklion.

✠

One after the other, the trains arrived in southern Greece bringing the formations for the operation. Rumors were rife and everyone was eager to find out when "H-Hour" was.

Unfortunately, the *22. Luftlande-Division* was not available for operations on Crete. It had been sent to Rumania in March to protect the oilfields at Ploesti, which were of vital importance to the Germans. In its place, the *5. Gebirgs-Division* of *Generalmajor* Ringel was trained for the invasion. The division had fought in Greece. It had been in the Balkans for six weeks, marched more than 1,500 kilometers across the peninsula and reached Athens. It had helped decide the Campaign in the Balkans. It was in Athens that Ringel saw the top-secret orders for the operation that accompanied a map of the island he received. Printed in bold on the map: *Unternehmen "Merkur"* — Operation "Mercury". Later on, Ringel wrote:

> A chill went down our backs. The few sentences that were to be read there described in utmost sobriety the most unimaginable adventure that anyone ever had to go through.

Generalmajor Ringel moved from Chalkis to Athens with his headquarters. It was there that he prepared the plan for the attack on Crete by his mountain troopers. His operations officer, *Major* Haidlen, and his logistics officer, *Hauptmann* Ferchl, worked long days at the famous high rise at Omonia Place, from whose roof one could see all of Athens at night.

Crete had become a point of refuge for the Commonwealth forces leaving Greece. There were English, Australians and New Zealanders there. Among the coastal cities of the island and its field positions and lines of antiaircraft weapons, the British Expeditionary Force had established a shield in front of Egypt, which also protected the Suez Canal at the same time. The island also served as a way station for the British naval force based in Alexandria. The British also considered Crete as a starting point for any invasion of the Balkans. The German Balkan Campaign had beat them to the punch.

BRITISH INTENTIONS
On 30 April 1941, New Zealand Major General Bernard Freyberg, V.C., assumed command of all of the Commonwealth forces on Crete. Together with the Commander-in-Chief Near East, General Wavell, who was based in Cairo, Freyberg came to the conclusion that there were only four landing zones of any consequence on the island in the event of a combined German air- and seaborne operation. Consequently, he devoted most of his attention to preparing those areas for defense. It was intended to emplace heavy weapons and keep the forces there in the highest state of alert.

The first zone under consideration was the western side of the island, with the Malemes airfield. The second area was Suda Bay. The airfield at Rethymnon on the eastern side of the island was the third possible landing zone. Finally, the town of Heraklion and its airfield was the fourth area.

After this round of talks—Wavell was on Crete on 30 April—the British Command Headquarters, known as CREFORCE, issued Operations Order 10 on 3 May 1941:

Heraklion Sector: Employment of the English 14th Infantry Brigade with the 7th Mediterranean Regiment. In addition, the Australian 2/4 Battalion, the British 156th Antiaircraft Battery and half of the Australian 7th Light Antiaircraft Battery. For coastal protection, B Battery of the 15th Coastal Artillery regimen is to be employed. Two Greek infantry battalions are attached in support. Commanding this sector is Brigadier Chappel.

Rethymnon Sector: Employment of the Australian 19th Brigade with the 2/2, 2/7 and 2/22 Battalions, as well as a machine-gun company. Two Greek infantry battalions are attached in support. Commanding this sector is Brigadier Vasey.

Suda Bay Sector: Forces for the protection of the supply center of the island and the Akrotiri Peninsula are the British 151st and 234th Heavy Antiaircraft Batteries and the 129th Light Antiaircraft Battery. In addition, there is half of the Australian 7th Light Antiaircraft Battery. For infantry protection, there is the Australian 2/8 Battalion, the Northhumberland Hussars, an antitank battery and the main body of the 15th Coastal Artillery regiment. Reinforcements are in the form of a Greek infantry battalion. Commanding this sector is Brigadier Western.

Malemes Sector and the Area West of Chania: Employment of all of the New Zealand 2nd Division with its 4th and 5th Brigades [Brigadiers Inglis and Hargest, respectively] and a battle group under Major Oakes. In addition, a battle group of the British 156th

Antiaircraft Battery and a section of the Australian Light Antiaircraft Battery. For reinforcement: Three Greek infantry battalions. Commanding this sector is Major General Puttick.[1]

The total number of forces on the island for the Empire numbered some 30,000 men, to which there were an additional 11,000 soldiers of the Greek Army. In order to reinforce the four defensive sectors, numerous convoys were dispatched from Cairo at the beginning of May, which continued to bring new elements to the island until the start of the fighting. For instance, the 2nd Leicester, the 1st Argyll and the Sutherland Highlanders were transported to the island from the Near East. On 13 May, Major General Freyberg ordered the establishment of the Australian10th Brigade. Colonel Kippenberger was named its commander.

In order to ensure the success of any defense, Winston Churchill pressed for the shipment of as many heavy weapons as possible to the island fortress. He was especially concerned that armored vehicles be delivered. With regard to that aspect of the defense, he wrote:

> If the Germans conquer the airfields on Crete and if they are able to use them, then they will be in a position to bring in reinforcements in unlimited quantities. A dozen infantry tanks could play a decisive role for us in just such a situation in preventing that from happening. Therefore, I asked the chiefs-of-staff to consider whether one could turn around a ship with tanks, which was already on its way to Egypt, in order to land a few tanks from it on Crete. My colleagues did not consider it advisable to endanger the rest of the ship's cargo for such a detour, even though they were in agreement with me concerning the value of tanks on Crete.[2]

But Churchill did not give up so easily. On 12 May, he telegraphed General Wavell in Cairo: "Would it not be advisable to consider whether an additional dozen infantry tanks with trained personnel should be employed against 'Schorcher'?"[3]

On 15 May, Wavell replied: "Have done my best to prepare 'Colorado' for defense against an infestation of beetles. The recently undertaken reinforcements consist of 6 infantry and 16 light tanks."[4]

This was a confusing message, since the Prime Minister had to have assumed that Wavell meant there were additional assets sent to the island. In reality, these 22 armored vehicles were the only ones on the island at the

---

1. Translator's Note: This excerpt comes from an unattributed source; therefore it cannot be verified and has been reverse-translated from the German.

2. Translator's Note: Reverse-translated from the German.

3. Translator's Note: These quotations are also reverse-translated from the German. "Schorcher" was the British codename for the anticipated German invasion of Crete.

4. "Colorado" was the British codeword for the defense of Crete.

time. They had not been sent there "recently". In reality, they had been there for some time.

The failure to meet the request of the Prime Minister turned out to be a gift for the invading forces. It was in large part responsible for the German victory there.

☩

Admiral Cunningham, the Commander-in-Chief of British naval forces in the Mediterranean, received directives to conduct operations to protect Crete from the sea. The focus was to be on the prevention of follow-on landings along Crete's coasts. In addition, of course, the British naval forces were responsible for running and protecting convoys to the island. For instance, during the night of 16/17 May, the cruisers *Gloucester* and *Fiji* took the 2nd Battalion of the Leicester Regiment, along with all of its equipment, from Alexandria to Heraklion. During the night of 18/19 May, the *Glengyle* transported 700 men of the Sutherland Highlanders from Alexandria to Timbaki. Admiral Cuningham had a fleet of four battle groups of cruisers and destroyers and a reserve group with the battleships *Warspite* and *Valiant* at his disposal. There was also a flotilla of fast boats in Suda Bay.

During the night of 19/20 May, Tank Landing Ship A2 brought three tanks ashore at Tribaki that promptly moved on to Heraklion, where they were incorporated into the defenses of the airfield.

The British air forces on the island had been subjected to aerial bombardment from the *VIII. Flieger-Korps* ever since 13 May. The air corps had received orders to eliminate the enemy's antiaircraft batteries, take out the British cruiser *York*, which was at anchor in Suda Bay, and interdict British naval traffic.

On 18 and 19 May, the hangars at Heraklion and Malemes were bombed, and German aerial reconnaissance indicated only a few aircraft left at those facilities. Despite the aerial campaign, the antiaircraft guns on the *York* continued to fire, as did the batteries located at the northern and southern ends of the bay.

On 19 May, General Wavell had the remaining seven aircraft on Crete return to Egypt.

On the same day, the Greek 1st Infantry Regiment, which was at Castelli, where it had been performing security duties, was attached to Brigadier Hargest and his 5th Brigade.

That was the state of affairs for General Freyberg's defenses as the German operation prepared to commence.

A few hours before the start of the German operation, British intelligence sources were unusually well informed about the German intentions, the strengths of the land, sea and air forces employed, the time of the attack, the landing zones, and the German's concept of the operation.

On 17 May, CREFORCE anticipated the employment of some 25,000 to 30,000 German soldiers, who would be employed from the air. In addition, another 10,000 men were expected to arrive by sea, protected by the Italian fleet.

The seriousness with which the British took the defense of Crete was echoed on 7 May, when Churchill spoke before Parliament: "We will defend Crete, our defensive outpost in the Mediterranean, to death and without a single thought given to retreat!"

ATTACK FROM THE AIR—THE HELL OF MALEMES

The attack on Crete, which had originally been scheduled for the middle of May, had to be postponed somewhat due to a lack of fuel. The attack date was first moved to 18 May, then 20 May.

By the evening of 19 May, all of the preparations for the largest airborne assault in history up to that point had been made. Both officers and men had been carefully briefed on their missions and were at the airfields, ready to take off. Student's headquarters was counting on a quick, decisive victory. The air order prepared by the *VIII. Flieger-Korps* of *General* von Richthofen contained a detailed time line for support. Fighters, destroyers and dive bombers waited for their orders to start.

Since the available lift capacity was insufficient to carry all of the battle groups at once, the attack was organized in waves, as mentioned previously. The first wave was to hit the airfields at Malemes and Chania and Suda Bay at first light on 20 May, while the next wave would not start until 1300 hours, after the aircraft had returned from their first drop. The wave launched at 1300 hours would strike the airfields at Rethymnon and Heraklion.

The *5. Gebirgs-Division* was spread out among three airfields in southern Greece: Euböa, Attica and Böotien. Two flotillas of boats and ships had been assembled—from motorized sailboats to small freighters. In short, everything that could be impressed into service from Greek ports, as well as assets from the German Navy. Light artillery pieces, *Flak*, equipment, vehicles, fuel and last, but not least, mountain troopers were to be loaded on board.

✠

"Comrades," *Oberleutnant* von Plessen, the commander of the *3./FJSR* greeted his assembled platoon and squad leaders on the evening of 19 May. "Let's review our mission one more time. We will be going in with 3 officers, 27 NCO's and 77 men. The rest of the company has been detailed to the regimental reserve under *Oberleutnant Osius*. We will be using 12 gliders; three for each platoon. Now our individual missions . . ."

After a short pause to look at the assembled men, he continued: "I will take the patch of woods on the western edge of the Malemes airfield with the company headquarters section. From aerial photography, it appears the enemy has dug in there.

"*Leutnant* Musyal attacks the heavy antiaircraft guns 800 meters west of the western edge of the airfield with the 1st Platoon and sets it out of commission.

"Arpke, you and the 2nd Platoon will take out the light antiaircraft guns on the northern and northwest edges of the airfield.

"*Oberfeldwebel* Scheel, you will land with your 3rd Platoon just southwest of the airfield and eliminate the enemy positioned there.

"It is imperative that we knock out the antiaircraft weaponry as soon as possible so that the parachute elements following us can jump as unimpeded as possible.

"After completing those missions, the company will set up along the west bank of the river valley, oriented west, and defend against any attacking enemy forces. To the right, we will be next to the sea. To the left, we will hold as far as and including the east-west road. We will establish contact with the 4th Battalion. We will also clear any obstacles we find on the western part of the airfield.

"Any questions? That's all . . ."

✠

Early in the morning—the sun had not yet risen—*Oberjäger* Erich Schuster left the tent that had been pitched on the edge of the airfield at Eleusis with his squad. The rest of the squads from Musyal's platoon also exited their tents. The *Leutnant* reported to *Oberleutnant* von Plessen. The remaining platoon leaders did likewise. Then the order came: "Mount up!"

The squads marched one after the other to their gliders. The 12 gliders formed the third to seventh flight of the battalion.

The *Ju 52's* came to life. The gliders bounced along behind them, and then they lifted off. The gliders dropped their wheels and rose into the morning skies. The machines headed south—the *I./FJSR* was on its way to Crete! To the left, the first rays of the sun felt their way into the small widows of the gliders. The formation climbed higher to reach the right release height. Red light filtered through the cabin. Perhaps inspired by the light, one of the paratroopers started singing:

Rot scheint die Sonne, fertiggemacht!
Wer weiß, ob sie morgen für uns auch noch lacht.
Werft an die Motoren, schiebt Vollgas hinein.
Startet los, fliegt an! Heute geht es zum Feind!

The sun shines red; we're ready to go!
Who knows if she'll smile for us again tomorrow.
Start up the engines; give her the throttle!
Let's go; head out! Today we meet the enemy!

An die Maschinen!— An die Maschinen!
Kamerad, da gibt es kein Zurück.
Fern im Osten stehen dunkle Wolken,
Komm mit und zage nicht—komm mit!

To the planes!—To the planes!
Comrade, there's no turning back.
There are dark clouds in the east,
Come along, don't hesitate—come along!

Below them was the Mediterranean; to their right and left were the remaining flights of gliders. There wasn't a lot of talking. Besides, you would have had to yell in order to be understood. Dust danced in the sunlight. Below them, the sea reflected back brilliant flashes of light.

Gradually, it became too hot for *Oberjäger* Schuster. He and his squad were wrapped up in their thick jumpsuits. The knee pads were tied on tightly. Someone was snoring. It was true! Someone in front of him was sleeping on the way to Crete. Was it Horn or Kellermann? Perhaps the slow-moving Schulz?

"Crete ahead!" The glider pilot shouted.

"Cinch up your helmets! Check everything out one more time!" Schuster barked to his squad. A glance at his watch revealed it was 0640 hours. The *Ju 52* suddenly gave a jerk. With some skill, the glider pilot ensured he did not lose the tow rope.

"How much altitude?" Schuster signaled to the pilot.

"2,600 meters!" he yelled back.

"Damn . . . much too high!"

A German fighter whizzed past them. The pressure tossed the glider about like a toy. Suddenly, there were gray balls of cotton appearing in front of and to the side of the aircraft and gliders. The *Ju 52* took evasive action. The glider pilot attempted to emulate him. Through the noise of the *Ju 52*, the men could hear the sound of the antiaircraft rounds detonating.

At that moment, the towing aircraft banked off to the left. At the same time, the tow rope was released. There was a hard jerk in the glider, which tossed the men forward. Then they started gliding on their own. The noise gradually subsided, to be replaced by the sound of crackling detonations.

In front of them, there was a brilliant burst of flame from one of the *Ju 52's*. A few seconds later, a glider spiraled downward, on fire. As it fell, both wings sheared off. It fell like a stone to the ground.

Then the men could see the detonations from the bombs the *Stukas* were dropping. The *Stukas* had reached the enemy positions right in front of them. By bombing them, they forced the enemy to take cover.

A *Bf 110* shot past the descending glider. Streams of fire were emitted from its cannon and machine-guns, which hammered away at enemy positions, which replied in kind.

Three or four blows registered next to Schuster's glider. Another group of comrades had been hit; the glider dove steeply to the ground.

The glider descended ever more sharply. The earth approached rapidly. Cliffs rose in the distance. That had to be Hill 107, Schuster thought. Then he saw the silhouette of a bridge. That was the bridge over the Tavronitis. The airfield had to be next to it.

The glider slipped past the bridge along with two other gliders. Then they touched down, the barbed-wire wrapped skids starting to brake the glider's forward momentum. The rocks and vegetation shook them. There was a crashing sound, a final jerk, and then they were stationary.

"Release the cockpit!"

The restraints were released and the men swarmed out of the glider, which had brought them safely to Crete.

While he was running, *Oberjäger* Schuster could hear the snarl of a twin-barreled machine-gun firing and the report of antiaircraft weaponry around the airfield. Intermixed was the sound of the fires from attacking German destroyers and fighters. Another glider whooshed earthward barely 10 meters above their heads. One of the plywood crates burst like a ripe fruit as it crashed into the cliffs.

Erich Schuster ran over to the glider from which *Oberfeldwebel* Arpke was being pulled. He saw that he was unconscious. One of the men from that same glider that had crashed into the cliff was holding his broken arm.

"I'm taking over the platoon!" Schuster called out. He told the man with the broken arm to stay with the unconscious *Oberfeldwebel*, who was being tended to by a medic.

The enemy antiaircraft weapons were firing as if possessed. Off to the right, two more gliders were putting down. The scene was repeated to the left.

"First Squad . . . to the right! 2nd, left . . . 3rd in the middle! Follow me to the edge of the runway. We're going for the antiaircraft positions!"

Erich Schuster and his platoon worked their way forward to the northwestern portion of the runway of Malemes. The enemy started firing at them. *Gefreiter* Penzberger, mortally wounded, collapsed behind Schuster.

The English soldiers fired from their positions and trenches on the paratroopers, who were advancing by leaps and bounds. When a twin-barreled machine-gun swung in on Schuster's squad, it dove for cover. Schuster crawled on by himself in the olive tree orchard, until he had a field of fire directly on the firing antiaircraft battery.

"Bring the machine-gun up here!" he called out. His order was passed on, from one man to the next.

Once the machine-gun was in place, it opened fire and allowed the other squads to advance by bounds. All six antiaircraft guns in that particular position were still firing.

"*Oberfeldwebel* Arpke is coming, *Herr Oberjäger!*" One of the men next to Schuster called out as he turned to look to the rear. Schuster also turned around, and he saw Arpke advancing toward him in a series of grotesque leaps. Schuster crawled a bit in Arpke's direction, when the latter was forced to take cover.

"West edge of the runway is full of the enemy, *Herr Oberfeldwebel!*" Schuster reported to his platoon leader. "The enemy has dug in all around the battery."

"We have to go back to the riverbed, Schuster." Arpke said. "From there we can work our way forward from two sides with assault groups."

Groaning, Arpke grabbed at his knee. He had suffered a contusion that was also leaking blood. Despite that, he supervised all of the preparations and had his platoon set up defensive positions oriented to the south and east.

He issued orders: "Machine-guns and mortars: Fire on the enemy positions in front of the antiaircraft guns. Schuster and Willrich, attack the positions from the left and right and smoke out the field fortifications. Everybody else give the two assault groups covering fire!"

Oberjäger Schuster took his group—at that point, with only six men left—and headed north, before he took aim at the enemy's gun on the right flank. They reached some vegetation, crawled through it and then inched their way forward to the cover afforded by a cliff outcropping.

Boom . . . boom . . . boom!

Rounds hammered into the ground in front of them. The enemy was shooting denial fires from the western edge of the runway, since he suspected something was happening there.

They continued crawling, until they were about 30 meters from the outer enemy field positions.

"Hand grenades!" Schuster ordered, pointing to the trenches.

The men armed the grenades and threw them simultaneously into the trench. After the six grenades detonated, they jumped up and ran the 30 meters to the enemy trench, jumping in. Schuster landed on a dead enemy soldier on the floor of the trench. He ran, bent over, to a bend in the trench line and fired with his submachine-gun when he saw enemy soldiers. The men then ran farther, reached the first gun and took it. The enemy started tossing hand grenades at them.

"Give me covering fire!" Schuster called out, as he crawled forward through a narrow communications trench. When he ran into some enemy soldiers, they were too surprised too fire. They raised their hands and surrendered.

When the first German mortar rounds began landing in the enemy's main position a few seconds later, Schuster rallied his men and they advanced. They fired as they ran. A round tore open Schuster's jump smock. The men overcame an intermediate position and then reached a 4-centimeter Bofors antiaircraft gun. Hand grenades ended all resistance there. The gun fell silent. The remaining two guns were taken out by Willrich's assault detachment.

The platoon had accomplished its initial objective. It occupied the western edge of the runway and waited for the arrival of the *Ju 52's*, which would bring the paratroopers who were going to jump in.

"Over there, *Herr Oberjäger!*" Kühlkens yelled, pointing to the skies. It was the eagerly awaited *Ju 52's*. The groups of transporters arrived in short intervals. They approached at low altitude over the coastal mountains, then came down even lower, flew through the fires of another enemy battery and the air was suddenly filled with the deploying silk. The paratroopers descended from the skies into a fire-spewing hell below.

As far as one could see, the skies were filled with parachutes. It was a breathtaking, unique picture that was presented to the soldiers who had landed previously. A short while later, *Oberleutnant* von Plessen, ordered the 2nd Platoon to move south and join up with the 1st Platoon and the company headquarters section near the bridge.

The 2nd Platoon remained in its location, however, because otherwise the company would not have had any more flanking cover. Moreover, the enemy could have advanced on the airfield from the north. *Oberjäger* Schuster and his squad were then given another mission from a company messenger, however.

"*Herr Oberjäger*, you are to move south to establish and maintain contact between the company elements there and with the 2nd Platoon."

"Good, Mesters. Tell *Oberjäger* Arpke what I'm doing!" Schuster said, since his squad was already separated somewhat from the rest of the platoon.

The men of Schuster's squad then worked their way south. They used the available cover and concealment and established contact with *Feldwebel* Ellersiek after an hour. Ellersiek informed Schuster that the platoon leader, *Leutnant* Musyal, had been shot in the thigh just 10 meters from the glider after it had landed.

"I've taken over the platoon, Erich," Ellersiek stated. "*Oberjäger* Schulz is leading my squad."

"What's going on with the antiaircraft position you had?"

"It was just a decoy."

"What's going on with the remaining platoons?" Schuster asked, trying to form a picture of the overall situation in the hour it had taken to work his way south.

It turned out that the company headquarters section, which had landed shortly after Schuster's platoon, had not been engaged. *Oberleutnant* von Plessen's glider crash-landed in the vicinity of the coast, but *Feldwebel* Galla's squad had landed completely intact and operational. *Oberleutnant* von Plessen had had Galla's squad come with him to advance southwest and take the antiaircraft position at the southwestern end of the runway.

Once the men from the three gliders had been assembled, they started to receive heavy fire. *Oberleutnant* von Plessen assaulted the antiaircraft position that had taken them under fire with an *Oberjäger* from one of the groups. The company commander did not reach the enemy's position, however. He was mortally wounded, as a burst of fire from a machine-gun swinging its way towards them hit him when he dove for cover. By the time his comrades had crawled their way forward to him, he was dead.

Feldwebel Galla then took charge. He reached the southwestern portion of the runway, where he saw the muzzle flashes of the antiaircraft guns, which continued to hammer away.

The men hit the ground and then crawled their way forward through the vegetation towards the fire-spewing barrels of the guns. They were almost deafened by the ear-shattering loudness of the firing. When they had approached to within 150 meters of the corner gun, the enemy started firing directly at them. The assistant gunner on the machine-gun was killed. *Feldwebel* Galla took his place. They engaged in a firefight with the enemy, until the English gun finally fell silent. The paratroopers then worked their way forward again.

Their way terminated 50 meters from the enemy's position, however. Whoever tried to advance any farther was hit by a machine-gun that had remained silent up to that point and which fired on the Germans from an elevated position. The German machine-gunner was the next one to be killed. Galla rolled to the side, throwing himself behind the weapon. He took aim at the enemy and let loose with a burst in the direction from which a burst of fire came screaming towards him at the same instant. Galla felt a hard blow to his left shoulder, which threw him back. He wanted to return to his machine-gun, when a second salvo hit him and flung him back.

Galla's assault detachment was completely wiped out. All had been caught by the deadly machine-gun and mowed down.

✠

The three gliders of the 3rd Platoon did not all arrive at the same time. At 0655 hours, the towrope was ripped loose from the glider in which *Oberfeldwebel* Scheel was sitting. The experienced glider pilot was able to put down on the island of Antikreta. The glider crash-landed. The men aboard suffered slight contusions, but they were all still combat capable. Under the leadership of *Oberfeldwebel* Scheel they made their way to Crete, although it was 24 May before they reached their company and fought with it.

The remaining two gliders landed at the village of Tavronitis, which was then cleared. The men took 30 prisoners and then advanced to the western end of the runway, where they linked up with the company. One of the squads was even able to make one of the captured antiaircraft guns serviceable again, where it was then employed against the enemy antiaircraft positions on the northwest edge of the Malemes runway.

✠

The company physician, *Oberarzt Dr.* Weizel, had distributed his medics among the various gliders, so that the loss of one glider would not mean the loss of the entire medic contingent.

The physician advanced with his medical personnel behind the 2nd Platoon in its advance on Malemes. Lewis machine-guns and submachine-guns extracted their first toll in blood. Two wounded men were attended to immediately. Behind a hedge, a wounded comrade called for a medic. *Dr.* Weizel and *Obergefreiter* Müller immediately went to the position, where they tended to the stricken comrade, who had been shot in the chest.

One of the medic NCO's had found an English tent and pitched it, once the forward advance of the Germans had temporarily come to a standstill. The wounded were taken there, in order to protect them from the burning rays of the sun.

"*Herr Oberarzt*, three wounded men are still at the runway!" Weitzel worked his way forward with two medics and recovered the three men. When the doctor heard that *Leutnant* Musyal was wounded and *Oberleutnant* von Plessen had been killed, he assumed command of the 3rd Company. He had the company assemble on the west end of Malemes and set up defensive positions there. The position was expanded by detachments moving both north and south. The securing of the east-west road, which had also been a part of the company's mission statement, was also soon accomplished.

When *Oberjäger* Schuster linked up with the company at 1000 hours, it held a sector running from the southern end of the runway along the western edge to the north as far as the coast.

An hour later, *Oberleutnant* Trebes, along with elements of the regiments 13th Company (Heavy Weapons) and the rest of the 1st Platoon of the 3rd Company, assaulted a British tent camp that was south of the road in an olive tree orchard. A German platoon had been encircled there. The camp was taken, the encircled platoon relieved and 30 prisoners taken.

Towards 1215 hours, *Oberleutnant* Dobke of the *IV./FJSR* arrived at the location of the 3rd Company with 15 men as reinforcements. He and his men took over the northern portion of the western edge of the airfield, helping to firm up the German defenses. It was Dobke's intent to then advance north and silence the enemy antiaircraft guns that were still firing there.

During that phase of the fighting, when no one really knew what was going on in the other battalion sectors, a message arrived at the *IV./FJSR* that a *Stuka* attack was imminent against the enemy antiaircraft battery at the northern end of the runway. *Dr.* Weitzel ordered Dobke to call off the planned attack, but the latter ignored the directive. Around 1300 hours, he went to the northern end of the runway with a few men and eight prisoners. Apparently, he was lured into an ambush by the prisoners, whom he had brought along as emissaries and whom he had allowed to roam freely, and was killed.

✠

By 1400 hours, the last wounded of the 3rd Company had been recovered and treated. The company improved its positions along the western edge of the Malemes runway. Weitzel went to find *Hauptmann* Gericke, the commander of the *IV./FJSR*, to get briefed and receive farther orders.

Gericke ordered him to hold the positions he was in. An enemy counterattack was expected shortly. Weitzel informed Gericke of the 3rd Company's precarious situation and received assurances that he would most likely receive about 50 men as reinforcements from *Reserve-Kompanie Osius*.

Dr. Weitzel had just returned to his company's location, when the enemy

opened heavy artillery fire from the high ground around the airfield and
farther to the east.

Let us now turn to some of the other actions that had occurred that
morning.

KAMPFGRUPPE GENZ ATTACKS

The battle group of *Oberleutnant* Genz, which had departed from the airfield
at Tanagra with a combat strength of 90 men divided among nine gliders, was
part of the advance guard for the Parachute Assault Regiment. The men of
the *1./FJSR* were also brought in by gliders in order to take out the enemy's
antiaircraft defenses. After completing his mission, Genz had two potential
options: 1. Hold his positions until *FJR 2* had advanced on Chania or 2.
Attempt to fight his way through to his regiment's 2nd Company, which was
to be employed in the area of Akrotiri. Genz's platoon leaders were *Leutnants*
Toschka and Mahrenbach. The company headquarters section was led by
Oberfeldwebel Kempke.

The gliders and their tugs had not even crossed the coastline of Crete
when they started receiving antiaircraft fire. It had been planned to fly over
the western part of the island after the initial approach and then steer onto
the objectives from the southeast, a measure designed to both surprise and
take advantage of the rising sun.

But the plans changed for unknown reasons and the aircraft headed
for Cape Spatha, just to the west of Chania. The tug aircraft, continuously
irritated by the antiaircraft fires, attempted even more evasive maneuvers.
A burst of antiaircraft fire exploded right next to the glider of *Oberleutnant*
Genz. Genz looked through the small porthole and saw how the glider on the
left was released from its tow line; then the one on the right was also released
itself. He could not see the other groups with the 1st and 2nd Platoons. Then
the gliders of the headquarters section released themselves.

At 2,200 meters, the gliders started a controlled descent on Crete. At the
same time, the antiaircraft weapons started to register exclusively on them.
Mixed among the incoming cannon fire were pearls of machine-gun tracers.

Oberleutnant Werner, who was piloting the glider, looked around
inquisitively at Genz. Straight ahead, directly below them, were powerful
detonations. Those must have been coming from the *Stukas*, whose mission it
was to prepare the positions for the assault of the gliderborne forces.

Then Genz saw an even more powerful explosion—apparently a direct
hit on an enemy battery. Genz tapped his comrade on the shoulder: "There it
is, Werner! Let's take this crate down!"

The pilot sized up what he had to do. He took the glider down in tight
spirals. The glider moved rapidly over an olive-tree orchard. The right wing
clipped a tree. The glider then touched ground, scrapped along a few meters
and came to an abrupt stop. "Out, men! Get out and assemble!"

Genz jumped out into the open, after the cockpit of the glider had
been opened up. Two "Tommies" were approaching. They started to raise

their weapons. A blast of fire from the submachine-gun of the company headquarters section leader took them down.

"Follow me!" Genz called out. The group of men headed for the closed cover. Up to the front, figures with flat helmets started to appear. The paratroopers fired as they ran, also tossing hand grenades. Barely 100 meters away and off to the side, the German fire was joined by the characteristic sound of other German submachine-guns.

"It's Stehfen and the mortar section!" one of the men called out.

"Let's go . . . attack!"

They assaulted, linked up with Stehfen's group and got to a better position, where they took up cover. They intended to wait there for the other squads to catch up with them.

✠

The glider with *Oberjäger* Hahn and his squad had been hit in the air by antiaircraft fire. Descending steeply, the glider's pilot aimed the machine directly for the enemy battery. In the middle of the curtain of fire, the glider crashed through, landing on the barrel of one of the guns in the northwest part of the position.

"Get out! . . . get out!" the *Oberjäger* roared. He jumped out of the machine. Rifle fire was cracking, joined shortly thereafter by the sounds of pistol fire. In the middle of jumping forward, Hahn was mortally wounded. *Obergefreiter* Holzmann heard his comrade scream in death's agony. He spun around to the side, escaping a salvo of submachine-gun fire, and tossed hand grenades over the wall of sandbags encircling the gun. He worked his way forward, step-by-step, and then eliminated the rest of the gun crew by himself.

✠

Leutnant Toschka's platoon flew past its designated objective. It landed in Chania, near an enemy assembly area. The enemy attempted to engage the glider, which had landed a short distance away, but Toschka and his men succeeded in destroying the two trucks full of English soldiers approaching them.

Leading his men, Toschka reached the enemy battery in Chania. The men entered the enemy's trench line and eliminated the enemy forces in close-in fighting. It was there that the *Leutnant* was badly wounded. He collapsed to the bottom of the trench, landing on some of the wounded enemy soldiers whom he had just shot a few moments previously. They then dressed each other's wounds.

✠

In the meantime, *Oberleutnant* Genz had succeeded in reaching his objective—the same antiaircraft battery that Toschka was engaging—with the two squads he had hastily assembled. Toschka could see his company commander standing upright and directing the actions of his men. Toschka tried to warn his commander to get down, even though every sound he uttered was sheer agony. Finally, Genz heard his junior officer and took cover. It was just in time—an English machine-gun had started to swing in on him. The English machine-gunners, who had lain in ambush and not fired until that moment, were barely 50 meters away. Despite the surprise achieved by opening fire first, they were quickly eliminated by hand grenades.

"We took the battery!" Genz exclaimed. "Set up an all-round defense!"

At the same moment, some of the members of *Leutnant* Mahrenbach's platoon showed up and reported to the company commander.

"What happened?" the company commander wanted to know.

✠

"There . . . up ahead . . . that's the crossroads . . . land . . . land!" *Leutnant* Mahrenbach rattled off, as he saw the objective.

Shell bursts exploded next to the descending glider. A hail of shrapnel entered the glider. *Leutnant* Mahrenbach was killed in the fraction of a second. The assistant platoon leader, Officer Candidate Bühl, was badly wounded in the head and blinded even before the glider touched down. The *DFS 230* then slammed into the earth; almost everyone on board was wounded. Despite that, the men ran to the designated rally point. Carrying and supporting one another, they attempted to carry out their mission. They took the badly wounded men into one of the buildings at the crossroads. Only one man on the glider had remained uninjured. *Gefreiter* Pfriemberger took up an ambush position at the crossroads. Virtually alone, he determined to stop the enemy who would have to approach up the road.

A short while later, Pfriemberger saw four English trucks approaching, crammed full of British soldiers. They were coming from Chania and intended as the relief force for the battery. Pfriemberger felt like running off and crawling into a hole somewhere. Instead, he took up the fight against all of them.

Using his submachine-gun, Pfriemberger fired a burst into the cab of the lead truck. The vehicle rolled off to the side and came to a stop with squealing brakes. The remaining trucks had to stop, since the lead vehicle was blocking their path.

Advancing on both sides of the road, the English soldiers attacked the building in which Pfriemberger had holed up. But the *Gefreiter* did not give up. He fired bursts into the group of attacking soldiers and forced them to take cover. Then he changed position and would show up at another point, opening fire from there. Wherever the English showed up, he forced them to take cover. The enemy, who assumed an entire squad of paratroopers was in the building, pulled back. A single man had accomplished the mission of an entire platoon. With unbridled trust in himself and his comrades, whom he knew would not leave him in the lurch, he had accomplished the seemingly impossible. By doing so, he had also saved his comrades in the gun positions at Chania.

✠

"Over there, *Herr Oberleutnant!* Our fighters!"

Exactly one hour after the landing of the advance guard, additional *Ju 52's* with gliders in tow surfaced on the horizon. They made their approach, were released, and descended down to the Akrotiri Peninsula.

"There's *Hauptmann* Altmann and the 2nd Company!" *Oberleutnant* Genz tried to rally his men. "That shows everything's going according to plan."

Just a few minutes prior to that, they had seen paratroopers from *FJR 3* jumping in.

The men Genz had with him attempted to man and operate the English antiaircraft guns. At that moment, two *Bf 110's* dove in and strafed the area around the battery positions. Luckily, no one was hurt. At that moment, the outposts reported English tanks moving around.

In all, Genz had 34 soldiers who were capable of fighting. Looking at his watch, he could see that it had only turned 0900 hours. Should he try to fight his way over to the 2nd Company, as one of his mission options had been? That would entail moving across open mountain terrain, however. At that moment, the *Oberjäger* behind the radio set reported: "*Herr Oberleutnant,* message traffic from the 3rd Regiment: We cannot get through to Chania. Fight your way through to us!"

That was the only radio message they received. A few seconds later, the radio set was destroyed by a rifle round. The enemy was still firing from other areas toward the battery positions.

"Tank, *Herr Oberleutnant!* They're coming directly towards us!" one of the outposts reported. The time for thinking was over.

"We're going through the olive trees to the southwest!" Genz ordered. The survivors tended to the wounded. While the heavy machine-gun fired, the remaining men took off in the designated direction. They reached a vineyard and were, for the time being, safe. When they reached the far side of the vineyard, Genz called the headquarters section leader forward. Just as Genz started to tell him what he wanted done, an English truck started approaching from the direction of Chania. Genz identified the machine-gun in the cab and also saw the soldiers standing in the cargo space, tightly pressed together.

"Fire!" he yelled.

The machine-gun started long, staccato bursts. Carbines and submachine-guns joined in. The truck stopped, rocking back and forth. The soldiers jumped down and sought cover.

"Let's go . . . before they get a chance to recover!" the company commander barked: "We'll run into the 3rd by going directly to the southwest."

Skillfully employing the terrain, the men of Genz's company worked their way in that direction. When they reached the open area of an olive-tree orchard, barely 150 meters south of the road, they started to receive rifle and machine-gun fire.

The paratroopers disappeared into the irrigation ditches. A paratrooper pointed out to Genz that the heavy machine-gun was being set up in a position that was exposed to the enemy. "Cover! Get behind cover!" He yelled. He then ran over to them when he saw they did not understand and continued with their work. He had barely covered half the distance when an enemy machine-gun salvo cut down the German machine-gun team. When Genz got to them, he saw that both were dead. He grabbed the machine-gun and ran in a zigzag pattern back to his original position, followed all the way by the fire of the enemy machine-gun.

Enemy patrols and assault detachments that attempted to enter the orchard were turned back. The hot Mediterranean sun burned down mercilessly on friend and foe alike. None of the paratroopers had tea or water. For the most part, the men did not have anything to eat, either.

"We need water, *Herr Oberleutnant!*" the medic said to the company commander. "Especially the wounded."

"Two volunteers!" Genz called out.

"I'll go, *Herr Oberleutnant.*" Kempke chimed in.

"I'll go with him!" the medic added.

Both of the men disappeared. On the way to the next visible structure, the two were attacked by Greek soldiers who had waited in ambush. Kempke killed one of the attackers with his pistol. Another one was overwhelmed by the medic in hand-to-hand combat. A machine-gun started to fire from one of the buildings in the farm complex. With a leap, both of the Germans landed in a ditch. They crawled back to the company.

"Can't get through, *Herr Oberleutnant!* The place is crawling with Greeks."

"We'll wait until dark and try again!"

OPERATIONS OF THE WESTERN GROUP
Generalmajor Meindl had to detach the 1st and 2nd Companies of his assault regiment to *Gruppe Mitte*, the middle group. He used the rest of the 1st Battalion—the headquarters and the 3rd and 4th Companies—against the antiaircraft positions at Malemes and to take the airfield there.

The *III./FJSR*, reinforced by regimental assets—one third of the 14th (Heavy) Company and one half of the 3rd Company of the Antiaircraft Machine-Gun Battalion—received orders to either jump or air-land 15 minutes after the original gliders had been employed.

To that end, the 9th Company of *Hauptmann* Witzig was to land just east of the airfield between the village of Malemes and the church on the eastern edge of the airfield. It was to support the 1st Battalion in its fighting to take the airfield.

The majority of the battalion was to jump north and east of Malemes, with the mission of clearing the village and screen the fighting for the airfield from the east. Following that, the battalion was to be prepared to continue the fight east and establish contact with *Gruppe Mitte.*

Additional elements of the 3rd Battalion, together with fighting elements from regimental headquarters, were to be brought in by gliders at H+15 at the large bridge west of the airfield. That group, under the command of *Major* Braun, and supported by *Oberleutnants* Schächter and Trebes, was to take the bridge over the Tavronitis, prevent it from being blown up and support the 1st Battalion in its attack against the enemy's antiaircraft positions west of the airfield.

The *IV./FJSR* was to jump in west of the aforementioned bridge. The battalion was augmented by elements of the regimental staff, elements of the regimental heavy companies, a medical platoon and one third of the 3rd Company of the Antiaircraft Machine-Gun Battalion. The regiment intended to establish its headquarters in the northern tip of the olive-tree orchard there and defend, if need be.

The 4th Battalion was also directed to support the 1st Battalion and those elements of *Major* Braun that were operating against the western edge of the airfield.

The 16th Company of the regiment, under the command of *Oberleutnant* Hoefeld, was directed to jump into the riverbed of the Tavronitis 600 meters southwest of the airfield and support the 1st Battalion in its attack against the British field camp.

The jump of the 2nd Battalion, supported by two-thirds of the 14th Company, was directed to commence at H+5 on the high ground east of Spilia. It was to screen to the west and along the road south. In addition, it was to act as the regimental reserve and, if necessary, be prepared to support the attack on the Malemes airfield. Following the capture of the airfield, it was to press on in the direction of Chania, after the area around Kastelli was determined to be clear of enemy forces.

A reinforced platoon from the 2nd Battalion, under the command of *Leutnant* Mürbe, was directed to jump in east of Kastelli, engaging the weaker enemy forces reported there and fixing him in place. If the enemy proved too strong, Mürbe's men were to fight their way back and join their parent battalion.

Those were the plans, at any rate. Let's see what actually transpired . . .

The *4./FJSR,* and the elements of the battalion headquarters that jumped with it, landed on the slopes of Hill 107 and suffered heavy casualties there, because they landed in enemy positions that had not been previously identified. The enemy forces around the Malemes airfield were considerably stronger than the aerial reconnaissance had determined. The enemy was not positioned at the previously identified field camp. Instead, he had set up in extraordinarily well-camouflaged positions that were surrounded by wire obstacles. These positions were only first identified when the enemy started firing from them. The effects of those surprise fires were devastating. The battalion commander, *Major* Koch, was wounded in the head. With the exception of the 3rd Company, the battalion was unable to execute its mission.

As has previously been described, the 3rd Company was able to take a few positions on the western edge of the airfield and the field encampment site. Hill 107, which had been the designated objective, remained in English hands. At 1500 hours, when strong enemy artillery fires started to fall on the company and the attached elements of the 13th Company, the men had to dig in.

The English attack that occurred at 1645 hours, which was conducted by a medium tank with infantry following, placed a great deal of pressure on the company, which was then under the command of *Dr.* Weitzel. Mortar and machine-gun fires were able to hold the enemy back. The tank rolling forward in the dry creek bed was brought to a standstill by a 3.7-centimeter antitank gun. Its escorting infantry were turned back with mortars. Although the Germans were able to hold, it was readily apparent that an energetically conducted attack with four or five tanks would have collapsed the German positions.

Between 2000 and 2400 hours on that first day of the attack, some 21 wounded men from the company were taken to the main aid station at Tavronitis, 15 of them badly wounded. The company set up an all-round defense. It had suffered 17 killed, among them *Oberleutnant* von Plessen.

The enemy did not attack that night. The 50 reinforcements that the 4th Battalion had promised did not arrive, because *Hauptmann* Gericke simply did not have them to send.

✠

The *III./FJSR* was widely scattered with all of its elements. It landed in the Malemes-Pyrgos area, west of Platanias, and as far as Marina, far to the south of Malemes. The battalion commander, together with his headquarters, along with the 10th and 12th Companies, were almost immediately decisively engaged, since they landed in the middle of well-established and fortified enemy positions.

Only parts of the 9th Company were able to fight their way through to the regiment in the course of the day. Even so, its commander, *Hauptmann* Witzig, was wounded. Because the landings had not taken place correctly, the mission of the battalion could not be accomplished.

Kampfgruppe Braun, with its nine gliders, reached the bridge west of the airfield on time. The battle group was able to clear the machine-gun defenses around the bridge and establish contact with elements of the 3rd Company of the 1st Battalion. Following that, it had to set up all-round defensive positions along the creek bed and the olive tree orchard located there due to the heavy fires it was receiving from Hill 107. *Major* Braun was badly wounded in the head. *Oberleutnant* Schächter was badly wounded when his glider crash-landed, with the result that *Oberleutnant* Trebes had to assume command of the remnants of the battle group.

The regimental headquarters and the 4th Battalion landed in the correct drop zones. After the regimental headquarters established itself at the designated location, the headquarters elements and the 4th Battalion advanced on the bridge and the western portion of the airfield. These elements were also heavily engaged from enemy firing from Hill 107.

In the midst of trying to establish contact between the regimental headquarters and the 4th Battalion and both *Kampfgruppe Braun* and the 1st Battalion, *Generalmajor* Meindl was badly wounded. The commander ordered *Hauptmann* Gericke to assume temporary command of operations in that sector.

Other elements had better luck when landing. The 16th Company, for instance, assembled with little enemy resistance at its designated objective on high ground, where it established security.

The *II./FJSR* more or less hit the appropriate drop zones. The 6th Company set up security to the west and the south along the pass in the vicinity of Spilia.

One of the company's platoons was dropped too close to the village of Kastelli, however, and started to receive heavy fire from insurgents and civilians while its men were still descending. The platoon suffered a horrific fate, since it was practically wiped out by constant engagements and ambushes. Of the 73 men whom *Leutnant* Mürbe had under his command and control, only 20 were later freed from captivity, most of them wounded.

The regiment's situation did not look too promising. Meindl, who had recovered enough from his wounds to resume command, personally gave instructions to *Major* Stentzler and *Hauptmann* Gericke. Meindl, who had a well-earned reputation as one of the toughest paratroopers in the business, told Stentzler and Gericke the following: "Stentzler, attack west of Gericke with your battalion [2nd Battalion], swinging out far to outflank the enemy. Gericke, continue to attack from the west and frontally with your battalion [4th Battalion, with the attached 3rd Company] on both sides of the improved road; aim for the airfield in the direction of Malemes."

The heavy weapons of the 2nd Battalion, which had arrived in the course of the afternoon, were attached to the 4th Battalion for its attack against the northern slope of Hill 107. Also supporting the 4th Battalion was the 1st Battalion, which was being led by the battalion physician, *Oberarzt Dr.*

Neumann, after *Major* Koch had been wounded. Neumann and his men assaulted the northern slope after sunset after the heavy weapons had succeeded in silencing most of the enemy's guns. The fighting doctor and his men then succeeded in actually taking the gun positions in close-in combat.

At the same time that fighting was taking place, *Major* Stenzler and his men assaulted the southern slope of Hill 107. They were able to take over the gun positions after a fierce hand-grenade duel within the redoubt. Four officers and 100 enlisted personnel surrendered to the Germans. The Germans had thus taken the southern and northern positions of the commanding high ground, but the English were fighting with the courage of desperation in the middle of the hill mass and continued to fire with their antiaircraft weaponry.

Later that evening, *Major* Stentzler assumed command of the tactical operations of the regiment in the front lines, while *Generalmajor* Meindl assumed overall command of the fighting forces on the ground.

IN THE CENTRAL AREA OF OPERATIONS: *OBERST* HEIDRICH JUMPS WITH THE 2ND BATTALION

Oberst Heidrich's *Fallschirmjäger-Regiment 1* had its mission targets in the center sector. To recap:

The *I./FJR 1* of *Hauptmann* von der Heydte was to jump into the area around the Agya Penitentiary. *Hauptmann* Derpa's 2nd Battalion was to jump east of the penitentiary and take the high ground at Galatas. The 3rd Battalion of *Major* Heilmann was also to jump in, serving as the regimental advance guard in the Galatas–Daratsos–Alkianou Road–Chania Area. Finally, the division's airborne engineer battalion, attached to the regiment, was to be employed north of Alkianou. The battalion, under the command of *Major* Liebach, was minus its 3rd Company.

After the orders conference, the regimental commander—short and stocky, with light-blue eyes that shone with vitality—informed Derpa that he intended to jump in with the 2nd Battalion.

He dismissed his commanders, wishing them good luck.

✠

Major Ludwig Heilmann would jump with his men of the advance guard at 0700 hours. Once the drop zone had been secured, the battalion was to attack as part of the regiment toward Suda Bay and the capital of Crete. Later on, the officer wrote about his mission:

> Just before dawn, the 9th Company took off from the airfield at Tanagra. It took lead position in the approach on Crete over the Mediterranean. The battalion commander was with it.[5] As the first

---

5. Translator's Note: As is often typical with German firsthand accounts, the author refers to himself in the third person.

section approached the coastline, we were able to unmistakably identify elements of the British fleet, which were at anchor in front of the coast. In the vicinity of the drop zone, columns of smoke arose, a sure sign that the *Stukas* had prepared the attack. Our approach into the island was from the west. The paratroopers standing in the doorways could hear rifle fire from below, despite the noise from the engines. The heights around Galatas came into view, and machine-gun fire also bellowed from that direction. We jumped the next moment.

Right after landing on Crete's soil, a fight for life and death ensued. Some of the paratroopers landed right in front of the rifle and machine-gun barrels of the enemy. Some got caught in the branches of the olive trees. One man crashed through the roof of a passenger bus. Another man got caught up in the lines between telephone poles. The first dramatic episodes of fighting took place among grape vines, agave plants and olive trees. There were crashes and booms in every direction.

Greek soldiers, who were positioned close to the road and had surrounded their positions with barbed wire, surrendered. On the other hand, well-aimed fire was coming down on the drop zone from New Zealand forces occupying the high ground. Individually, armed only with pistols and hand grenades, my paratroopers worked their way up the slopes. After some difficult close-in fighting, I worked my way across the battlefield in leaps and bounds. In a defile, I saw the wounded leader of the 1st Platoon of the 9th Company, who was next to a wounded New Zealander. They were helping each other in dressing their wounds.

Then something happened that was unexpected. Going up the slope, the New Zealand soldiers were standing behind trees, their rifles down at their sides. I moved forward with an *Oberjäger*. It looked as if they wanted to surrender. But since there was no one else following us, the New Zealanders seized the opportunity and opened fire. We ran up the hill. Just as I saw the first few buildings of Galatas in front of us, the *Oberjäger* running behind me collapsed to the ground, hit. About 20 New Zealanders were approaching me from the direction of Galatas.

Without having noticed him, my adjutant had also climbed the hill at the same time, off to the right. He silenced a machine-gun with hand grenades. Off to the left of me, the commander of the 9th Company was assaulting with his men, but he was hit and badly wounded.

All that had occurred in the first half hour of the landing. The enemy's resistance appeared to be stiffening. Suddenly, a section climbed up the defile behind me, breathing heavily from the exertion. The section had a machine-gun with it. Thus, we were able to open fire on the approaching 20 New Zealand soldiers at the last minute.

The enemy group had approached to within bounding distance of the position where the wounded *Oberjäger* was lying. After the first burst had been fired, the flat helmets of the New Zealander had disappeared. More paratroopers arrived, and I was able to establish a deliberate defense of our forward-most position. A hundred meters behind us, the battalion physician set up his collection point for the wounded.

The battalion adjutant arrived with 80 prisoners. He reported in to me. We left the prisoners behind the wall of a cemetery. The wounded company commander of the 9th Company was still under enemy fire and could not be recovered. When we attempted to advance farther on Galatas, we started to receive rifle fire from the rear. One after the other, my men started to be wounded.

At that point, two hours of intense fighting had passed. The sun burned down mercilessly on the paratroopers, who had dug their way into the earth. Although the hill had been taken, the fate of my other companies was still unknown. I succeeded in personally establishing contact with the regiment and report on my situation. The farther attack on Galatas was discussed. On the way back to the forward positions, I brought a few reinforcements along with me to the hill.

The enemy started launching immediate counterattacks during the afternoon. The situation became more critical with each passing hour, and I still did not have any contact with my 10th, 11th and 12th Companies. Heavy attacks were starting to flare up against our position. We did not give up a single meter of ground. But as the sun descended into evening, exhaustion arrived and our situation looked desperate. Ammunition was already running low. The commander of the 9th Company died of his wounds in the front lines. Night came and none of us had any great expectations for the next day. *Oberst* Heidrich ordered us to evacuate the hill. He wanted his regiment to be drawn up closer. Only a squad remained behind to screen. It turned back several nighttime attacks and was able to hold on until the following morning.

The expected enemy attack did not materialize. In fact, German close-air support aircraft arrived at 1000 hours and strafed the castle positions. Supplies were dropped; confidence increased.

What the battalion commander did not know at the time was the fate of his other companies. The 11th Company had been dropped in the mountains, where it advanced and linked up with the regiment's 1st Battalion and fought with it. Unfortunately, as was later determined, the company commander and his headquarters section landed separately and apparently were taken prisoner, whereupon they were shot out of hand along the side of a road. The 12th Company suffered heavy losses. Some of the paratroopers landed in a reservoir and drowned. The 10th Company landed in enemy positions at Daratsos and in an enemy encampment. The company commander was badly wounded and when he attempted to stand up, he received a second, mortal wound. Although the fight appeared hopeless, one of the company's platoons actually entered an enemy barbed-wire encircled position and took a few hundred prisoners. When the platoon moved back through the enemy lines with its prisoners, it was engaged from high ground on two sides and wiped out.

THE I./FJR 3 OF HAUPTMANN VON DER HEYDTE

The *I./FJR 3* of *Hauptmann* von der Heydte flew in the second wave of *Ju 52's*. The officer later recounted his exploits in memoirs entitled *Daedalus Returned*[6]:

> We flew over the sea. It reflected back up to us in shades of blue. The mountains of Crete rose in front of me. Like gigantic birds, our machines glided directly towards the mountains. Then we swung past them and, at that moment, the voice of the pilot sounded: "Prepare to jump!"
>
> I was at the door in two steps. The air stream seized me. Below me, I recognized the village of Alikianou. I could see people on the streets. The shadows from our machines hovered like the hands of spirits over the sun-drenched white houses. In the valley under me, a large, dark mirror reflected: The water reservoir. The machine flew more slowly. The moment had come: "Jump!"
>
> I pushed off with my hands and feet and threw my arms as far in front of me as possible. The air stream from the descent grabbed a hold of me; the air was rushing in my ears and, as I looked up, I could see the white chutes of my paratroopers as far as the eye could see. Only someone who has jumped before can gauge what kind of feelings I had.
>
> As I looked around, I had a shock. I was being driven by the wind with increasing speed towards the reservoir. I had thought about death before, but it was a death on the battlefield. Would that be my fate—to drown there? In the end, however, I landed on the edge of the water basin in a fig tree.

The fight on Crete had thus started for von der Heydte's battalion as well. Assaulting rapidly, it attacked the high ground at Chania. It was mostly men from the 2nd Company of *Oberleutnant* Straehler-Pohl and the 3rd Company of *Oberleutnant* Knoche, both well-proven company commanders. The men assaulted the so-called Castle Mountain with unbelievable élan. Supporting them was Ackermann's heavy machine-gun platoon.

---

6. Translator's Note: This book, apparently in English, was not available to the translator for cross-checking. Therefore, the extended citation is a reverse translation into English from the German.

But just getting up the high ground had its fair share of obstacles. In front of the large penitentiary complex, a heavy machine-gun had been emplaced. It fired and forced the men of the heavy company to take cover. The men rallied around *Feldwebel* Gabbey and *Feldwebel* Ackermann. The battalion headquarters assembled and messengers from all four battalions arrived. A short while later, radio contact was also established. *Hauptmann* von der Heydte was just in the process of writing an attack order when three paratroopers brought him a Greek prisoner who had offered his services as a translator. He spoke perfect German.

The men heard machine-gun fires from the Galatas Hills; from Chania were coming the sounds of machine-gun salvoes and the crack of rifle fire.

"We're going to advance!" von der Heydte ordered. But the men were stopped by machine-gun fire after only a hundred meters. The men took advantage of the concealment offered by an olive-tree orchard and continued the advance. With the 2nd Company in the lead, the Cladiso was crossed. Then, in energetic bounds, the men moved up the Cladiso Valley.

Oberleutnant Knoche's 3rd Company continued the fight to clear the drop zone. Two machine-guns encountered on the way to an isolated outbuilding were eliminated.

When the 1st Company got bogged down in heavy enemy fire, von der Heydte transferred temporary command of the battalion to his adjutant and crawled and leapt to his 1st Company. He identified the two machine-guns that were pinning down the 1st Company between the road and the deep Cladiso Valley. The battalion commander immediately sent a messenger to the 4th Company (Heavy) with orders to bring up a mortar section to knock out the machine-gun nests.

Joined by his liaison officer, von der Heydte crawled forward in order to determine the exact location of the machine-guns. As they briefly exposed themselves, however, they also started to take fire from the olive-tree orchard in front of them.

Casualties mounted. The mortars finally got forward and established a firing position. When they opened fire, the English answered with their own artillery on the paratrooper positions. The English fires were so intense that the battalion was incapable of making any more advances in that direction.

In order to better observe the fires of the mortars and give corrections to his guns, the section commander, an *Oberjäger*, stood up to get a better view of the house where the English had set up their machine-guns.

"Get down!" von der Heydte yelled over to him.

"But, *Herr Hauptmann*, I can observe a lot better this way," the *Oberjäger* replied.

The first mortar rounds landed right on the enemy positions and, after the fourth salvo, the enemy no longer stirred in that location. At that point, a report was passed from mouth-to-mouth among the paratroopers, until it finally reached the battalion commander: The commander of the 4th Company had been badly wounded.

Then another ominous message arrived: The commander of the 2nd Company had also been badly wounded. The battalion liaison officer recommended to his commander that contact be established with the 3rd Battalion. *Hauptmann* von der Heydte had already been thinking that for some time. But a thick patch of woods separated him and his men from their sister battalion. If he sent some elements through there they might be caught in an ambush and wiped out. He turned to his messenger. The messenger sensed what was up. "I'll go!" von der Heydte announced.

"Are you crazy, *Herr Hauptmann*?" Knoche asked him, distraught. Initially, the *Hauptmann's* blood boiled and he wanted to dress down the seemingly insubordinate officer. But then he controlled himself and realized that his company commander was right. Later on, he found out how right he had been, since any movement through those woods would have probably cost him his life.

All of a sudden, there was a crashing and bursting front of them. "Tanks up front!" one of the men called out. A few seconds later, a small armored vehicle rolled around the bend in the road into view. Fires were concentrated on the vehicle. It approached to within 50 meters of the paratroopers, before it was stopped by an antitank rifle, whose round penetrated the side of the vehicle. An explosion thundered from within the vehicle. The tank jerked about, ran into a telephone pole and remained stationary. It was not until later, when the fighting subsided in the area a little, that the two dead British tankers inside could be recovered.

In the meantime, *Oberleutnant* Hagl of the 2nd Company had reached the battalion commander with his platoon. He and his men had had to fight their way through the English to get through. The powerfully built Bavarian, who had risen through the ranks as an enlisted man, assumed security for that portion of the battalion sector. *Hauptmann* von der Heydte and his liaison officer then headed in the direction of the battalion command post.

When they reached the command post, located in a defile off the Cladiso, the adjutant approached them. He reported that the command post had received a direct hit and that two men had been killed. In addition, the radio equipment had been damaged by the artillery round. *Oberleutnant* Mäckh had already been sent to establish personal contact with the 1st Company.

A short while later, the platoon leader of the signals section reported that the radio equipment had been repaired and that *Oberleutnant* Mäckh was already on his way back from the 1st Company. Since he had not been heard from for a while, von der Heydte sent two men out to find him. The men found the officer unconscious. The battalion signals officer had been shot in the throat and was lying beneath some vegetation at the edge of the defile. When they tried to lift him up, Mäckh told the men to leave him there and that there was a report for the battalion in his pocket.

The men took the message to the command post, whereupon another detail was sent out to get the wounded officer to the clearing station. On 25 May, the brave officer finally succumbed to his wounds. *Oberfeldwebel* Jeier took over the duties of battalion signals officer.

The reports that started to come in from the companies indicated that all had taken ground. An assault detachment from the 1st Company had advanced as far as the village of Peribolia and identified strong enemy forces southwest of the village. The 3rd Company had taken a hill with ruins from the Middle Ages on it and established defensive positions there. Greek forces, which had defended those hills, had been taken prisoner.

Barely 100 meters from the battalion command post was the clearing station of *Oberarzt Dr.* Petrisch. The battalion's second physician had gone forward to render immediate first aid on the battlefield. When von der Heydte showed up at the clearing station at noon, *Dr.* Petrisch was already operating on men. Twelve badly wounded men were waiting their turn to go under the knife. The less grievously wounded had been sent to a field hospital that had been established at the Agya Penitentiary. The battalion commander moved among the men and spoke a little to each of them. He also went over to a badly wounded English soldier. When the British soldier discovered that the battalion commander was in front of him, he said: "Sir, the war is over for me. I hope that it will also be over for you and your men soon."

In the afternoon, around 1500 hours, the enemy was arrayed in a deeply echeloned front ahead of the battalion and prevented it from breaking through in the direction of the plains of Chania. For the time being, the enemy did not counterattack any more, however. He only strengthened his artillery fires, which were augmented by naval artillery from the ships anchored in Suda Bay.

All of a sudden, flares rose into the air in front of the positions of the 2nd and 3rd Companies. The enemy had started to attack again. He attempted to shoot past the 1st Company across the slope where the 2nd and 3rd Companies had dug in. The enemy approached to within close-combat range. Man-to-man fighting flared up, and the losses of the battalion increased. The enemy was able to be thrown back, however. In the afternoon, it was even possible for the 1st Battalion to establish contact with the 3rd Battalion.

✠

The regimental order for continued operations directed the 3rd Battalion to cover both flanks of the route running along the Alikianou-Chania road. The 2nd Battalion was to remain as the regimental reserve in the vicinity of the command post, which had been established near the penitentiary. The 1st Battalion was ordered to establish defensive positions on the high ground to the right Cladiso.

When it turned dark, the enemy fires ceased in the sector of the 1st Battalion. The 1st Battalion had survived its first day of battle on Crete.

✠

The regimental commander had jumped with the *II./FJR 3* of *Major* Derpa in the vicinity of Chania. The battalion was able to jump in safely. Its mission was to take the fortress hill of Galatas.

Oberst Heidrich ordered the attack to commence right after the landing had been completed. He personally participated along with *Major* Derpa. While assaulting the high ground, Derpa was killed next to the regimental commander in the rifle fires of the defenders. Despite the severe loss, the paratroopers succeeded in taking possession of the high ground. *Oberst* Heidrich established his command post there.

To the rear of the 3rd Regiment, the elements of the airborne engineers jumped into the area around Alikianou with their commander, *Major* Liebach. The men landed between the road leading to Chania from Alikianou and the riverbed of the Jaroanos. The battalion, minus the elements it had attached elsewhere, had the mission of covering the rear of the regiment, conducting reconnaissance in the direction of Aliakianou and fixing enemy forces.

Shortly after jumping, *Leutnant* Schoemperlen and his men assaulted the bridge at Aliakianou. It was his mission to take it and establish a blocking position. Patrols from the 1st and 4th Companies, the platoon of *Leutnant* Hardt and a squad under *Feldwebel* Maluche covered the advance of Schoemperlen's platoon as well as the entire drop zone of the engineers.

The 2nd Company of engineers had started from the airfield at Topolia. They departed in the second wave around 0900 hours and had to jump under heavy artillery fire.

In advancing on the bridge, a farmstead on the periphery was attacked and taken. Some 60 Greek soldiers and civilians surrendered. In the midst of the enemy positions along the road, *Leutnant* Schoemperlen was killed by a round to the head before the bridge was reached. *Oberjäger* Schwab, who then continued leading the attack, was forced to ground by rifle fire about 50 meters from the bridge.

Major Liebach directed a patrol into Alikianou, which was led by *Leutnant* Fiedler. He moved through Kufos and approached to within 200 meters of Alikianou, when he encountered British outposts, which were driven back with hand grenades. The enemy artillery fire that then commenced forced the patrol to pull back and then retreat back to the battalion command post. On the way back, it linked up with *Leutnant* Heiduschke and four other paratroopers of the 1st Company of engineers, which had jumped at the wrong spot. The men were happy to have established contact with comrades.

Major Liebach reinforced the patrol that had returned around noon and sent it off, with an added machine-gun section, in the direction of Alikanianou again. In addition, he had four squads, supported by six machine-guns, move out against the bridge. But that renewed attack also proved futile, when it bogged down about 150 meters from the bridge.

At 1245 hours, *Oberleutnant* Tiedjen, the commander of the 2nd Company of engineers, which was fixed in place in front of the bridge, requested *Stuka* support. He also asked for them to attack the enemy-occupied high ground to its south. *Major* Liebach submitted the request and had the two patrols led by *Leutnant* Bültmann and *Leutnant* Hardt pulled back.

Leutnant Fiedler had started on a second patrol in the direction of Kufos-Alikianou in the meantime. Just outside of Kufos, he encountered the enemy. His patrol was turned back, but Fiedler refused to give up. Taking four men and a junior noncommissioned officer with a flamethrower, he attacked the village again. He penetrated the enemy's defenses that time, and the handful of paratroopers followed the *Leutnant*, who was about 300 meters ahead of them, in the direction of Alikianou. There, however, they were received by fires from snipers. *Gefreiter* Hermann was hit in the head. At the same time, the outpost in Kufos was attacked by civilians, including women, and *Unteroffizier* Rhode was wounded by birdshot.

Leutnant Fiedler's patrol had to yield to the north and reached the battalion command post around 1830 hours, where it reported in to *Major* Liebach.

During that time period, the 1st and 4th Companies of the Airborne Engineer Battalion had advanced to the northeast. Since the bridge could not be taken, *Major* Liebach had the 2nd Company and the attached antitank platoon dig in around the battalion command post and screen to the west, south and east. By doing so, one of the battalion's missions was accomplished: Guarding the regimental command post.

During the night of 20/21 May, *Major* Liebach received a directive to also guard the division command post with his battalion. The division headquarters was in morning, since *Generalleutnant* Süßmann had been killed. Like many others on that costly morning of 20 May 1941, he had also landed in Crete, starting with his battle staff on five gliders from the airfield at Eleusis. Both of the division adjutants and both of the division liaison officers were with the general in the same glider.

After about 20 minutes of flight—the formation had just reached the island of Ägina—the gliders were passed by a single *He 111*. When the *He 111* moved in front of the lead aircraft, the wings of the glider it was towing were sheared off, apparently as a consequence of the turbulence that had resulted. The tail section of the glider lurched violently downward, the tow cable tore and all of the occupants of the glider were killed upon impact on the cliffs of Ägina. The remaining aircraft of the divisional headquarters landed, as planned, about 600 meters from the reservoir. *Oberst* Heidrich assumed command of the division, while still retaining command of his regiment.

AT THE HEADQUARTERS OF THE *XI. FLIEGER-KORPS*

Around noon on 20 May, all of the soldiers at the corps headquarters waited for positive reports from the island. *General der Flieger* Student had sent *Oberstleutnant* Snowadzki to Malemes in a *Ju 52* that morning. Snowadzki had the mission of landing there and establishing an airfield command, which was to coordinate the takeoffs and landings for all of the aircraft of the 5. *Gebirgs-Division*, which were to be landed there.

Generalmajor Schlemm, the corps Chief-of-Staff, knew little of the situation on the island. Neither did *Major i.G.* Trettner, the corps Operations Officer, or *Hauptmann* Mors, the corps Intelligence Officer, who had been unable to intercept any enemy communications of importance. Everything was shrouded in an oppressive cloak of mystery until Snowadzki finally returned from Crete. The news he brought was shattering. The airfield at Malemes continued to be in enemy hands, as was Hill 107, which flanked the airfield. The remaining airfields were out of the question. No machine could land unscathed in Crete at that point.

Snowadzki had succeeded in landing at Malemes, but he noticed the airfield was still occupied by the enemy as he was taxiing. He had the battle-damaged aircraft rev up and take off, fortunately able to escape. The second *Ju 52*, which had landed with him and carried the ground personnel for airfield operations, was also able to get out safely, with both machines later returning to Athens.

Although only 7 of the 502 *Ju 52's* that had started the operation in the morning had been destroyed, the entire matter seemed to hang in the balance. *Oberstleutnant Dr.* Weyland, the corps Signals Officer, was unable to establish contact with either the western group or the central group. The radio operators attempted to establish contact every two minutes, but their efforts were in vain.

Then came even more devastating news: The *Ju 52's*, which had returned between 0900 and 1000 hours, could only be refueled manually, which delayed the start of the next wave by hours. The fuel had to be hand-pumped into the aircraft from drums.

The start time of 1300 hours for the second wave could not be met. In addition, the telephone connection between the transport formations and the corps command post had been rendered unserviceable by acts of sabotage.

The bombing attack that was to precede the second wave went on as scheduled, however. The *VIII. Flieger-Korps* directed the *Stuka* attacks, which had been scheduled for exactly 1515 hours, to continue in the third and fourth target areas. The *Ju 87's* screamed earthward with sirens howling at Rethymnon. Gigantic clouds formed from the detonating bombs seemed to reach skyward after the rapidly climbing aircraft. The bombs also fell at Heraklion, the fourth target area. The enemy had been paralyzed by the bombing, but the paratroopers, who were supposed to take advantage of the attack by jumping in and taking the two airfields, were not there. The advantage of surprise was lost.

✠

Just before the first attack by these *Stukas* took place, the corps received its first radio message from Crete. It came from *FJR 3*: *Oberst* Heidrich reported that he had taken the fortress hill, but that he did not have enough forces to conduct the designated attack on Chania. He requested the *FJR 2* of *Oberst* Sturm as reinforcements so as to be able to take the capital, which was also serving as the enemy's command and control center. But *FJR 2* could not be redirected. That regiment had no information concerning the proposed new area of operations. Moreover, the pilots had no means for navigating there.

Consequently, *FJR 2* started out at 1515 hours that afternoon for its original target of Rethymnon. It only had two battalions available to it for its mission, since the *II./FJR 2* of *Hauptmann* Schirmer had been detailed to participate in the taking of Heraklion with the east group.

THE JUMP AT RETHYMNON
The objective of *FJR 2* was the city of Rethymnon and its airfield. It was intended for the *II./FJR 2* of *Major* Koch to jump on both sides of the airfield, along with the attached *2./Fallschirm-MG-Bataillon 7*[7], a platoon from the *2./FlaMG-Bataillon 7* and a platoon each from the regiment's 13th and 14th Heavy Companies. The battalion was to take the airfield, get it operational again, if necessary, and hold it open for the air-landed forces of the *5. Gebirgs-Division.*

The first element to get airborne was *Gruppe Kroh* at 1330 hours. It started from the airfield at Megara. The 4th Company of *Hauptmann* Morawetz was the lead element of that group. He was followed by the 3rd and 1st Companies. Bringing up the rear was the 2nd Company (MG).

✠

"We are the tip of the spear, gentlemen!" *Hauptmann* Morawetz said to his paratroopers as they climbed aboard the machines. "We'll be jumping together with the battalion headquarters."

A short while later, they were in the air and were headed for their second airborne operation on Greek territory. The first one had been the bridge at Korinth.

The aircraft had left behind huge clouds of dust and dirt from their propellers and wheels as they had taken off, and the thick red clouds delayed the takeoff of the companies that followed. But that was all behind the men of the 4th Company.

When the target area appeared below them and the signal horn blared, the men moved rapidly to the open doors and jumped into the open. They felt the dramatic tug of their chutes as they deployed and were able to see puffs of smoke as machine-guns and antiaircraft weaponry fired up towards them. The company began to take losses as it was still in the air. Among those killed

---

7. Translator's Note: 2nd Company of the 7th Airborne Machine-Gun Battalion. The following unit is the 2nd Company of the 7th Antiaircraft Machine-Gun Battalion.

before they touched the ground were the company commander, Morawetz, and his executive officer. In fact all of the officers of the company were killed before they could even fire in return.

Feldwebel Brenninger assumed acting command of the company. He called out to his men: "We're attacking the airfield!" They jumped up, ran a few dozen meters and were then forced to ground by the massed fires of the defenders. Paratroopers from other elements joined up with the 4th. They worked their way forward in short leaps and bounds. Among them was *Gefreiter* Erich Lepkowski, who has provided the following firsthand account:

We propelled ourselves up again and ran forward. We were able to move perhaps 50 meters forward, before the renewed enemy fires forced us into cover again. When we saw the *Feldwebel* jump up again, we followed him. A machine-gun started firing that we had not identified before. I saw the flaming spear of tracers and wanted to take a dive. But before I could get out of the danger zone, I felt a hard blow against my left thigh and collapsed to the ground. I put some weight on the leg. Contrary to my expectations, it held. I heard screams to the right and left of me: "Medic . . . medic!"

All at once, I heard another sound: "Hands up!" I saw the Tommy helmets. They were Australians. Two of them had reached me and held their submachine-guns under my nose. "Get up!" one of them said. I shrugged my shoulders and indicated my leg. The two of them picked me up and carried me back to the hill with the vineyards, where they had their command post. I saw *Feldwebel* Brenninger there. He had also been wounded. The medic, who had looked after him, came over to me.

Help the *Feldwebel* first, I told him. The medic shrugged his shoulders sympathetically: "Sorry! The sergeant is dead!"

He looked after my leg and told me that the bullet had lodged. "We'll cut it out, and you can have it for a souvenir!" he stated. "You'll be the ones going into captivity!" I replied, even though I wasn't convinced of that myself. The medic looked at me inquisitively for a few seconds.

"You bastards!" he said. His voice registered unwilling admiration. "You do the craziest things, but we'll toss all of you in the ocean!"

"Just wait," I replied. "Perhaps you'll be the ones taking a bath. I hope you can swim."

The medic laughed and told his comrades what I had said, and they got a kick out of it as well.

The 3rd Company, which followed behind the 4th, was set down some 7 kilometers from its intended drop zone. It jumped into the cliff country west of Hill 217 and many of the men suffered jump-related injuries.

The 1st Company landed close to the 4th in the vicinity of the airfield, however. When it attempted to advance on the airfield along with the 4th, it also received heavy fire and took heavy casualties. Before the 1st Company was even able to reach its weapons containers, it had already been badly battered. Despite that, it attacked. In front of the vineyards, a location that also had fateful consequences for the 4th Company, the 3rd Company also bogged down, some 600 meters from the airfield.

Major Kroh, who had jumped along with his headquarters with the 3rd Company of *Oberleutnant* von Roon, immediately assembled those elements that he could. Together with the *2./Fallschirm-MG-Bataillon 7*, they advanced in the direction of the airfield. By 1730 hours, that group had reached the road, which went past the vineyard hill, 400 meters to its east. The brutal heat also took its toll on the men. Despite that, *Oberleutnant* von Roon spurred his men of the 3rd Company on. He wanted to take the day's objective under all circumstances, and that was the airfield, which was vitally necessary for the air-landing of the mountain forces.

Supported by mortars, von Roon and his men were able to assault the northern slope of the vineyard around 1800 hours and establish positions there. These were to be used for the attack with the rest of the battalion that was to follow. Just a half hour before von Roon and his men had reached their jump-off positions, *Major* Kroh had directed the commander of the *2./Fallschirm-MG-Bataillon 7* to take the hill in a combined effort with the elements of the 1st and 4th Companies, which were fixed in position in an olive-tree orchard south of the vineyard.

The battalion attack started 90 minutes later, with von Roon's men the first to reach the crest of the hill. In a combined effort, the enemy was pushed back. By 1930 hours, the hilltop vineyard was completely in German hands. The prisoners taken by the Australians, including *Gefreiter* Lepkowski, were liberated. The prisoners were able to tell their liberators that elements of the Australian 19th Brigade of Lieutenant Colonel Campbell had been defending there.

As darkness fell, *Kampfgruppe von Roon*, supported by fires from a captured antiaircraft gun, advanced once more in the direction of the airfield. The battle group reached the edge of the airstrip, and then advanced to its middle, engaged in bitter fighting all the way. Once there, however, fires from well-camouflaged positions on the high ground forced the men to take cover again.

By this time, *Major* Kroh's force had suffered a total of 400 casualties in dead, wounded and missing. It had also not accomplished its mission, since the airfield was still in enemy hands. It would be left for the next day to decide whether they would accomplish their goal and secure the airstrip for the following forces.

Gruppe Wiedemann, which consisted of the 3rd Battalion of *FJR 2*, along with the attached *1./Fallschirm-MG-Bataillon 7*, the *2./Fallschirm-Artillerie-Abteilung 7* and the *2./Fallschirm-Fla-Bataillon 7*, was not able to depart its airfield at Megara until 1400 hours. As it entered Crete air space, it started to receive fire. The alerted enemy was firing with everything he had, when the jump horn sounded at 1610 hours and the men of the reinforced battalion landed on both sides of the bridge over the Platania.

In the broken up terrain, only a portion of the air-dropped weapons containers could be found. Three *Ju 52's*, badly damaged by antiaircraft weapons, had to make emergency landings.

Right after landing, *Hauptmann* Wiedemann advanced on Rethymnon with the 9th Company, along with elements of the 11th Company, antitank guns, antiaircraft weapons and a 10.5-centimeter light infantry gun from the 2nd Battery of the divisional artillery battalion.[8] This force succeeded in breaking through the Greek-held defensive positions east of the city and fought its way forward to its eastern outskirts. The advance bogged down there in the face of strong defensive fires. Artillery fire was slamming into the German positions from the British guns on the flanks in the hills to the south. The men were fixed in their cliff positions by the artillery fires from the high ground.

Around 1800 hours, the enemy launched an immediate counterattack. The British forces ran into the southern flank of the German forces. The *Kampfgruppe* was able to hold firm for an hour, before Wiedemann had to issue the order to pull back. By 2000 hours, the *Kampfgruppe* had pulled back to its start position, along with all of its wounded. It established a strong blocking position around the village of Peribolia to ward off the pressing enemy forces. As night fell, the enemy launched his first attacks against the blocking position, but he was turned back.

✠

Gruppe Schulz, which consisted of the headquarters of *Fallschirm-MG-Bataillon 7*, the regimental signals platoon, the *2./FJR 2* and a platoon each from the 13th and 14th Heavy Companies, started from Tanagra at 1330 hours. When the lead aircraft reached the air space over Rethymnon, it started to receive heavy antiaircraft fire. One *Ju 52* with men from the 13th Company crashed to the ground in a fiery blaze. Most of the remaining elements made it through, however, and jumped as planned at 1550 hours just to the west of the airfield. Only the 2nd Company was prevented from jumping at the proper place as a result of the heavy ground fire. It had to jump farther to the west.

---

8. Translator's Note: At this point, the divisional artillery consisted of only one battalion (and not a regiment).

Around 2230 hours, *Major* Schulz reached the area of the proposed regimental command post with the majority of his headquarters. It was there that he was informed by the regimental adjutant that his headquarters had jumped at the wrong location and had been widely dispersed during the jump. As was later determined, some elements had jumped into the middle of enemy positions and had suffered heavy casualties while still descending. *Oberst* Sturm, the 52-year-old senior serving officer of the airborne corps, was missing. When he was finally liberated after 10 days of captivity, it was discovered that he had jumped with 10 other men into an area completely isolated from the others. On the evening of the second day, the small group had to surrender after it had engaged in a firefight lasting several hours and all of its ammunition had been expended.

Major Schulz assumed acting command of the regiment. He advanced west with his weak battle group and reached *Gruppe Wiedemann*, which was fighting at the Plantania Bridge on the night of 20/21 May.

ATTACK ON HERAKLION

Oberst Bruno Bräuer's *FJR 1*, with the attached *II,/FJR 2*, the *1./Fallschirm-MB-Bataillon 7* and the *2./Fallschirm-Sanitäts-Abteilung 7*, had the mission of taking the city and airfield of Heraklion in the second wave, commencing at 1515 hours. It was to hold open the airfield for the air-landed forces to follow. To that end, the colonel had task-organized his forces as follows:

- The *II./FJR 1* of *Hauptmann* Burckhardt was to jump with attached heavy weapons over the Heraklion Airfield and take it, while receiving air cover from German ground attack formations.
- The *I./FJR 1* of *Major* Walther was to take the enemy radio station at Gournes, 8 kilometers east of Heraklion, where it was to screen to the east.
- The *II./FJR 2* of *Hauptmann* Pietzonka was to be dropped to the west of the 3rd Battalion, where it would screen to the west and be available to the regiment as its reserve in the event of a crisis.
- The *III./FJR 1* of *Major* Schulz—not to be confused with the *Major* Schulz who jumped at Rethymnon—was to jump in near the city of Heraklion and take it.

The success of this portion of the operation was contingent upon a massed jump by all formations over the drop zones at 1515 hours and the protection afforded by the destroyers of the *VIII. Flieger-Korps*. This prerequisite was not met. It was not possible to get the *Ju 52's*, which had departed between 0900 and 1000 hours, cleared for takeoff again at 1300 hours, the designated start time. The difficulties experienced in refueling, the clearing of aircraft that had crash-landed upon return and the monstrous clouds dust clouds that had formed all contributed to the delay, in some cases up to three and a half hours. In addition, the telephone communications between the airfields had been interrupted, thus making comprehensive and immediate communications among the commanders concerning the onset of delays and the coordination of new start times impossible. As a result, formations took off in improper order and did not appear over the drop zones *en masse*. At the most, squadrons appeared over the respective drop zones anywhere between 1500 and 1800 hours. Since the destroyers were only able to provide air cover until 1615 hours due to range limits, most of the forces therefore had to jump without any air cover.

The bombing raids conducted by the *VIII. Flieger-Korps* had not destroyed the enemy; instead, they had only forced him to take cover temporarily. Finally, as a result of the loss of aircraft during the first wave and the return flight home, the combat strength of *FJR 1* had been reduced by 600 men.

The enemy was also well prepared for an airborne insertion against the airfield at Heraklion. Exploiting the caverns in the surrounding terrain, the enemy had established a deeply echeloned defensive system. He controlled the low ground, which was the only terrain that was suitable for aerial insertion, by flanking and frontal fires.

The *II./FJR 1*, which was supposed to take the airfield by simultaneously attacking it from two sides, was greeted during the approach and jump with intense antiaircraft cannon and machine-gun fires. Several machines crashed to the ground on fire. Because of the high ground, the jump took place at 200 meters, with the result that many paratroopers were killed or wounded as they hung defenseless in the air.

The eastern group of the battalion, led by *Hauptmann* Burckhardt, was unable to conduct a massed attack. The commanders of the 5th and 8th Companies, *Oberleutnant* Hermann and *Oberleutnant* Platow, rallied all of the available soldiers together and attacked uphill towards the airfield. *Oberleutnant* Platow and several other officers were later found dead on the high ground.

Oberleutnant Hermann had been shot in the head while still in the air, which caused him to go temporarily blind. Despite that, he continued to lead his company. Supported by a *Hauptfeldwebel* and a *Gefreiter*, he was helped forward until he collapsed.

By the time darkness fell, *Hauptmann* Burckhardt had succeeded in gathering some 60 to 70 men of his battle group at the base of Hill 182.

The western battle group, under the command of *Hauptmann* Dunz, jumped along the western edge of the airfield. The *Kampfgruppe* consisted of the 6th and 7th Companies, as well as the *1./Fla-MG-Bataillon 7*. Within 20 minutes, it was wiped out. Those who had not been wounded or killed while jumping, succumbed on the ground shortly after landing to an enemy attack by several light and medium tanks, which rolled into the positions of the paratroopers and shot to pieces anything and everything offering resistance. Returning to the regiment were only three soldiers from the 6th Company and two soldiers from the antiaircraft company. They reported the news of the disaster. Within the battalion, 12 officers and 300 men were killed; an additional 8 officers and 100 men were wounded.

Within the 1st Battalion of *FJR 1*, only the 3rd Company was dropped on time in its designated area around Gournes. The battalion headquarters and the 1st and 2nd Companies did not arrive until three hours later. Because it was so late in the day, the 4th Company did not receive permission to even take off. It had to be employed later and at a different location. Fortunately for the 1st Battalion, its jump was without enemy interference. In the case of the 2nd Company, however, it jumped 5 kilometers east of its target of the radio station at Gournes, when it was originally supposed to land 2 kilometers to the west. The company later linked up with its parent battalion after a long delay. The radio station was captured, however, and the battalion then screened to the east and south.

Oberst Bräuer, who arrived with his regimental staff at 1840 in the area east of Gournes, immediately decided to advance on the airfield, screened by elements of the 1st Battalion under *Oberleutnant Graf*[9] Blücher. The regimental commander thought that the airfield had been taken by the 2nd Battalion. Around 2340 hours, he reached the eastern slope of the airfield plateau and encountered strong enemy forces, much to his surprise. That night, *Oberleutnant* Blücher and his platoon fought their way to the high ground on the eastern part of the airfield. The regimental command post was established on the high ground north of the road, 2 kilometers east of the airfield.

In accordance with the overall plan, the *II./FJR 2* of *Hauptmann* Pietzonka, which had been attached to *FJR 1*, jumped into its drop zone. Without encountering the enemy, he started screening to the west and south. Even so, his battalion was not very strong, since two of its companies, the 5th and the 6th, had had to remain behind due to the losses sustained in *Ju 52's*.

During the night, *Oberst* Bräuer attempted to assemble his widely scattered forces—at least those that could be reached—for a concentrated attack on the airfield in the morning. In order to focus on that action, we will be following the exploits of the *III./FJR 1* of *Major* Karl-Lothar Schulz.

THE WAY TO HERAKLION

"Get ready!" *Major* Schulz ordered, as he looked at his watch, which told him it was already 1600 hours. He stood in the open door of the *Ju 52* and the air-stream battered him. Then the tooting of the Bosch horn sounded. With a broad leap, the officer jumped out. He felt how the satchel with equipment and his weapons dragged him towards the earth. Then he felt the jolt of the deployment. He swung towards earth, just like the other soldiers of his battalion.

The initial individual fires soon grew to a wild crescendo. The antiaircraft guns fired rhythmically. Behind him, Schulz heard a jarring detonation, as a *Ju 52* broke apart after receiving a direct hit. He saw another machine fly past him overhead. It was drawing a long trail of ground fire after it.

The white chutes of the paratroopers were visible by the hundreds to the

---

9. Translator's Note: Count.

west over the skies above Heraklion. They fluttered to earth, inviting targets for the defenders to fire at.

Major Schulz hit the ground, conducted a parachute landing fall, extricated himself from his chute and crawled into a grain field, which offered him and the other paratroopers who landed there some concealment. They had landed barely 100 meters from the walls of the city, from which the enemy was firing with rifles and machine-guns.

Crawling, *Major* Schulz worked his way back. When he reached a vineyard, he encountered an English combat force. A burst from his submachine-gun caused them to disappear. Farther to the left, two more German submachine-guns joined the firing. Hand grenades exploded.

A few minutes later, Karl-Lothar Schulz had assembled his men. From the reports he had received from individual groups, he determined that they had landed in the middle of a large concentration of enemy forces outside of the city. *Hauptmann* von der Schulenburg, the *Graf*, showed up. Behind him was a group of paratroopers.

"What do you think, Schulenburg?"

"The battalion is assembling 400 meters farther to the rear to attack the village along the road, *Herr Major*."

"What about the casualties? Are they heavy?"

"A lot, *Herr Major*. But *Oberarzt* Langemeyer is already operating."

They reached the rally point. *Oberleutnant* Kerfin was giving instructions to the groups that were showing up. The weapons containers were starting to pile up. Medical containers had also been found.

"We'll attack the village. It is the jumping-off point for the attack on the city!" the *Major* announced.

The attack moved out and made good progress. The paratroopers proved to be the superior of their enemy in house-to-house fighting. English and Greek forces, including some civilians, fired at them from the city. The medics took care of the wounded and evacuated them. The Scottish snipers on the city walls were extremely good shots, however. Many a paratrooper fell to them through head wounds. A bitter struggle had started for the city of Heraklion. When one of the assistant battalion physicians attempted to cross one of the roads, he was also felled by a wound to the head.

The village was taken by the paratroopers, but the subsequent attack on the city bogged down. As the cries for help emanated from the wounded in the evening, *Dr.* Langemeyer was no longer able to contain himself. Accompanied by several paratroopers and two medics, he ran forward. He was forced to take cover, but he then discovered a group of paratroopers that had wounded with them behind a low wall.

"Give me cover!" he said, turning to the men who had accompanied him.

When the firing commenced, the doctor ran forward, bent over as far as he could. Up front, from the walls of the city, there were muzzle flashes. The machine-gun there was soon covered by the German fires and quieted.

Rifle fire started up. Another 10 meters for the physician! He made a sharp turn and tossed himself forward with a mighty leap taking all of his remaining strength. He had reached the low wall!

The doctor saw immediately that things were not good. One had taken a round to the belly, another had been hit in the chest and a third hit in the thigh. Langemeyer injected morphine to at least soften the fierce pain of the wounded. He then dressed the wounds the best he could along with the two medics who had run up behind him.

When it started to turn dusk, *Major* Schulz showed up at the provisional clearing station. He asked the doctor how they could save the badly wounded.

"We can only help them if we take the hospital, where it's possible to actually operate" he replied.

"Well, then. I guess it's into the city" he said. A few minutes later he announced he needed three volunteers for a patrol.

Three medics volunteered. They got to the city gate, which was on the western side and protected by barricades. They reported this information back to the commander when they returned.

Langemeyer had returned to the tent where *Oberarzt Dr.* Kirsch had been bedded. Kirsch had been shot on the right side of his chest and badly wounded. He would make it through if there were no complications, but his loss meant that the jaw specialist was not available in case any soldiers with those types of injuries were brought in.

✠

In the meantime, *Major* Schulz had gathered his company commanders together. He started his briefing by announcing that they would enter the city through the west gate. "We will not be able to get over the wall. But if we go this way . . ." he said, both pointing to the map and giving a hand gestures, " . . . across the cliffs above the gate, we will have the opportunity to take out the guards in the watchtowers."

"We should split up then, *Herr Major!*" von der Schulenburg interjected. "We'll only get into each other's way if we're all at the gate at the same time."

"Good, Schulenburg!" the commander responded. "You'll take the 'beach group' with *Oberleutnant* Becker, bypass the city and approach from the sea side. I'll take the west group along with *Oberleutnant* Kerfin. The 'beach group' moves out at 0230 hours. The west group at 0245 hours. Make the necessary preparations. It is imperative that we act quickly and decisively."

✠

It had turned night over the desperate and bloody fighting for Crete. The situation for the attackers was more than critical. Up to that point, *General der Flieger* Student had only heard ominous reports. Flying in the face of his concepts and plans, his men had not succeeded in a single place to take one of the three designated landing fields for the mountain forces.

As a result, the battle for Crete could go either way. Student seriously considered calling off the operation. But that would have meant losing the 7,000 paratroopers that were already on the island. At an evening conference, the Commanding General wrestled his way to a decision: "We need to concentrate all available reserves for an attack on the airfield at Malemes to secure at least one landing strip for the mountain troops."

The men, who stood around the corps commander in the headquarters, knew that that was the sole option left; otherwise, he would not have taken it.

Later on, Student commented on this decision:

> That decision really was not an easy one for me. The airfield at Malemes, which shimmered red like a clay tennis court, was small and had only been used by the English just as a fighter base. That much was known. To undertake an air-landing operation with 500 heavy transporters—with all of the unforeseen incidents—was to place everything on one card. But there was no other path for me to take. The unmistakable *Schwerpunkt* was placed on Malemes.

The first night on the island tugged at the men's nerves. Facing the 7,000 paratroops, of whom a large portion was either dead, wounded or missing, were 43,000 enemy soldiers. If the enemy initiated an immediate counterattack during the night with all of the armor at his disposal, he would undoubtedly push the small band of paratroopers into the sea.

MAJOR-GENERAL FREYBERG'S COUNTERATTACK

Even though the attack orders of *FJR 3* had fallen into the hands of the commanding general of the Commonwealth forces on Crete, Major-General Freyberg, on the first day of the attack, he failed to draw up the necessary countermeasures, even though the missions of the remaining waves of paratroopers and other battle groups were also outlined in broad strokes.

There were several reasons for that. One of them was that the field-telephone links from his headquarters to his subordinate commands had been destroyed by the aerial bombing attacks. He had too few radio sets to make up the difference. As a result, his headquarters was not informed at all or only insufficiently informed about critical developments on the island. That led, in the end, to the loss of the airfield at Malemes, which was to prove so crucial for the landings that would follow for the Germans.

Immediate counterattacks: That was the only option for countering the enemy forces that landed. No matter how strong they ultimately were, it was during the landing process that they were at their weakest. The British leadership was of one accord in that thought. As a result, counterattacks had been practiced against both sea- and air-landed forces.

It was during those counterattacks that the armored forces on the island were earmarked to play a decisive role. But when the paratroopers started to land, these basic rules of engagement seem to have been forgotten. Although there were immediate counterattacks conducted among the smallest of elements, for the most part, the defenders stayed put where they were. Of course, there were reasons for that as well. British intelligence forces had long since realized that not all of the German forces earmarked for the invasion had landed and that paratroopers could land at any moment at another, quieter place.

For example, when one of the company commanders of a unit positioned along the edge of the airfield at Malemes requested the advance of the battalion reserve along with all of the tanks at around 1000 hours on 20 May, the battalion commander denied the request. It was not until 1700 hours and *after* the critical situation of the paratroopers had passed that an attack with two infantry tanks and a platoon of fusiliers was allowed. The small British force was promptly eliminated by the paratroopers.

This failure, which he himself had caused by the scattershot employment of his forces, caused the British battalion commander to pull his forces back. As a result, it was only a matter of time before Malemes would fall.

That first night, only local counterattacks with limited objectives were conducted by weak Allied forces. As a result, the British gave away their unique chance of chasing the German paratroopers from the island.

The British maintained strong forces along the coast to the east of Malemes in order to receive and hold up the expected seaborne assault by the Germans. The Germans, however, had no intention of landing seaborne forces there.

During those late evening hours of 20 May, the fate of Crete had already been decided, even if it did not appear that way initially. In fact, at that point, everything appeared to be heading for a giant fiasco on the part of the Germans.

✠

The headquarters of the *XI. Flieger-Korps* had gained the impression on the evening of 20 May that the enemy resistance had been considerably more intense than had been expected. From that point forward, all efforts at the corps headquarters in Athens were directed to supporting the assault regiment at Malemes so that the airfield could be taken.

By then, the radio contact with the forces at Malemes, Chania and Heraklion was good. It was only with the group at Rethymnon that no radio communications could be established. The radio section of the group had been badly damaged during the jump, and the two attempts that were made to drop replacement equipment failed. Student then had a Fieseler *Storch* fly to Rethymnon. The aircraft was able to penetrate the antiaircraft fires and land near there. Despite the successful landing, the aircrew was then captured by the Allied forces when it attempted to establish contact with *Gruppe Kroh*. That night, Student summoned *Hauptmann* Kleye to his headquarters. Kleye was a well-known daredevil within the headquarters staff. He gave the young officer the mission of flying to Malemes early in the morning of 21 May to personally report on the situation and establish contact with the *Sturm-Regiment*.

Kleye was enthusiastic in accepting the mission. While he prepared for his solo flight to Crete, the headquarters staff busied itself with new plans for allowing the corps to finally start landing forces of the 5. *Gebirgs-Division*.

Let us return to operations on the island during the night of 20/21 May.

ON THE ROAD TO VICTORY: OPERATIONS OF THE *STURM-REGIMENT*

The night of 20–21 May 1941 had already fallen, as the survivors of *Kampfgruppe Genz* crawled through a roadside ditch in the Chania area. After 90 minutes, they reached a ditch that was overgrown with vegetation, almost like a tunnel. Once there, they were able to move forward upright, albeit somewhat hunched over. *Oberarzt Dr.* Stehfan and *Oberjäger* Kempke moved ahead of the group, scouting the way. After an hour, they returned and reported that there was a fairly large settlement in the valley, but it was swarming with English. They could not bypass the settlement, however, since the mountains closed up to it on both sides.

While the men were still discussing the situation, they were fired at by a group of about 30 civilians. The civilians, who were assaulting the position of the paratroopers, were held at bay with bursts of submachine-gun fire and hand grenades. Eventually, they were driven off.

The men then took off, one after the other, in the direction of the village. As a precautionary measure, they took off their telltale helmets, so as not to be recognized in the darkness. At the outskirts of the village, they ran into a building that had been converted to a signals center for the enemy. They were addressed by someone in the house and asked who they were. Alfred Genz, who could speak English, replied that he was Captain Miller from the Yorkshire Antiaircraft Battery. While Genz engaged the man in conversation, the remaining men filed past and disappeared into a grain field. Genz soon followed after his ruse was discovered and the English started firing at him.

They felt their way forward, moving along a creek. When the creek started to bend, they left it and climbed up a hill, from whose crest the paratroopers suddenly stated to receive fire.

"Stop firing!" Genz shouted through the crackling of the small-arms fire and the explosions of the hand grenades. "We're English!"

The firing slowed down, and the paratroopers used the brief respite from the gallows to run back down the hill. They reached the opposite slope, but they were greeted by machine-gun fire there. Once again, Genz called out in his best English that the Germans were on their heels and that they would attempt to catch them in the flank.

They pulled back off to the side. A few minutes later, the English troops that had been pursuing them were engaged in a firefight with their comrades on the hill. This was followed by an adventurous march at night that took the last reserves of strength the men had. They moved through enemy-occupied villages, past encampments and through deep, stony defiles. When the men started falling to the ground in exhaustion, Genz ordered a two-hour rest.

Early on the morning of 21 May—it had already turned light—Genz was awakened by a guard. He awoke, startled, and the guard reported in an excited voice: "*Herr Oberleutnant*, there's Germans over there!"

Electrified by the news, Genz shot up. He looked through his binoculars in the direction he had been given. It was true. Some 3 kilometers away, German paratroopers were going into position on a hill slope.

"Fire a recognition signal!" Genz ordered the *Feldwebel* of his company headquarters section. A short while later, a countersignal was sent rocketing into the air from the opposite slope.

The men marched through the valley and then ascended the hill. When they linked up with a company from von der Heydte's group, they started to receive machine-gun fire from the direction where they had just come. The enemy had gotten as far as where Genz's men had been, and they had escaped in the nick of time. Genz and his men were assimilated into the *I./FJR 3* for the remainder of the fighting.

✠

The 1st Battalion of the *Fallschirm-Sturm-Regiment*, which was under the acting command of *Oberstabsarzt Dr.* Neumann after *Major* Koch had been wounded, prepared to continue the attack forward into the center of the English positions on Hill 107 that morning from its positions along the northern slope of the hill. From there, it was directed that it take the airfield at Malemes.

Shortly before that, *Hauptmann* Kleye had succeeded in landing on the beach three kilometers west of Malemes at Spilia. He inquired about the situation, found that it had remained unchanged and also received the news that ammunition was starting to run low within the regiment. He took off and, once in the air, radioed a message that ammunition was needed and that it was possible to safely land along the beach at Spilia.

A short while later, six *Ju 52's* took off to bring in the urgently needed ammunition. They were able to land safely, unload their cargo and then return safely to the Greek mainland.

Neumann's men ran right into the withdrawal movements of the British when they launched their initial attack. The Germans pressed hard and they succeeded in taking the high ground. It was only along the far slope of the hill mass that the enemy continued to hold, reinforced by an antiaircraft gun.

About the same time that the hilltop was taken, *Hauptmann* Gericke received the following orders from the corps:

The airfield at Malemes must be taken under all circumstances on 21 May. Attack time is 1500 hours. To support the attack, paratroopers will jump in behind the enemy at Malemes and Pyrgos and also participate in the fighting for the airfield. The assault regiment will be reinforced by two companies of paratroopers, who will jump in. Heavy aerial preparation will start at 1400 hours to initiate the attack.

A short while later, the paratroopers heard the sound of naval artillery, which soon increased vastly in intensity within a few seconds. But the naval fire was not intended for them. Instead, it was directed at a light German naval element that had entered the area.

Two enemy antiaircraft guns on Hill 107 were captured intact. The paratroopers directed their fires against a neighboring piece of high ground, which was still being held by the enemy and from which he was engaging the Germans of the 4th Battalion, who were positioned along the edge of the airfield.

The men of the 4th Battalion had taken the enemy's bunkers along the airfield after close combat. All of a sudden—it was around noon—the men heard the droning of aircraft engines. It was a *Ju 52*, which descended from the clear skies, moved across the mountains and then made an approach over the crowns of the trees of an olive tree orchard. But the airfield was still not clear of the enemy. Enemy firing commenced; machine-guns hammered.

Taking evasive action, the *Ju 52* swung out of the firing area and then proceeded to land! It rolled across the hot sand. Paratroopers ran to the machine, and the doors were opened. Crates of ammunition were tossed out.

"Grab the badly wounded, and we'll take them back!" *Leutnant* von Koenitz barked to the men on the ground. He then left the aircraft and made his way over to *Hauptmann* Gericke.

The badly wounded, including *Generalmajor* Meindl and *Major* Koch, were loaded onto the aircraft. The machine started up, taxied and took off. It made it out safely, then climbed ever higher until it disappeared from the sight of those still on the ground.

On the western side of the airfield, which could not be reached by the enemy's antiaircraft weaponry, three *Bf 110's* landed around 1400 hours. They were briefed on the location of the English battery, which was still firing, and directed to eliminate those positions.

The three destroyers took off and approached the hill with the enemy positions. They opened fire with their machine-guns and automatic cannon, whizzed past the defenders, turned and returned to strafe the positions again. After the third run, the enemy fires ceased and, waving their wings, the three *Bf 110's* returned to the Greek mainland.

✠

For the 3rd Company of the assault regiment, the night had gone by in tortuous slowness. An English patrol was identified and engaged. Would the enemy attack? That was the worried question for the paratroopers of the company. They all knew they were in a critical situation. Around 0500 hours, a messenger arrived from the battalion with orders for it to be prepared to move out at 0530 hours. *Oberarzt Dr.* Weizel received instructions to act as guides for the mountain forces that would be landing in the afternoon.

The men moved into their positions. Around 0900 hours, heavy enemy artillery fire started coming in. They saw the individual *Ju 52's* and *Bf 110's* land and take off. When the sun reached its high point early in the afternoon, it burned down on the men with full intensity. It was 1600 hours before the first *Ju 52's* appeared over the mountains. The British antiaircraft guns opened up with everything they had. But the aircraft flew in at low altitude and through the fire to make their approach. The enemy then started firing on the airfield. English double-barreled machine-guns joined in, and the landing aircraft were riddled with bullets.

The men of the 3rd Company directed the men streaming out of the aircraft. Farther off to the right, Erich Schuster saw one of the *Ju 52's* go up in flames. Another one rolled across the tarmac with a long train of brilliant flames following it. As it taxied to stop, the doors opened and mountain troopers, some with their uniforms on fire, jumped out and rolled to the ground, trying to extinguish the flames.

Erich Schuster ran with his squad to one of the men laying on the tarmac. They reached the wounded man and pulled him back to the edge of the airfield.

The second wave of *Ju 52's* started their approach. Clouds of dust and dirt soon rose high into the sky. A motorcycle with sidecar, which had just been unloaded, rolled between the landing *Ju 52's* and reached the position where their wounded battalion commander was laying and evacuated him. He was placed into the sidecar, and the machine raced off to the relative safety of the edge of the airfield.

Erich Schuster ran with *Gefreiter* Kellermann to one of the mountain troopers who had collapsed. An artillery round came screaming in towards them. They took cover. The crushing blast of the explosion made them feel as if their eardrums were about to explode. A few seconds later, they were on their feet again, but they were forced to take cover again by machine-gun fire.

That time, the German machine-guns at the airfield's edge were quicker than the enemy. Its burst of fire wiped out the lives of those men behind the other machine-gun, who had also been trying to kill others in order to survive.

Behind them, a *Ju 52* exploded, and a gigantic fireball rushed skyward. Then Schuster and Kellermann reached the unconscious man. He had been hit in the upper thigh. Blood was spurting out of the wound. Schuster applied a tourniquet above the wound. They then dragged the man back through the fire, which had abated somewhat, to the edge of the airfield.

Schuster and Kellermann are just illustrative of all of the other men of the 3rd Company, who did their utmost to retrieve the wounded. They guided the mountain troopers to positions and helped out whenever they could.

Landing and taking-off aircraft threw up huge yellowish-red walls of sand and dust across this place of destruction. Landing way at the far end of the runway, one of the last *Ju 52's* hit the ground with its nose and started to burn.

With pick axes and iron bars, the paratroopers ran toward the flames, which hissed and singed. They attacked the doors of the aircraft, which were jammed shut, and helped the mountain troopers get out. They then ran for cover. They made it just in the nick of time, because the aircraft exploded in a huge ball of flames a few seconds later.

Two bulldozers, which had been captured, clattered towards the wreck from the edge of the airfield. They pushed the downed aircraft off the landing strip.

Malemes proved to be just the first step in a fiery inferno for the mountain troopers. But they had made it from the heavens to join the hellish fighting going on on the ground. They had arrived and soon the word spread like wild fire: "The mountain troops are here!"

KAMPFGRUPPE RAMCKE IS COMING!

On 19 May, *Oberst* Ramcke and his adjutant, *Hauptmann* Vogel, arrived at the airfield at Topolia, 40 kilometers north of Athens. Bernhard Hermann Ramcke, like *Oberst* Sturm, 52 years old, was one of the senior officers of the fledgling airborne corps. Just a few days previous, he had received permission from Student to jump in to Crete with a *Kampfgruppe* in case of any eventualities. In the meantime, he went with the corps headquarters to Greece to assist the *5. Gebirgs-Division* in its preparations to be air-landed.

When the fighting on Crete started early on 20 May, Ramcke and Vogel were busy assisting in "packing" the mountain troopers. During the night of 20/21 May, under the guidance of Ramcke, the *Ju 52's* were loaded out with ammunition, heavy weapons and all the assorted equipment needed for their operation. At the time, however, there was still no available landing strip for the mountain forces.

"Damn! If we don't get the mountain guys over early in the morning, then our guys will be in some deep shit! We've got to get at least one airfield open . . ."

Ramcke turned round as someone cleared his throat behind him. "*Oberleutnant* Voßhage, *Herr Oberst!*" the paratrooper officer reported. "What . . . Voßhage . . . I thought you were already over there!" Ramcke said, surprised.

"My company was unable to follow, *Herr Oberst*. We would like to request for you to try to get us over there, *Herr Oberst!*"

"What's your story, Kiebitz!" Ramcke asked the *Hauptmann*, who was standing next to Voßhage.

"Same here. *Leutnant* Klein is gathering the remaining men."

A thought shot through Ramcke's brain, a way to get around Student's directive to him. "Grab every paratrooper you can find and report back to me in an hour!" he told the two officers.

"Vogel," Ramcke said a minute later. "Get ready! We're going to Crete!"

"How's that, *Herr Oberst?* We don't have any transporters."

"Let me handle that," he answered with a smile.

Oberst Ramcke hurried over to the radio communications center, closely followed by his adjutant. He had the signals personnel put him in touch with the corps headquarters. A short while later, Student was on the phone. Ramcke reported to the Commanding General: "We're ready, *Herr General!* I have a reserve battalion with 500 men and we're ready for orders!"

"Where did you get the men, Ramcke? Everything's already out."

The *Oberst* reported briefly on what he had done. When he finished, there was silence for 30 seconds. Then Student came back on the line: "Good, Ramcke. You win. You'll jump with the first wave on the second day to relieve the forces on the ground at Malemes. The airfield needs to be taken as rapidly as possible so that the mountain forces can follow on. Have the aircraft unloaded. Good luck!"

Like a bolt of lightning, Ramcke was outside again. "Get going, Vogel . . . over to the aircraft. Tell everyone to unload immediately. Gather the paratroopers, give them rations. Get ready to go!"

Oberst Ramcke raced from group to group of paratroopers in his motorcycle-sidecar combination. Cursing, the mountain troops unloaded their heavy weapons. When the paratroopers had all been assembled, *Hauptmann* Kiebitz and *Oberleutnant* Voßhage were able to report 550 men.

Despite their hurried preparations, *Kampfgruppe Ramcke* was unable to take off first. *Hauptmann* Schmitz and two companies of his antitank battalion were finished and ready to go first.

Around 1400 hours, the first *Stukas* descended on the remaining British positions at Malemes. Around 1500 hours, the first wave of *Ju 52's* reached the jump zone with the antitank forces. They jumped. *Hauptmann* Schmitz and his men were thrust into combat operations immediately. Then some mountain troops arrived that had taken off from other airfields on the mainland. These were followed by the *ad hoc* battle group of *Oberst* Ramcke.

✠

When the aircraft approached the rocky shores of Crete, Ramcke turned to his adjutant. "Jump close. Good luck, men!" He then added: "We'll do it!"

The order came to get ready to jump. Ramcke announce he would be the first out the door.

Ramcke stood in the open door and observed the landscape below, first the silvery green olive trees and then a vineyard. The sound of the jump horn penetrated through.

With a leap, the small figure of Ramcke jumped into the unknown. Following closely on his heels were the 550 men who had been "collected" at Topolia. As they floated to earth, they were not engaged.

Ramcke landed 2 meters behind an agave plant that was as tall as a man and armed with thorns on pointed leaves. He executed a parachute landing fall over his left shoulder and released his parachute. He pulled his pistol and ran a few dozen steps forward to have a better field of vision. He looked skyward and saw the white domes of the parachutes above him and a final *Ju 52*, which still had not released its "cargo."

"Jump! . . . Jump now!" he yelled, but no one could hear him, of course. But as if they had heard them, the men started tumbling out and the parachutes deploying. But it was too late. The men were pushed out to sea by the wind, where the men faced certain death by drowning due to their heavy loads.

"*Herr Oberst! Herr Oberst!*" Paratroopers were running over to the colonel. Among them was *Oberleutnant* Reil, another adjutant.

"Reil, assemble everyone over there in front of the house with the well."

German paratroopers were waving from the direction of the house. Ramcke hurried over to them. An officer from the group approached Ramcke. It was *Oberleutnant* Göttsche, the signals officer of the assault regiment.

"It's great that you're here, *Herr Oberst!*" he said between short breaths, precipitated by the run. "The regiment is in need of command and control. *Generalmajor* Meindl has been badly wounded. *Major* Braun, in the headquarters, has been killed. Many of the officers are dead. We have taken heavy losses. But the majority of the airfield is in our hands. The first mountain forces have already landed as well, but they have also taken heavy casualties. *Generalmajor* Meindl and *Major* Koch, who was also wounded, have been flown out."

"Thanks, Göttsche! Brief me on the situation!"

The signals officer reached into a pocket on his knee and pulled out a map: "*Hauptmann* Gericke and his battalion are on the east side of the airfield and on both sides of the coastal road engaged in hard defensive fighting with the enemy. *Major* Stenzler, who has assumed acting command of the regiment, is with his battalion on the southeast side of Hill 107. A half hour ago the mountain forces coming in from Tattoi have started landing. The airfield, however, is still under enemy fire. The enemy is still firing from a portion of Hill 107."

"We have to completely clear Hill 107," the colonel responded. "We'll set up our command post here in the olive garden." He summoned Reil and then told Göttsche to take them up front.

Ramcke, his messenger, Engler, Reil and Göttsche then headed rapidly towards the fighting. The closer they got to the airfield, the louder the sounds of combat became. The buildings on the western edge of the airfield, which they soon reached, were filled with equal numbers of German and English wounded. In front of them were the dead. *Oberst* Ramcke began to develop his plan of attack.

When he returned to the command post, he received the report that only two of the four companies he had assembled had been able to take off. He turned to his messengers.

"*Kompanie Kiebitz* reports immediately to *Hauptmann* Gericke along with its attached antitank guns. Orders for Gericke and his battle group: Pressed the attack hard—even after nightfall—along both sides of the coastal road. Push the enemy back as far as possible so that he can no longer reach the airfield with his artillery. The company will advance to the area of operations of Stenzler's battalion and reinforce that company."

Ramcke paused as a messenger came running into the command post: "*Herr Oberst, Hauptmann* Schmitz has linked up with us with his antitank personnel. His battle group is at company strength."

Shortly afterwards, Schmitz showed up and reported to the colonel that his men were assembling near the command post.

"Thanks, Schmitz! Stay here until I see where you are needed the most."

A minute later, *Oberst* Utz, the commander of *Gebirgs-Regiment 100*, arrived at the command post.

"Good that you're here, Utz!" Ramcke said in greeting. "Listen to what I think your first mission should be!" After a slight pause, Ramcke continued: "You'll go with your forces at first light to bypass the southern wing of the enemy by moving through the mountains. As soon as you have gone around them, you'll shoot a signal: Two star bursts. At that point, *Kampfgruppe Gericke* and *Kampfgruppe Stenzler* will move out to attack. First objective: Eliminate the artillery. After that, we'll continue the attack east until we establish contact with *Kampfgruppe Heidrich* at Chania."

"Good plan, Ramcke! We will set out immediately. You can depend on us!" Utz concluded.

By the evening of that 21 May 1941, all of the airfield at Malemes was in German hands. This was a pivotal moment for the entire Crete operation.

That evening, Ramcke went to visit *Kampfgruppe Gericke*, where he was briefed on the situation. Everyone was confident that everything would turn out well, now that additional forces had landed.

Ramcke then went on to see *Major* Stentzler, where the mood was also good. On the way back to the airfield, Ramcke linked up with the mountaineers from *Gebirgsjäger-Regiment 100*. Fully equipped, they moved past him into the mountains.

The *Ju 52's* landed and took off from Malemes without a break. Paratroopers continued to jump in and mountain troops were landed.

A few minutes after Ramcke had returned to the airfield, the main body of *Major* Bode's divisional artillery battalion landed. The Chief-of-Staff of the

XI. Flieger-Korps, Generalmajor Schlemm, arrived soon thereafter. He wanted to get everything ready for the arrival of Student on Crete.

The situation in the area around the western portion of Malemes had stabilized. The trump card that Student had played had worked. The airfield was in German hands and the reinforcements for the various groups started to arrive.

As it dawned on the second day of the attack, the area around the drop zone of the assault regiment's 3rd Battalion was a disaster. Parachutes were spread over olive trees and agave plants; dead paratroopers were still hanging in the branches of the trees. Everywhere one looked, there were dead. Hundreds of paratroopers had been killed in the area of operations of the western group.

Of the 580 men who jumped from the battalion, 250 were killed immediately. One hundred and fifteen soldiers were wounded, and 135 were missing. Only 80 of the men were able to make their way through to the other units of the regiment.

When the *Stukas* attacked around 1400 hours, the paratroopers advanced against the village of Malemes. It was cleared, house by house. The enemy continued to hold out in the few remaining houses of the village, however. It was not until the antitank guns of *Hauptmann* Schmitz arrived that the village was finally taken.

During the evening of 21 May, Ramcke had outposts established along the beaches to await and guide the seaborne landing of other mountain forces. Among the outposts was *Kapitänleutnant* Bartels, who had arrived among the first *Ju 52's* to land at Malemes. He would act as a liaison officer for the seaborne forces.

THE ODYSSEY OF *OBERARZT* DR. HARTMANN'S GROUP

During the evening of 20 May, *Oberstabarzt Dr.* Neumann had radioed the corps headquarters in Athens for reinforcements of medical personnel. Student immediately had elements of a medical company that had remained on the mainland alerted and earmarked them for a jump the next day at noon. That group was under the command of *Oberarzt Dr.* Hartmann.

The group took off at 1300 hours on 21 May for Crete. It was the last element that *Oberstabsarzt Dr.* von Berg, the energetic commander of *Fallschirm-Sanitäts-Abteilung 7*, had available. The group came from the battalion's 2nd Company; the remaining elements of the company had already jumped during the afternoon of 20 May as part of the eastern group, *Fallschirmjäger-Regiment 1*, at Heraklion.

Hartmann's group consisted of two platoons with a total of 60 men. They had been directed to reinforce Dietzel's medical company. It was planned for them to jump in the vicinity of the main clearing station to the east of Tavronitis in the area near the river bridge. The enemy was also located not far from the clearing station on the eastern, western and southern sides.

At 1430 hours, Crete came into view. Exactly five minutes later, the drop zone of the 5th and 6th Companies of the assault regiment came into view. The word went out: "Get ready to jump!"

Oberjäger Sieber, standing in the open door of the aircraft, saw that the aircraft carrying the second platoon were hanging back a bit. The jump horn sounded and he tossed himself forward. He floated towards earth and, all of a sudden, there were flashes on the ground. Rounds started whizzing past him. Ten meters in front of him was another parachute. A dead man was swinging in his harness. The transport aircraft turned, and the medical personnel were surround by small-arms fire from the ground.

The men had jumped too far to the east and were landing in the middle of English field positions. Hartmann was among the first to touch down, followed closely by Sieber and a few others. *Oberjäger* Geisberger, who had dropped in some 200 meters farther to the rear, came running up to them. Behind him were a few figures.

Oberjäger Schrumpf said what the others were thinking: "Dropped too far off in the direction of Platanias, *Herr Oberarzt*!"

"We need to get to the weapons containers" Sieber called out. "I will crawl with my men as far as the agaves over there and put down covering fire!" The doctor nodded in agreement, and Sieber started out.

After crawling about 2 meters, he reached a tangle of agave plants, which were perhaps 4 meters tall. The sound of machine-guns hammering away seemed omnipresent, especially from the area where *Unterarzt* Geißler had landed with his section. Sieber then saw movement off to the right. He pointed in that direction and Schuth, the machine-gunner, placed the barrel of his weapon on top of the cover he was behind. When he could identify the enemy, he pulled the trigger.

The rattling of the German machine-gun scattered the enemy, who disappeared. Sieber fired with his submachine-gun in their direction as well. Despite all their efforts, however, the path to the weapons containers remained blocked. The English were attacking from three sides. Geisberger, who attempted to get to the weapons containers by going around to the right, was killed by rounds to his head and chest.

When the small group started to move forward again in order, at least, to get to a narrow drainage ditch, for better cover, it ran into massed enemy fires. Only seven of the paratroopers reached the ditch, where they set up for defense. *Gefreiter* Kurostin, who was next to Sieber, collapsed. There was a small hole in his forehead from a sniper's round.

Oberjäger Sieber has provided a firsthand account of his actions:

We finally reached the drainage ditch with seven men. We only had pistols and hand grenades. We fought for our lives there for two and a half hours. We turned back the enemy attacking on three sides over and over again. But there were less and less of us. More and more comrades were killed or wounded. Then our ammunition ran low. *Oberarzt Doktor* Hartmann had only two rounds left in his pistol. We were the only two left, and he said to me: "Sieber, these are the last two bullets, and then it's all over!"

He fired his last two rounds. As he bent forward and then straightened up, he was shot in the head, collapsing dead next to me.

I had only two hand grenades left. I charged them and tossed them in the direction of the sounds of the English weapons. The English replied in kind, tossing back their own hand grenades. Then they assaulted from three sides. I was taken prisoner.

The fighting of Hartmann's group was over. One of the English soldiers gave Sieber a cigarette. Another one gave him his canteen, from which the parched Sieber drank thirstily. They recovered the six dead men from the ditch. When they pulled the *Oberarzt* out, Sieber took his helmet off and held a hand in front of his eyes, so the enemy could not see that he was crying.

The group of 25 soldiers under *Unterarzt* Geißler, which had dropped somewhat farther back, succeeded in reaching Tavronitis the following night by heading west. At the village of Tavronitis, it was suddenly held stopped by German voices: "Halt, who goes there . . . advance and be recognized!"

"*Reichsmarschall!*" Geißler croaked out. That had been the password for the previous night; he did not know the current one. But it was enough. They were told to advance with their hands in the air. The two men of the outpost received them with weapons at the ready. *Oberleutnant* Nagele, the commander of the 6th Company of the assault regiment, arrived and turned to the *Unterarzt*: "Where are the others? Wasn't *Oberarzt Dr.* Hartmann with you?" Hearing no response, we waited a second, then continued: "There were two platoons of you. Where are the others? Do you need help?"

The *Unterarzt* answered slowly: "You can't help the others. They're dead!"

"Good God!" *Oberleutnant* Nagele stammered out. "Good God!"

THE DECISIVE FIGHTING OF *FALLSCHIRMJÄGER-REGIMENT 3*
Early in the morning of 21 May, the men of the 3rd Battalion of *Fallschirmjäger-Regiment 3* of *Major* Heilmann expected an attack by the English. The enemy was on the hill with the fortress. An attack would have swept away the weak German forces. But, for some reason, the enemy did not attack. When close-air support aircraft began attacking the fortress around 1100 hours, Heilmann had aerial recognition panels set out.

After the fighter-bombers, the *Ju 52's* showed up, which dropped supplies. Heidrich's regiment was ready for operations again and prepared to attack in the direction of Galatas. Although Hermann's battalion was still widely scattered, the 11th Company had been able to push its way through to the 1st Battalion. The news that came in concerning the 12th Company was shocking, however. For the most part, it had jumped over a reservoir. A number of paratroopers drowned. The 10th Company, which had jumped over Daratsos and had landed in the middle of enemy positions, had to finally yield to the enemy's superiority.

The 3rd Battalion had also ceased to exist. Jumping at the wrong location sealed its fate, and *Oberst* Heidrich ordered the 100 or so men around *Major* Heilmann to advance in the direction of Malemes and establish contact with the paratroopers there.

At the same time, the regiment attacked the fortress on the hill. The German attack was repulsed by the enemy. Heidrich had to content himself with transitioning to the defense and fixing as much of the enemy as possible.

At the same time, *Major* Heilmann marched with his 100 men through the wildly broken mountainous terrain in the direction of Malemes. In the middle of the night of 21/22 May, they heard powerful sounds of fighting at sea, all accompanied by naval artillery of extremely heavy caliber. It was a one-sided and bloody fight, in which the British Mediterranean Fleet put an end to one of the two light German troop convoys.

The first convoy, which consisted primarily of fishing vessels escorted by one Italian torpedo boat, was almost totally annihilated by a British force of three cruisers and four destroyers. However, about 100 of the mountain troops did make it to shore with their equipment. The second convoy was also discovered by the Royal Navy but was saved by the intervention of the *Luftwaffe* at dawn. During this day and the next the *Luftwaffe* extracted its revenge by sinking two cruisers (*Fiji* and *Gloucester*) and four destroyers.

Hauptmann von der Heydte, the acting battalion commander of the *I./FJR 3*, was awakened by machine-gun fire early on the morning of 21 May. Once the firing died down, he headed down to the Cladiso to wash up. His battalion positions had been well selected. Right in front of him were the villages of Peribolia and Pyrgos. In the background, Suda Bay could be seen. Off to the left, the peaks of the Akrotiki arose, on whose slopes light-colored houses and villas could be seen.

At the base of the foothills was Chania, which looked to be a confused mass of roofs and chimneys from the distance. The city was surrounded by a powerful wall from the Middle Ages. The tower of a minaret jutted skyward from the middle of the city.

The commander went from position to position with *Leutnant* Riese. When a few *Ju 52's* dropped supply canisters around 1100 hours, the tense ammunition situation was alleviated.

On that sector of the fighting on Crete, the English restricted themselves to patrolling activities on 21 May. From Malemes, however, the sound of fighting could be heard the entire day. The assault regiment and the mountain troops that had just landed were in action constantly.

It was not until night fell that the firing stopped. Night took over, clear and warm, with a heaven full of stars. But that meant no rest for the men around von der Heydte. They needed to remain alert for the enemy, if he decided to do something that evening.

✠

Kampfgruppe Kroh from *FJR 2* prepared to assault the airfield at Rethymnon the morning of 21 May. But before *Major* Kroh could issue his final orders, the English attacked around 0400 hours. The English attack against the west side of the airfield was turned back. The enemy attack, however, did prevent the Germans from carrying out their own.

The second British attack followed at 09000 hours. The British bypassed the southern wing of *Kampfgruppe Kroh* and could not be stopped. The vineyard on the hill, which had been captured by the Germans the previous evening, was lost. The battered battle group pulled back, actively pursued by the enemy. It moved to an olive oil factory, which was located approximately 1,800 meters east of the airfield, just east of the village of Stavromanos, directly on the sea.

The battle group set up for the defense within the factory and the houses and buildings around it. One antiaircraft gun oriented west, while a second one was set up to cover to the southeast. Over the next few hours, formations of the Australian 19th Brigade attacked. They were turned back.

When a paratrooper showed up and reported to Kroh that a number of paratroopers had been left behind on the beach and had been taken prisoner by the enemy, Kroh formed a strong combat patrol and sent it to the scene. The patrol was able to enter the enemy positions by surprise and liberate their 56 comrades.

Oberleutnant von Roon received orders to set up a logistics point 7 kilometers east of the olive oil factory. Supply canisters had landed there and could be recovered. It was imperative to safeguard the supplies from the Greek forces and fifth columnists.

It was imperative in that sector, where it had also proven impossible to take the airfield with the forces available, to fix as many enemy forces as possible to prevent them from reinforcing their comrades at Malemes.

✠

Major Schulz, who had assumed acting command of *FJR 2* after *Oberst* Sturm was reported missing, linked up with *Kampfgruppe Wiedemann* on the morning of 21 May. With him was his headquarters. *Kampfgruppe Wiedemann* was defending east of Peribolia and had to fend off numerous enemy attacks the previous night. Schulz assumed command of both groups, while *Major* Kroh continued to be responsible for the operations of his battle group.

Kampfgruppe Schulz continued to reinforce the defensive positions around Peribolia. The defensive sector in the west, reaching from the sea to the road to Rethymnon and the airfield, was defended by the 9th Company. One platoon from the same company occupied the fortress on the hill, some 500 meters south of Peribolia. From the road to that hill was the 11th Company, while the 14th Company defended towards the south. Elements of the *7./Fallschirm-MG-Bataillon 7* and the *2./Fallschirm-Fla-Bataillon 7* oriented east. The entire battle group was subjected to British artillery fire the entire day. Australian snipers and Greek partisans fired at any paratrooper who left his cover.

At 0730 hours, *Do 17* light bombers appeared in the sector and bombed enemy positions in a succession of attacks until 1400 hours. About half of the bombs fell on the German positions, however, and caused casualties.

The Australians attacked in the south and southeast around 1600 hours. The Commonwealth attack bogged down in the combined fires of the 9th and 11th Companies about 400 meters in front of the German positions.

Six *Ju 52's* had appeared just before the attack and had dropped supply containers, of which a portion landed in no-man's-land. Volunteers were able to recover them.

Just before midnight, the Australians attacked again against the fortress on the hill. The enemy was turned back there as well, suffering heavy casualties.

That signaled the end of the second day of fighting on Crete for *FJR 2*.

THE FIGHTING IN AND AROUND HERAKLION

Two mortars from the *III./FJR 3* opened fire against the western gate to Heraklion at 0230 hours. The mortar rounds smashed into the gate and also impacted on the watchtowers of the city wall that were occupied by the enemy.

Karl-Lothar Schulz had ordered the city gate to be taken under fire to make sure the area around it was not mined. When it was determined that it was not, he had the mortars concentrate on the watchtowers. The first enemy machine-gun fell silent. The second one also fell silent after a direct hit.

"Fire smoke!" Schulz ordered after he looked at his watch.

The smoke rounds placed a thick veil over the intended site of the attack on Heraklion. *Major* Schulz then ordered his paratroopers to attack, and he stormed forward with them. They took the barricades in a duel of hand grenades and pressed on to the city gate, which was sent skyward with two *Teller* mines.

At the same time, the hammering of automatic weapons could be heard coming from the harbor, and it indicated to the commander that Schulenberg's and Becker's companies had also started their operations.

The paratroopers entered Heraklion through the destroyed city gate. By the time it had turned light, they had reached the market place and pushed the British forces back. Assault detachments moved farther into the city in an effort to reach the group at the harbor. They cleared the buildings from which they had received fire in close combat. Using small-arms and hand grenades, they fought meter by meter for nine hours. Then they achieved their immediate objective: Both battle groups linked up. They had reached the middle of the city, but the enemy was still located in pockets of resistance there as well.

Schulz established his command post at the market place. Ammunition became scarce again.

A short while later, the local commander of the Greek forces and the city's mayor appeared at Schulz's headquarters. The surrender document was signed by both sides. The paratroopers moved through the city in four groups. Suddenly, new enemy activity flared up. Employing his reserve platoon, Schulz headed for the direction of the sound of fighting. He got to Becker's group, which had had to pull back somewhat under enemy pressure.

"What's going on, Becker?" Schulz asked the company commander.

"We've been attacked by strong English forces, *Herr Major*. The English do not recognize the surrender of the city, because they did not sign the document."

"The Citadel!"

The attacked in the direction of the Citadel, where the enemy fires increased. They were able to hit the enemy in the flank, since von der Schulenburg's group had fixed them in place.

Close-in fighting started. Each building had to be wrested from the enemy. The enemy, who was putting up a tough fight, then disengaged from the elements fighting with Schulz, penetrated through von der Schulenburg's group and raced back into the Citadel.

"We'll pull back to the command post. Send messengers to both the east and west gate. Our forces there are also to pull back to the vicinity of the command post!"

At the command post, it soon became clear that *Kampfgruppe Schulz's* time in Heraklion was limited. There was only one way out of the dangerous situation: Withdrawal and evacuation of the city, which had cost so much sacrifice to take.

Leaving behind rearguards, which covered the withdrawal movement, *Major* Schulz pulled back with his battalion. Prior to leaving, he informed the mayor that *Stukas* would come "and attack the Citadel and all those positions where the enemy had barricaded himself. Tell the civilians to leave those places so that they do not become casualties."

Late in the afternoon of 21 May, *Stukas* flew in to attack Heraklion. The air was filled with the sirens of the dive-bombers for 10 minutes. For those 10 minutes the bombs detonated and the enemy positions were torn apart. The Citadel shook under the explosions. That signaled the end of the second day of fighting for *Major* Schulz and his men in and around Heraklion.

Around 2330 hours on 20 May, *Major* Walther, the commander of the *I./FJR 1*, received orders from *Oberst* Bräuer to consolidate and march in the direction of Heraklion. It was directed to clear the airfield. Passing the subsequent orders to the companies, which were screening to the north, east and south took the better part of the night. *Leutnant* Lindenberg's platoon from the 1st Company could not even be found. The officer had advanced into the mountains south of Gournes, where he was ambushed by Greek detachments. As was later found out, his platoon was wiped out to the last man.

As a consequence of these delays, Walther's battalion could not be employed as a whole. Instead, it entered the battlefield as platoons and companies. *Oberst* Bräuer had the individually arriving elements immediately committed to the attack. That appeared to be the only way to establish contact with *Oberleutnant Graf* Blücher's platoon, which was having a difficult time of it on the eastern edge of the airfield.

Extremely heavy small-arms fire commenced on the morning of 21 May. The enemy had nine artillery pieces, a number of heavy mortars ad numerous light and heavy machine-guns. Moreover, he could not be identified in his well-camouflaged positions. Facing the enemy initially were only 5 heavy machine-guns from Walther's *I./FJR 1*. The remnants of Burckhardt's battalion, the *II./FJR 1*, which had joined those forces, did not have any heavy weapons.

Due to the punishing defensive fires of the English, the attack bogged down. Blücher's platoon was able to hold out until noon. Then he was attacked by infantry supported by armor and the entire platoon was overrun by the enemy. *Oberleutnant Graf* Blücher was killed.

After darkness fell, the *I./FJR 1* was pulled back to the western slope of the high ground 2 kilometers southeast of the airfield, where it set up defensively.

A difficult day for the battalion had come to a close. Even though the airfield could not be taken, the German contingent was at least fixing enemy forces around Heraklion. Enemy immediate counterattacks were turned back, and *Oberst* Bräuer proved an obstinate opponent who did not give up. He knew he had to fix as much of the enemy as possible in order to assist the operations of the other forces elsewhere.

During the evening of 21 May, the headquarters of the *XI. Flieger-Korps* considered the crisis on Crete as having been mastered, even though there had been many failures. Student ordered the attack on Chania to commence on 22 May, while still paying close attention to the security of the airfield at Malemes. *Generalmajor* Schlemm was sent with a small headquarters advance party to Malemes on the morning of 22 May.

THE TRAGEDY OF THE LIGHT BOAT CONVOYS

On 20 May 1941—it was Ascension Thursday—the first light boat convoy sailed out of the harbor at Piräus. That signaled the start of a tragedy that could not have ended worse than it did. On board the barges, sailboats and other less-than-exactly seaworthy craft was the *III./Gebirgsjäger-Regiment 100* of *Oberstleutnant* Ehal. Along with its attachments, there were some 800 men.

At about the same time, the barges and sailboats of the second light boat convoy with the reinforced *II./Gebirgsjäger-Regiment of Major Dr. Treeck,* hauled anchor at Chalkis on Euböa.

There were a total of 50 sail- and motorboats that were heading in the direction of Crete. Also at sea were four battle groups of Admiral Cunningham's forces. The A-1 group was 100 sea miles west of Crete. Rear Admiral King's 15th Flotilla was southwest of the bottleneck at Kaso. Rear Admiral Glennie's Force D reached the narrows at Kithera during the night of 19/20 May and was striving to link up with Force A-1.

Force B, consisting of the cruisers *Gloucester* and *Fiji,* had refueled in Alexandria and was also underway to join Force A-1, which was planned for the evening of 21 May.

The aircraft with the paratroopers aboard flew over the light vessels of the German flotillas, and the mountain troopers waved to the aircraft as they flew by.

Around Cape Sunion, the southern tip of the Greek mainland, the Italian torpedo boat destroyer *Lupo* approached the first German convoy, while the *Sagitarrio* linked up with the second convoy. Both boats provided convoy escort from that point forward.

A third convoy, consisting of heavier vessels, was prepared to sail from Piräus, where it was a reserve element. There were some ships among this convoy, which also had some tanks on board.

While the *Lupo* cruised around the boats of the first convoy, the convoy reached the Island of Milo, after a scorchingly hot day at sea. The convoy dropped anchor and did not set out again until the next morning, 21 May. It later returned to harbor, however, when the second convoy did not join it, as had been planned.

At 1500 hours, the second convoy came into sight. At that point, the first convoy lifted anchor and continued on its way to Crete. As it started to turn dark the island drew ever nearer and the mountain troops started to breathe easier. Another two hours and they would be at their objective. *Korvettenkapitän* Bartels was prepared to greet them in the bay at Cape Spatha.

In the meantime, Force D under Rear Admiral Glennie, which had the cruisers *Dido, Orion* and *Ajax,* as well as the destroyers *Janus, Kimberley, Hasty* and *Hereward,* had been on a crisscross search cruise and had advanced as far as the northwest coast of Crete. At that point, they swung north. When the radar of the command vessel reported enemy boats, battle stations were ordered. When they had approached to within range, Glennie ordered the searchlights to be turned on.

The English ships were ready for combat. The three-gun turrets of the cruisers and the two-gun turrets of the destroyers swung onto the visible targets. Then the order was given: "Fire when ready!"

Muzzle flashes lit up the night sky from a few dozen barrels. After every salvo, the ships pitched back. In the distance, among the boats that also became visible in the nighttime moon, there were impacts. The first detonations resounded and geysers of flames rose skyward. The night was transformed into a ghostly flickering hell.

"Alert . . . alert!"

The mountain troops were torn from their exhausted sleep. They jumped up, went topside and stared to the south, where a terrible storm was brewing and flame after flame jerked through the darkness and rose as if trying to split the night asunder.

Mountain troopers Sepp Gnadler and Xaver Atternberger helped each other put on life jackets, after the battalion commander ordered them on. Off to the right, barely 600 meters away, the *Lupo* fired with everything it had, including a salvo of torpedoes. But it was then covered with the fires from four destroyers. Rounds impacted, and the boat was on fire. The boat maneuvered wildly. It escaped the fire from the English boats, only to return to the fray again.

"Look . . . they're coming this way!" Atternberger called out, when he saw a destroyer swing in their direction. While the first one started to attack, it was followed by a second one. Rounds from the naval artillery landed to the right and left of Atternberger's craft. A round landed where *Oberstleutnant* Ehal was standing on the bow. Personnel, equipment and bits and pieces of the boat shot skyward.

"Help . . . help!" one of the Greek crewmembers called out. Then another round landed square in the boat and ripped the mountain troopers from their feet.

"Everyone overboard!" the senior coxswain called out, who was the captain of the ship at that point. Shortly after Atternberger jumped into the water, he was followed by Gnadler. They swam for their lives, because the destroyer was turning in their direction. It came across an another group of Germans and, when it finished passing, there was nothing to be seen of them anymore. It then rammed the boat and cut it in two.

Searchlights were blazing from the bridges of the attacking boats. Whenever one of those fingers of light settled on a German boat, the artillery soon sent it to the bottom. The turret guns of the cruisers soon started in on the *Lupo*. Although hit 19 times, the Italians did not give up and continued the fight. A two-masted boat was lit up like a burning torch before it sank. Three, then four, other boats were alight.

Horrified, the men in the water watched as the overwhelming English force ran roughshod over each of the remaining boats for the next two and one half hours. It was not until 0330 hours that the English force turned east. After sinking the majority of the German vessels, Admiral Glennie had ordered his force to assemble 30 sea miles west of Crete at 0600 hours.

The few boats that had succeeded in fleeing north ran into the boats of the second convoy later on and joined them.

The British naval forces had spent too much time on the "rabbit hunt", however. Long-range aerial reconnaissance of the *Luftwaffe* had sighted 33 enemy vessels from all four naval groups at sea and reported them.

The 1st Squadron of *Lehrgeschwader 1* of *Hauptmann* Hoffmann, the *III./ Kampfgeschwader 30* and several *Do 17's* of *Oberst* Rieckhoff's *Kampfgeschwader 2*[10] prepared to take off and intercept the British. It was imperative to hold back any British naval force that might be approaching the second light boat convoy.

Around 0830 hours, what was left of the first convoy and the main body of the second convoy were sighted by the lead vessels of Rear Admiral King's Force C. The *Sagitarrio* of Commander Cigala immediately engaged the lead vessel and started to cover the convoy with smoke. The cruiser *Perth* sank one of the boats of the convoy with a salvo, while the cruiser *Naiad* attempted to turn back the first German aircraft that had arrived on the scene. The *Stukas* and the bombers were able to land several hits on the *Naiad* and, a short while later, the cruiser *Carlisle*, which was also participating in the defense against German aircraft, was also hit. Captain Hampton, the ship's commander, was killed on his bridge.

The mountain troopers observed the attacks of the *Luftwaffe* against the British vessels. They saw the huge water spouts created when the bombs exploded and the resulting tongues of flames, whenever they it something solid. One *Ju 88* crashed. When it hit the water, it burst apart in a cascade of flames.

The *Lupo* and the *Sagitarrio* continued to provide smoke for the defenseless boats of the light convoys.

Force C turned away, but not before one of its destroyers had sunk a second German craft. The British ships and boats had been ordered to link up with the heavy covering force of Rear Admiral Rawlings. Rawlings had also ordered a cruiser and a destroyer to steam ahead to assist the badly damaged *Naiad*.

As those vessels moved ahead, they were attacked by *Ju 87's* of *Sturzkampfgeschwader 2* of *Oberstleutnant* Dinort and *Ju 88's* of the *I.* and *II./ Lehrgeschwader 1* of *Hauptmann* Kollewe. In addition, a few *Bf 109* fighter-bombers joined the fray.

The main target of the attacking aircraft was the British battleship *Warspite*. The battleship was hit several times, mostly from a fighter-bomber section from the *III./Jagdgeschwader 77* under the command of *Oberleutnant* Huy.

Ju 87's dove on the destroyer *Greyhound*, which was located between Pori and Antikithera. Hit directly by two bombs, the ship sank within 15 minutes. The cruiser *Gloucester* received a severe blow at 1530 hours and was soon burning brightly. The cruiser *Fiji*, which attempted to sail away, was hit by a *Bf 110* and lost power. A half hour later, it was hit so badly by two *Bf 109* fighter-bombers of *Hauptmann* Ihlefeld of the *I./Lehrgeschwader 2*, that the

---

10. Translator's Note: *Lehrgeschwader* = Instructional Wing, a formation normally stationed in the homeland for training purposes, but elements of which were occasionally sent to combat zones for a "refresher" experience to keep them from becoming unacquainted with evolving tactics, techniques and procedures. *Kampfgeschwader* Bomb Wing.

134   JUMP INTO HELL

ship's captain, William Powlett, had to abandon ship. The *Kingston* and the *Kandahar* rescued 523 survivors from that ship. The *Naid* and the *Carlisle* were hit several more times in the course of the rolling attacks from the air. The battleship *Valiant* of Captain Morgan also suffered some damage.

The English naval flotilla had succeeded in scattering the two light boat convoys and sinking a few of the boats. The mountain troops, whose comrades had already gone though the hell of Malemes, had to undergo yet another ordeal, which again cost them heavy casualties.

But the British side had to pay for that success with its own heavy casualties in both ships and men. Two cruisers and two destroyers were lost, with two battleships being slightly damaged and two cruisers being heavily damaged.

That evening, Read Admiral Rawlings dispatched the destroyers *Decoy* and *Hero* to the southern coast of Crete, where they were to pick up the Greek king at the village of Roumeli.

King George II of Greece had hidden himself away up to that point in the country estate of Minister President Tsouderos in the vicinity of the road to Alikianou. On 21 May, German paratroopers were close to capturing him. But he escaped from them and issued a proclamation to the citizens of Crete to open a fifth-column movement against the Germans. That proclamation contradicted the rules of the Haag Convention, which Greece had also signed. Many Cretans followed the exhortation. They killed German soldiers in ambushes and frequently paid for it with their lives.

During the night of 22–23 May, the German light convoys wanted to make another try. They set off to the south and approached to within four kilometers of Cape Spatha. Once again, they were caught by British naval forces, blown to bits, set on fire, rammed and cut in two by destroyers.

One boat crew attempted to swim the 4 kilometers to land. In a rubber dinghy, which they towed, they brought along 15 wounded mountain troopers. Another 15 lightly wounded mountain troopers held on to the lines attached to the dinghy or brought along by comrades who were not wounded. Thanks to their life vests, they could not sink.

In all, there were some 100 mountain troopers. When they finally reached the coast line after unimaginable duress, they were unable to climb the steep cliffs. They attempted to go farther down the coast. They were still swimming on the morning of 23 May, when German search-and-rescue aircraft approached, touched down and recovered the men. The aircraft saved 178 mountain troopers from death by drowning, while another 84 were saved by Italian fast boats.

Out of *Oberstleutnant* Ehal's battalion, more than 300 remained at sea, with another 100 wounded but rescued.

In addition to the 15 mountain troopers who landed on Crete during the night of 22–23 May, another *Leutnant* and 35 men reached the peninsula of Cape Spatha. Half naked, at the end of their strength, they climbed the cliffs and survived.

The unfortunate chapter concerning the light boat convoys, which was written in blood and filled with horror, was finished. Among the heavy casualties that were suffered in the assault on Crete, theirs were among the most tragic. They saw death coming and could do nothing about it. They went down in the barrage fires of the British naval forces.

THE THIRD DAY OF OPERATIONS OF THE ASSAULT REGIMENT AT CHANIA

Right after the two light boat convoys had been destroyed, the enemy also attacked at Malemes in the sector of the assault regiments 4th Battalion. He attempted to break through between the road and the coast with trucks and armored vehicles. Tanks advanced in the sector manned by Kiebitz's company. *Oberst* Ramcke had sent antitank elements there to reinforce Kiebitz. It proved to have been a wise decision.

Two tanks were knocked out. The enemy was turned back, and he suffered heavy losses. On that day, the west group assembled for its decisive attack east. The attack was to be launched as soon as the mountain troopers of *Oberst* Utz had completed their bypass maneuver. When *Generalmajor* Schlemm arrived on Crete around noon on that 22 May, he immediately began directing the bringing up and employment of reinforcements in close conjunction with the corps headquarters in Athens.

While the German Armed Forces High Command had yet to issue a single bulletin concerning the operations on Crete, Winston Churchill let the cat out of the bag in an address to the lower house of Parliament, in which he stated:

> Heavy enemy aerial attacks took place in the Chania area and along Suda Bay Wednesday morning [21 May 1941]. They were continued over the course of the entire day and accompanied by the landing of new airborne forces to the southwest of Chania. It appears the enemy has occupied the airfield at Malemes, 10 miles from Chania, and has also occupied the area west of Ceres; although the airfield there is under fire from British colonial forces . . .
>
> There has been extremely difficult fighting. I wish to send those fighting there words of encouragement. They need to know that this is one of the most important battles, which can be decisive for the Mediterranean.[11]

ATTACK OF THE MOUNTAIN FORCES

Ever since the morning of 22 May, *Oberst* Utz and his battle staff had been reconnoitering the English battery positions outside of Modion and in the village of Malemes. The enemy needed to be ejected from both positions.

Utz was able to determine that the English blocking positions only extended 2.5 kilometers south as far as a communications center on Hill

---

11. Translator's Note: This passage was reverse-translated from German back into the original English without access to the original quotation.

295. Correspondingly, he sent a portion of his regiment south to bypass the position. Utz ordered his 7th Company, commanded by *Leutnant* Bachmaier, and the heavy weapons attached to it to support the paratroopers in their fighting for the village of Malemes.

The infantry guns that the paratroopers had succeeded in getting to the top of Hill 107 opened fire on the heavy English battery located at Modion. The English battery had to be taken out if the subsequent landings at the airfield were to succeed.

The New Zealand 4th Brigade, which opposed the paratroopers and mountain forces there, had tough farmers' sons among its ranks, who fought shoulder to shoulder with their fierce Maori comrades.

At the start of the attack, Bachmaier's company had all of its heavy machine-guns fire in order to suppress the enemy's machine-guns. The paratroopers and mountaineers assaulted. Defensive fires whipped past the attackers from the ruins of the village, from window frames, from rooftops and from trees.

While the German forces attacked, the infantry guns on the hill engaged the heavy English battery and suppressed its fires.

When Bachmaier and his men started to enter Malemes, two fresh companies of New Zealand forces were committed to an immediate counterattack. They ran into the midst of the German formations, yelling their battle cry. The khaki-yellow figures with the flat helmets appeared from behind agave plants and holm oaks. They fired on the German attackers, ran on and then their attack bogged down in the concentrated defensive fires of the Germans. The New Zealanders were unable to break through to the west edge of the village.

At the same time, the *8./Gebirgsjäger-Regiment 100* of *Oberleutnant* Zwickenpflug encountered the enemy advance guard that had been advancing from Paläochora The previous evening, the mountain unit had moved forward to the village of Mulete, 5 kilometers south of the Malemes airfield, where it had established a blocking position. The enemy troops pulled back after a short firefight, whereupon they were pursued by the Germans. The fighting from a movement to contact lasted until noon on 22 May. It then followed upward along the slopes of the road serpentines that led from Anoskeli. Early in the afternoon, the fighting concentrated around the village proper. The mountain troops dug in, since they could see the main body of what appeared to be two British battalions approaching. When they encountered the German outposts, however, they pulled back after a short firefight. Zwickenpflug's men then took up the pursuit again.

On the morning of 24 May, this small element of mountain forces reached the coast, where no more enemy forces were to be found. Apparently, the English had been picked up by a naval convoy waiting for them.

ADDITIONAL LANDINGS BY MOUNTAIN FORCES

It was exactly 1000 hours on 21 May when the first group of *Ju 52's* bearing the *I./Gebirgsjäger-Regiment 85* started their approach to the Malemes airfield. The English batteries were still firing in a steady rhythm on the airfield. Thick clouds of red dust rose skyward and interfered with the pilots' visibility. Once again, aircraft were hit and there were dead and wounded. Frequently, the pilots in their transport aircraft had to circle around the island for 15 minutes or even longer before they could land. The completely overloaded machines then set down in the middle of a Hell's Gate consisting of bursting artillery rounds and where visibility was nonexistent.

More and more *Ju 52's* were lost. On the first day of the landings, it was 20 aircraft. On the second day, however, the number rose dramatically to 123 aircraft. In all, some 143 *Ju 52's* were scattered along the edges of the tarmac by the evening of 22 May. The self-sacrificing spirit of those transport pilots was praised by *General der Gebirgstruppen* Julius Ringel in an interview with the author:

> In the 12 days they were employed from the mainland to Crete, some 200 *Ju 52's* were destroyed, damaged or remained unaccounted for. In all, the aircraft covered 2,400,000 kilometers. They transported 23,463 personnel, 539 artillery pieces and mortars, 5,358 weapons containers, 711 motorcycles and 1,090,130 kilograms of supplies. They took 3,173 wounded men back to the mainland from the island. Never before had such a similar movement been attempted from the air. Never before had a campaign been waged like that. The mountain troopers of the *5. Gebirgs-Division* were always aware that we owed a debt of gratitude for the greatest adventure of our lives, and its successful outcome, to those men who had flown hundreds of kilometers to Crete and then took back the wounded. Some may consider themselves lucky not to have to carry around such memories with them; we considered ourselves fortunate to have been part of it.

Towards noon on 22 May, the *I./Gebirgsjäger-Regiment 85* had been landed. It was attached to the forces under *Oberst* Utz. It was directed to advance south and take the dominant high ground of Hill 259. It was then to swing out farther to the east, maneuver around Malemes and take the enemy in the village in the rear. If the battalion succeeded in doing that, then the solitary British battery that was still firing on the airfield would be taken out of commission.

Between 1200 and 1400 hours, the *I./Gebirgsjäger-Regiment 100* also landed. It was likewise sent south. Moving with the mountain battalion was also a motorized battery from the airborne division's artillery battalion.

Towards evening, *Gebirgs-Pionier-Bataillon 95* of *Major* Schätte landed. It was joined by *Major* Bode and the rest of his airborne artillery battalion, as well as elements of the division artillery of the *5. Gebirgs-Division*.

During the decisive phase of that eventful day, the New Zealanders attempted to take back Malemes for the last time, and another group of *Ju 52's* landed. On board that flight of aircraft was the mountain division's headquarters and the division commander, *Generalmajor* Ringel.

Just before him, *Hauptmann* von Richthofen from the headquarters of the *VII. Flieger-Korps* had landed so as to pick up the target list of the paratroopers for the bombers and *Stukas* and conduct the final coordination for the employment of all of the air formations that had been committed.

Shortly after landing, Ringel assumed command of all of the forces of the west group. Both *Generalmajor* Schlemm and *Oberst* Ramcke briefed him on the overall situation and the fighting around Malemes. *Oberst* Utz also reported personally to his division commander.

That afternoon, the enemy battery at Modion was attacked by *Stukas* and silenced by some direct hits.

As darkness fell that day, all preparations had been made for the big attack on 23 May.

Fallschirmjäger-Regiment 3 had held on to all of the areas it had previously taken. Heilmann's battalion was reached by mountain forces at 1700 hours and relieved. Paratroopers and mountain troopers greeted one another at Stalos.

THE RETHYMNON AREA OF OPERATIONS

In the sector of *Kampfgruppe Kroh* in the vicinity of the olive oil factory, the enemy started firing again on the morning of 22 May. The Australian 1st brigade started attacking in the direction of the factory at 0700 hours. The Australians were supported by the Greek 4th Brigade, which also had two tanks attached. The attackers were able to approach to within hand-grenade range before the enemy attack bogged down.

In order to look after the wounded and dead in no-man's-land, the enemy offered a ceasefire at 1011 hours, which *Major* Kroh accepted. The weapons fell silent, and the Germans were able to recover 50 of their own. Seventy wounded German paratroopers were evacuated and cared for by English medics.

At 1423 hours, the enemy artillery commenced firing again. The Germans replied with their own antitank and antiaircraft guns. An English mortar that had been abandoned on the beach was manned by the Germans and used successfully against its former owners.

The small-arms fires of the snipers continued without a let up the entire day. They had infiltrated the area southwest of the olive oil factory at Hill 254 and also came from the area around Kamiri. Despite the heavy sniper fires, the German battle group was able to hold on to its positions.

The morning of 22 May also started with artillery fire in the sectors of *Kampfgruppe Schulz* and *Kampfgruppe Wiedemann*. A *Stuka* attack hit the enemy as he was in the midst of his attack preparations. The *Stukas* were guided in from the ground by means of directional arrows and hand-and-arm signals. The *Stukas* had a devastating effect. An enemy attack against the fortress hill south of Peribolia was turned back by the 11th Company.

One hour later, the enemy attacked in the direction of Peribolia in battalion strength from the southeast along the river valley and from the roads leading in from the south and southeast. That fight raged the longest. It did not start to abate until 1842 hours, after the attackers had already suffered heavy losses.

Exactly 20 minutes later, the Australians attacked for a third time. They confused the defenders by firing German signal pyrotechnics and they were able to penetrate into the positions of the paratroopers. They had to pull back to Peribolia and, finally, back to the road itself that ran through the northern portion of the village and ran along the coast from west to east. The paratroopers were able to reestablish themselves there. Using assault detachments, the Germans were able to push back the Australians in house-to-house fighting. By 2140 hours, Peribolia was back in German hands again.

On the other hand, the situation in the sector of the 9th Company had turned critical. On fortress hill, where the company was defending, the English had approached dangerously close to the German positions. They had even been able to penetrate the line in several places. The company had to pull back to the centrally located cemetery. They set up an all-round defense there.

At the same time, *Oberleutnant* Begemann, coming from Peribolia, reached the positions of the 9th and reported that the entire battalion had been wiped out and that he would try to break through to *Kampfgruppe Kroh* in the west. *Leutnant* Kühl, the acting commander of the 9th, decided to remain at the cemetery and defend, however.

When *Oberleutnant* Begemann and his men tried to break out, they mistakenly came under friendly fire from the 11th Company, which thought it was being attacked by the enemy. Both sides suffered losses, before they realized that it was German fighting German.

Then the British attacked the cemetery with reinforced elements. They got to within hand-grenade range of the cemetery wall. Launching an immediate counterattack with a handful of men, *Leutnant* Kühl was able to drive the enemy back. His attack was driven home with such intensity that the English started running, despite their superior numbers.

As evening approached on that memorable day of 22 May, the cemetery on that high ground had taken a heavy toll on both sides.

The paratroopers at Rethymnon were involved in a hopeless struggle, but they could not give up if they did not want to endanger their brother paratroopers in other sectors.

WITH *FALLSCHIRMJÄGER-REGIMENT 1* AT HERAKLION

The 22nd of May was also a day of bitter decisions and equally bitter operations in the sector of *Fallschirmjäger-Regiment 1*. A British emissary approached the positions of *Kampfgruppe Schulz*. He brought with him the offer of the British commander at Heraklion:

German Paratroopers!
You have fought bravely. But continued fighting has become senseless.
You are the only group on the island that has not yet been destroyed.
Resistance is senseless. As much as I recognize your courage, I must
ask you to surrender honorably. You will be treated well.

The answer that Karl-Lothar Schulz sent forward with his emissary was
short and to the point: "The German Armed Forces have the mission of taking
Crete. It will accomplish this mission."

A short while later, Schulz received orders from his regimental commander
that the taking of Heraklion was to be put on hold. Schulz's battalion was
to screen along the road to the west. In addition, Schulz was to bypass the
city to the southeast with his main forces, advance on Hill 491 and silence
the battery that was engaging the main body of *Kampfgruppe Bräuer* from its
positions there.

The group that was left behind to screen the road was also given charge
of the lightly wounded. *Major* Schulz took off as darkness fell with his main
body. He had to cross the main road twice, but his force did not appear to
have been discovered. As day dawned on 23 May, he was at the jumping-off
point for his assault on Hill 491.

✠

Oberarzt Dr. Langemeyer had set up his battalion clearing station in the
mountain village of Telikakä. The clearing station also tended to the wounded
of *Bataillon Schirmer*, which had been attached to Schulz. Schirmer's men had
fought it out all day on 22 May against Greek fifth columnists. The wounded
Dr. Kirsch had also been taken to that clearing station. As the first cases of
dysentery surfaced and fevers set in, something started to become in short
supply that no one had thought of during preparations for the campaign:
Toilet paper! The doctor immediately sent a request in the clear to the corps
headquarters in Athens for the much-needed item. The corps headquarters
then spent hours trying to discern what the supposed code word "toilet paper"
meant, until someone finally understood it was not a code word. *Ju 52's* later
dropped not only the necessary medical supplies for the 2nd Medic Company
but also the much needed paper.

Dr. Langemeyer worked day and night at the clearing station. It was a
time for improvisation and for everyone to give his all. Exemplary among the
medical personnel was *Dr.* Kirsch, who operated on two paratroopers badly
wounded in the jaw, even though he himself was badly wounded. Although
he almost fainted several times, he finished the operations. Before he was
finally evacuated to the mainland on 30 May, he helped out again and again
when needed.

✠

When the English news announced on the morning of 23 May 1941 that the "reputation of the German Armed Forces was being endangered on Crete", the situation had already shifted in the other direction, despite the reports emanating from General Wavell's headquarters in Cairo or the report of Winston Churchill before the lower house of Parliament. It was only a matter of time before the island was in German hands. Despite that, there would still be some heavy fighting before that change would become noticeable.

KAMPFGRUPPE GERICKE ATTACKS

During the early-morning hours of 23 May, the enemy facing *Kampfgruppe Gericke* pulled back to the east. *Hauptmann* Gericke, who saw an opportunity, attacked with all of the forces he had available on both sides of the road.

Kampfgruppe Schmitz and *Kampfgruppe Stentzler* joined the attack of the 4th Battalion by moving out to both its right and left.

The paratroopers pursued the withdrawing enemy from defile to defile and hilltop to hilltop. They battered the enemy whenever he attempted to dig in and took all of the high ground until the area just west of Platanias in a single rush. That signaled the end of the remaining enemy batteries that were still able to fire on Malemes. *Oberleutnant* Horst Trebes made a name for himself during this phase of the fighting. He led his company from the front and continuously spurred his men on in order to exploit any and all weaknesses of the enemy.

All of the battle groups participated in this thrust. Since the start of the day, they had all been formed into *Gruppe Ramcke*, while *Generalmajor* Ringel had assumed overall command of the western group. That evening, the paratroopers dug in along the limits of their advances. They received orders to move out again for the attack on 24 May after the mountain forces of *Oberst* Utz had completed their bypass maneuver.

OPERATIONS OF THE MOUNTAIN FORCES ON 23 MAY

From his command post, *Generalmajor* Ringel directed the employment of his mountain combat engineers on the morning of 23 May. They were directed to take the small coastal town of Kastelli. The town was defended by Greek forces, augmented by a few platoons of Australians. It was there that Mürbe's platoon had jumped on 20 May and had been almost completely wiped out.

While the engineers replied to the enemy defensive fires they were receiving from Kastelli, they waited for the *Stukas* that had been requested by *Major* Schätte. When they arrived, flipped over to initiate their dives and started howling towards earth, the defenders attempted to leave the town. But the machine-gun fires from the engineers kept them fixed in position.

The bombs fell in the middle of the enemy positions in the town. Flames and smoke headed skyward. Following the *Stukas* were the fighter-bombers, which circled around the town and sought out any pockets of resistance, bombing and strafing them. When the last aircraft dropped a red pyrotechnic to signal the end of the aerial attack, Schätte gave the signal to start the ground attack.

The field-grade officer moved out to attack at the head of his men. Extremely heavy defensive fires were being received by the engineers from the high ground to the west of Kastelli, which was the home of a Byzantine church, surrounded by massive walls.

Schätte later told the author the following in an interview concerning the operation:

> Skillfully using camouflage, the Greeks had transformed the church into a veritable fortress. They fired at us with everything they had. The tall vines [of the vineyard] initially offered us good concealment. Exploiting every depression in the ground, we worked our way forward in bounds. Our machine-gun provided covering fire. Two platoons of mountain troops went around the structure and approached ever closer. The first group of hand grenades flew over the walls. The forward-most soldiers jumped forward. In a final group bound, we were in. A white flag started to wave on the wall. The enemy, Greek soldiers, surrendered.

While that group reached its designated objective, the main body of the battalion assaulted in the direction of the large factory in Kastelli. The attackers were greeted with German weapons there, just as they had at the church. The weapons had been recovered from weapons containers that had not reached their intended targets. In addition, fifth columnists ran about with German aerial recognition panels, causing farther confusion. Despite all that, the factory was taken.

On the east side of Kastelli and the high ground to its southeast, the attack came to a standstill. Forces on the left wing made some progress, but the casualties were heavy.

Major Schätte decided to go around the town with a section of engineers and enter it from the north. His maneuver succeeded. The section was able to enter the town, and it was eventually taken in house-to-house fighting.

All of a sudden, a woman appeared at *Major* Schätte's side. She informed him that German prisoners were still being held in the police barracks. The entire battalion immediately moved out to free the prisoners. The guards, who opened fire, were overpowered.

When the mountain troops entered the area in the basement, they ran into three New Zealand officers who, with drawn pistols, held the Greek fifth columnists at bay and kept them from murdering the captured paratroopers. One of the officers said: "Good that you showed up! We'd rather leave the island as prisoners than permit such a massacre."

A true act of military heroism, since they had done it at the risk of their own lives as well. One bright moment during the bitter fighting that seemed to characterize the struggle on the island.

The 20 men freed were the survivors from Mürbe's platoon.

The taking of Kastelli marked the clearing of the last obstacle to unimpeded landing at Malemes for the Germans. Engineers, antitank elements and motorcyclists pursued the withdrawing enemy in the direction of the White Mountains and forced the groups of fifth columnists farther and farther south. They did not encounter any British forces. It appeared as if the enemy had left the western portion of the island.

The remaining groups of mountain forces were also on the offensive that day. *Major Dr.* Treeck reached the jumping-off point for the assault on Hill 259 with his *I./Gebirgsjäger-Regiment 85*. The high ground was taken without a fight and then occupied.

The paratroopers also attacked in the direction of Modion. One of the companies got as far as the road, whereupon *Oberst* Utz moved up to the company to check on its progress. At that point, he was engaged from Hill 259 on the right. His motorcycle-sidecar had to take cover. The firing led the Germans on the low ground to believe that the paratroopers had not taken Hill 259 after all. Instead, they had probably taken the high ground across the way at Wryses. That meant that Hill 259 had to be taken as quickly as possible, since it was of vital importance for the continuation of the attack. *Major* Schury's *II./Gebirgsjäger-Regiment 100* was supposed to advance to the low ground near Hill 259 and establish contact with *FJR 3*, something the battalion could not do if the hill were still occupied by the enemy.

Oberst Utz had the 1st Company of Treck's mountain battalion attack the hill. *Oberleutnant* Pröhl's men worked their way forward across rocky ground under a searing sun for four kilometers. They moved across hilltops, through thorny bushes and across defiles. When they finally reached the attack objective, they had a direct view to the village of Platanias, where other paratroopers were fighting. By the time the men got there, the "real" Hill 259 was clear of the enemy. Had the enemy been there, he could have had a decisive impact on the fighting on the lower ground.

The mountain troops continued their assault. They took the village of Kuros in a *coup de main* and then advanced towards the coast in the direction of Stalos. As it started to turn dark, they were addressed in German. It was men from *FJR 3*, who greeted the mountain troopers with a great deal of relief. The Germans had succeeded in bypassing Platanias and Agya Marina, establishing contact with *Kampfgruppe Heidrich*.

✠

On that same 23 May, additional elements of the mountain division landed. Among those landing was *Oberst* Krakau, the commander of *Gebirgsjäger-Regiment 85*. Everything on Crete was pointing towards victory, but the decisive blow would not fall until the next day, 24 May.

THE SITUATION AT RETHYMNON
The enemy opened fire with artillery on *Kampfgruppe Kroh* at the olive oil factory at 0600 hours. When the Australians attacked, they were turned back. Launching an immediate counterattack, assault detachments under *Leutnant* Fellner and *Leutnant* Rosenberg set out after the enemy. They reached the jumping-off point for the enemy's attack, pushed the enemy farther back and then occupied his former positions. They then held their positions after several attempts by the Australians to retake them.

Around 1600 hours, elements of *Kampfgruppe Kroh* succeeded in establishing contact with other elements that had jumped at the wrong location in the mountains. *Oberleutnant* von Roon received orders to take these elements, advance toward the battalion and occupy the group of buildings at the bend in the road 400 meters southeast of the olive oil factory, forming an outer bastion for the German position.

Oberleutnant von Roon cleared the houses, thus creating the prerequisites for attacking the village of Kimari, a few hundred meters farther south, which was held by both British and Greek forces.

✠

The day also started with heavy artillery fire for *Kampfgruppe Wiedemann* in the Peribolia area. The artillery fires increased in intensity until noon.

Around 1600 hours, the enemy attacked from the south in the direction of Peribolia and also attempted at the same time to retake fortress hill. When it appeared this enemy attack might meet with success and cause a severe setback for the Germans, fighter-bombers, bombers and *Stukas* joined the fray at 1700 hours.

The individual groups of aircraft operated to good effect. They bombed the enemy positions, scattered an enemy concentration and took up field fortifications in their bombsights. The aerial attacks, directed from the ground with hand-and-arm signals and pyrotechnics, lasted until 1830 hours. Finishing out the attacks were strafing runs on the enemy. The enemy pulled back to his start positions. The Germans retrieved the supply and ammunition canisters that had been dropped. Unfortunately, the airborne artillery did not receive any rounds. Despite that, the two battle groups in the Rethymnon area were certain that they could hold out against farther enemy attacks and fix a large number of enemy formations.

THE HERAKLION AREA OF OPERATIONS
In the area of operations around Heraklion, the individual battle groups of *FJR 1* had been forced over to the defensive. They faced numerically vastly superior enemy forces everywhere.

The *III./FJR 1* of *Major* Schulz worked its way through the wasteland of cliffs towards Hill 491. At the edge of exhaustion, the men reached the foot of hill as the sun went down on 23 May. They ascended the high ground from three sides after darkness had fallen.

After a short, sharp firefight, the paratroopers took the hilltop and the British gun positions on the first assault. The enemy had been completely surprised. He had not thought it possible that the Germans would reach the hill so rapidly and was surprised when the enemy attacked the very position that they had considered to be the most difficult one.

The enemy was disarmed and outposts were established. The rest of the battalion then fell into an exhausted sleep.

When the patrol dispatched by *Oberst* Bräuer arrived at the hill, it saw most of the men of Schulz's battalion sleeping. Only *Hauptmann* von der Schulenburg, as the officer of the guard, and his outposts were awake and ready for action. Von der Schulenburg accompanied the patrol to the east group and reported to *Oberst* Bräuer: "*Kampfgruppe Schulz* has taken Hill 491, in accordance with orders. The battle group is sleeping."

DAY OF DECISION: WITH THE AIRBORNE ASSAULT REGIMENT

During the early-morning hours of 24 May, a patrol under the command of the assault regiment signals officer, *Oberleutnant* Göttsche, advanced along the road toward Platanias. Göttsche could tell from the enemy's fire that the town was still in enemy hands, as were the slopes to the west. From the paratrooper's command post, one could observe the advance of the mountain forces. A short while later, the paratroopers also began to attack. The 2nd Battalion and all of *Kampfgruppe Gericke* pursued the withdrawing enemy and took the village of Platanias and the high ground on either side that same morning. Following hard on the heels of the enemy, the airborne soldiers moved through Agya-Marina and advanced as far as the high ground east and southeast of Stahana-Chania. *Kampfgruppe Gericke* was able to establish contact with the airborne engineer company of *Oberleutnant* Griesinger on those hills. The engineers were part of Heilmann's battalion, which, in turn, was part of *FJR 3*. The entire airborne battle group that was supposed to take Chania was centered around the reservoir located about 6 kilometers to its southwest.

After some fighting, the 2nd Battalion, which had moved in front of *Kampfgruppe Gericke*, reached the high ground just east of the road that led from Agya-Marina to the south. By means of a messenger, *Major* Stentzler heard that Gericke and Utz had established contact with the middle group.

Late in the afternoon, the enemy opened heavy artillery fire, which climbed to a crescendo by evening. *Major* Bode, the commander of the airborne divisional artillery, replied with everything he had. When he was at the outpost of one of his forward observers, he was caught in the middle of a heavy barrage There were dead and wounded. *Hauptmann* Gericke later told the author the following in an interview:

On 24 May, our battalion command post was located in a large cave. There was water in small, stinking puddles on the ground, and it smelled of decay and mold everywhere, but it was rock solid against any incoming rounds. Outside, the mountain troopers moved past

146

with their antitank guns. The airborne artillery was also changing positions.

The artillery commander had established his observation post behind a cliff line that jutted forward. *Major* Bode carefully raised the scissors scope over the edge of the cliff. Despite that, the enemy had noted the movement.

One of the men next to the scope had barely shown his helmet when fate dealt its blow. Head shot—dead! Snipers took everything under fire that exposed itself.

It did not take too long before the first salvo of English mortar fire fell behind the cliffs. The artillery commander collapsed, dead, from shrapnel. The adjutant, *Oberleutnant* von Bültzingslöwen, was bent over, badly wounded.

The fire shifted farther towards the village. Walls collapsed, windows rattled and mortar crumbled, giving off white clouds of dust. Very heavy shells were singing their song as they passed over the forward-most positions. They were coming from the English warships in Suda Bay.

Hauptmann Gericke went to the clearing station with his adjutant. When they came out of the defile and onto the asphalt road, they started to receive fire immediately. Moving as fast as they could, they approached the bridge. Just before they reached it, the fire intensified. When they crossed the bridge, the concussion from the detonating rounds threw them and their motorcycle-sidecar combination over the railing of the bridge and into the dry creek bed.

Mountain troopers, who had gone into position nearby, recovered the paratroopers. They had to first push the heavy machine to the side. Amazingly, the two men had not been injured. *Hauptmann* Gericke only had a bruise on his foot.

On the afternoon of 24 May 1941, Student arrived at Malemes. He had not been able to remain on the mainland any longer. He immediately took off for the forward command post, where *Oberst* Ramcke was the first to brief him and discussed the planned attack for the next day. Enemy artillery fire fell around the command post. The mortar rounds were falling close by. In the inferno of the artillery rounds, Student presented Ramcke with the award of the Iron Cross, First Class, for those who had already earned it in the First World War.

On 25 May 1941, the German Armed Forces High Command made the following announcement on the radio to the people of Germany:

The Armed Forces High Command makes the following announcement:

German paratroopers and air-landed forces have been in battle against elements of the British army on the island of Crete since the morning of 20 May.

In a bold assault from the air, they conquered tactically important points on the ground on the island, supported by fighter, fighter-bomber, bomber and dive bomber formations. After additional reinforcement from Army formations, the German forces have transitioned to the attack. The western portion of the island is already firmly in German hands.

The *Luftwaffe* destroyed efforts by the British fleet to intervene in the decision on Crete, drove it from the sea to the north of Crete, sunk or damaged a large number of enemy ships and achieved air superiority over the entire area of operations. The entire operation is running according to plan.

Early in the morning of 25 May, the command post of the assault regiment was moved from Agya-Marina to Stalos. *Oberst* Ramcke moved the 2nd Battalion to the right and the 4th Battalion to the left along the designated line for the attack on the high ground north of Galatas. The 1st Battalion, under the acting command of *Oberleutnant* Stoltz, remained as the reserve for the battle group behind the right wing. Ramcke assembled *Kampfgruppe Schmitz* between the two forward battalions. Off to the right, *Major* Stentzler and his 2nd Battalion established contact with mountain forces.

It was intended for the attack to start at 1600 hours. *Stukas* and fighter-bombers were to soften up the enemy targets. The *Ju 87's* appeared at first light, bombing enemy positions at Galatas. In between the *Stuka* sorties, the fighter-bombers appeared, which strafed heavy machine-gun and antitank gun positions at low level. They were followed by the bombers.

The aerial attacks lasted the entire morning. The attack was moved back to 1650 hours, because additional *Stuka* attacks were planned for 1630 and 1645 hours. But only one *Stuka* attack actually materialized. The mountain forces and the paratroopers were ordered to attack. It was exactly 1700 hours when the decisive fighting for Galatas started.

Led by *Major* Stentzler, the 2nd Battalion assaulted the olive tree orchards and hills northwest and north of Galatas. The snipers in the trees were engaged with bursts of machine-gun fire, and the machine-gun nests were enveloped and taken out with hand grenades. Position after position was rolled up. The New Zealanders and Maoris surrendered.

When Stentzler discovered that the mountain forces that were advancing directly on the high ground of Galatas next to where his men were bogged down, he had *Oberleutnant* Barmethler's company on the right swing south and attack the enemy in the rear. The maneuver succeeded. The enemy pulled back, and the mountain troopers were able to continue their advance.

After Stentzler's men had advanced far enough, *Kampfgruppe Gericke*, supported by attached antitank forces, started its attack. In hand-grenade duels of sometimes considerable intensity, the ridgelines at Koljenvithra, which ran parallel to one another, were taken. Four paratroopers were killed in those attacks. They had closed to a short distance of New Zealanders, who were displaying a white flag. Once near, they were fired upon from ambush positions.

The 2nd Battalion had borne the brunt of the attack. It had taken the hills that were so important for the enemy that were north of Galatas. That meant that a bulwark of Chania had been ripped out of Chania's defenses.

WITH THE MOUNTAIN FORCES IN GALATAS

On that 25 May, the mountain forces also attacked in small assault detachments in their sector. Concealed by vegetation and olive trees, they worked their way forward in small bounds and eventually took terrain, meter by meter.

The mountain artillery of *Oberstleutnant* Wittmann—*Gebirgs-Artillerie-Regiment 111*—antitank guns and mortars from all of the battle groups registered on the enemy pockets of resistance on the high ground. Under the covering fires provided by the artillery forces, the mountain troopers advanced. Greeks, English, Australians, New Zealanders, and Maoris were all fighting around Galatas. In addition, there were also British commando elements.

The mountain troopers had to advance frontally against the well-camouflaged system of trenches, machine-gun nests, mortar positions and antiaircraft artillery batteries and through wire entanglements.

While bitter fighting raged there, the men of the *1./Gebirgsjäger-Regiment 100* climbed the hill at Galatas with the church on it. It was north of the fortified Hill 103.

The sun burned down mercilessly on them. The smell of decay filled the air and myriad flies, green with iridescence, buzzed into the air like colored clouds whenever the mountain troopers hastened by.

The men reached the church courtyard and climbed over the walls. But the enemy had already left this formidable position. His rearguards withdrew in the face of the mountain troopers. From the church hill, the Germans were able to employ antitank guns that had been brought up, as well as heavy machine guns, which fired into the flanks of the fortress hill, which was still occupied by the enemy.

The remaining companies of the mountain regiment climbed up the slopes of fortress hill. It was the same hill that *Oberst* Heidrich and his men had stormed on the night of 20/21 May and had had to abandon again the following night to fall back to the penitentiary at Agya.

The enemy had set up his positions in the ruins on top of fortress hill. They opened fire when the Germans had approached to within 50 meters. At the same moment, however, German artillery on cemetery hill and church hill opened fire on the enemy positions.

The enemy defending there were Australians. They were terrific soldiers with a lot of grit. They even started an immediate counterattack. They stormed out of their trenches and from behind buildings and tossed hand grenades as they ran or fired from automatic weapons. Mountain troopers collapsed to the ground, mortally wounded or dead. They had to turn to flee downhill, pursued by the Australians.

When the men on church hill realized the enemy was attacking, they turned their heavy machine-guns on the Australians. The attack was broken up in the streams of deadly fire being poured upon it. Only a few of the Australians returned to the hilltop from the attack, where they again had good cover.

The church hill was held. Despite that, the situation was all still far from critical. *Generalmajor* Ringel wrestled with the decision to call off the attack. Then a message arrived from Athens that the *Luftwaffe* would launch one more attack at 1800 hours. The enemy's latest positions were reported, including those on fortress hill, and, a few minutes later, the dive bombers dropped their deadly cargoes to good effect. Following the *Stukas* were the bombers which, in turn, were followed by the fighter-bombers.

After the effective close-air support, *Oberst* Utz raced over to the men of his 3rd Company, who had been forced off fortress hill. "Men!" he said in his broad Bavarian accent, "We're going to attack one more time!"

Leading his men, Utz raced up the hill against the positions between Galatas and the church hill. They reached the plateau and took the buildings and positions of the enemy in a rush. Fortress Hill proper was taken by the men of the 2nd Company, who rolled up the enemy positions from the south. *Feldwebel* Graindl later provided this firsthand account:

> I was calm, at least my men thought so. The assault on Fortress Hill was difficult. The 3rd [Company] had already discovered that ahead of us. They had been ejected by the Australians.
>
> I had my platoon disperse. We then advanced by leaps and bounds. The heavy machine-gun canisters had to be taken along, even though we were crawling. Sweat poured into my eyes, salty, and down my body in small puddles. Suddenly, a burst of tracer ammunition from a machine-gun shot past our heads to the right. A sign that there was an enemy machine-gun on the left flank of the platoon. Rapid bursts of fire, joined by individual rifle rounds from snipers in the trees, whizzed all around us. They were constantly being interrupted by the distinctive hammer blows of our machine-guns. The barrels were glowing hot. The machine-gunners called for more ammunition. Every man was firing. The men, who had seen four different campaigns, knew this would be their most difficult fight.
>
> They advanced, meter by meter. Every tree, every piece of vegetation and every fold in the ground was used for cover and concealment. Fifty meters in front of us was a bald piece of flat ground with no vegetation on it and traversed by a wide band of wire entanglements. Moving individually, the men reached the last trees before the open area. Lungs were bursting; our hearts hammered wildly in our chests.

"Machine guns, right and left . . . give covering fire!" I cried. "Give me the wire cutters!"

The cutters went from man to man to me. Bursts of fire were directed against the English positions and held the enemy down. I had to approach the wire obstacle like a snake. But the enemy was unable to force me back. One of the Tommies, who was manning the machine-gun on the right, fired tracer ammunition into the wire obstacle.

Feldwebel Graindl cut the successive strands of wire. In quick spurts, the men raced through the small gap he had created and crossed the open area, as German mortar fires raked the enemy positions. They reached the crest, where they were again taken under fire. It was coming from the buildings in Galatas, which was in front of them. When a few machine-guns fired at them from a depression off to the right as well, Graindl and six volunteers worked their way to the edge of the depression, jumped in at the same time and silenced the defenders.

The men then advanced from one piece of vegetation to the next. When they got to within 50 meters of the enemy's rearward positions, they were greeted by a veritable wall of defensive fires.

At the same time, warning cries were heard from behind them: "The Tommies are attacking!"

The enemy also started attacking in the depression as well. The *Feldwebel* and his handful of men were unable to stop them until they had approached to within 20 meters.

On the hilltop plateau, the fighting continued on relentlessly. German antitank guns and mortars fired into the enemy concentrations, and the fires started to show effect. The Australians, who had advanced the farthest, were driven back with hand grenades. The shell-shocked and wounded surrendered. The mountain troopers owned fortress hill.

With the onset of darkness, Stentzler's battalion had approached as far as the northern and western edges of Galatas. *Oberfeldwebel* Max Burghartswieser stormed the western outskirts with his platoon from the 7th Mountain Company. With the 19 men who had survived the fighting of the afternoon, the platoon sergeant stormed into the town proper. He later recounted this action:

We simply overran the first position, with no mercy or quarter given. Every pocket of resistance had to be taken with hand grenades and pistols. Of the 40 English soldiers there, only two escaped with their lives. Australians, New Zealanders and English were pushed back. Many of the enemy fought onto death; the remaining ones fled. Firing submachine-guns and machine-guns from the hip as we ran, we succeeded in entering the main position. The enemy began to weaken. Whoever did not sink to the ground—hit—was pursued. The last trench line was cleared. The way into Galatas had been opened.

It had turned dark, when we received orders to occupy Galatas and get to the southern outskirts of the village. Paratroopers and mountain troopers from another company joined us.

Suddenly, Tommies appeared in all the alleyways. Small-arms fire and hand grenades chased them away. We headed for the northern outskirts. Then we heard an unusual noise: Were those tanks?

Firing with everything it had, the first tank approached. We did not have any antitank guns with us. It approached to within 20 meters. Also bothering us were two mortars, which had been brought up and were firing constantly. We were blinded and deafened; we tossed individual hand grenades against the tank, as well as bundled charges. Finally, one of its tracks broke. Despite that, it continued to fire and tore great gaps in the company, which had arrived in the meantime.

By then, it was 1930 hours. Among the first men in Galatas was the machine-gun section of *Oberjäger* Kerer. He had been directed to set up position in the middle of the village and cover the concentration of the 7th, 8th and 9th Companies, which had become widely dispersed.

He had just reached the village square, set up in position and fired his first burst of machine-gun fire, when he heard the following called out: "Enemy tanks attacking along the main street!"

A few seconds later, Kerer sighted the silhouettes of two armored vehicles emerging from the darkness. Fighting started there, as well. The enemy, supported by the two tanks, moved rapidly forward. Kerer had to stop the tanks if he did not want to succumb to them.

"Everybody except for the lead machine-gunner report to me!" he called out through the noise of battle.

"We're going to attack the tanks and hold them up!"

The tanks were already rolling towards the wall where Kerer and his men had set up. They had to pull back to the next closest building, where they ran into Burghartswieser and his remaining men.

"Give me covering fire!" Kerer called out to the others. Then he ran into the open with a bundle of hand grenades. He slung them towards the lead tank, but rounds from the automatic cannon forced Kerer to the ground and his aim was off. The grenades exploded relatively harmlessly to the side. The tank had approached to within 5 meters of the building the Germans were in. It then turned in place, coming to a stop in front of the building. It started firing with both its machine-gun and automatic cannon. Enemy infantry appeared behind the second tank. They reached the gardens and attacked the building, where Burghartswieser organized the defense. He was soon joined by *Feldwebel* Bruno Faltermeier, who had approached the building from the rear. With him was a section of riflemen, who joined in the fighting.

Both of the tanks were engaged by the German forces. They moved back somewhat, to take up positions a bit farther to the rear. The movement of the tanks afforded the German forces the opportunity to leave the building and work their way back to the wall.

One of the tanks broke a track all of a sudden. At that point the English started to pull back under the pressure of the massed fires of the Germans. The second tank turned and disappeared into the night.

The enemy attacked in full force again, somewhat later. Kerer's section was decimated. Two heavy machine-guns were lost. Kerer had only five men left, all of them wounded. At the last minute, a messenger arrived and brought the news that the companies had assembled in the center of the village and were ready to defend. Kerer had thus accomplished his mission.

The high ground around Galatas—the main line of resistance for the enemy—had fallen. By daybreak, the mountain battalions of *Oberstleutnant* Schrank and *Major* Schury had Galatas firmly under German control. The village presented a horrific scene at daybreak on 26 May. Dead were laying everywhere, Germans next to new Zealanders, English and Australians, who all held their weapons still in their now stiff hands.

The English defeat at Galatas was the start of a battle of pursuit that lasted all of the next day. On 26 May, the day after the bloody fighting at Galatas, Churchill stated the following before the lower house of Parliament:

> The fighting around Chania raged with indescribable ferocity, and just as vehemently, if on a smaller scale, around Rethymnon and Heraklion. General Freyberg's forces have received reinforcements in men and materiel and continue to receive them.[12]

At that point, the Prime Minister was interrupted by long, sustained applause. He continued:

> At *the* moment I am speaking, the success of their heroic resistance is still uncertain. However the battle may eventually turn, the defense of Crete, as an outpost of Egypt, will remain in first place among the annals of the British Army and the Royal Navy.

When *Generalmajor* Ringel received word from *Oberst* Utz on the morning of 26 May that all of Galatas was in German hands, he ordered the continuance of attack operations:

> We will pursue the enemy across a broad front to the east. He has been weakened. He can no longer be permitted to establish himself anywhere. We will remain static in front of the blocking position at Chania, since it appears advisable to support the attack on this position from the flanking movement from the south by the 85th

---

12. Translator's Note: Reverse-translated from German back to the original English without access to the original text.

Regiment. To that end, we have to wait until the bypass maneuver from the south has been completed.

RETHYMNON BETWEEN COLLAPSE AND LIBERATION

During the night of 25–26 May, *Major* Kroh at the olive oil factory made all of his preparations for the ordered attack and breakthrough to Heraklion. Two light antiaircraft weapons, which could not be brought along, were dispatched to the rear. The 17 badly wounded men had to be left behind in the factory under the care of a few medics.

At 0200 hours, the men departed towards the original drop zone, which was reached after three hours. At the drop zone, Kroh reorganized his force of 250 men into three units: The 1st Company under *Oberleutnant* Schindler, the 2nd Company under *Oberleutnant* Rosenberg and the 3rd Company of *Oberleutnant* von Roon.

In addition, there was Hinz's company, which consisted of the remnants of the 10th, 11th and 12th Companies, as well as the heavy company of *Oberleutnant* Marr, who had a combined force of *Flak*, antitank elements and the antiaircraft machine-gun company.

The order to break through to Heraklion was rescinded by the corps on the evening of 26 May, however: "*Fallschirmjäger-Regiment 2* continues to hold in its old positions and fix the enemy."

The battalion command post was established on Hill 217, east of the drop zone.

✠

The enemy attacked on the morning of 27 May in the sector of *Kampfgruppe Wiedemann* in the Peribolia area. He hit the eastern portion of the German defenses with strong forces. With support from four tanks, the enemy almost succeeded in breaking through. Thorbecke's battery—the *2./ Fallschirm-Artillerie-Abteilung 7*—set the first tank alight. The second tank was immobilized and then blown up with demolition charges by the paratroopers. After a long firefight, the third tank was also knocked out, with the fourth tank turning away and disappearing after being hit.

The enemy's infantry were bogged down in the defensive fires of the machine-gun sections. The enemy called off his attack; it had cost him too many casualties. More attacks were launched later, but they were all turned back.

When the enemy attacked fortress hill on the night of 27–28 May, his assault was stopped cold. However, at 0200 hours, he did succeed in penetrating in the southeast between the 9th and 14th Companies and advancing as far as the village of Peribolia. He was able to establish himself in several buildings there.

Major Schulz, who was in command of *Kampfgruppe Wiedemann*, gathered together messengers, radio operators and other communications personnel and launched an immediate counterattack, which drove some of the Australians back. Schulz and his men took 30 prisoners. Despite those efforts, his attack did not meet with complete success, since the enemy was still defending from some of the houses.

Three assault detachments from the 9th Company did not succeed in dislodging them. In the process, the paratroopers also suffered extremely heavy losses.

Hauptmann Wiedemann was wounded during the morning of 28 May in the course of the fighting, as was *Oberleutnant* Paul. *Oberleutnant* Pabst, *Oberleutnant* Begemann and *Leutnant* Molsen were all killed.

The fact that the men were able to hold out was in large measure due to the support provided by the *Luftwaffe's Stukas*, bombers and fighter-bombers. But the situation looked grim, and the men knew the next day would signal their end if they did not get help from somewhere.

THE SITUATION AT HERAKLION

The *II./FJR 2*, which had jumped at Heraklion to reinforce *Kampfgruppe Bräuer*, occupied Hill 296 on 26 May. With that, *Hauptmann* Schirmer's men had taken the high ground that dominated Malemes airfield. When the English attacked there during the day, they were driven back after hard fighting.

The German battalion physician assembled the wounded in an olive orchard. Three prisoners volunteered to help take care of them. It did not matter whether they were German or English. When the dressings and medicines started to run low, the physician decided to take the badly wounded through the lines to the field hospital of the enemy. A medical noncommissioned officer, two medics and two men from the 11th Company accompanied the doctor, who led the way, waving a white flag and also accompanied by one of the wounded English.

When they had approached to within 200 meters of the English positions, they were engaged by a machine-gun. "Don't fire. We're friendly."

The firing stopped. The small group approached the positions, until the surgeon stopped the group and asked for an officer. A 1st Lieutenant from New Zealand appeared, and the German told him of his desire to transfer the wounded to the English for medical treatment. The Commonwealth officer hurried towards the rear to report the incident to his commander.

Those remaining behind were searched by New Zealand soldiers, who relieved them of their decorations. After the lieutenant returned, the enlisted personnel had to return the decorations to the Germans. Then, under guard, the group was escorted to a deep defile and the command post. The wounded were delivered to the enemy's field hospital. The surgeon, who had been promised safe passage earlier, however, was retained.

That night, the New Zealand 1st Lieutenant appeared and took the German medical officer back to the front, in contravention of the orders he had received from his commander.

"I gave you my word of honor to take you back," he said, "and I am accustomed to keeping my word, even if someone wanted to prevent me from doing so. At first light, place your wounded in front of our positions, and I will ensure that all are cared for and go to the field hospital. Use a large white flag so that our men know that it is you. I will give them instructions."

The German thanked his officer counterpart and was deeply moved by his behavior.

ATTACK ON THE CAPITAL

During the early-morning hours of 27 May, assault detachments of the 4th Battalion of the Assault Regiment advanced on the capital. The detachment under *Feldwebel* Weiß was immediately engaged and reported back to headquarters that the enemy positions were still occupied.

Hauptfeldwebel Barnabas's assault detachment of the 2nd Battalion succeeded in cleverly exploiting the terrain and breaking through the forward lines of the enemy.

"We are going to take the machine-gun position. Once there, we'll have a view of the entire area!" he called out to his subordinates.

They stormed the first pocket of resistance using pistols, submachine-guns and hand grenades. Two paratroopers took and manned the machine-gun and opened fire on the next strongpoint, while the *Hauptfeldwebel* continued storming forward and took another two machine-gun positions. They reached a parapet, where Barnabas showed the flag he had brought along, so that they would not be taken under fire by their own people. As a precautionary measure, however, Barnabas had his men move the prisoners they had taken move into a defile and take cover a minute before a promised *Stuka* attack was to take place. The *Stukas* arrived and dropped their bombs on the enemy positions. The parapet that Barnabas and his men had been in just a moment before was not spared either.

The enemy was softened up by these combat raids against his positions. When the actual assault on Chania started after artillery preparation, the mountain forces were able to break through. The 2nd Battalion of the Airborne Assault Regiment also reached its objective of the day: The final sections of high ground southwest of Chania.

Kampfgruppe Gericke, reinforced by elements of *Kampfgruppe Schmitz*, advanced to the western slope of the hills east of Maurotrixas. From that position, they continued to attack after the guns of the artillery preparation fell silent. In a quick thrust, they succeeded in taking the high ground as far as the western edge of Chania. The fighting was hard, however. It was thanks to the German heavy machine-guns, which had been employed on the flanks, that the paratroopers were able to get as far as they did. Antitank guns and machine-gun positions were eliminated. Gericke then issued his orders to signal the actual assault on the capital of the island: "Pursue vigorously. Don't give the Tommies any time to set up. Chania needs to fall today!"

Bomber squadrons flew over Chania and dropped their deadly cargoes. The detonations echoed over to the location of the paratroopers. Gigantic plumes of smoke, flames and ash jetted skyward, collapsed upon themselves and then rose again. Then a terrific explosion shattered the air. The British main ammunition depot had received a direct hit.

The mountain troops ran down slope from the hilltops. They were also involved in the assault on Chania. The ring around the city was closed.

Major Stentzler's 2nd Battalion of the Airborne Assault Regiment had also moved out at the same time as the other formations. When the mountain troopers and the men of *Kampfgruppe Gericke* became entangled, however, *Oberst* Ramcke held up Stentzler's men on the western edge of the city in order to establish a reserve force in case the fighting in the city proper required its employment.

Paratroopers and mountain troopers moved into Chania, shoulder to shoulder. The motorized elements of *Kampfgruppe Schmitz* were in the lead. They moved forward rapidly to the city center without encountering significant resistance. They raised the flag they had brought along on the red steeple of the church.

Kampfgruppe Heidrich advanced on Chania from the south. *Hauptmann* von der Heydte's 1st Battalion was the lead formation. It was later determined that the enemy had abandoned the city under pressure from the heavy bombardment and had only left a few rearguards behind. The enemy had pulled back to the Akrotiri Peninsula in the direction of Suda. Gericke later provided this firsthand account of the fighting:

> A large fuel depot was burning along the way. Thick clouds of smoke were spilling out of the oil containers and formed huge mushrooms. Individual rounds were heard being fired in our direction. The streets of Chania started to fill with paratroopers. They were lucky to be among the survivors. In the middle of the marketplace was the commander, surrounded by his battle staff. The individual units filed past him in small groups. One of them called out: "*Herr Major*, see our flag over there?"
>
> The man pointed to the church tower. He had barely gotten the words out of his mouth, when the church bells started to peal. The antitank gunners from *Gruppe Schmitz* were responsible; they were ushering in the sound of victory.
>
> English prisoners by the hundreds filed through the streets. The throng at the marketplace grew ever larger. A stream of humanity poured into the open from a small alleyway: Barefoot, without headgear, ripped uniforms. Italians who had been taken prisoner by the English in Greece. They had been freed by the mountain troopers.
>
> A short time later, the commander of the local prison camp told Gericke

that he had 300 German prisoners that he wanted to release to him. The men went to the prison. The *Major* pulled on the door bell and informed the amazed English guard that the war was over for him. He had the guard force move outside and disarm. Gericke then went with some paratroopers up to the prisoner area. He opened the first cell door. Paratroopers moved out into the open, saw their comrades and started cheering.

"Comrades, you are free. Chania has fallen!"

There were about 300, just as the British major had said. They stormed out of the prison and formed up. They surrounded the major and his guard force and then marched off. One of them started singing; the rest of them joined in, including the paratroopers of the assault regiment:

"We're the old hands of the Assault Regiment!
When an old paratrooper
jumps through the door—oha-ohaa!
Then the devil runs away!"[13]

The night of 27–28 May passed quietly. On the morning of 28 May, the corps ordered *Oberst* Ramcke to assume command of the entire western portion of the area of operations, from Suda Bay to the western tip of the island. The mountain forces, which had performed so magnificently there, were taken out of sector and used to advance on Rethymnon and, at the same time, relieve *Kampfgruppe Kroh* and *Kampfgruppe Wiedemann*, which had jumped there. Only *Gebirgs-Pionier-Bataillon 95* remained in the western sector. Ramcke established his headquarters on the outskirts of the city, a kilometer northwest of Chania. Stentzler's 2nd Battalion was responsible for the city. Gericke's 4th Battalion and *Hauptmann* Schmitz's antitank forces defended along the coastline. The prison camp was taken over by the decimated 1st Battalion.

The first situation report that Ramcke released in his new capacity read as follows:

During the period from 20–27 May, the Airborne Assault Regiment took considerably more than 800 English prisoners. Up to the evening of 27 May, the assault regiment's casualties were:
34 officers and 272 noncommissioned officers and enlisted personnel were killed.
31 officers and 499 wounded.
4 officers and 395 missing [Most of the missing paratroopers were killed.]
3 prisoners.
The Airborne Assault Regiment and its attached elements have accomplished the missions given to it: Clearing the airfield at

---

13. Translator's Note: *Das sind die Alten vom Sturmregiment! / Wenn so ein alter Fallschirmjäger / springt zum Loch hinaus—oha-ohaa! Da reißt der Teufel los!*

Malemes, accomplished on 21 May after hard and casualty-intensive fighting, and, in continued heavy fighting, taken terrain as far as the village of Malemes to the east.

From 21 May until the morning of 23 May, several strong enemy counterattacks from the east were turned back.

After that, the regiment fought side-by-side with the mountain forces—main effort to both sides of the coastal road—from one attack to the next, until, the evening of 27 May at 1900 hours when Chania, the capital of the country, was taken.

This extremely difficult mission, which was mastered in spite of heavy casualties and an especially high loss rate among leaders, can only be attributable to the high state of training and the unsurpassable offensive *esprit de corps* shown from the most senior officer down to the youngest assault soldier.

/signed/ Ramcke

THE MOUNTAIN TROOPERS IN THE STORMING OF CHANIA

For the assault on Chania, the initial positioning of forces had been similar to that during the assault on Galatas. The paratroopers of *Oberst* Ramcke stormed long the left wing of the front. Adjoining them was *Bataillon Forster* of *Gebirgsjäger-Regiment 141*, followed by the *II./Gebirgsjäger-Regiment 100*. Paratroopers of *Gruppe Heidrich* then adjoined farther to the right. Rounding out the frontage was *Gebirgsjäger-Regiment 85*, which was farther to the south and still in the middle of its flanking movement.

Around 1000 hours on 27 May, the first flights of *Ju 87's* appeared, flew to the western edge of Chania and bombed identified enemy positions. As they climbed and turned away, the signal was sounded for the mountain forces to attack.

The attack advanced rapidly. From patch of woods to patch of woods, from defile to defile, the mountain troopers advanced. The enemy put up bitter resistance in farmyards and tangles of cacti. The English were pushed back in hand-grenade duels and the attendant close combat.

Towards 1300 hours, the *I./Gebirgsjäger-Regiment* of *Oberstleutnant* Schrank reached the village of Platanias. One hour later, the *II./Gebirgsjäger-Regiment 100* of *Major* Schury was in Paligoria, just outside of Chania. The paratroopers, on the other hand, had bogged down in front of the positions of the new Zealanders. The *6./Gebirgsjäger-Regiment 100* swung against the enemy from the south. They showed up to the rear of the New Zealanders and surprised them, breaking their resistance. *Major* Schury's entire battalion then attacked. The men climbed aboard the trucks that had been captured in Paligoria, and the antitank guns were limbered to them. The mountain troops assaulted into Chania in this impromptu manner.

Just before this attack, *Generalmajor* Ringel had ordered the forces under *Oberst* Utz to bypass the city to the left and head straight for the important military harbor of Suda. By the time the messenger had reached *Major* Schury, however, he was already rolling through Chania on his captured vehicles. At 1530 hours—before the paratroopers—the *Major* raised the *Reich* war flag on the main square of the city.

While *Kampfgruppe Heidrich* and *Kampfgruppe Utz* then pursued the enemy who was withdrawing in the direction of Suda, *Major* Schury had his 6th Company attack the city's citadel. In an interview with the author, former *Gefreiter* Feutner of the *6./Gebirgsjäger-Regiment 100* provided the following firsthand account:

> The heat of the day—it was already 1400 hours—bore oppressively down on our tired bones. The water in our canteens was long since gone; our thirst practically unbearable. Despite all of that, we were again under cover awaiting orders to attack again.
>
> While a squad screened the "Yellow Hill" up front, we established contact with a platoon from a neighboring company and covered its advance on the village of Paligoria. What would be waiting for us in Chania? Were there even enemy forces still in the city after the heavy bombardment? Would we encounter armed civilians and rooftop snipers again?
>
> *Major* Schury, who was on the hill, gave orders at 1415 hours to take and hold the fort in the middle of the city.
>
> The company moved out immediately to attack. The edge of the city was reached by moving through gardens, over walls, through marshy terrain and past blooming agave plants. We kicked in the first house doors. Emptiness everywhere.
>
> The streets were empty of people; the buildings and rooftops torn to pieces. Remnants of walls were lying in the streets. The white, dead city seemed eerie to us in its blazing heat and silence. Nothing, absolutely nothing, could be heard in that tangled mess of wires, wall ruins, heaps of rubble and remnants of houses.
>
> We snuck forward, rifles at the ready. Occasionally, a shot was fired and a hand grenade burst.
>
> A gap in the row of houses to the left revealed the imposing old Turkish fortress. The entrances had been barricaded with stones. We saw a person behind the wall, who was spying on us. Before a round could be fired, he had disappeared. A few seconds later, a call from many voices echoed over to us from behind the stone walls: "*Italiani, Siamo Italiani!*"
>
> It was our brothers-in-arms, the Italians from the Campaign in Greece. We raced down the ditch, broke the slight resistance of the English guards and fetched a hundred Italians from the fortress.
>
> There was a mad rush of excitement among them to have been freed. They had gone through a lot there.
>
> The fort was occupied and secured. We then advanced to the

main plaza and, at 1530 hours, the *Reich* war flag was raised on the flagpole.

When an English rearguard set up positions on the east side of Chania, the noise of battle swelled again. The enemy was firing at the attackers, who were approaching across the road of the Akrotiri Peninsula. We joined in. The last remaining resistance was broken on hand-grenade duels and the close combat that followed.

When *Oberst* Utz entered Chania around 1700 hours, the mayor of the city officially surrendered the city to him and requested that he spare the city's citizens. Utz responded in his open and laconic fashion: "Although the German soldiers have entered Chania as victors, they have not entered as enemies. There will be no talk of plundering and retribution. Any soldier who plunders will be shot."

✠

By evening, the mountain troopers advancing towards Suda had reached the bay, where the enemy had set up for one final, stubborn defense. Since the Germans did not know what kind of forces they were dealing with, *Generalmajor* Ringel ordered *Oberstleutnant* Wittmann, the commander of the divisional artillery, to form a battle group with forces he was given and clear Suda Bay. The intent was to remain on the heels of the enemy, advance along the main road to Rethymnon and relieve the encircled paratroopers of *Kampfgruppe Kroh* and *Kampfgruppe Wiedemann* there.

In addition, Wittmann was to establish contact with the forces of *Oberst* Krakau, which were attempting to bypass the enemy and advance on Stylos. Those orders and directives initiated the movements and operations that would bring the fighting on Crete to a close four days later.

✠

Kampfgruppe Wittmann, 400-men strong, reached its lines of departure on the coastal road between Chania and Suda Bay at 0300 hours on 28 May. Patrols moved forward and reported that the enemy had evacuated his positions in front of the city of Suda.

Oberstleutnant Wittmann had his battle group move out, and it left Chania to advance at high speed towards Suda. It reached the enemy's initial obstacles, but they were unmanned. By noon, Mega Chorafia was reached. At that point, the road branched, one way leading to Georgiupolis and the other towards Stylos.

The advance guard raced ahead on its motorcycles along the mountain road to Stylos. When it reached the village, it found *Kampfgruppe Krakau* engaged in combat with the enemy, who was still holding there. The motorcycle infantry immediately joined the fray, and the English pulled back.

Generalmajor Ringel had *Kampfgruppe Jais* advance in the direction of

Rethymnon, while *Kampfgruppe Utz* rolled forward to the southern Crete harbor of Sfakia, in order to clear the coast of the enemy there.

THE FINAL FIGHTING AT RETHYMNON

Because it was quiet in the Heraklion area and the enemy limited his activities to holding his positions, *Major* Kroh decided on 28 May to advance with his battle group to the west and into the area that had been abandoned two days previously and which was close to the airfield at Heraklion. His 2nd Company, which was farthest to the south, moved out in the direction of Prinos. Greek soldiers were positioned there. They were able to hold back the German advance with light and medium mortars. Combat activities on both sides abated.

On 29 May, *Ju 52's* dropped rations and ammunition. Kroh had elements conduct combat raids in the direction of Panormon, to the south into the mountains and again towards Prinos. Prinos was bypassed; a patrol advanced as far as Kimari.

By 1800 hours, the Germans had finished their preparations for an attack on both Prinos and Kimari. The 1st Company, the battle group headquarters and Hinz's company moved out at 1930 hours to assault Kimari. During the first rush by the Germans, the enemy forces pulled back to the olive-tree orchard north of the village.

The 2nd Company, advancing on Prinos, entered the village and cleared the houses. *Major* Kroh then had the company prepare for the breakthrough to the west. He intended to attack early on the morning of 30 May. *Major* Kroh was unaware of the other events that had happened on the island. No one in his battle group knew that mountain forces were already headed in their direction to relieve them.

At 0630 hours on 30 May, Kroh's men started their attack on the olive oil factory. After a few hundred meters, after rounding a bend in the road, they ran into motorcycles, antitank guns and trucks. Figures in field gray were manning them. It was the lead elements of the mountain division's *Kradschützen-Bataillon 55*. On their way to help relieve Kroh's men, they had contained a force of some 1,200 Australians and then headed towards Kroh's beleaguered force.

After 10 days of hard fighting and many a critical situation, the men of *Kampfgruppe Kroh* had finally been relieved. The battle group had sustained extremely heavy casualties, but it had held out and fixed in place a large number of enemy combatants.

GRUPPE WIEDEMANN

The Australian forces that had entered Peribolia during the course of 28 May broke out on the following morning and forced their way through the thin lines of *Kampfgruppe Wiedemann* to rejoin their comrades.

In the same area around Peribolia and fortress hill, the enemy renewed his artillery fires a few minutes later in an effort to demoralize Wiedemann's men. The artillery preparation was followed by an attack, which could only be turned back by employing all of the forces at his disposal. Things looked grim for the paratroopers, when their ammunition started to run out. At 1200 hours, however, they started to hear small-arms and machine-gun fire from the west.

"Those are German machine guns!" one of the men called out. He was not wrong. A short while later, German pyrotechnics were visible as they rose brilliantly in the clear skies over Crete. A platoon from the mountain motorcycle battalion blazed a path into Peribolia. It was followed a short while later by the main body, which also had artillery with it.

The German guns immediately began firing on the Australian positions. The Australians replied in kind, and the artillery duels lasted until the following morning. Then the motorcycle infantry, supported by two tanks, which had been barged over from the mainland, attacked after an artillery preparation. The enemy was dislodged from his positions, eventually pulling back in a panicked flight. By 1100 hours, some 1,100 Australians surrendered to the Germans. That signaled the end of the fighting in Wiedemann's sector around Peribolia. It is doubtful whether those paratroopers could have held out another 24 hours.

✠

At Rethymnon, *FJR 2* had lost 550 men dead, not including the 2nd Battalion, which was employed at Heraklion. In all, some 500 men were taken prisoner, but all of them were later released.

The mobile battle group of the mountain division hurried on to Heraklion, but the decision had already been reached there.

On 29 May, *Oberst* Bräuer ordered the second attack on the city. The advancing sections received only limited fires. The enemy was also pulling back there. Within a few hours, the withdrawal was transformed to a wild flight to the southern coast. Heraklion was firmly under German control.

✠

Just beyond Rethymnon, the mountain forces received heavy fire from Greek soldiers on 30 May. After they surrendered, the mountain troops learned that there were 300 paratroopers being held prisoner in Rethymnon. Among them was the regimental commander, *Oberst* Sturm. The motorcycle infantry raced towards the city, but the men had already been freed by other mountain elements.

When the advance guard moved out again, the Commanding General of the *XI. Flieger-Korps* was with them. In his history of the division, *Hurra, die Gams,* *Generalmajor* Ringel later wrote of the experience:

Nothing demonstrates better that the creator of the German airborne corps, *General* Student, was more than just a great soldier and organizer—that he was a man in whose breast a warm heart beat for every last one of his soldiers—than the night he spent sleepless at the command post of *Kampfgruppe Wittmann.*

Militarily, what would the fate of a few hundred have meant for someone else of his rank? If they fell, they fell as the shattered work tool of an event that demanded millions of sacrifices.

For this man, however, every one of his soldiers was priceless; he worried about all of them, as if each were his own son, and that was seldom seen during those hard and terrible times.

"THE HIGH COMMAND OF THE GERMAN ARMED FORCES ANNOUNCES . . ."

On 1 June 1941, the High Command German Armed Forces announced the following concerning the fighting on Crete:

> The powerful airborne operations that had started on 20 May to take the British bulwark of Crete are coming to a conclusion. Enemy resistance has collapsed everywhere. The attack group on the western portion of the island, consisting of paratroopers and mountain forces, have beaten and scattered the enemy after very heavy fighting, enduring extreme heat and extremely difficult movements. The paratroopers encircled at Rethymnon have been relieved.
>
> The remnants of the scattered British units have fled towards the southern coast, pursued by our forces, to escape farther fighting by embarking on ships.

That same day, General Wavell's headquarters issued the following:

> Crete: New German reinforcements were brought into Crete by air on Thursday. The operations by the dive-bombers lasted the entire day. Our forces once again occupy new positions. They have given the Germans heavy casualties.[14]

When the German High Command statement was released on 1 June, as the taking of the island was drawing to a rapid conclusion, the British War Ministry announced the following:

> After 12 days of fighting, which was undoubtedly among the bitterest of this war, it has been decided to pull our forces back from the island. Although heavy losses in men and aircraft were inflicted on the enemy, it has become clear that we cannot hope to continue operations with our land and sea forces in Crete and its waters for an unrestricted time without greater air support than that which can be employed from our African operating bases.
>
> Fifteen thousand men have already arrived in Egypt, but it must also be stated that we have suffered heavy casualties.

Major General Freyberg was flown to Egypt in a Sunderland flying boat

---

14. Translator's Note: This passage and the next were reverse-translated from German back into English.

on the night of 30–31 May. Major General Weston followed him the next night. Weston had been given command of the remaining forces on Crete in the absence of Freyberg. That was a thankless task, since 10,000 English and Commonwealth soldiers remained behind on the beaches at Sfakia and were taken prisoner.

On 2 June, *Reichsmarschall* Hermann Göring issued the following order-of-the-day:

> Crete Warriors, Comrades!
>
> A glorious deed in the history of our new branch has come to a conclusion. Victory flags wave on Crete. You, paratroopers and air-landed forces, together with comrades from the Army, have accomplished once-in-a-lifetime deeds under your tried-and-true leaders of all ranks.
>
> Airmen, paratroopers and mountain troops, in the spirit of brothers-in-arms, have forced the island of Crete in a manner reminiscent of those great days at Narvik and, as a result, have ejected England from important positions in the Mediterranean.
>
> Comrades! All Germans are filled with the deepest admiration and unending thanks for your latest victory. Along with the *Luftwaffe*, all of German Army is moved by and proud of the heroes who sacrificed their lives and their well being in the fighting for Crete.
>
> Forward in the spirit of the victors of Crete!

The Commander-in-Chief of the German Army, *Generalfeldmarschall* von Brauchitsch, also issued an order-of-the-day for the German forces employed on Crete.

The after-action report of the German Armed Force High Command concerning the Campaign in the Balkans summarized the losses suffered on Crete. Army personnel suffered:

> Dead: 20 officers and 301 noncommissioned officers and enlisted personnel.
> Missing: 18 officers and 596 noncommissioned officer and enlisted personnel.
> Wounded: 13 officers and 274 noncommissioned officers and enlisted personnel.
> Total: 51 officers and 1,171 noncommissioned officers and enlisted personnel.
> *Luftwaffe* losses among aircrew and airborne forces were as follows:
> Dead: 105 officers and 927 noncommissioned officers and enlisted personnel
> Missing: 88 officers and 2,009 noncommissioned officers and enlisted personnel
> Wounded: 104 officers and 1,528 noncommissioned officers and enlisted personnel

Total: 297 officers and 4,464 noncommissioned officers and enlisted personnel.

According to the German report, the British losses in prisoners were 10,700 personnel of all ranks. Greek prisoners: 5,000. The Commonwealth dead totaled some 5,000 personnel, not counting those lost at sea.

New Zealand sources place the total casualties among the Commonwealth ground forces at 15,743 men. They list the naval losses at 2,011 men.

The fight for Crete, the biggest operation of German airborne forces actually employed from the air, was over. It was as if a revolution had occurred, and no one has described that better and in more precise terms than Major General J. F. C. Fuller:

> Of all of the operations of the war, the attack from the air on Crete was by far the leader when it came to audaciousness. Neither before or afterwards was something similar attempted.
>
> It was not an air attack but rather an attack from the air. The fighting was also not decided in the air. Instead, it was decided on the ground and without the support of a land army.
>
> Its most salient feature was the aerial transport and the lifting of an army in the air. Just like the Battle of Cambray in 1917, this attack signaled a revolution in tactics.[15]

The fighting on Crete, which also turned out to be the main aerial employment of the airborne corps in the entire war, was legitimized, in the final analysis, by this praise. But the consequences that Crete had for the German airborne corps were so important and so decisive that this operation had to be presented in great detail. Let us examine some of the consequences of this operation.

CONCLUSIONS DRAWN FROM THE CRETE OPERATION

It is difficult for me to write about the Battle for Crete. For me, as the commander of the German air-landed forces that conquered Crete, this name is a bitter memory. I miscalculated when I recommended this attack, and this not only meant the loss of many paratroopers, who were my sons, but also, in the end, the death of the German airborne force, which I had personally created.

That was the conclusion drawn by Student after the war. What happened after Crete? Crete was considered a grandiose victory of the airborne corps. It was also, at the same time, the defeat of the same. Once again, Student:

On 19 July, on the occasion of the presentation of the Knight's Cross

---

15. Translator's Note: Unknown source. Presumably reverse-translated from German into English.

recipients for the Crete Operation at the *Führer* Headquarters in Rastenburg, Hitler said to me:

"Crete proved that the days of the airborne corps are over! Airborne forces are a weapon of surprise. Your surprise factor has since worn out."

He had the highest words of praise for the performance of the men. Over the next few months, I would feel the greater import of those words of Hitler's, when the airborne forces were sent to Russia as ground forces.

✠

Some of the airborne forces still on Crete and others returned to their peacetime garrisons on Germany, where they were greeted with great jubilation, when the war with the Soviet Union started.

For instance, the *III./FJR 1* heard the special report concerning the start of *Barbarossa* as it was crossing the Danube south of Budapest on its way to the Wildflecken Training Area, where the entire regiment was to be given some rest and be reconstituted.

The General Staff of the Army and the *Führer* Headquarters as well seemed to focus on the losses sustained in the taking of Crete. The *Reich* Air Ministry was shocked by the amount of transport aircraft that had been shot down or crash landed, even though the considerably smaller operations over Holland had cost more machines. But the loss of 143 *Ju 52's*, not including 8 that disappeared without a trace (presumably lost at sea) and 121 damaged aircraft was a number that cut to the quick.

Soon there were more than enough advice givers who attempted to convince Hitler that the employment of airborne forces was something akin to a lottery. Hitler allowed himself to be convinced by this whispering campaign, especially since he also considered the losses at Crete too high and did not want to initiate another operation that was so doubtful. He directed that the paratroopers were to be employed in the Soviet Union on the ground.

That might have worked well if the entire airborne force had been employed as an organic whole. Instead, however, the forces were split up into small contingents and employed piecemeal on different parts of the front.

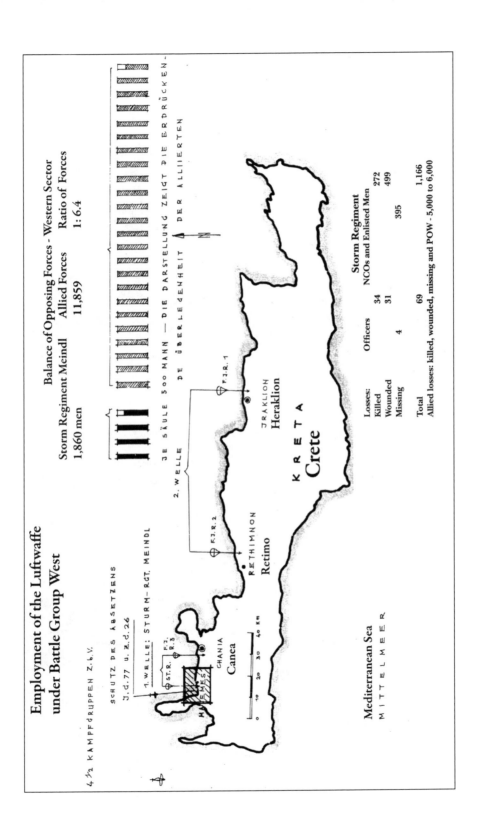

Employment of the Luftwaffe under Battle Group West

Balance of Opposing Forces - Western Sector

	Storm Regiment Meindl	Allied Forces	Ratio of Forces
	1,860 men	11,859	1:6.4

JE SÄULE 500 MANN — DIE DARSTELLUNG ZEIGT DIE ERDRÜCKEN-
DE ÜBERLEGENHEIT DER ALLIIERTEN

SCHUTZ DES ABSETZENS
J. G. 77 u. Z. G. 26

4 ½ KAMPFGRUPPEN Z. b. V.

1. WELLE: STURM-RGT. MEINDL

2. WELLE

F. J. R. 1
F. J. R. 2
ST. R.
F. J.
R. 3

K R E T A
Crete

JRAKLION
Heraklion

RETHIMNON
Retimo

CHANIA
Canea

MALEMES

N

0 10 20 30 40 Km

Mediterranean Sea
MITTELMEER

Storm Regiment

Losses:	Officers	NCOs and Enlisted Men
Killed	34	272
Wounded	31	499
Missing	4	395
Total	69	1,166

Allied losses: killed, wounded, missing and POW - 5,000 to 6,000

An assault glider prior to the flight to Crete.

The remains of a glider that landed at Malemes on 20 May 1941.

The first wave jumps over Crete.

The edge of the airstrip at Malemes became a graveyard for *Junkers Ju 52's*.

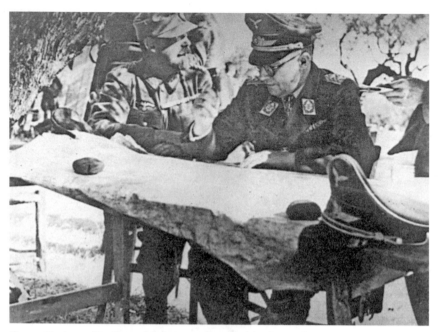

Generalleutnant Student (right) on Crete with *Generalmajor* Ringel, the commander of the *5. Gebirgs-Division*.

With the division headquarters of the *5. Gebirgs-Division*: Ringel (facing inward on the left) and Student (middle).

General Student prepares to ride in a motorcycle sidecar.

Mountain troops on the move. *General* Student in the sidecar passes the column.

A field camp in the mountains of Crete.

Air-dropped weapons canisters are recovered. German paratroopers jumped without weapons, except for a pistol or gravity knife. Consequently, they were effectively defenseless until the weapons containers were recovered.

Chania, after the assault.

Oberst Ramcke presents awards to paratroopers in Chania.

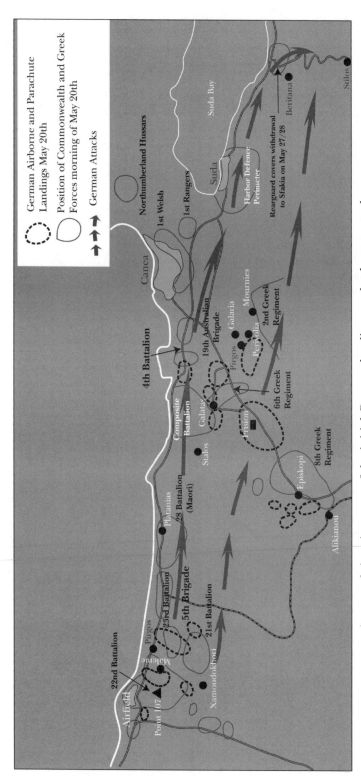

A general situation map of the initial German landings and subsequent advance.

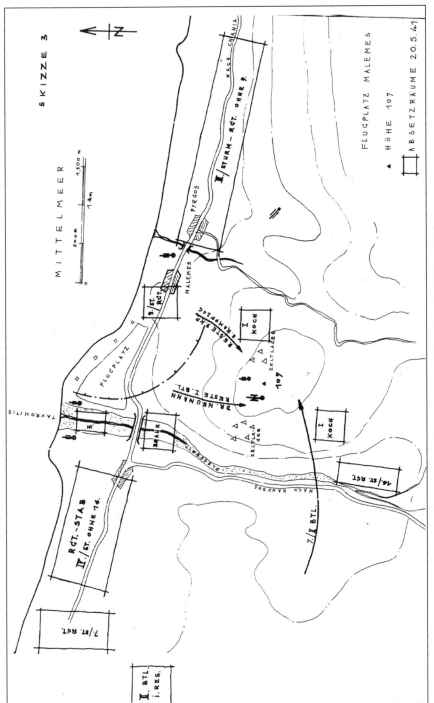

German positions surrounding the airfield at Maleme.

The Conquest of the Airfield at Maleme by Sturm-Regiment Meindl of the XI. Flieger Korps

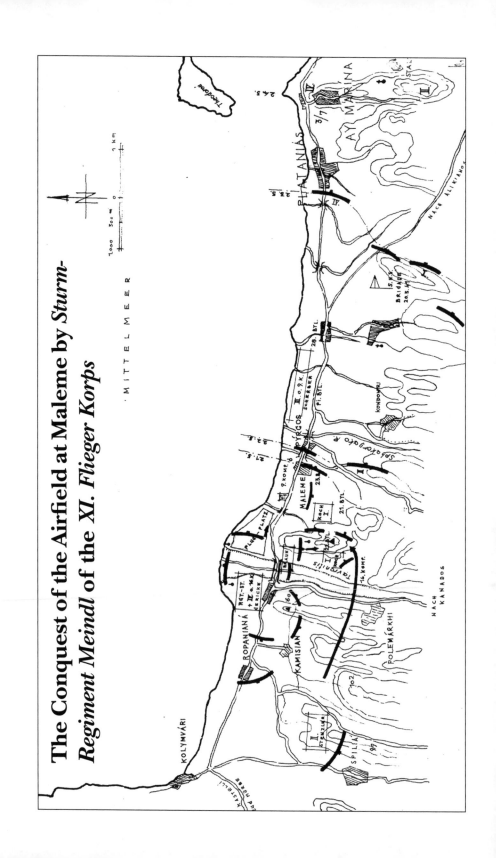

The End of the Fighting for Cania, the Capital City of Crete

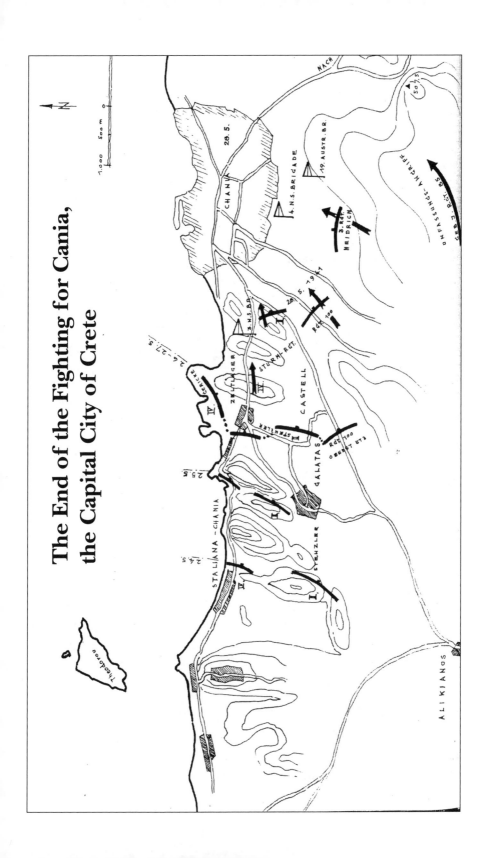

Air-dropped medical containers recovered at Dr. Langemeyer's aid station in Heraklion.

Chania on 26 May 1941: A heap of rubble.

The Bay of Suda after the German air attack.

Paratroopers take a break.

Major Schulz with his battalion in Heraklion.

Negotiations with the mayor of the city. To the left of the mayor is *Major* Schulz.
Oberleutnant Kerfin is seen talking to the soldier standing at attention and reporting.

Major Schulz warns the mayor of Heraklion of an impending *Stuka* attack.

Major Schulz (left) and his regimental commander, *Oberst* Bräuer.

Paratroopers wounded at Rethymnon.

Rudolf Witzing.

Alfred Schwarzmann.

Martin Schächter.

Fritz Prager.

Erich Schuster.

Wolfgang *Graf* Blücher.

Walther Koch.

Walter Gericke.

The Tavronitis Bridge at Malemes.

English surrendering at Malemes.

Reichsmarschall Göring presents awards to his paratroopers.

Oberst Ramcke presents awards to the Crete warriors.

Oberst Ramcke in front of his command post in Chania.

Reichsmarschall Göring discusses the operation with officers of *Sturmabteilung Koch*: *Hauptmann* Witzig (far left) and *Major* Koch (far right). To Göring's right is *General* Milch. With his arms crossed is *Generalmajor* Jeschonnek.

Adolf Hitler talks to officers of *Sturmabteilung Koch*: *Oberleutnant* Meissner, *Hauptmann* Witzig and *Major* Koch.

CHAPTER 6

Paratroopers in the Soviet Union

In September 1941, the 2nd Battalion of the Airborne Assault Regiment was the first formation earmarked to go to the Soviet Union. It departed from Goslar, its garrison city and where it had been reconstituted, to the Eastern Front near Leningrad. It was to be committed against the Soviets near Petruschino, where they had forced a bridgehead over the Newa River, and which started to have dangerous consequences for the entire front. The battalion, which was still under the command of *Major* Stenzler, flew to Russia.

Other units and formations from the division followed at the end of September. Both *FJR 1* and *FJR 3*, as well as the divisional engineers *(Major Liebach)*, the division artillery battalion, the antitank battalion and the division's medical battalion, were all transported by air to the front around Leningrad.

The headquarters of the division had nothing to command, since all of its subordinate elements had been farmed out to other formations. The division had a new commander, *Generalleutnant* Petersen, who was assisted by *Oberstleutnant i.G. Graf* von Üxküll, the division operations officer; *Oberleutnant* Tappen, the intelligence officer; and *Oberstleutnant* von Carnap, the divisional adjutant. As soon as the subordinate divisional elements landed at Ljuban, they set off to be attached to other formations.

It was not until the end of October that Petersen had regained command and control of some of his divisional formations. The division was finally able to be employed as such along the Newa. The fighting around the Soviet bridgehead at Wyborgskaja was especially intense. Through 17 November 1941, the paratroopers had had to fend off some 46 Soviet attacks in their sector. In the process, the airborne troopers eliminated 41 tanks and took 3,400 Red Army men prisoner. Five Soviet aircraft were shot down with infantry small-arms.

Before the end of the year, the 1st Battalion of the Assault Regiment—once again under the command of *Major* Koch, who had recovered from his wounds—also made the trek east and into the area of operations around Schaikowka. It was directed that the battalion defend the important airfield at Anissowo-Gorodischtsche, where bitter fighting was being waged at equally bitter temperatures of up to 40 degrees below zero.[1]

Before we look at some of the operations that the paratroopers were involved in during that coldest winter in generational memory, let us turn

---

1. Translator's Note: The exact same temperature in both the Celsius and Fahrenheit scales.

to the employment of other airborne assets in the Campaign in the Soviet Union. These airborne forces were not part of the *Luftwaffe*. Instead, they were Army elements part of the famous *Regiment Brandenburg*, a special forces formation.

LÜTKE'S AIRBORNE PLATOON IN ACTION

On 20 June 1941, *Leutnant* Lütke's airborne platoon was alerted by *Lehrregiment Brandenburg z.b.V. 800*[2]. The officer had just finished his parachute training in Brandenburg.

"We're going to Russia, men." *Leutnant* Lütke said to his platoon as they started to receive their equipment.

After loading the weapons containers, the platoon headed east toward East Prussia a short while later. Once he arrived there he was informed by the commander of the division that he was attached to that his platoon was to take an important bridge near the frontier and hold it until the division's troops could arrive.

At first light on 22 June 1941, the paratroopers waited along the east side of the airfield at Suwalki for the green light to go. But the platoon was not alerted; neither did it receive other orders. No parachutes and no transport aircraft were available!

When three *Ju 52's* finally arrived, bringing with them the needed parachutes, it was already too late. The bridge under discussion had already been taken in a *coup de main* by motorized ground forces.

On 23 June, the platoon was ordered to the airfield at Varene. The paratroopers were briefed on *Unternehmen "Bogdanow"*—the taking of both railway bridges along the two-tracked railway line from Lida to Molodeczno and preventing their demolition.

The platoon was ready to go on the morning of 25 June. Ten minutes after being alerted, the first *Ju 52* was in the air. It circled over the airfield until the remaining two machines could get airborne and join up.

The aircraft flew nap-of-the-earth style, barely clearing the crests of the trees, until they got to the area of operations. The men were supposed to jump 1,200 meters beyond the bridge on a small plateau. The platoon was then to work its way back to the bridge through a small strip of woodline.

When the orders were issued to prepare to jump, the enemy started intense fire on the *Ju 52's*, which were at an altitude of only 30 meters at the time. The pilot of the lead machine was wounded in the mouth. The glass in the cockpit shattered.

Despite that, the orders were issued from the jumpmaster to prepare to jump. The *Ju 52's* climbed to a jump altitude, reached the bridge at 55 meters, and the paratroopers started jumping without waiting for the plateau or the jumpmaster.

---

2. Translator's Note: The 800th Special-Purpose Instruction Regiment "Branden-burg" was the code name for the special-forces regiment. *z.b.V. ("zur besonderen Verwendung")* For Special Employment (literally).

The jumpmaster was the only one left on board when he noticed that the weapons containers had not been dropped. He had the wounded pilot fly around, whereupon the jumpmaster dislodged the containers and also jumped himself, albeit at a very low altitude.

The other two *Ju 52's* also had their paratroopers jump when they saw what was happening with the lead machine.

This incident actually rebounded to the Germans' favor, however. If the platoon had actually jumped on its intended target, it would have landed on 16 tanks that had assembled there, which would have then taken it under fire.

All of the paratroopers landed safely, despite the jump height of only 55 meters. They were on both ends of the bridge.

The Soviet tanks then attempted to blow up the bridge with high-explosive rounds, but the embankment nearby offered a certain degree of protection. It was only when mortar fires joined in that some of the rounds landed dangerously close.

Both the bridge and its approaches were in the hands of the German paratroopers. At that point, however, Red Army men started to attack. The machine-guns that had been retrieved from the weapons containers opened fire. They were joined by the sounds of submachine-guns firing. The first enemy attack went to ground. A handful of Soviets attempted to crawl to the bridge. They were discovered by an *Obergefreiter*. His submachine-gun fire warned his comrades, and *Leutnant* Lütke immediately went towards the sound of the firing with three other men. The *Obergefreiter* suddenly stopped firing. He had been hit in the head. When the officer found him, he was still alive. The men dressed his wound and carried him to a safer location. The Soviet soldiers had been thwarted in their effort to sneak up on the bridge, however.

As it started to turn dusk, the Russian tanks pulled back.

Leutnant Lütke ordered his men to set up an all-round defense, a so-called hedgehog position. During the night, armored cars from a division's reconnaissance battalion made it through to them. Once there, the paratroopers had communications to the rear. That did not mean the danger was over, however.

✠

In the middle of the night, *Obergefreiter* Henning, who was one of the outposts on the bridge, saw a movement and heard noises, which suddenly fell silent. He shook awake the machine-gunner, who had dozed off. "They're coming!" he whispered.

In the space of a few seconds everyone was awake and prepared to defend. Their nerves stretched to the breaking point, they waited for the attackers to appear. Suddenly, Henning saw two flashes from some vegetation barely 30 meters in front of him. He raised his submachine-gun and let loose with a long burst.

The machine-gun joined it with its rattling, then another one. The earth-brown-clad figures, which seemed to spring up out of nothingness, reeled back under the impact of the bullets. Hand grenades were tossed, and one landed barely half a meter from Henning. He grabbed it instinctively and tossed it back. It burst in the air on its way back.

Then, all of a sudden, it was quiet again. The Soviet raiding party had been turned back. "It'll be quiet, now!" one of the men said. But *Leutnant* Lütke had a different opinion. "They'll be coming back . . . they most certainly will be coming back again!"

The office was proven right. Two hours after the disastrous first attack, the Soviets followed up with a larger, more intense one. Once again, the machine-guns opened up, joined by the automatic weapons on the armored cars. The muzzle flashes shone brilliantly in the night and streamed in the direction of the charging Russians.

The night was filled with the racket from the weapons. Orders in Russian were barked, but this attack also came to a standstill. The wounded Soviets were evacuated a short while later by their comrades.

Until first light, the minutes seemed like hours. A feared third attack, which would have put the platoon, whose ammunition supplies were dwindling rapidly, in a precarious position, never materialized.

The fighting had also taken its toll on the Germans. Up to that point, the platoon had lost four men and another 16 had been wounded. Radio communication with the division was lost, but the armored car crews did succeed in contacting a motorcycle infantry battalion. Acting on its own initiative, elements of the battalion swung up from the south to the two bridges and relieved the paratroopers.

Both bridges remained intact, and the division used them to advance farther to the east. For the time being, the paratroopers remained with the motorcycle infantry battalion and participated in its operations. On 4 July, the remaining seven men of the original platoon were sent back to a collection point at Vilna. *Leutnant* Lütke was not among the seven; he had been killed in some fighting in a patch of woods while with the motorcycle infantry.

FALLSCHIRMJÄGER-REGIMENT 1 OUTSIDE OF LENINGRAD

On 25 September 1941, *Major i.G.* Trettner, the operations officer of the *7. Flieger-Division*, made a surprise visit to *Bataillon Schulz* in Wildflecken and stated that the division was about to be committed on new operations.

"Africa?" *Major* Walther asked.

"No sun this time, comrades! We'll be seeing snow and ice." Trettner replied.

"That means Russia!" *Oberleutnant* Becker chimed in.

"You'll be moving out early tomorrow. The area of operations is Leningrad, on the northern wing of the Eastern Front. The forces there are in danger of being cut off by the Soviets advancing from Leningrad. In addition, the enemy is threatening to break through to Tosno and the airfield there. The Red

Army has succeeded in crossing the Newa at several points and establishing bridgeheads. We'll start tomorrow at 0530 hours. Make your preparations. Everything needs to go like clockwork. You'll be flying from here directly to Stendal. There you'll refuel and take on your weapons."

Ten minutes later, all of the paratrooper elements at Wildflecken had been alerted. *Generalmajor* Bräuer briefed the assembled regiment on its new mission. The regimental commander had just returned from Fulda, a half hour away, also surprised by the news.

✠

In the command post of the *III./FJR 1*, *Major* Schulz bent over the map. He pointed to a spot marked in red with his index finger.

"I don't like that, Kerfin!" he said. "If the Russians get over the Newa there, they'll get the whole shooting match!"

"I don't think they'll attack there!" *Hauptmann* Kerfin replied.

The *III./FJR 1* was in a position behind the Newa, which abutted the Mga River on its left. In front of them, the German front extended 12 kilometers east along a narrow tongue. If the Russians succeeded in crossing the Newa in the middle of the tongue, they could cut off and eliminate the German forces farther to the east.

Artillery shells could be heard occasionally whistling past the command post overhead. Then the field telephone rang. The command post received a report from the infantry regiment farther east along the tongue. A Russian breakthrough was reported.

"The Russians got through the river with tanks. They simply rolled through . . ."

Then the line went silent.

"Alert the battalion!" Schulz ordered. While *Hauptmann* Kerfin sent out the alert message, Schulz turned to the signals man on the telephone.

"Contact regiment! Urgent!"

When *Generalmajor* Bräuer came on the telephone, *Major* Schulz briefed him. Schulz received orders to stop the Soviets who had broken through, eliminate them and restore the former lines.

A short while later, the battalion advanced. Both of the 5-centimeter antitank guns were towed by prime movers, as they moved forward through the vegetation in the early-evening twilight.

"Tanks ahead!" One of the paratroopers called out. Three tanks were rolling along the river's edge in the vegetation. Occasionally, they halted. But they did not fire. Schulz's battalion then reached the area of the breakthrough.

"Spread out . . . bring the antitank guns forward. Establish tank hunter/killer teams!" the commander ordered.

The paratroopers disappeared in the dense vegetation and woods. The sound of fighting that they had previously heard fell silent. But the rattling of tracks on armored vehicles became louder and louder. The antitank guns had been brought forward by the prime movers, unlimbered and set up in positions offering the best fields of fire available in areas where the enemy would most likely employ his armor.

The tank that was advancing along the river line suddenly stopped. Its turret with its long trunk of steel started to traverse. Then, a long lance of flame shot out of the barrel. The round slammed into the ground behind one of the prime movers for the antitank guns.

The enemy tank farthest to the left rolled into a deep hole in the marshland. It attempted to get out by moving in reverse. At that moment, the first rounds cracked from the German antitank guns. One direct hit to the rear of the tank set it on fire. Figures sprang from the hatches and jumped to the ground and rolled around in an effort to extinguish the flames on their uniforms, which had also caught fire.

The steady rhythm of heavy Maxim machine-guns joined in. They had been brought forward on small carts. The fires increased in volume and intensity and climbed to a true crescendo. The two remaining tanks were firing with everything they had. The German antitank guns replied in kind.

"Bound your way forward! Cut off the enemy infantry and eliminate the two tanks!" *Major* Schulz barked.

The men jumped up and ran from one concealed position to the next. Three hunter/killer teams ran forward, after the machine-guns had been set up in flanking positions and started to provide covering fire.

Feldwebel Ahrens crept through the underbrush with his men. Next to him, closer to the river, *Oberjäger* Hollmann and his section were also advancing.

Ahrens and his men had not yet reached the tank, when the vehicle located next to the river was visited by a mighty blow. Ten seconds later, it was completely engulfed in flame.

When the remaining tank started to turn, it was hit in the rear by a 5-centimeter antitank-gun round. A few seconds later, it was also engulfed in flame.

With the tanks out of the way, *Major* Schulz led the assault of his battalion against the enemy infantry. In close-in fighting, the Red Army men were driven from the former positions of the German infantry regiment that had been forced back. The paratroopers then oriented towards the tip of the tongue, the most threatened sector for the Germans.

In the nights that followed, the Soviets attempted to get across the Newa several times in assault boats. But the paratroopers were on the alert. They waited until the Soviets were in the middle of the water before they opened fire with machine-guns. Russian snipers, located in trees on the far side of the river, were taken down by airborne snipers. The German paratroopers, who had been rumored by Army units that they were only capable of fighting in the warmer climes of the south, showed just what they were made of.

Wherever they were employed, the paratroopers defended successfully. All of the Soviet bridgeheads, with the exception of one, were reduced. The last remaining one—the bridgehead at Petruschino—was attacked by the 2nd Battalion of the Airborne Assault Regiment of *Major* Stentzler on 19 October.

In murderous combat—due to the narrowness of the front, only one company could attack in the sector at a given time—the Soviets were pushed back meter by meter. There was horrific man-to-man fighting before the enemy was ejected once and for all. Stentzler's battalion was practically wiped out in the nighttime fighting. Stentzler himself died a day later from wounds sustained to his head. But he had accomplished his mission and eliminated the Soviets' bridgehead leading to Tosno.

These operations were among the hardest the paratroopers ever participated in. The enemy had to be ejected from every position in man-to-man fighting. The Soviet machine-gun positions were rendered combat ineffective by the use of demolitions.

THE RUSSIAN ODYSSEY OF THE AIRBORNE ASSAULT REGIMENT

Under the command of *Generalmajor* Meindl, the airborne assault regiment was reconstituted after operations on Crete. The time for resting was short, however. On 26 September, *Major* Stentzler's 2nd Battalion had already moved out for the Eastern Front.

Four days later, the battalion was in its first operations against Soviet forces. During the successful breakthrough through the Soviet field positions at Petruschino, it was *Hauptmann* Reinhart's 8th Company that stood out. He became one of the first paratroopers to receive the newly created German Cross in Gold.

Through the 18th of November, the battalion was in frontline positions in the vicinity of Schlüsselburg.

The 4th Battalion of the regiment was sent to Krementschug in November. Soon, the regimental headquarters and the 1st Battalion joined the sister formations in the Soviet Union. *Major* Koch, who had recovered from the wounds suffered on Crete, resumed command of the 1st Battalion. The regimental headquarters was flown to Juchnow, where *Generalmajor* Meindl commanded a division equivalent for a while that consisted of *Waffen-SS*, *Luftwaffe* ground formations and other infantry elements. The 1st Battalion was sent to the area around Schaikowka. It was intended for that battalion to defend the airfield at Anissowo-Gorodischtsche.

The 10th Company of *Leutnant* Vogel was employed a little later, fighting in the area northwest of Rshew, near Sobakino, from 7 January until 6 April 1942. On 15, 17 and 21 January, the company launched successful local attacks and sealed off Soviet penetrations near Sobakino.

OPERATIONS OF THE 1ST BATTALION OF THE AIRBORNE ASSAULT REGIMENT

The 3rd Company of the 1st Battalion was dug in along the northeast corner of the airfield at Anissowo-Gorodischtsche. *Hauptmann* Jungwirt's 2nd Company adjoined it.

Oberfeldwebel Schuster and his platoon had raced out to the trench line from the warm bunkers after the alert had been sounded. It was turning first light on 16 January 1942. As Schuster turned around in the trench, he could see the airfield buildings and the structures of Schaikowka jut skywards. To the right of him was *Oberfeldwebel* Ellersiek's platoon. To the left in the trench line was *Feldwebel* Dudda's platoon.

To the right of Schuster was the Maxim machine-gun that had been captured the previous day during the attack on Gorodischtsche. A pyrotechnic climbed into the ashen morning sky.

"Get ready!" Schuster called out when he saw the first batch of Soviets on skis approaching. Both of the platoon's machine-guns opened fire. The Maxim then joined in, distinguishable by its comparatively slow rate of fire.

The first group of attackers—ski personnel with white coats—turned off to the side and headed for Mithinka.

New groups of Soviets appeared from a depression 600 meters in front of the main line of resistance. This time, it was infantry. When they reached the area that had been laid with mines by the engineers, powerful detonations roared through the early morning. Schuster saw a group of Soviets crawling towards the wire entanglements. He fired four bursts from his submachine-gun, pressed the magazine release and slammed another magazine home.

One of *Oberjäger* Bühren's men was hit in the head, collapsing to the ground, dead. Then hand grenades started coming in. The sounds of the Soviet battle cry—"Urrä"—penetrated through the sounds of fighting, but it suddenly fell silent as two more heavy machine-guns joined in the fight. One squad of Red Army men reached the forward trench before they were mown down in a burst of fire.

Leutnant Arpke moved through the communications trench to reach Schuster. "Erich, get ready to move out! The company's going to launch an immediate counterattack on Mithinka in 15 minutes. The enemy had penetrated there." Arpke left no time for a response; he was already moving forward through the trenches to alert the next platoon leader. Little did he know it, but that would be the last time Schuster ever saw him alive.

"Get ready!" They pulled their chin straps tight. Hand grenades were made accessible. *Oberjäger* Kruse took demolitions with his group.

The preparatory artillery fires started, joined by the *Flak.*

"Let's go!"

They jumped up and ran across the firmly packed snow to the northeast in the direction of Mithinka. Schuster took long leaps over the craters in the ground. He collapsed in a mound of snow at one point, but forced himself up and ran on. Ellersiek's platoon joined his.

The first few Soviet riflemen started firing. Geysers of steel, mud, dirt and snow shot skyward. They picked up their pace. They started to gasp for breath, and the cold air felt like needles in their lungs. A platoon of Red Army men appeared at the edge of Mithinka. They wanted to put some mortars into position.

Both of the machine-guns were being fired from the hip as the men ran. Off to the right, *Oberjäger* Kruse joined up and was also firing as he ran.

The firing of the paratroopers was returned from hedges and buildings around the village. Despite that, they were able to reach the outskirts, crawl through the gap in a dilapidated fence and take out a heavy machine-gun that was firing out of a blockhouse.

The sound of fighting could be heard from off the flank, as well. *Leutnant* Arpke was assaulting with his men against the neighboring village of Jekolewka. During the next bound forward, two men were cut down. The rest made it, however, and eliminated pockets of resistance with hand grenades. The men then set up in the buildings they had just taken.

Feldwebel Schuster then rallied his men forward again, this time in the direction of two or three machine-guns that were still firing. Rounds whizzed past them. Finally, they reached the heavy machine-guns and tossed hand grenades. They then continued assaulting until they reached the far side of the village. Mithinka was in German hands. *Major* Koch had the former positions reoccupied. A platoon and a mortar section were positioned there. Exhausted and happy that they were able to free some captured comrades, the men of Schuster's platoon headed back to their positions. Once they got there, they ran into *Feldwebel* Dudda.

"Erich," he said, his voice thick with emotion. "Erich, we lost Helmut."

"Where is he?" Schuster asked, without realizing that tears were rolling down his cheeks.

"We took him to the battalion command post," Dudda replied.

Leutnant Helmut Arpke, recipient of the Knight's Cross, was killed in the assault on Jekolewka on 16 January. He was buried at the regimental cemetery at Schaikowka. His platoon provided the honor guard.

✠

The fighting over the next few days did not allow the paratroopers to get any rest. *Hauptmann* Hans Jungwirt's 2nd Company was able to take a portion of Belnja-South from the Russians. A short time later, the experienced company commander demonstrated his mettle again at Michailewo. He was able to push back the enemy forces that had penetrated and hold his position against seven Soviet attacks. For those actions, the young officer received the German Cross in Gold.

On 18 January, the village of Borez was taken from the enemy, only to be followed by an attack of Soviet ski forces late in the evening of 22 January. Prior to the Soviet attack, the battalion's positions were peppered with rockets from

Stalin organs, which transformed the positions into an exploding and flaming inferno. Swarms of rockets howled through the nighttime skies. Their impacts shook the earth. Schuster heard the powerful detonations, as they slammed into the earth. He thought his eardrums would burst; the concussions seemed to suck the air out of his chest.

Up front, the *Teller* mines exploded and the wire entanglements were torn apart from the impacting rocket salvoes.

The paratroopers fired at the attacking Russians from their positions in Jekolewka and Mithinka. Two four-barreled *Flak* also fired at the charging Russians.

The enemy had approached to within penetration of the German positions across the battalion's entire defensive sector. But then their assaults collapsed in the crescendo of defensive fires.

Not more than five minutes later, however, a second wave attacked. That attack was also turned back. The 3rd Company, reinforced by the 2nd Company, which had been the ready reserve, were then ordered to attack the western outskirts of Gorodischtsche. If they were successful, then the main line of resistance would have been moved up enough that the corner positions would no longer be threatened.

Ten minutes later, the three platoons of the 3rd Company moved forward stealthily. *Feldwebel* Schuster moved at the head of his platoon. The reached a defile running across their path, encountered a Soviet outpost and put it out of action with hand grenades. The Soviets opened fire again with their rocket launchers. But the 3rd Company had already moved past the beaten zone and was not in any danger from them.

Suddenly, the men saw Soviet earthen bunkers in front of them. Bursts of fire were headed toward them from the bunkers on the flanks. The paratroopers ran on, reached a shallow depression in the snow, jumped in and then worked their way to the first bunker.

The 1st Company, which had been held back somewhat, finally closed up on the right flank of the 3rd Company and also started to attack the bunker line. The individual bunkers were taken out with bundled charges. Soviets exited into the open with their hands up; most of them were wounded.

Schuster ordered his men to move on to the outskirts of the town.

They continued to run, as did all of the other platoons. They had made it through the bunker line and approached the initial buildings. The defending Soviets had to fall back. A machine-gun was brought forward and put into position; the units started to set up strongpoint defenses.

Ellersiek's platoon was briefed. Dudda also linked up with the other platoons and took an additional strongpoint, with the result that the three platoons could support one another with covering fires.

When the enemy attempted to take back that portion of the town he had just lost 30 minutes later, he entered the kill zone of the paratroopers and had to pull back. The western portion of Gorodischtsche was held by the airborne forces from 22 to 28 January. Combat patrols wrested additional houses and buildings—one after the other—from the enemy. *Feldwebel* Schuster often led the combat patrols. When Schuster and his men got into a crisis situation on 26 January, an *Obergefreiter* was able to use a Soviet automatic weapon to blast a path through the Russians and into freedom. *Obergefreiter* Walter Funk went on to earn the German Cross in Gold for this and other similar actions.

Over the next few days, it was *Oberfeldwebel* Heinrich Orth who was the talk of the battalion. During the fighting for Anissowo, the taking of the village and the successful defense against the enemy's counterattacks on 3 and 4 February, his platoon of 50 held its own against an entire elite battalion of Soviets, taking 126 of them prisoner. *Major* Koch submitted him for the Knight's Cross. *Generalmajor* Meindl also recommended approval and the noncommissioned officer was approved for the high award on 18 March. Unfortunately, he was killed eight days prior to that in the taking of Philippkowo and Silkowitschi, where he, once again, had contributed significantly in their conquest.

✠

The evening before the assault on Anissowo, *Major* Koch appeared in the area of Schuster's platoon. As he started to leave, he made an offhand comment to Schuster: "Big secret for the time being, Schuster, but you can let your platoon in on it: the regiment is going to be reconstituted and will be sent to Germany for it."

When Schuster returned to his command bunker and was all set to tell the good news to his men, the empty shell case at the bunker entrance started to make a sound. It was connected to the outposts in the trenches by wires, who could signal an alert by pulling on them.

Schuster grabbed his helmet and slipped it on. Then he ran out into the open. The individual squads arrived in the trenches at about the same time, where they saw attacking Russians about 400 meters away. It was Siberians who were attempting to overrun the German positions there.

They got as far as the wire entanglements, where some of the *Teller* mines went off and tore apart any attacker who was in its danger zone. The Germans fired with everything they had. Schuster saw the enemy decimated but continue to attack. Soon tall Siberians were in the trenches. The close combat had begun! The man-to-man struggle lasted for 10 minutes, until all of the Siberians who had entered the trench line had been overcome. Wounded men called for medics. The dead were removed from the trenches.

The fact that things had turned out reasonably well was in no small measure thanks to Ellersiek's platoon, which had attacked the enemy in the right flank and essentially wiped him out.

Major Koch took his leave of those wounded, who had to be evacuated to Germany. He then ordered a counterattack on Anissowo by the 3rd and 4th Companies. The remaining two companies had to hold the line.

The two companies took Anissowo and set up for the defense there. But the Soviets did not launch an immediate counterattack, however. Instead, they shelled the town with artillery, the length and intensity of which overshadowed anything the paratroopers had seen before. Following the artillery, a regiment of Soviets attacked in four waves, one after the other. The four waves were each turned back.

When some houses on the northeastern side of Anissowo were lost, two squads of paratroopers assaulted with two flamethrowers and ejected the enemy forces that had taken them.

It was then quiet until 10 February. On 11 and 12 February, Koch's battalion launched an attack into Belnja-South. The 3rd Company, commanded by *Oberleutnant* Hoefeld, was able to defeat an enemy force 10 times the size of his own and then establish defensive positions there.

On 19 and 20 February, Koch's men were again in action. *Major* Koch led his headquarters company to Michailowo. At the same time, Jemikowo and Orlofka were attacked. Towards midnight, Koch ordered his battalion to attack Dimitrowka.

The lead attack element was led by *Feldwebel* Schuster. Ellersiek's and Dudda's platoons were about 50 meters to his rear and off to the flank, providing security. They started to receive fire. Two 7.62-centimeter antitank guns were firing at them from a large bunker. Ellersiek's platoon took the bunker and put it out of commission. Then the battalion continued its assault on Dimitrowka. The captured weapons of the Soviets were manned by the paratroopers and turned on their former owners.

The fighting around Schaikowka increased in its intensity. The paratroopers were no longer receiving reinforcements, and their numbers dwindled. Despite that, they still launched an occasional local attack, an example of which was the taking of Wypolsowo on 22 February. The battalion was then granted a few days of rest.

March started out with a Soviet attack, which was supported by armor. The paratroopers were able to turn it back. The attack on Salowo on 2 March failed, but it was possible to enter the town on 9 March. In addition, Anissowo-Gorodischtsche, which had been lost, was taken back.

On 18 March, the men of Koch's battalion went above the call of duty one more time, when they attacked the enemy-occupied Hill 238 west of Postdnakowo and took it.

On 1 April 1942, M*ajor* Koch was transferred back to Germany. He had been directed to form a new airborne regiment—*Fallschirmjäger-Regiment 5*—from volunteers and veterans from the Campaign in the East.

He told the comrades he left behind that he would ask for all of them: "We will remain together, comrades!"

The remnants of the battalion defended against the Soviet attacks along the main road at Fomino from 14 to 24 April. *Hauptmann* Reinhart had been given acting command of the battalion. Once again, the Red Army men experienced firsthand the determination and grit of the German paratroopers. Lieutenant Colonel Rotkirilow stated the following after he was captured: "If the entire German 1st Airborne Division had opposed us, then we never would have broken through in that sector with an army corps."

On 26 April 1942, the battalion was pulled out of the front and sent by rail back to Germany. There weren't nearly as many on that trains as had started. The comrades who had been killed remained behind at the military cemetery at Schaikowka. Before he left, Schuster visited the cemetery, where he saw the following on a wooden sign: "After immortal feats-of-arms at Narvik, in Holland, at Eben Emael, at Korinth, on Crete and at Leningrad, these men held the encircled airfield at Anissowo-Gorodischtsche in bitter close combat against Soviet divisions."

Two Knight's Cross recipients of the battalion were buried there next to their comrades. During that round of fighting in the Soviet Union, 16 men of the battalion also received the German Cross in Gold.

OBERSTABSARZT DR. NEUMANN

Until the middle of February, the Red Army did not attack very much in the regimental sector. Combat raids and patrols attempted to place the paratroopers in the sector on edge, but there were no major activities. It was only later that the situation again became critical. The partisans blew up the rail facilities at Kossnaki and, a short while later, Soviet battle groups were reported in the Issnoski area. They also broke through along the boundary between the *4. Panzer-Armee* and the *4. Armee.*

Generalmajor Meindl received orders to seal off the enemy forces that had broken through and eliminate them.

Meindl's men succeeded in getting about three-quarters of the way around the Soviet force. It was only in the east that the ring remained open, since Meindl lacked the necessary manpower to close it completely.

The enemy was stopped and defeated in a series of local actions. The main mission—the stopping of the breakthrough—was accomplished. One combat raiding party from Meindl's group also succeeded in breaking through on the road to Gshatsk and establishing contact with the cut-off *20. Panzer-Division.*

A short while later, another Soviet battle group of about two divisions was cut off and decimated.

The next operations concerned the German military hospital at Juchnow, which had been surrounded on three sides by the Red Army. The regimental surgeon, *Oberstabsarzt Dr.* Neumann, proved a master of the situation and was able to save thousands of wounded. Some 2,000 men, whose care and handling had not been safeguarded, were then in his hands. It was impossible to move back along the road to Rosslawl, because the Red Army was blocking it with armor formations; it then appeared grim for the wounded being evacuated. *Dr.* Neumann, who had been forced to become a combatant on Crete and had commanded the forces that took Hill 107, turned to *Generaloberst* von Richthofen, whom he knew from the War in Spain. In a telegram to Richthofen, Neumann explained:

Some 2,000 soldiers in Juchnow are condemned to death, if they cannot be flown out by air transport as soon as possible. They fought with great devotion to duty and placed their lives on the line more than once.

We remain the only ones who can help them, and we can thank them by flying them out of the ring of encirclement that grows tighter with each passing day. If they remain in the pocket, then it is almost certain they will be killed.

Von Richthofen immediately established an aerial bridge. For two days in a row, *Ju 52's* landed one after the other at Juchnow. After some 1,000 men had been saved in that fashion, *Dr.* Neumann organized a large medical convoy, which he personally led back to the rear when the *Bf 109's* of *JG 51 Mölders* were able to sweep the roads clear of the Soviets.

The paratroopers were thus able to carve a narrow channel through the Soviets, through which the last medical transports carrying the wounded were able to roll. While still at Juchnow, *Dr.* Neumann was promoted to the next higher medical grade on 6 February 1942—*Oberfeldarzt.*

NIGHTS ALONG THE MIUS

Fallschirmjäger-Regiment 2 was sent east in November 1941 under *Generalmajor* Sturm. It was employed on the right wing of the Eastern Front, deep in the south. It reached Stalino at the end of November, and the hot spots of its commitments over the next few weeks would be centered around the towns of Woroschilowka, Iwanowka and Petropawlowka.

The men had been sent to support their allies, the Italians. Their command post was located in Woroschilowka. The Italian regiment consisted of two Black Shirt Battalions and a battalion of *Bersaglieri* (mountain troops). It was in that environment that *FJR 2* spent the worst Russian winter for 50 years. There would be no lack of dramatic events!

✠

It was 17 January 1942, when *Oberjäger* Erich Lepkowski reported to his battalion commander. *Major* Pietzonka shook hands with the young noncommissioned officer, who had grown combat hardened at both Korinth and Crete.

"Lepkowski, I want you to relieve the radio team in Woroschilowka and establish a standing patrol there."

"With the Black Shirts, *Herr Major?*" the East Prussian Lepkowski responded, skeptically.

"That's right . . . with the 63rd Black Shirt Battalion. I want to know immediately if something's happening there. Be on your toes, though. The village is about a kilometer in front of our positions."

On his way back to the trench line and bunkers of the *4./FJR 2*, Lepkowski had to take cover several times due to impacting mortar rounds. When he reached the bunker, he was greeted by a glowing red field stove. Bierbaum was standing right next to it. He had pulled his shirt above his head and was pulling lice from it and tossing them on the glowing top, where they burned up, stinking all the while.

"Get ready to go to the Black Shirts!" he told his radio section and squad.

"Shit!" one of the men exclaimed.

They picked up their weapons and equipment and left the bunker, which another squad would inherit. Lepkowski led his men through a small patch of woods, which helped keep the bitterly cold wind somewhat at bay. The snow crunched under their footsteps. Off to the left, a village was burning.

"Over there's the battalion of *Hauptmann* Schirmer," *Obergefreiter* Schmauder said, matter-of-factly. Stock, who was carrying the backpack radio, shoved him to get him going again. They continued to move towards the Italians, undergoing some artillery fire along the way. They finally reached the outskirts of Woroschilowka. They were received there by *Feldwebel* Kohl in an artillery-proof dugout. Kohl seemed relieved to see the men.

Kohl took off with his two radio operators after the sound of fighting had abated somewhat. An hour later, the nightly harassment raid from the Russian Air Force arrived. The aircraft were usually outmoded types that could no longer be employed during the day. They appeared with such regularity, however, that the frontline soldiers had a host of nicknames for them. This time, the biplane dropped two bombs, causing no damage, and disappeared.

Early on the morning of 18 January, however, the Soviets attacked Woroschilowka. Stock, the radio operator, a college student from Hamburg, passed on a report of the attack to the battalion. A short while later, friendly artillery opened fire on the Soviets, who drew back. The local attacks continued through 22 January. Then, however, on 23 January, the Soviets launched a major attack.

When the Soviet attack started, Lepkowski rendered a report to both *Major* Pietzonka and *Hauptmann* Schirmer. The Black Shirts had been relieved by the *Bersaglieris* in the meantime, and this was the first time they had experienced a large-scale Soviet attack. A short while later, the first Italians started to flee. They abandoned their six antitank guns and heavy machine-guns and ran to the rear.

At the same time, the *I./FJR 2* was also attacked. *Major* Pietzonka allowed the enemy to approach to within 100 meters before he gave orders to fire. The enemy attack in the German sector came to a standstill.

When the Soviets started to move directly on the *Bersaglieri* positions, the time had come for Lepkowski to act and participate in the fighting. Stock ran through the first belt of ammunition as he fired a long burst against the assaulting Soviets. The Italians that had remained in their initial positions also began streaming back.

"They'll get us as well shortly . . . we're getting out of here . . . Blow up the radio set, Stock!" Lepkowski ordered.

They fired a last belt through the machine-gun. The Red Army men in the field of fire of the machine-gun dove for cover.

Lepkowski and his section ran to the rear, followed by a hail of Soviet rounds. When Stock suddenly screamed, Lepkowski and Schmauder dove for cover.

"I'll provide covering fire . . . see what's wrong with Stock!"

Schmauder dressed the chest wound of his comrade the best he could, threw him on his back and then took off running, Lepkowski firing all the while. Taking huge strides, they made it back to the German positions. Afterwards, they could no longer explain how they had done it. The main thing: They had made it back!

On Sunday, 25 January, the Italians launched an attack to retake Woroschilowka. Lepkowski's patrol also followed them in the heavy fire. He went first to Hill 331.7 to the German observation post. There he encountered *Leutnant* Schönicker, who informed Lepkowski that the Italians had retaken the village. Lepkowski and his section then went towards the village, only to find Italians already moving past them to the rear. They were pulling back again. The Italian attack had failed, and Lepkowski reported the miserable state of affairs via radio to *Hauptmann* Schirmer.

On 30 January, two platoons from the *II./FJR 2* attacked Woroschilowka. The paratroopers were able to enter the village. The Russians were at an advantage in the house-to-house fighting, however, since they were able to take advantage of every possible hiding space and managed to get off the first round in most engagements. *Leutnant* Kober was killed. Eleven other paratroopers followed him in death. The survivors pulled back.

When it started to thaw a little on 8 February, the command post breathed a collective sigh of relief. With the resulting deep, soupy mud, the front came to a complete standstill on both sides.

It was not until Saturday, 21 February, that the Soviets attacked again, this time at 0300 hours against Hill 292 after artillery preparation. The hill was defended by about 20 paratroopers, who had a few machine-guns in support. Two paratroopers were wounded while defending, but the men held the position. After the enemy pulled back, he left behind 140 dead.

A Soviet patrol on the night of 26 February was turned back. Prisoners stated that there would be a new attack launched against the 2nd Battalion from the northwest. The Russians did, indeed, attack the following morning in thick fog. Initially, however, they only attacked in the sector of the 4th Company. Schmauder saw the enemy first and opened fire. Lepkowski was not a part of the defense. He had taken ill on 2 February and was sent to the battalion infirmary. *Oberjäger* Kuhn led the radio section in his place. Hill 292 was held by *Feldwebel* Piepenburg and his platoon.

When Lepkowski returned to his men, it was quiet again at the front. The men were positioned at Petropawlowka until 6 March. Lepkowski discovered that he had been recommended for the German Cross in Gold by *Major* Pietzonka. For some reason, however, the award was not approved at this time.

Rumors surfaced that all of *FJR 2* was to be pulled out of the line by 16 March. But it was not until 18 March that the regimental reserve was moved by truck to Iwanowka and then on to Orlowo-Stalino. On 23 March, the 1st Battalion arrived in Stalino, where it was loaded on trains. Were they heading home? Many of the men, who were at the end of their rope, mentally, emotionally and physically, secretly hoped that was the case. It truly looked as though they would spend spring in Germany, far from the front and in some homeland garrison.

The train initially moved through Dnjeprpetrowsk and Fastow in the direction of Kiev. When the train continued to move northwest once it had reached Gomel, the logical place for a movement west to Germany, the mood sank. They were not headed in the direction of Germany. On 4 April, the Lithuanian-Russian frontier was reached and, a day later, Easter Sunday, the train cars were at Krasnogwadeisk. Lepkowski showed some gallows humor: "Children, we're being kept by Mother Russia!" The movement to a new area of operations caused a panic in some of the men. A *Gefreiter* from Leipzig tried to commit suicide; he shot himself in the mouth.

The men detrained at Tosno; the regimental command post was established at Lipowik. It was there on 18 April that *Oberfeldwebel* Lepkowski was wounded in the eye by artillery shrapnel.

Instead of going to the field hospital, Lepkowski showed up at the command post on 21 April and was reassigned to the 5th Company, which was commanded by *Oberleutnant* Ewald.

Along the Wolchow River, where the regiment was positioned, the spring thaw had started. Shortly afterwards started what was later to be called the "green hell along the Wolchow". The planned encirclement by the Soviets had failed but, despite that, scapegoats were needed on the German side and *General der Infanterie* von Chappius, the Commanding General of the XXXVIII. *Armee-Korps* and *Generalmajor* Altrichter, the commander of the *58. Infanterie-Division* were relieved. Von Chappius took his own life later that year.

Despite the initially precarious position of the Germans, there were some 180,000 Red Army men in the pocket at Wolchow by then, most of the Soviet 2nd Shock Army of General Vlassov. Ten German divisions had encircled them. The paratroopers had arrived as reinforcements, along with an airborne antitank company, a machine-gun company and the 4th Battalion of the Airborne Assault Regiment.

The wooded and marshy terrain demanded everything of the paratroopers. *Oberfeldwebel* Lepkowski seemed to be the jack-of-all-trades for the company. One night, he advanced into no-man's-land with seven other paratroopers to determine where the Soviets had started their actual main line of resistance. After about 200 meters, they ran into a Soviet patrol. After a short, sharp firefight, the Soviets were forced back.

Over the next few weeks, Lepkowski was always on the go. Every night saw new firefights with the Soviets, who were desperately trying to find a way out of their encirclement.

One night, Lepkowski and his patrol crossed a stinking pool of tepid water on a bridge made from tree trunks. *Gefreiter* Rohloff slipped and fell into the water. Gasping for breath and cursing, he pulled himself out, only to be subjected to the cutting comments of Samkohl, an East Prussian known as a surly type: "Once again it looks like you had to have something extra. Didn't you already take a bath before Christmas?"

There was suppressed laughter, which immediately quieted down when Lepkowski raised his arm. The men immediately disappeared into the thick wall of green and silently became one with the earth. They waited.

A short while later, in the pale moonlight, they saw three Red Army men approaching the bridge. They were overwhelmed and Samkohl, who spoke Russian, interrogated them. They stated there was a collection point barely 300 meters farther on that had weapons and ammunition. Everyone was assembling there for an attempted breakout.

In a single file, they moved in the given direction. The Russians remained behind with one man guarding them. When they covered the last 100 meters by crawling they saw a few field-made huts. In front of them were two guards with a heavy Maxim machine-gun.

An hour later, Lutz's radio section arrived. The *Obergefreiter* established radio contact. Then he turned to Lepkowski. "They're almost ready!" he whispered.

"As soon as the artillery starts, we'll take out the machine-gun," Lepkowski ordered.

When the first few salvoes landed in the enemy camp and gigantic geysers of dirt rushed skyward, they tossed hand grenades at the guard post and took it out of commission.

Artillery shells hammered the Russian camp. All of a sudden, a mighty detonation shook the very heavens. The stockpile of ammunition went up in a garish flame. Of the 120 Russians who were supposed to have been in the camp, none were to be seen.

✠

A few nights later, Lepkowski received orders from *Major* Pietzonka to lead a combat patrol with *Leutnant* Fischer. They headed in the direction of the Russian camp, which had apparently been reoccupied. They took off at midnight. The encountered a strong Russian patrol, drove it back in the direction of the enemy camp and reconnoitered.

The days and nights were spent with similar missions against the surrounded Russians. *Major* Pietzonka again recommended Lepkowski for the German Cross in Gold, but the award seemed cursed. The paperwork was again apparently lost. Lepkowski was promoted for bravery in the face of the enemy, and he pinned on *Oberfeldwebel* rank on 1 April.

The fighting continued, seemingly endlessly. The men of *FJR 2* discovered what it meant to be engaged against an enemy who was familiar with all of the tricks of the trade in this type of terrain.

The short nights started. Swarms of mosquitoes seemed to be everywhere and spread malaria. Despite brutal wars of extermination against the troublemakers, everyone killed seemed to be replaced by tenfold more.

As spring turned to summer, the enemy fought with incredible intensity to escape from the threatened captivity. It turned brutally hot, and one of the paratroopers was heard to say: "Whoever goes to Hell from here better bring along a pair of blankets!"

On 21 June, the 5th Company of *Oberleutnant* Ewald was pulled from the line. The fighting around Wolchow was drawing to a close. It would not be until Monday, 6 July, before the regiment was moved back to the homeland.

That did not signal the end of the fighting in the Soviet Union for all of the paratroopers, however.

WITH *FALLSCHIRMJÄGER-REGIMENT 1* IN THE CENTRAL SECTOR OF THE EASTERN FRONT

After being reconstituted in Germany, *FJR 1* was sent to France in the area of Avignon. The regimental commander, *Generalmajor* Bruno Bräuer, met with *Oberstleutnant* Karl-Lothar Schulz shortly after their arrival there.

Schulz knew that Bräuer had something on his mind. They were about to be deployed again. Perhaps it was to Africa?

"You know, Schulz, there's no one better I can think of to transfer the regiment to. I'm being transferred. I recommended you for command, and the recommendation was accepted. You need to lead it like you led your battalion."

"*Danke, Herr General!*" Schulz replied, smiling broadly.

"Your march orders are for Russia. I would have liked to have taken the regiment there, but my transfer is fixed in cement." He paused a bit, thinking about the command he was about to give up. Then he continued: "How will you structure your regiment?"

"Von der Schulenburg will take the 1st, *Major* Gröschke the 2nd and *Hauptmann* Becker the 3rd. Kerfin will remain my right-hand man."

"I couldn't agree with you more, Schulz. Good luck!"

☩

The new area of operations for *FJR 1* was Smolensk and the rear areas of the central sector of the Eastern front. They were employed against partisans, whose activities seemed to grow daily. They blew up rail lines and bridges and ambushed German supply columns on the way to the front. A hot bed of partisan activity was the area southeast of Smolensk and to both sides of Wjasma. General Below, who was responsible for the partisan forces in that area, had more than 20,000 men just in the woods around Jelnja, east of Smolensk.

☩

When *FJR 1* moved from Vitebsk, where it had been transported by air, towards the east along the main supply route, some of its lead elements turned off too soon and wound up in the woods, which were swarming with partisans. The partisans attacked, and it was only through determined immediate counterattacks that they were turned back. When the men continued on, they ran into a heavily fortified *Organization Todt*[3] camp. The men there were amazed that the paratroopers had made it through after their wrong turn in the woods. Nonetheless, the *OT* men were happy to see those temporary reinforcements.

Divided into small, mobile battle groups, the regiment opened its campaign against the partisans. To help it in combating main strongpoints of the partisans, the regiment had a battalion of *Flak* attached to it, with both heavy and light pieces that could be used in a ground role. In the area round Lake Bakanowskaja they were guided by Finnish scouts, tough, hard men who knew the woods like others knew their backyards.

The regiment scored enormous successes. The combat activities of the partisans in that area dried up. Once the first snow fell, their activities resumed, and the paratroopers again had their hands full. They often had to fight at night, the preferred operating time for the partisans, and often stood in mortal combat against those cunning foes.

General der Flieger von Greim, the future Commander-in-Chief of *Luftflotte 6*, often visited Schulz. He was able to land just about anywhere in his Fieseler *Storch*[4]. The men hit it off, and Greim would frequently talk about the overall situation in the East. He also never forgot to bring long something good for the men.

By December of 1942, the Russian resistance movement in that sector was completely paralyzed. Correspondingly, the regiment was moved to the Orel area, where it was once again employed on the front lines. In the Duchowtschina area it was able to turn back several breakthrough attempts by the Soviets. When a regiment of the *12. Panzer-Division* was encircled there, the paratroopers launched an immediate counterattack. In bitter nighttime fighting, the enemy was defeated at Alexajewska and forced back to his original line of departure, thus relieving the trapped regiment from the armored division.

The following night, as part of its continued attack against the enemy, the regiment succeeded in penetrating into the enemy's main line of resistance. It blew up bunkers and dugouts and eliminated a rear-area artillery firing position, including a battery of "Stalin Organs". During those operations, however, *Hauptmann* Horst Kerfin was killed on 22 January 1943.

---

3. Translator's Note: The *OT* was a paramilitary organization responsible for constructing military-related infrastructure in occupied territories.

4. Translator's Note: The "Stork" was a light utility aircraft capable of landing and taking off in extremely short distances.

When the regiment was pulled out of the line in that area of operations, *Generaloberst* Rudolf Schmidt, the Commander-in-Chief of the *2. Panzer-Armee*, which was employed in the Orel area, wrote *Oberstleutnant* Schulz a handwritten letter of praise, part of which read:

> I extend my thanks and praise to you for the operations of your paratroopers. They sealed off the penetrations of the enemy and eliminated those forces that had broken through. You paratroopers, my dear Schulz, were the salvation of Orel. You saved the *2. Panzer-Armee* from sustaining high casualties.

The regiment went back to the homeland for reconstitution. Once that was completed at Gardelegen, the regiment was then sent to France, initially to the Normandy area. It was then moved farther south and established quarters in the Avignon area.

At the airfield, the paratroopers took part in jump training with the *Me 323*, where they jumped from the aircraft by means of a slide instead of an open door.

The new *1. Fallschirmjäger-Division* was being assembled in that area as part of the *XI. Fallschirm-Korps*. By that date, it was no longer considered necessary to have misleading names for the airborne formations.

✠

What had been going on with the *XI. Fallschirm-Korps*, which had only had the bare bones of a division at its disposal up to that point? Had *General der Flieger* Student succeeded in getting more forces? Had his voice been strong enough to succeed in establishing a true airborne corps with fully equipped formations?

Map of the combat area of the Leningrad and Narwa Front.

The paratrooper regiment returns to Hildesheim (from the left): *Oberfeldwebel* Festerling, *Oberfeldwebel* Schelling, unidentified, *Oberfeldwebel* Reisinger, *Oberfeldwebel* Herter.

Major Koch is greeted in Hildesheim.

Men of the assault regiment in Russia near Schaikowka. An *MG34* is emplaced in the heavy machine-gun role.

The first dead in Russia. The German field cemeteries were quite elaborate given the circumstances. The Russians destroyed all traces of these memorials to fallen comrades.

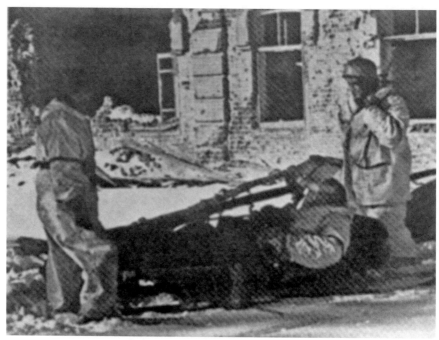

Wounded are evacuated in Russia by sled.

Oberst Schulz presents awards to paratroopers in Russia.

CHAPTER 7

Rebuilding the Airborne Corps

ATTACK PLAN FOR MALTA

It was the spring of 1942 before *General der Flieger* Student could tackle the task of rebuilding his decimated airborne forces. The first formations were returning from the East, where they had been badly battered. Von der Heydte's battalion was sent to the Döberitz-Elsgrund Training Area, where it was redesignated as an instructional battalion. Experiments were conducted with night jumps and descents on wooded areas. Efforts were also undertaken to allow the paratroopers to jump with their main small arm instead of having to retrieve one from a weapons container. Trials were also conducted starting in May of that year with a new generation of gliders such as the *Gotha Go 242*[1].

There was a purpose to all of those efforts. Von der Heydte's battalion was earmarked for the initial assault on Malta, where it would jump into the British antiaircraft defenses six hours before the main body arrived and take them out of commission.

The attack plan for Malta and several other operations had recently been discussed in Rome. *Generalfeldmarschall* Kesselring had summoned Student to Italy's capital. Student saw *Generalmajor* Ramcke there as well, as the latter had been sent to Italy to help train that country's fledgling airborne corps. The airborne division *"Folgore"* and the air-landed division *"Superba"* were being formed and trained in accordance with German doctrinal principles.

Together with Ramcke, Student worked out the first draft for an assault on the island fortress. In theory, command and control of the operation was under the Commander-in-Chief of the Italian forces, Colonel General Cavallero. By involving the Italians in this way, the Germans hoped to secure access to all of the Italian fleet to support the operation.

Ramcke and Student came up with an operation that was broken down into four parts:

Part One: After a surprise landing by gliderborne forces from von der Heydte's battalion on the antiaircraft batteries of Malta and the subsequent elimination of them, the main body of the paratroopers and air-landed forces will arrive as the advance guard under the personal command and control of *General* Student to the south of

---

1. Editor's note: The *Gotha Go 242* was a heavier glider than the *DFS 230* and up to 21 fully equipped troops could be carried in the *Go 242*, compared to 10 in the *DFS 230*. Over 1,500 of the *Go 242* were constructed but they were mostly used to carry supplies and evacuate casualties.

213

La Valetta on the high ground there. It will establish a broad landing zone on the island and attack the airfields and city of La Valetta in rapid, decisive action.

Part Two: Seaborne landings of the main body of the attack forces south of La Valetta, which will advance in conjunction with the airborne forces from that area.

Part Three: In order to deceive the enemy and divert his attention, there will be a deception operation against Marsa Scirocco Bay.

Part Four: The safety of the seaborne transports is the responsibility of the Italian fleet. The securing of the air space is the responsibility of *Luftflotte 2*. The formations of that tactical air force will conduct massed attacks on the airfields and antiaircraft positions on Malta prior to the airborne landings, defeat the enemy's air forces and paralyze the enemy's antiaircraft defenses.

For the operation, 12 of the *Gigant* transporters were available for planning purposes. The *Me 323* had six engines and were able to take a complete *Flak* platoon or 130 fully loaded soldiers in one lift.

The operations received the codename *Unternehmen "Herkules"* and lived up to its name, both in size and ambition. The chances for success were good, better than those on Crete had been. The point of debarkation for the identified forces was Sicily. The *II. Flieger-Korps* of *General der Flieger* was earmarked to support the airborne forces. In addition, the entire Italian Air Force was designated to support the operations. Mussolini also promised the use of all of the Italian Navy, including its capital ships.

The Italian airborne division *"Folgore"* was based in Viterbo and Tarquinia and under the command of General Frattini. Thanks to the help received from Ramcke, he was able to imbue the fledging Italian airborne force with true airborne spirit. The air-landed division *"Superba"* was also a formidable combat formation. In addition, there were four well-equipped Italian infantry divisions to be added to the mix. That was a force that outnumbered the one used to take Crete by many fold.

In the middle of these preparations, a telegram summoned Student to the *Führer* Headquarters in Rastenburg. Student had just arrived, when *Generaloberst* Jeschonnek, the new Chief-of-Staff of the *Luftwaffe*, greeted him with these words: "Listen to me, Student. Tomorrow morning you'll have a hard audience with the *Führer*. *General der Panzertruppe* Crüwell from the *Afrika-Korps* was just here. With regard to the *esprit de corps* of the Italian forces, he had delivered a shattering verdict. As a result, the Malta Operation is in danger, since Hitler doubts the resoluteness and devotion of the Italians more than ever."

Despite that, Student hoped to be able to convince Hitler. In front of a large audience, Student presented the final plans for *"Herkules"* the next day. Hitler listened attentively and asked a number of questions. When Student finished his presentation, Hitler aired his opinion. After the war, Student provided the author with the following:

A torrent of words flowed from Hitler: "The establishment of one of the bridgeheads with the airborne forces has been assured. But I guarantee you the following: When the attack starts, the British ships at Alexandria will sail out and also those from the British fleet at Gibraltar. Then see what the Italians do: When the first radio messages arrive about the approach of the British naval forces, the Italian fleet will run back to its harbors. The warship *and* the transporters with the forces to be landed will both head back. And then you'll be sitting alone with your paratroopers on the island."

Student was prepared for just such an objection. He stated:

Generalfeldmarschall Kesselring has taken that eventuality into consideration. Then the English will experience what happened to them a year before on Crete when Richthofen came in and sank a portion of the Alexandria squadron. It will probably be even worse for the enemy, since Malta is within the effective range of the *Luftwaffe*. The air routes to Malta from Sicily are considerably shorter than those from Greece to Crete were. On the other side, the distances for the British naval groups are twice as far as those to Crete. Malta, *mein Führer*, can thus become the grave of the British Mediterranean Fleet.

Hitler could not make up his mind. With the specter of Crete still haunting him, he vacillated. Malta most certainly should have been a priority in the larger sense, since the British 10th Submarine Fleet operated from the island, which was responsible for sinking so much Axis shipping bound for Africa.

But, in the end, he decided against it, and even Student's assurances that even in the worst case the airborne forces could take the island all by themselves, because Malta had already been badly battered by the German aerial attacks. In the end, Hitler decided: "The attack against Malta will not take place in 1942."

As a result of this decision, Hitler cancelled an operation that would have lent an entirely new face to the overall conduct of the war in the Mediterranean and would have decisively influenced the war in Africa in favor of the Germans.

FALLSCHIRM-BRIGADE RAMCKE IN AFRICA

Student initiated the conversation: "Rommel has taken Tobruk. In order to conduct the attack on Alexandria, he has requested another armored division form the *OKH*,[2] but only the initial elements of the 164th Light Division have arrived." Student paused and then continued: "You, Ramcke, will also be sent to the desert with a combat brigade."

---

2. Translator's Note: *OKH* = *Oberkommando des Heeres* = High Command of the Army.

"Where's the brigade?" Ramcke asked, surprised. As far as he knew there was no such brigade, and he was right. It would be Ramcke's job to form it and then lead it in Africa. Paratrooper elements from all over Europe were tasked to start sending personnel by train to Athens. They were then transported to Crete by air, from which they would then be sent to Tobruk.

Student instructed Ramcke to fly ahead to Athens to start the task of forming the brigade. He was to coordinate with the local *Luftwaffe* commanders to arrange for transportation of his men. Student also provided Ramcke with a list of personnel and potential commanders, which his staff had already prepared for this eventuality. After leaving the corps headquarters, Ramcke looked at the list:

Commander: *Generalmajor* Ramcke
Operations Officer: *Hauptmann* Schacht (later: *Major* Kroh)
Adjutant: *Oberleutnant* Wetter
Brigade Surgeon: *Stabsarzt Dr.* Cohrs
Translator: *Sonderführer* Wesselow
Airborne Artillery Battalion: *Major* Fenski
Airborne Engineer Company: *Oberleutnant* Hasender
1st Battalion: *Major* Kroh (later: *Major* Schwaiger)
2nd Battalion: *Major* von der Heydte
3rd Battalion: *Major* Burckhardt

✠

After making the initial preparations in Greece, Ramcke flew on ahead to Africa. When he landed at the headquarters of the air commander for Africa, it was the end of July. A liaison officer greeted Ramcke with the words: "The *Generalfeldmarschall* will see you tomorrow at 1000 hours."

During the night, Ramcke experienced his first aerial attack on African turf. At 1000 hours on the dot, Ramcke was standing in front of Rommel and reported that he was bringing a brigade with him to Africa. He informed Rommel of the brigade's strength and organization. When he ended his report, Rommel extended his hand: "Thank you, Ramcke! I am happy that you are here. The situation and mission here in Africa is something you already know. Get here with your men as soon as possible. This theater of war is not so simple. It has its own rules."

A short while later, Ramcke was on his way to the front to get oriented before his flight back to Greece the next day. When he returned to the capital, *Major* Kroh and his 1st Battalion were already there. Working closely with the Air Transport Commander for the Mediterranean, all movement issues were quickly and satisfactorily resolved. A few days later, Kroh's battalion was deplaning in Africa and moving towards the front from Tobruk. It was employed on Ruweisat Ridge.

The 2nd Battalion of *Major* von der Heydte followed soon thereafter, with the remaining elements of the brigade coming in quick succession. They took up positions at the Deir el Shein strongpoint and relieved the garrison at Fort Bab el Quattara.

The paratroopers dug in along the edges of the *wadis*, the dry creek beds. The paratroopers had to learn to adjust to the glowing heat of Africa quickly; they were given no time to acclimate. They took up positions in stony foxholes, which were covered with shelter halves as protection against the sun. They held out in temperatures of 55 degrees (131 degrees Fahrenheit), surrounded by myriads of flies and hit by the *Ghibli*, the raging sandstorm that covered everything in extremely fine sand.

As if that weren't enough, the enemy also made their stay uncomfortable: artillery fire, nightly bombing raids and constant enemy patrols. The Malays and Indians, who were positioned across from them, appeared at night, treading softly and carrying dagger-like knives between their teeth. Whoever fell asleep often did not wake up. But after a few of those incidents, the paratroopers knew the score.

To the south of the airborne forces were the Italians of the *"Bologna"* Division. Next to them were the Italian paratroopers of the *"Folgore"* Division. The two Italian divisions had also been sent to support Rommel.

Both of the Italian divisions proved resolute in the defense. The attacks the Commonwealth forces launched at night were always driven back. Despite that, casualties were taken among the Italians and the Germans.

On 30 August, the men of Ramcke's brigade heard the order-of-the-day from Rommel:

Soldiers!

Today, *Panzer-Armee Afrika*, reinforced by new divisions, moves out to attack the enemy and eliminate him once and for all. I expect that every soldier of this army gives his all during these decisive days.

/signed/ Rommel, Commander-in-Chief

An hour after sunrise, Ramcke had his commanders gathered around him. Ramcke briefed them on his concept of the operation for the attack:

We attack as follows: The assembly area and the brigade command post will be at Fort Bab el Quattara. Von der Heydte's battalion will conduct a limited-objective attack along the Ruweisat Ridge to fix the enemy. Hübner's and Burkhardt's battalions will be led by me. They will be formed into *Kampfgruppe Ramcke*, along with the brigade's heavy weapons and two battalions from the *"Folgore"* Division, which are commanded by Lieutenant Colonel Camosso, whom I welcome here.

We will advance to the northeast from Bab el Quattara on the northern point of the entire offensive. We will overrun the enemy, reach a designated line along Dir el Ankar and the northern edge of Deir Munassib, dig in there and hold the position.

In addition to the two *Folgore* battalions, *Major* Boekmann's heavy artillery battalion [*schwere Artillerie-Abteilung 408*] has been attached. The *"Trieste"* Division is attacking to our north. Right to the south of us, the 164th Light will advance. The attack objective is 14 kilometers in front of us at the designated line. We can count on the attack zone to be heavily mined.

The battalion commanders took notes of the salient points. Just 24 hours earlier, *Major* Kroh had transferred command of his battalion to *Hauptman* Schwaiger in order to become the brigade's operations officer. The original operations officer, *Hauptmann* Schacht, had contracted dysentery. The new adjutant was *Oberleutnant* Wetter, who had been transferred in from *Flak-Regiment 135.*

In his *Kübelwagen* [3], which was driven by *Feldwebel* Börner, Ramcke headed for the assembly area that evening. The attack started at 2200 hours. *Oberleutnant* Wagner's company was the first to move out. It was guided through the gap in the minefield that had been created by the engineers. It was quickly followed by the second company.

During the previous two nights, the *Deutsches Afrika-Korps* had moved south, while only deception positions remained in the north. It was Ramcke's mission to keep the deception alive.

Ramcke next had heavy weapons taken through the gap. He wanted to fix the enemy forces in the north through artillery fire and a rapidly executed attack long enough for the motorized elements of the *Afrika-Korps* to encircle the enemy through their outflanking maneuver to the south.

In the pale moonlight, the paratroopers snuck forward, bent over at the waist. The last few squads of Wagner's company and the main body of Knacke's company were still in the minefield gap when the enemy started firing mortars. Those were soon joined by antitank guns and heavy machine-guns.

The German antitank guns that had been brought forward opened fire on the enemy positions, which could be identified by their muzzle flashes. Within a few seconds, there was the ear-deafening roar of battle. The first English dugouts were identified. The individual sections approached the bunkers and knocked them out of commission with demolition charges. When the lead company reached the foothills of the Wadi Deir el Ankbar early in the morning, it had almost reached its objective. At that point, however, the lead elements ran into a previously unidentified minefield. The mines went up with mighty detonations and flung the bodies of the paratroopers through the air.

"Send mine-clearing parties forward!" Ramcke ordered, who, as always, was in the thick of things with his men. He had *Major* Kroh request engineer reinforcements from the *164. Leichte Division,* so that his men could get through the minefield while it was still dark. After daylight, they would be in a shooting gallery.

---

3. Translator's Note: The *Kübelwagen* was the German equivalent of the jeep.

Salvoes of heavy artillery fire started to come at the Germans from the direction of Alam Nayl.

The company commanders ordered their men to dig in while they awaited the arrival of the engineers. When the engineers arrived they were able to clear a lane through the minefield under the protective covering fires of the paratroopers. Hübner's battalion took over the lead and was the first formation to reach Deir el Munassib. It fought uphill and then dug in. Ramcke's men had thus reached their objective for the offensive.

Ramcke then had his men construct deception positions about 200 meters in front of the actual positions. He set up his command post right behind the Italian formations. Mine-clearing parties then cleared paths to and among the positions.

When *Generalfeldmarschall* Rommel appeared on the morning of 2 September, Ramcke showed him the work that had been done on his brigade's positions. Rommel appeared satisfied. He then asked Ramcke: "What do you expect will happen, Ramcke?"

"The enemy will attack soon. He would be ill advised not to, *Herr Feldmarschall.* We have prepared ourselves for his attack. His artillery is already feeling out our positions, meaning they are registering their guns."

"That's what I think too, Ramcke. Keep your eyes peeled. Turn back the enemy. It is important that you stop him here, otherwise the *Afrika-Korps* will be in a tight spot."

Rommel then filled Ramcke in on the fighting in the other sectors over the past few days, before he took his leave of the paratroopers.

An hour before sundown on 3 September 1942, the enemy attacked Ramcke's sector. Ramcke raced to the artillery battalion with his battle staff, messengers and assistant. Once there, *Hauptmann* Wiechmann reported that his guns were ready.

When the enemy appeared close to the front lines, Ramcke ordered the protective fires to be initiated. In the sector of Hübner's battalion, he also attacked with armor. The German antitank guns posted there opened fire. A deadly duel started between the tanks and the guns. When the enemy infantry appeared, machine-guns hammered away all along the front.

The night was filled with the sound of howling artillery shells and the dull thud of detonations. Hits were registered among the enemy forces. The English then showed up again in front of the German lines, this time at a distance of only 200 meters.

A short while later, the sound of close-in fighting could be heard: Hand grenades and pistols, interspersed with bursts of submachine-gun fire.

Ramcke saw danger: "The enemy's penetrated over there . . . Kroh, have Kiebitz's company launch an immediate counterattack."

A few seconds later Kiebitz's men stormed forward. The close-in fighting started anew, and the penetration was sealed off in hand-to-hand combat. The enemy pulled back; those who weren't fast enough or had been wounded were taken prisoner.

A messenger showed up: "*Herr General*, the commander of the 164th has called for help. His command post has been encircled."

"Take an order to *Major* Hübner: Tell him to form an assault detachment of platoon size and launch an immediate counterattack to relieve the command post."

Leutnant Schäfer led the assault detachment that was formed. He was able to push back the enemy and relieve *Generalmajor* Kleemann's command post. *Leutnant* Schäfer did not live to see the fruits of his efforts, however.

By first light on 4 September, the British 132nd Armoured Brigade had been pushed back. In all, the antitank guns and artillery had knocked out 16 British tanks. An addition 80 personnel carriers, prime movers and armored cars were also destroyed, smoking ruins in the desert wasteland.

Rommel showed up at the brigade command post again to express his thanks to Ramcke and his paratroopers. The Italian allies of the *"Folgore"* Division on the right flank had also fought bravely. Both of the battalion commanders, Major Rossi and Captain Carugno, were killed conducting defensive operations.

Over the next few days and weeks, Ramcke's brigade was in the center of the defensive fighting. Making a name for himself during these operations was *Oberleutnant* Tietjen and his airborne combat engineers who never gave up in their willingness to perform their duties and fight. Tietjen's platoon leaders were *Leutnant* Thiemens, *Leutnant* Treue and *Leutnant* Hermann. The company first sergeant was *Hauptfeldwebel* Mross.

A short while after that, the brigade and the *"Folgore"* Division were sent to the southern sector of the front at El Alamein. It was there that they would undergo one of the toughest tests they would face in the African desert.

During the night of 22/23 October 1942, Bernard Montgomery, the new Commander-in-Chief of the British 8th Army, launched an offensive from the El Alamein position. His bomber formations traversed the southern portion of the German front and dropped their deadly cargoes there. The fortifications at Quattara and Ramcke's command post were hit by 250 bombs. Despite that punishment, there were relatively few casualties.

The brigade was alerted. It was ready to defend in its positions, but it turned out that the British actions were only deception measures. The English placed their main effort in the north along the coast. More than 1,000 British tanks rolled forward under the protective cover of the Royal Air Force, which enjoyed local air superiority. When the reports of successful penetrations in the north increased at the beginning of November, all of the officers of the brigade were convinced that they would be sitting in a trap if strong Commonwealth forces broke through to the north.

During one commanders' conference, *Hauptmann* Hübner said what the other officers were thinking: "*Herr General*, we'll simply be policed up by

British prisoner details later on since we are not motorized."

"Entirely possible," Ramcke agreed. "How many vehicles do we have, Kroh? And what can we transport with them?

The available vehicles are just enough to keep the antitank guns and the artillery mobile, *Herr General,*" the operations officer replied.

Ramcke took a compass and placed the point on Bab el Quattara so as to measure distances.

"As far as the coastal road at El Daba, it is 70 kilometers, as the crow flies. To Fuka, it is more than 130 kilometers. By moving all available vehicles in leaps and bounds, we can make the foot march of the brigade somewhat easier."

A few minutes later, a radio message from the field-army headquarters was brought in by the signals officer. Ramcke skimmed it quickly and then turned to his assembled officers.

"We're at that point, gentlemen!" After a short pause, he continued: "It has been directed that the brigade disengage from the enemy this evening and occupy a new defensive position between Duweir el Tarfa and the minefield at Deir el Quata . . . Kroh, make the necessary preparations!"

One of the officers excitedly chimed in: "That means a night foot march of more than 30 kilometers for the brigade, *Herr General!*"

"We will conduct the disengagement in such a manner that the enemy does not notice what's happening. A few patrols will remain behind to deceive the enemy of our departure, keep him busy and act as if there is a completely occupied main line of resistance in front of him. They will then also depart with the trucks that will be provided."

In a night march that will never be forgotten by those paratroopers who participated, the brigade reached its new positions on the morning of 3 November and dug in. That same evening, the brigade received new orders that it was to move again, distance itself from the enemy and occupy new positions at Fuka, some 100 kilometers away on the coast. Without trucks, that would take four long night marches. If the men attempted to move during the day, the enemy air force would certainly see them and attack.

On that 4 November, all of the field army under Rommel's command disengaged from the enemy, in contravention of a *Führer* order.

Within Ramcke's command, *Hauptmann* Straehler-Pohl's battalion was to first to move out on trucks. The men did not head out in the direction of the general retreat, however. Instead, they occupied new positions in accordance with orders received from higher headquarters. Ramcke's men were acting as rearguards for the field army and had to fend for themselves in the desert.

When the brigade's 1st and 2nd Battalions attempted to disengage from the enemy, they were attacked. The antitank guns, which were serving as rearguards for the battalion movements, opened fire at a short distance and knocked out a group of English tanks. The English attack collapsed, and the two battalions were able to continue their movements without enemy interference.

While Fenski's and Hasender's battalions screened the continued march of the brigade, all of the remaining vehicles leapfrogged to the west. Burkhardt's battalion was then employed as a rearguard. When the enemy approached at first light, he was held back by the brigade's antitank guns. Three English armored cars went up in flames, before the English kept a respectable distance.

Any of the enemy tanks that pursued, with the exception of one, which turned away in time, were knocked out. As it turned night on 5 November, however, the antitank guns had to be blown up, because they had run out of ammunition. The antitank personnel were reassigned within the brigade.

Oberleutnant Haseneder and *Hauptmann* Kagerer were captured by the British in their shot-up vehicle just prior to nightfall. *Oberleutnant* Tietjen had been employed during the day on the north of the brigade with his men and an attached antitank gun with a *Kfz. 15* prime mover to act as flank guard. They fought against superior English armored forces the entire day. He was cut off from the main body and, after all of his ammunition had been expended, he and his men entered British captivity. *Leutnant* Tiemens assumed command of Tietjen's company.

During the night of 4–5 November, elements of the brigade ran into an English vehicle column, which also had a few armored vehicles.

During the evening conference, Ramcke gave the order to capture the column. He had the requisite combat raiding parties formed. The groups worked their way forward to the unsuspecting and resting British. At midnight, they all attacked at once.

The enemy was completely surprised and overrun. The enemy soldiers were disarmed and forced out of their vehicles. Then the paratroopers drove off with their intact booty. They picked up the other comrades waiting for them and continued to head west through the desert, guided by a compass. After they had moved some 40 kilometers, Ramcke had the men take a rest.

When the brigade arrived at Fuka on the morning of 7 November and encountered a German reconnaissance battalion there, the reconnaissance commander could barely believe what he saw. Just like everyone else, he had written off Ramcke's brigade as having been cut off, encircled and destroyed or forced to surrender.

A half hour later, the wiry airborne commander entered the command post of *Panzer-Armee Afrika*. Just when Rommel was in the process of writing off the airborne brigade, Ramcke arrived to announce he was very much still alive, indeed.

On 13 November, 1942 Ramcke received the Oak Leaves to the Knight's Cross to the Iron Cross for his operations in North Africa.

While elements of Ramcke's brigade were shipped back to the continental main land, von der Heydte's battalion stayed on—replenished by personnel details from other elements of the brigade—and fought with the *90. Leichte Afrika-Division* as its rearguard. It participated in the entire retreat. On 18 November, it faced New Zealand forces at El Nofilia. The battalion found itself again fighting a foe that had caused it so many casualties during the operations on Crete. For the fighting there, which Field Marshal Montgomery later described as a "sharp engagement", *Major* von der Heydte later received the Italian Bravery Medal in Silver.

Among the forces that were attached to von der Heydte was the brigade's 2nd Engineer Company. As they continued the retreat, however, more and more of the specialists, such as the engineers, were taken away from the battalion and sent back to Germany. They soon gained the impression that Africa had already been written off by the high command as a theater of war. By the time the remaining paratroopers reached the Gabes Position, the battalion had been so battered that most of the men had to be hospitalized or given convalescent leave.

By then, the Allies had also landed in Northwest Africa as part of Operation "Torch". This created a new crisis that once again called for the "firemen" of the airborne corps. It was the reconstituted *Fallschirmjäger-Regiment 5* that would answer that call.

EMPLOYMENT OF *FALLSCHIRMJÄGER-REGIMENT 5* IN TUNISIA

After the Allies had landed in Northwest Africa at Casablanca, Oran and Algiers and started to advance towards Tunisia with the objective of creating a second front in the rear of *Panzer-Armee Afrika*, Hitler ordered *Generalfeldmarschall* Kesselring, who was the overall Commander-in-Chief for the southern theater, to send everything he could to Africa to stabilize the situation.

Oberst Harlinghausen, the air commander for Africa, was among the first to land at the El Aouina airfield at Tunis. After his *He 111* arrived then the first aircraft of *Jagdgeschwader 53* arrived. There were no other German soldiers in Tunisia. The Germans had to try to get as many forces to northwest Africa as possible. If that did not occur in a timely manner, the enemy would be able to march to Tunis without any opposition. That would mean that *Panzer-Armee Afrika* would be in the grips of a vise and its downfall only a matter of time.

Fallschirmjäger-Regiment 5 was earmarked to be the advance guard for the German ground forces headed for Tunisia. The regiment was not at full strength, however. In the summer, its 2nd Battalion had been detached and reassigned to *Brigade Ramcke*. The remaining two battalions were alerted in Normandy, where they had been preparing for the invasion of Malta, and sent by train to Caserta, near Naples. The battalions were commanded by *Hauptmann* Jungwirt and *Hauptmann* Knoche. When the 3rd Battalion arrived in Naples on the evening of 10 November, it received orders for its 10th Company (*Leutnant* Baitinger) to head to the airfield at Naples with an advance party.

Early on the morning of 11 November, that small party flew via Trapani to Tunisia, where it landed at El Aouina. It was subsequently ordered to move through Tunis and screen the road leading into the city from the west.

Leutnant Baitinger executed his orders. To notify this higher command what he had done, he sent Viktor Fink, a medic, back to the airfield. Armed with his submachine-gun, Fink took the streetcar to the airfield and reported to *Oberst* Harlinghausen: "Order executed! Access road to the west screened!"

At about the same time, the paratroopers that had arrived at Caserta were informed of the Allied invasion of Northwest Africa. Elements of *Hauptmann* Langbein's 3rd Company were immediately sent as an advance guard for the regiment to Tunisia. *Hauptmann* Schirmer flew with them. He was with the regimental headquarters and he wanted to oversee the arrival and employment of the paratroopers for the regimental commander when they landed.

During the evening of 11 November, those elements headed for Catania. The next day, they went on to El Aouina. *Oberst* Harlinghausen used the company to safeguard the airfield at La Marsa, which was especially important for the follow-on landings of the incoming German forces.

On 12 November, farther elements arrived: The headquarters of the 1st Battalion, the *10./FJR 5* of *Oberleutnant* Jahn and a third of the *12./FJR 5* of *Hauptmann* Knoche. The paratroopers landed at La Marsa after a stop at Trapani. Thus, a combat-capable force began to be assembled in Tunisia.

Oberst Harlinghausen discussed the situation with the three captains who had arrived and then divided the greater Tunis metropolitan area into a western and a southern security zone. *Hauptmann* Schirmer became responsible for the western zone, while *Hauptmann* Sauer received the southern zone.

The remaining elements of the regiment's 3rd Battalion were flown to Tunisia on 14 and 15 November. The *I./FJR 5* landed on 15 November.

During the morning of 16 November, *Hauptmann* Knoche and *Oberleutnant* Quednow, who spoke fluent French, and *Leutnant* Klein, the acting commander of the attached *14./Infanterie-Regiment 104*, went by a motorcycle-sidecar combination on reconnaissance. They ran into French positions and were taken by the local commander to the commander of the regiment, Colonel Le Couteux, who was in Tebourba.

Calling upon a directive by Marshal Pétain, *Hauptmann* Knoche asked the French commander to evacuate the area along the Medjerda River and allow the establishment of three bridgeheads on the far side, from which the advancing Allies could be turned back, since they had illegally entered Tunisia. *Hauptmann* Knoche wanted to establish the bridgeheads at Djedeida, Tebourba and Medjez el Bab.

Hauptmann Knoche hoped to achieve some room to maneuver for his regiment with this plan. But the French Colonel turned down his request. He referred to orders received by the French high command at Béja. *Hauptmann* Knoche offered to personally go to Béja and speak with General Barré, which he was permitted to do. Béja was reached at high speed and the negotiations with the French staff officers started.

In the end, the French were prepared to give up Tebourba and Djedeida and pull back as far as Medjez el Bab. They did not want to give up Medjez el Bab proper, since it was an important transportation nodal point along the river.

The French were negotiating so stubbornly, since British paratroopers had jumped into the area around Souk el Arba and were attempting to take Béja themselves.

While *Hauptmann* Knoche was negotiating on his own initiative, the *Ju 52's* carrying the regimental headquarters were landing at El Aouina. The regimental commander, *Oberstleutnant* Walther Koch, was in the lead aircraft. Next to him were the regimental surgeon, *Stabsarzt Dr.* Weizel, and the regimental signals officer, *Major* Graubartz.

The aircraft landed without incident, and the *Ju 52's* started back to Italy after the engines were checked. *Oberstleutnant* Koch had the 10th Company of *Hauptmann* Becker head for Djedeida to safeguard the bridge over the Medjeda River there.

Up to this point, no shots had been fired on either side.

On 14 November, *General der Panzertruppen* Walther Nehring also landed in Tunisia. Accompanying him in landing at La Marsa were his operations officer, *Major i.G.* Moll, *Major* Hinkelbein and an aide, *Leutnant* Sell. Nehring had been given responsibility for establishing the *XC. Armee-Korps* in Tunisia and conducting the defensive fight there. *Oberst* Harlinghausen reported to him and briefed him on all of the ongoing measures. Nehring then flew on to Bizerta in order to establish contact with the forces that had been shipped there. Nehring ordered the senior officer present, an *Oberst*, to move all of the forces that had already landed and all of the ones to follow as far forward to the west and southwest as possible.

Nehring then flew back to Sicily on a *Ju 52* after the promised *He 111* did not arrive. He then flew on to Frascati, where he reported to *Generalfeldmarschall* Kesselring and told him what he required, if he hoped to be able to carry out the difficult mission.

The race for Tunis had started and paratroopers would be employed on yet another and different field of battle.

THE OPERATIONS OF *FALLSCHIRM-KORPS-PIONIER-BATAILLON 214*

The corps engineer battalion, commanded by *Major* Witzig, had also been originally earmarked for employment as part of *Brigade Ramcke*. It received orders for deployment in October, and it was supposed to be sent to the El Alamein positions. But the battalion was redirected while it was inbound, with only the 2nd Company eventually linking up with Ramcke's forces. (During the retreat it was also badly battered.)

The engineers were told to await new orders. *Major* Witzig was well aware that things were hot at Alamein but that new dangers had appeared in Northwest Africa. With the Allied landings there, he knew that was most likely the future area of operations for his battalion. When he reported to *Generalfeldmarschall* Kesselring, the theater Commander-in-Chief personally informed him that his battalion was going to Bizerta.

The initial transport for the battalion to Africa left the harbor at Piräus at 0600 hours on Sunday, 15 November, on board a *BV 222* six-engined flying boat. Riding in the aircraft were the battalion headquarters, the signals platoon and the 1st Platoon of the 1st Company. Going with the men were parachutes, equipment and weapons.

After a stopover in Trapani, where the flying boat was refueled, the air movement continued to Bizerta, where it landed without incident.

The next day, the remainder of the 1st Company was carried over to Africa on the same flying boat.

The 3rd and 4th Companies had boarded *Ju 52's* in Italy in the meantime and had also landed at Bizerta. After all the forces had landed, the battalion reorganized. On the next day, two companies headed towards Tabarka, moving via Mateur. The enemy's advance was to be stopped as far west of Tunis as was possible. The 3rd Company of *Oberleutnant* Friedrich remained behind in Bizerta as the battalion reserve.

Attached in support of the battalion was an Army tank company, an Italian antitank company with antitank guns mounted on tracked vehicles, a platoon of 2-centimeter automatic *Flak* and a battery of 10.5-centimeter guns.

When the small battle group arrived in Mateur, it was greeted enthusiastically by the Arabs there. The next morning, 17 November, the group advanced another 18 kilometers west, where it encountered advanced motorized elements of the enemy, who pulled back after the first exchange of fire. The battle group started to pursue and reached Djebel Abiod, where it was engaged by the waiting enemy, who was in fortified positions. It was the headquarters and three companies of the Royal West Kent Regiment, elements of the 138th Royal Artillery Regiment and B Company of the Northhamptonshire Regiment.

When the light armored cars, followed closely by the *Panzer IV's* of the attached tank company, rolled up at Sedjenane around 1430 hours in completely open terrain, they were fired upon by enemy artillery and mortars. Eight German tanks were immobilized. The fighting started, and the 2-centimeter *Flak* took up the fight against the enemy from open positions. Their salvoes registered among the enemy positions, but they soon received direct hits and were lost to the fight.

The engineers from the companies immediately took cover, but they took their first losses in killed and wounded. The engagement was continued until the fall of darkness by the German battle group, which had deployed in the meantime. All of its weapons were employed, and the enemy also suffered heavy losses.

The engagement at Sedjenane signaled the westward limit of advance for the Germans. The paratroopers had been stopped decisively. The objective they had sought—Tabarka, just a few kilometers from the Algerian frontier—could not be taken. The battalion dug in and defended its positions, especially from the "Cactus Woods", which at least offered some cover and concealment. The heavy weapons were pulled back over the next few days and sent to von Broich's *10. Panzer-Division*, which was also being rushed in. Witzig's airborne engineers were also attached to the division command.

After that first engagement, it remained quiet for a few days. An English patrol that surfaced in the middle of the positions of the 1st Company at first light on 20 November was driven back.

The following night, the 1st Company sent out a combat patrol under *Oberleutnant* Hünichen. The objective was Djebel Abiod. The patrol succeeded in the bright moonlight in approaching the outskirts of the village without being noticed by the enemy. When the engineers started to lay pressure-sensitive mines, they were discovered by the enemy and engaged. The patrol took some of the buildings of the village on the outskirts by means of bundled charges and hand grenades; an English artillery piece and four machine-guns were destroyed. Hünichen was wounded in the assault on one of the houses. The patrol had one man killed. *Feldwebel* Wenzel, who had assumed command of the patrol after Hünichen had been wounded, pulled his men back, being able to recover the dead and three of the wounded in the process.

FALLSCHIRMJÄGER-REGIMENT 5: LEUTNANT KEMPA ON THE WAY TO GABES

Leutnant Kempa, a bicycle platoon leader in the *10./FJR 5*, assembled his men early on the morning of 17 November at the La Marsa airfield in Italy and prepared for operations. With their bicycles next to them and in their jump outfits, the men waited on the wet, muddy ground for their platoon leader to come back with orders. No one knew which way they would go. When *Leutnant* Kempa returned from the regimental command post, he was able to satisfy their curiosity: "Men, we're flying south, taking the airfield at Gabes and holding it open for subsequent landings."

"Not just us?" one of the men asked.

"No, the 3rd Company of Kesselring's guard battalion is also coming along."

✠

A short while later, 12 *Ju 52's* headed south. There were 50 paratroopers and 100 men from the guard battalion on board the aircraft.

When the machines attempted to land at Gabes, they were engaged by the airfield antiaircraft defenses. The machines were jolted by hits.

"Abort! Would you finally abort!" *Oberleutnant* Salg, the commander of the guard battalion's soldiers insisted. The pilot relented and gave the signal. All of the *Ju 52's* climbed and headed north. The six aircraft with the paratroopers stayed together. *Hauptmann* Grund, who was to be the airfield commander after it had been taken, turned to Kempa: "What do you recommend, Kempa?"

"We should look for a suitable landing spot nearby, land there and then attempt to chase the French away from the target airfield, *Herr Hauptmann!*"

"Fine . . . let's do it!" Grund instructed the other pilots of the new plan. A short while later, a suitable patch of terrain was found where the aircraft could land. It was about 40 kilometers from Gabes. The aircraft made their approach and landed without incident, except for one. It suffered damage to its landing gear when it set down.

The paratroopers deplaned and, a few minutes later, a patrol was sent in the direction of Gabes. Just before reaching the city on the coastline, the six men were discovered by a French armored-car patrol. The men turned and peddled away, followed by fires from the French vehicles. The men sought cover in a narrow defile, where they hid.

Leutnant Kempa waited in vain for the return of the patrol. He then sent a second patrol out, that one led by *Gefreiter* Kuntze. The seven men also encountered the armored cars, but they were captured and taken to Gabes. The patrol leader told the interrogating French major that the airfield needed to be surrendered. Otherwise, *Stukas* would come and wreak havoc. The French major had the men put in custody.

Early on the morning of 19 November, as the seven men were being led back to an interrogation session, *Ju 52's* raced overhead. Neither the Germans nor the French on the ground knew that the aircraft carried the force with it that had attempted to land there the previous day. Two fighters were with them for air cover. The airfield commander took that as confirmation of what the *Gefreiter* had told him the previous day, and that the *Stukas* would be appearing shortly. He had his personnel mount up immediately, whereupon they abandoned the airfield in wild flight.

The French left the seven paratroopers behind. *Gefreiter* Kuntze was able to find his flare gun, whereupon he fired a flare to indicate that the airfield was clear of the enemy. The *Ju 52's* then landed.

The airfield was taken and secured. When the first U.S. armored vehicles showed up two days later, they were greeted by light airborne artillery, which managed to immobilize them. The two days had been enough time for the Italians to bring in two battalions to reinforce the few paratroops and the company from the guard battalion.

✠

In the meantime, the remaining elements of *FJR 5* were sent in the direction of Medjerda Valley. *Hauptmann* Knoche, who was officially sent back to Medjez el Bab to negotiate with Colonel Couteux, also dispatched his 10th Company (*Oberleutnant* Hoge), half of the 12th Company and half of the attached *14./Infanterie-Regiment 104* (*Leutnant* Klein) towards the same location. The battle group was directed to take the crossings over the Medjerda in the vicinity of the town.

Hauptmann Knoche succeeded in convincing Colonel Couteux to move his regiment, which had been reinforced with artillery and armored vehicles, to the far side of the river. The French colonel insisted on retaining control of the bridge, however.

The next day, 18 November, *Hauptmann* Becker's 9th Company had expanded its area of operations to include the airfield at Djedeida. They cleared the field to the extent that at least German fighters could land there.

During the evening of the same day, the French forces in the Medjez el Bab area started preparing for combat. Their outposts were directly across from the German ones of the 3rd Battalion. Through personal observation, *Hauptmann* Knoche detected the presence of U.S. tanks in the French assembly area that same day. Knoche's force, which were about one kilometer east of Medjez el Bab in positions, consisted of the following elements:

• Headquarters and one-third of the signals platoon of *FJR 5*

• *10./FJR 5* (minus one squad)

• One half of the *12./FJR 5* with heavy machine-guns, 8-centimeter mortars and the Model 1 airborne infantry gun

• One half of the *14./Infanterie-Regiment 104* with five 5-centimeter antitank guns and

• Two *Flak* sections

Hauptmann Knoche ordered preparations for an attack that night. At 0400 hours on 19 November, the individual unit leaders reported they were ready. After *Stukas* dropped bombs at 1130 hours, Knoche ordered his men to attack.

Under the covering fires afforded by their machine-guns, the paratroopers assaulted into the portion of the town east of the river. After some fighting, only the train station was still under French control.

Oberleutnant Bundt then took a combat patrol across the river. It continued along the west bank, avoiding the enemy's machine-gun nests. The patrol received fire from a bunker near the bridge. Two men, *Gefreiter* Seidel and *Gefreiter* Heine, were wounded. With the remaining men he had, Bundt assaulted the bunker. After taking the bunker, he sent the wounded back along with the prisoners he had taken. As the patrol continued its movements, it took fire again and again. *Oberleutnant* Bundt was mortally wounded with a head wound. Only four survivors managed to swim back across the river and return to the battle group.

Towards 1800 hours, the *Stukas* appeared for the second time. Italian reinforcements also appeared, including a platoon of antitank guns. Arriving with the Italians was the regimental commander, *Oberstleutnant* Koch. He brought demolitions with him from Tunis and had 10 combat patrols formed, which were to penetrate into Medjez el Bab during the night, spreading panic and blowing up targets.

The 10 groups started out at midnight. Exactly one hour later, at 0100 hours, the detonations from demolitions, bundled charges and *Teller* mines could all be heard going off at the same time. Fires flared and a depot went up in smoke. The French forces abandoned the town in wild flight and rolled away at first light along the Oued Zarga–Béja road. Medjez el Bab, the "key to Tunis," was in German hands. Led by *Hauptmann* Schirmer, a pursuit group of paratroopers chased after the French as far as Oued Zarga. They received orders there to turn around and return to Medjez el Bab.

That night, the German outposts of the *10./FJR 5* were attacked by a *Spahi*[4] squadron at the *Ferme Smidia* in the northern outskirts of the western part of the town. The mortars in the courtyard of the farm took the attacking light cavalry under fire. Machine-guns joined in, firing long bursts. The enemy was turned back with bloody losses.

The situation stabilized somewhat, even though it was obvious that the handful of defenders there could not hold out for long against the more than 100,000 Allied troops that had landed. Nevertheless, time had been won, and it was time that was used to get the initial elements of the *10. Panzer-Division,* which had been in France for reconstitution purposes, after having been battered on the Eastern Front, to Tunisia. Those elements were capable of holding up the Allied armor for a while.

On 21 November, *Kampfgruppe Schirmer* evacuated the western portion of Medjez el Bab and returned to the east side of the river. Because it was possible for that force to be outflanked by mobile enemy armored formations, Nehring had the entire front pulled back to an area about 30 kilometers southwest of Tunis.

OPERATIONS OF *KOMPANIE SCHUSTER*

Under the acting command of *Leutnant* Schuster, the *1./FJR 5* had landed in Tunis on 21 November. The *Ju 52's* were attacked as they approached to land by both British and U.S. fighter-bombers. A few of the machines taxied in on fire, and the paratroopers had to jump out as the aircraft were still moving. *Leutnant* Schuster, who emerged unscathed, was forced to recall a similar situation at Malemes, when he had to help mountain troopers escape from burning aircraft.

The company was loaded on trucks in the afternoon and driven up and down the streets of Tunis to deceive the enemy, who had a number of spies there.

After a lice-infested night at the Marshal Foch garrison, the 1st Company formed up the following morning. *Hauptmann* Jungwirt, the acting battalion commander, was on the scene to greet them and give them their first set of orders. After that, they rolled out of the French garrison.

The company went to El Kasbate, moving through Abd el Asker, Bin Mcherba and Teli el Kaid. They had to take cover there from an air attack. The movement then continued through Depienne. In the area around Pont du Fahs, the company dug in. The company command post was established in an abandoned French farm.

The days that followed were quiet. A portion of the company was dispatched to go after an English parachute detachment that had landed (see next section). At the end of December, there was a series of combat patrols, which drew the attention of even the regimental headquarters. Among the boldest was the one launched by the battalion trains!

4. Translator's Note: *Spahis* were light cavalry of the French army recruited primarily from the indigenous populations of Algeria, Tunisia and Morocco.

Leutnant Schuster briefed the patrol as follows: "We're going to take the French battery positions behind the hills at El Aroussa tonight. Initially, we'll move forward to the outposts by truck. The outposts are located 10 kilometers from the front, next to a knocked-out tank. From there, the patrol will move by foot. Approximately 35 kilometers have to be covered during the night."

Three hours later, the commander's *Kübelwagen* and a truck loaded with the patrol and demolitions set out. Thirty men went with *Leutnant* Schuster through no-man's-land. They dismounted at the outposts and went on by foot, heavily loaded down. Towards midnight, they reached El Aroussa, where the men were given a brief rest.

"Over there . . . behind the hills . . . is where the road goes . . ." Schuster explained to the men. The enemy has to be in those courtyards that we can see through the olive tree orchards. We'll start our search with the farm on the right. We will form two groups, which will advance to the left and right of me and my messengers and also provide flank guard."

The officer paused for a moment, then continued: "Heilmann, I want you to stay on the road. If vehicles approach, give a blink. Pöhl, your machine-gun section will cover the road. Schmalholz will take the wire cutters."

Schuster left nothing out in his briefing. He gave his orders confidently and without hesitation. When he took off, his four messengers—Koch, Baum, Kuhn and Bauer—followed him. The train's personnel moved out. Heilmann and the three machine gunners remained on the road, as directed. The first fence appeared, and Schmalholz went to work. They went through and then disappeared in an olive tree orchard.

"*Herr Leutnant?*" Baum whispered behind the officer.

"What is it?"

"Light signals from the road."

Leutnant Schuster turned around and saw a vehicle approaching from the west. It suddenly stopped and then moved out wildly, honking its horn. Two rifle rounds cracked in the night. They saw the vehicle slide to a stop.

"Heilmann got him. Danger's past. Let's go, men!"

Then Schuster had an idea. He decided to move on the road, since the enemy would think it was his own.

The paratroopers formed up. Schuster took the lead, his submachine-gun at the ready in his arm. The lieutenant, who had been in the vehicle and was now a German prisoner, also marched along with them. Schuster signaled to Heilmann and his group to rejoin the main body.

When the group was addressed by a guard, the French officer answered with "*Bon ami!*". The guard advanced somewhat, raised his rifle to the sky and fired. He apparently just wanted to warn his comrade. He then threw down his rifle and ran towards the Germans. The paratroopers dragged him into the roadside ditch, and Schuster asked him: "What's going on in the farm there? How many are there?"

"There are 15 and . . ."

At that instant, firing was initiated from the farm.

Schuster ordered the captured French lieutenant to be brought to him. Schuster ordered him to go to the farm and ask his comrades to surrender. Schuster gave a warning: "If they don't, then they'll probably all be killed."

The lieutenant nodded and headed towards the farm. But he had barely advanced five steps when a single rifle round echoed in the night. The lieutenant threw his arms in the air and collapsed to the ground, mortally wounded.

Then all hell broke out. The French fired with 7.7-centimeter cannon from out of the farm's courtyard and a few machine-guns rattled away, sending a stream of fire into the night.

Leutnant Schuster fired a signal flare. In its light, he could make out two vehicles and a prime mover next to the farmhouse under the trees.

"Set the vehicles on fire," he ordered. "That will give us some light."

Rounds poured into the vehicles. A short while later, there was an explosion, and the burning fuel turned night into day. A few seconds later, the second vehicle was also burning.

The paratroopers advanced, meter by meter. When they had approached close enough, they flung hand grenades through the shattered windows of the farm.

"Attack the house. Machine-guns: Give covering fire!"

Schuster stormed ahead. *Oberjäger* Schulze followed him. Suddenly, there was a howling in front of them. "Take cover!" someone yelled. They jumped into a shallow ditch. Not a moment too soon, either, because an impacting artillery shell tore big chunks of masonry out of the walls of the building they were next to. That was just the prelude. From a flanking hill on the right, a British battery started firing. The artillery fired on that portion of the farm that was still occupied by the French. The British probably thought it had fallen to the Germans.

The farm was fired on for half an hour. When the artillery ceased firing, everything that had been under its murderous impact had been wiped out. Schuster entered the building and found 24 dead French soldiers. The Germans took the automatic weapons with them and destroyed the French guns.

That patrol was followed by more, equally audacious ones. The 1st Company became known at the patrol company. When British paratroopers jumped in one night, Schuster alerted all of his platoons. The enemy was quickly attacked and taken prisoner.

During the early-morning hours of 10 January 1943, the company moved along a line running from the Bu Arada–Medjez el Bab road to the foot of Hill 311. The following morning, Schuster summoned his platoon leaders and his headquarters section leader.

He announced: "In half an hour, I'm taking vehicles and motorcycles to reconnoiter in the direction of Bou Arada. *Leutnant* Löbmann, *Oberfeldwebel* Krassek and *Feldwebel* Kurze will take the lead. Stahnke is my driver and

Gietmann my messenger. In addition, we'll take a machine-gun section."

Schuster informed *Leutnant* Flemming, the platoon leader of the 3rd Platoon, who had not been given a direct mission, to follow the patrol in half an hour.

Shortly after the men had departed, a telephone call was received from the regiment indicating that Schuster had been promoted to *Oberleutnant.*

The reconnaissance proceeded rapidly. Positions were identified on Hill 305. From there, the men went to Hill 306. It was there that they realized for the first time that the hill of Djebel Rihane, just across the way from them, was occupied by the enemy. They started receiving machine-gun fire. Then, a short while later, enemy tanks appeared, which were rolling towards them from the flank.

"Gietmann, determine the number of tanks and then report what's going on to Flemming!" Schuster ordered his messenger. Schuster left the high ground. He wanted Flemming to stop the British advance and to do that, he needed to buy Flemming time. Gietmann spied down from the hill on the moving tanks.

"Eight tanks, *Herr Leutnant!*" Gietmann reported aloud, while Schuster was still in hearing range. Then Gietmann counted another 4. In the end it was a total of 18, an entire company. Schuster was long gone by then, however.

Gietmann headed back toward Flemming's location. Gietmann knew where the tanks were headed, and that was where Schuster was in his improvised blocking position. Gietmann ran as fast as he could to carry out his mission.

An hour later, Gietmann reached Flemming's position. He reported what was happening.

"I hope the commander can make it. He should have been back by now." Flemming said.

The sound of fighting could suddenly be heard. Tank main guns were firing. Flemming's platoon was hit by the tanks and forced back. One of the outposts reported that he thought he had seen *Leutnant* Schuster captured by the enemy. When the word reached the regiment that Schuster had been captured, *Oberstleutnant* Koch had fly bills scattered over the English positions:

> Release *Oberleutnant* Schuster free immediately, in exchange for an
> officer. If he is not released by 1900 hours, a *Stuka* wing will bomb
> your positions at Bou Arada.

But the English did not have Schuster. It was not until the 1st Company finally succeeded in blunting the English armor attack and turning it back that the paratroopers were able to move forward and look for wounded in no-man's-land. That was where they found him; he was dead.

Schuster's remains were taken to the military cemetery at La Mornaghia along with the other paratroopers who had fallen and were buried there on 13 January 1943. Eulogies were given at the grave site for him and the other 12 fallen paratroopers by *Hauptmann* Jungwirth, *Hauptmann* Knoche and *Oberstleutnant* Koch. *Oberleutnant* Kleinfeld was given command of the orphaned company.

OPERATIONS BETWEEN MEDJEZ EL BAB AND THE "CACTUS FARM"
On 26 November, *Oberstleutnant* Koch issued orders to start withdrawing from Medjez el Bab, because there was a danger that the paratroopers could be outflanked from the south. Koch took his regiment to the area west of Massicault, where new positions were occupied on both sides of the road. Koch personally inspected every foxhole over the next few days. When Koch encountered an unshaven *Oberjäger* Karlinger one day, he dressed him down: "So that's how you want God to see you, Karlinger, if you happen to be killed here?" The *Oberjäger* started shaving so rapidly that he cut himself in several places. Over the days that followed, it was quiet. Because there continued to be danger in the Djedeida-Tebourba area, Nehring ordered one of the tank battalions of the *10. Panzer-Division* that had arrived in the meantime to be inserted into the line north of Tebourba.

When some 1,000 British paratroopers under the command of Major Frost jumped at the airfields of Pont du Fahs, Depienne and Oudna, with orders to take them by surprise, the German paratroopers were alerted.

Early on the morning of 30 November, elements of the 1st and 10th Companies, as well as an armored car platoon under the command of *Feldwebel* Hämmerlein, were sent to eliminate the enemy at Depienne. The intent was to bypass the airfield on the left and then swing around, attacking north. *Hauptmann* Jungwirt was to attack frontally with the rest of his 1st Battalion.

Hämmerlein's men took the lead in front of the 10th Company (*Oberleutnant* Jahn). The lead armored vehicle was knocked out and its commander killed. The paratroopers, who had mounted up on the vehicles, dismounted and advanced on both sides of the road, covered by the remaining armored vehicles. As they closed with the enemy, *Oberleutnant* Jahn ordered the men to attack: "Everybody up . . . Charge!"

The men jumped up and ran hunched over towards the enemy. With weapons at the hip, they fired while running at the muzzle flashes they could identify. After firing a burst from his submachine-gun, Jahn was hit in the head and collapsed to the ground, badly wounded. His enlisted orderly, *Obergefreiter* Oswald, crawled over to him and saw that he had been shot in the right temple. Three minutes later, he was dead.

That signaled the start of the first engagement ever between British and German paratroopers. The "Red Devils" were fighting the "Green Revils"[5]. English mortars lobbed rounds at the advancing Germans.

Major Frost and his men were able to turn back the first German assault. When the Germans attacked a second time, they were forced back a bit.

---

5. The British paratroopers were called the "Red Devils" because of their distinctive red berets and the Germans the "Green Devils" because of their green-colored jump smocks.

The third attack, launched on 1 December, inflicted heavy casualties on the British. In a bit of luck for the English, *Bf 109's* appeared over the battlefield during the decisive phase of the attack. Mistaking the forces, they engaged the Germans and knocked out two of the armored cars.

A group of some 70 British paratroopers were able to escape the area around Depienne and move to a farm 5 kilometers south of El Bathan. An Arab reported the group to *Kampfgruppe Knoche.* Knoche recognized the danger those paratroopers posed to his own forces and immediately initiated countermeasures.

Leutnant Johann Ismer volunteered to lead a combat patrol. Ismer was both the battalion adjutant and Knoche's personal friend. Ismer wanted to wrest the position from the British. Late in the evening of 1 December, Ismer and his patrolled worked their way to within 20 meters of the enemy strongpoint. But they were then identified, and the English opened up with murderous fire. One of the first to be killed was Ismer, with a round to the head.

Despite that, the patrol was able to advance. As darkness fell, Major Frost pulled back with his surviving men in the direction of Massicault. He had lost 150 men so far, either killed or wounded.

The fighting between the German and British paratroopers lasted until the next day. *Leutnant* Schuster, a platoon leader, was able to take an officer and two enlisted personnel prisoner. The officer was most likely Lieutenant Charteris, Frost's signals officer. According to British accounts: "Lieutenant Charteris and his men were ambushed and killed."

That account is incorrect. In actual fact, *Leutnant* Schuster, along with *Oberjäger* Koch and *Oberjäger* Bauer, captured the men while on patrol. On 4 December, they were taken with the other prisoners to Tunis and placed on an aircraft that was to take them to Berlin for interrogation. The Germans wanted to learn more about British parachute and air-landed forces, and the capture of these men was the first opportunity to interrogate personnel firsthand.

They never arrived in Germany, however. Apparently, the transport aircraft was shot down. The losses of several *Ju 52's* were reported that day.

In the end, only a small portion of the British paratrooper forces that had participated in the operations were able to make it back to their own lines.

PARATROOPERS IN THE FIGHTING AROUND TEBOURBA

When *Major* Oskar Berger from the German Army High Command arrived in Tunis at the end of November in order to get a firsthand impression of the situation in Tunisia for the Army's General Staff, he was given an unvarnished presentation of the facts by the headquarters of the *XC. Armee-Korps.* Berger promised to do everything he could to get the thoroughly justified requests of Nehring fulfilled.

The Commander-in-Chief South, *Generalfeldmarschall* Kesselring, also showed up at the corps command posts. Nehring briefed him as follows:

The shallow front from Bizerta to Tunis cannot be held over the long haul with the present forces against the expected enemy. The enemy will attempt to break through between Bizerta and Tunis. In contrast, an expanded bridgehead in Tunisia can be held for a limited period. That is also doubtful over time, however, if forces are not brought in soon to give depth to the bridgehead.

By the end of November, a few new forces were introduced to Tunisia. On 30 November, Nehring issued orders for attacking Tebourba. He intended to have *FJR 5* moved through El Bathan to employ it against the rear of the enemy positioned in the greater Tebourba area so as to encircle the enemy forces. In addition, the regiment was to relieve a paratrooper company and an airborne engineer platoon that had been encircled there.

All available forces were directed to attack from the north and northeast. These included *Panzer-Regiment 7* of the *10. Panzer-Division, Panzerjäger-Abteilung 90* and a *Tiger* company under the command of *Hauptmann* Nolde. Only 30 German soldiers remained behind in all of Tunis.

The Commonwealth and American forces, for their part, were in a race to see who could get to Tunis first.

On the first day of fighting, on 1 December, the Germans made good progress. The 2nd of December saw the high point of the battle. The *10. Panzer-Division* succeeded in defeating Combat Command B and the 11th Armoured Brigade.

As for the paratroopers, they had gone into their assembly areas on 30 November. To deceive the enemy, the regiment initially advanced along both sides of the road to Medjez el Bab. Koch intended to swing north towards El Bathan during the night of 30 November/1 December.

When *Oberstleutnant* Koch climbed aboard an armored car on 30 November to reconnoiter in front of the marching paratroopers, one of the men said: "We'll never see him again. He'll be snapped up by the Tommies!"

But the man was proven wrong. He returned after 20 minutes. His armored car was crowded with captured British soldiers. Koch had simply driven into an English outpost, selected his prisoners and returned with them!

One of the prisoners was wounded. He had a piece of artillery shrapnel in his skull. Despite all of the best efforts of the regimental surgeon, *Stabsarzt Dr.* Nödl, to get it out, he was unable to remove it with the instruments at his disposal. In the end, he used a pair of pliers from the tool box of an 8.8-centimeter *Flak* to remove the offending piece of metal! The shrapnel was given to the soldier as a souvenir on his way to the field hospital.

The German paratroopers were facing infantry form the Derbyshire Yeomanry of the 78th Infantry Division. In the area of Fourna, the *III./FJR 5* turned to the north. To the right of the road at Bjord Frenndj, the 2nd Platoon of the 10th Company occupied a large vineyard. *Feldwebel* Engelmann pointed to one of the huge concrete drums, from which a stream of wine, as thick as a man's arm, was shooting out.

"Help yourselves, comrades! The wine is good!"

A hit from an English antitank gun had "ventilated" the container. After enjoying the liquid refreshment, the company was ordered to leave behind all of its heavy equipment and establish contact with the encircled engineer platoon, which had carried out a special mission at El Bathan on the previous day behind enemy lines. The engineers had been instructed to take a bridge four kilometers west of El Bathan and establish a blocking position.

While elements of the *III./FJR 5* still advanced along the road to Medjez el Bab, the main body of the regiment had started swinging towards El Bathan. The closer the paratroopers approached El Bathan on the morning of 1 December, the more the fires against them intensified. Jungwirt's, Schirmer's and Knoche's battalions were able to advance together for the first time.

Leading the 12th Company was *Leutnant* Kautz with the men of his platoon. When they saw muzzle flashes in front of them, they took a detour over a pothole-filled road and found themselves a short while later in the rear of the village. Cork and olive trees concealed the route of the advance towards the headquarters of the U.S. battle group, which the young officer had received as his objective.

Suddenly, the sound of aircraft engines droned overhead. Nine *Stukas*, covered by two *Bf 109's*, raced towards the enemy positions, dove on identified targets and dropped their bombs. Mushroom clouds from the detonations rose above Tebourba and El Bathan. A U.S. ammunition depot in Tebourba went up with a shattering blast.

Leutnant Kautz and his men continued on, but their trucks got stuck in a mud-filled depression a short while later. They dismounted, pushed the vehicles free and then rolled onward to an olive tree orchard, where the continued advance was carried out on foot.

The paratroopers advanced by bounds. They reached a farm, took it and went from house to house in search of the U.S. headquarters. Suddenly, they saw it. Behind the men, however, four enemy tanks rolled out of an alleyway and took them under fire.

Kautz ordered his men to attack. Paratroopers Bohley and Vogel went down when a tank round exploded barely 3 meters from them. *Leutnant* Kautz was felled a few seconds later as well. The other men continued to run, firing from the hip and reached the buildings of the U.S. headquarters. Hand grenades flew through the windows. After they detonated, the men rushed the buildings.

In man-to-man fighting, all of El Bathan was captured by the paratroopers. Only one enemy battery continued to fire at the west end of the village. Four German tanks approached and eliminated it. Then six Churchill tanks appeared. Three of them were knocked out; the remaining tanks turned and disappeared.

English and American headquarters vehicles rolled across the road to the southwest. Armored vehicles, artillery pieces and signals vehicles followed in a dense mass. The *12./FJR 5* of *Oberleutnant* Wöhler pursued them.

They raced through Medjerda Valley, at whose edges the knocked-out and abandoned vehicles of the enemy were scattered about. They got as far as the two hill masses of Djebel Lanserine and Djebel Bou Aoukaz, where the enemy forces positioned there took them under fire.

Late in the afternoon of 4 December, the paratroopers assaulted the leading hill mass. The German tanks preceded them and eliminated the machine-gun nests. The paratroopers of the regiment and the airborne engineers under Witzig, as well as men form Barenthin's regiment, assaulted the high ground and drove out the enemy.

What had happened to *Feldwebel* Arent's airborne engineer platoon, however?

ARENT'S ENGINEERS AT EL BATHAN

On 30 November, *Oberstleutnant* Koch had summoned *Feldwebel* Arent to him: "Arent, you need to establish contact with Barenthin's regiment. Two companies of his regiment have been encircled in Tebourba. As soon as you have established contact with him, block the connecting road between Medjez el Bab and Mateur with your platoon."

Leading his platoon, Arent broke through the remaining rear-area outposts of the British that same evening. Using hand grenades and demolitions, the platoon of 50 men fought its way through to El Bathan. When it had reached the important bridge 4 kilometers west of El Bathan, Arent had machine-guns take up positions to the left and the right of the bridge. The bridge was then mined with the demolitions that had been brought along.

When the first English truck convoy from Medjez el Bab came rolling up, it discovered the area had become a minefield. The first vehicle rolled over the bridge and ran over two *Teller* mines. It flew into the air with a mighty blast. The second vehicle tried to get around the first one and also drove upon a mine. That sealed the bridge for good, and the supply columns of both the British 11th Armoured Brigade and the U.S. 1st Armored Division were stopped.

During that same night, the enemy attempted to take back the bridge with infantry forces that had been brought up. Arent's men gave the enemy a bloody nose. When the English crossed over the Medjerda during the night of 1–2 December, in an effort to get Arent's men in a pincers, the noncommissioned officer and 10 men attacked the enemy force at the moment it was trying to cross the river and threw it back with hand grenades. The situation soon became precarious, however, since more and more Commonwealth forces were showing up. Peter Arent breathed a sigh of relief just after noon on 2 December when men of the *10./FJR 5* appeared and reinforced his platoon. *Feldwebel* Engelmann had reached his engineer comrades in the nick of time.

A short while later, the paratroopers watched as an English bomber force of about 30 machines flew directly along the road from Medjez el Bab to Tebourba and dropped their deadly payloads with precision on the American armored formation that were pulling back there. A supply column was also bombed and destroyed.

Two paratroopers took the 35 prisoners that Arent's men had taken back to German lines. During the afternoon of the next day, when the two platoons discovered that the battle had ended, they pulled back towards the German positions. The engineer platoon remained on the high ground at Khoumet el Diab. When it began to move out again that evening, it started to receive fire. Artillery began to fall, and the sound of small-arms fire could be heard between impacting shells. Peter Arent, who had seen so much in so little time, suddenly fell face forward. His men raced to him, but it was already too late. He had been hit in the head.

That same day, radio traffic was received that stated he had been awarded the Knight's Cross. *Oberstleutnant* Koch placed the high award on the casket of his fallen leader, when he was buried at the military cemetery at La Mornaghia.

✠

The Battle for Tebourba was over. In the official English history of the conflict, the following was laconically noted concerning it: "The Germans won the race for Tunis."

AT THE "CACTUS FARM"
During the farther course of the fighting that lasted another six months in Tunisia, German paratroopers were always committed in the thick of things. At Hill 107, all three battalions of Koch's regiment were committed one after the other. In the "Blue Mountains" of Bou Arada, they experienced dramatic fighting. During *Operation "Ochsenkopf"*[6], they formed the southern attack group along with the *10. Panzer-Division*. It would go well beyond the scope of this book if all of the individual engagements of the paratroopers in the sands of North Africa were discussed. Just one action will be cited here at the end that is intended to be illustrative of all of the others, since it shows that a small group of paratroopers in good terrain were in a very good position to inflict heavy losses of the enemy and fix him for a long time.

✠

While the airborne engineers of *Major* Witzig dug in on Djebel Achkel, a platoon from the *4./JRHG* of *Oberfeldwebel* Heinrich Schäfer defended farther south on Hill 107. The 48 men of the platoon had established themselves on a contributory ridgeline of that hill mass, which overlooked and controlled the Medjez el Bab–Bou Arada fork in the road, and was dubbed the "Cactus Farm."

During the first few weeks of holding that position, the men thought they were in a "sanitarium". After the failed paratrooper attack on 20 April in the direction of Djebel Djaffa and Medjez el Bab and the subsequent withdrawal,

---

6. Translator's Note: "Ox Head", the last major German offensive in Africa.

the enemy pressed hard on the Germans' heels. He attempted to take Hill 107 several times by storm. When he was unable to do that, he went around the hill, assaulted it from the east and took the surrounding hills, with the exception of the "Cactus Farm".

On the evening of 28 April, the English assaulted the "Cactus Farm" directly for the first time. The attack was preceded by a massed artillery preparation, followed by a ground assault by four companies.

"Sight in the mortars for the shortest possible distance," Schäfer barked, when he saw the English come into sight. Schäfer did not give the order to fire until the closest English group had approached to within 50 meters. The machine-guns rattled and five mortars started lobbing rounds. The impacting 8-centimeter mortar rounds ripped the rearward attack groups right off their feet.

The lead English company almost got as far as the German lines. It ran into the wire obstacles and the trip mines there, which Schäfer had emplaced. *Teller* mines detonated and bundled charges went off. The enemy attack came to a standstill, and the survivors were forced to pull back.

The English attacked again the following morning, this time with 15 armored vehicles. Suddenly, German armor came to the rescue in the form of nine *Tigers*. The heavy tanks knocked out a number of enemy vehicles, but they also lost two of their own to track and transmission problems. The *Tigers* pulled back for some reason, and the remaining enemy tanks were able to reach the crest of the hill, where their machine-guns and main guns fired without interruption. Schäfer personally attacked one of the tanks with a Molotov Cocktail and put it out of action. The remaining paratroopers also jumped up and attacked with Molotov Cocktails and bundled charges. The airborne soldiers were able to take out six of the enemy tanks that way.

On the afternoon of 29 April, 30 bombers approached the "Cactus Farm" and bombed the entire plateau. They were followed by fighter-bombers, which strafed anything that moved. Vehicles from the 4th Company, which had been parked in and around vegetation for concealment, were also hit and destroyed.

All that was followed by the third direct assault on the "Cactus Farm." Close-in fighting ensued. The enemy was pushed back by the individual sections. An English soldier taken prisoner later said: "It was hell! There must have been at least 500 bloody, damn paras up there. They didn't give us a chance to reach their damned positions at all!"[7]

The enemy attempted again at first light on 30 April. The three tanks that participated in the attack were immobilized by German artillery that Schäfer had requested.

That afternoon saw the most intense attack up to that point. Tanks ascended the hill from three sides and overran the strongpoint. One after the other, however, they were taken out with *Teller* mines, bundled charges and shaped charges.

---

7. Translator's Note: Reverse-translated from the German without access to the original source.

In the meantime, Schäfer had also received the company headquarters section as a reinforcement, and he went with it to attack three of the tanks that had reached the top, destroying all of them. By the time evening fell, there were an additional 14 enemy tanks scattered on the hilltop.

That evening, the battalion adjutant, *Leutnant* Endlich, arrived and informed Schäfer that he needed to hold out one more day to screen the withdrawal movements.

When the English demanded the platoon's surrender, and the platoon refused, they attacked with an entire regiment, supported by tanks. The final protective fires of the German artillery stopped that attack as well. At 1400 hours on 30 April, Schäfer was asked to surrender one more time. But Schäfer did not bother to respond. He continued to fight until he received orders from the regiment at 1800 hours to pull back to his battalion. Thanks to the resoluteness of Schäfer's small element, the regiment had been able to reach a new blocking position. *Leutnant* Endlich accompanied the group back. On the plateau, he had counted 37 knocked-out and destroyed English tanks. When the adjutant rendered his report of what had happened to the regimental commander, Koch responded: "That's the Knight's Cross for Schäfer!"

✠

The fighting in Tunisia ended on 12 May 1943. The majority of the paratroopers there, along with their comrades from other Army formations and the *Luftwaffe*, went into captivity.

On 8 August 1944, *Oberfeldwebel* Heinrich Schäfer was presented the Knight's Cross in a POW camp in Harne, Texas, by the camp commander, a colonel. It had been sent to him by the Red Cross.

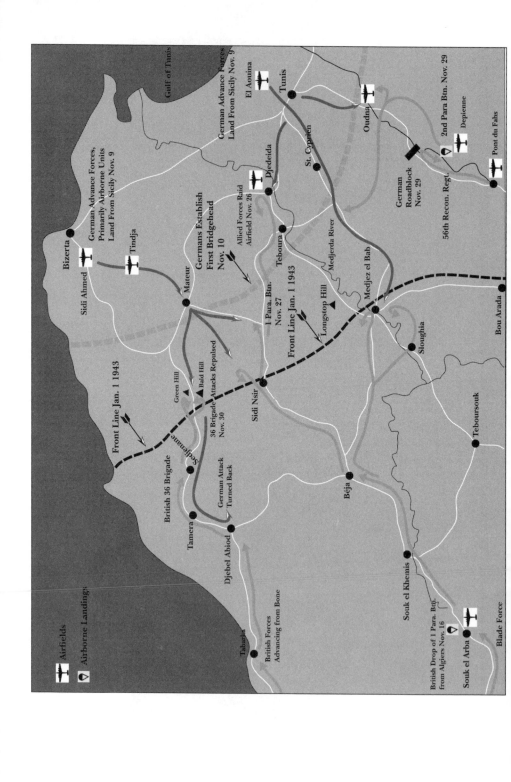

At the location of *Brigade Ramcke* in North Africa. *Generalfeldmarschall* Rommel talks to a captured New Zealand officer. *Major* Burckhardt is to the right of the captured officer.

A paratrooper in a shallow slit trench on the Ruweisat Ridge.

Stoßtruppe Arent in Tunisia (Arent is third from the left).

Peter Arent, who blocked the bridge at El Bathan.

Feldwebel Zimmermann of *Fallschirmjäger-Regiment 5*. As a medic, he saved many a man from enemy fire.

Men of *Fallschirmjäger-Regiment 5*:
Gerhard Schirmer.

Wilhelm Knoche

Hans Jungwirth

Heinrich Schäfer

Defensive position in Tunisia.

Tiger I in an assembly area near Tebourba.

The advance on Kairouan in Tunisia.

CHAPTER 8

Sicily and Italy

INTERLUDE

While *FJR 5* was conducting its bitter fighting in North Africa, the *7. Flieger-Division* was redesignated as the *1. Fallschirmjäger-Division* at the end of November 1942. At the end of January, a second division started to be formed from personnel levies of different formations. The commander of the *2. Fallschirmjäger-Division* was *Generalleutnant* Ramcke. The official date of activation, based on orders form the German Armed Forces High Command, was 13 February. The cadre base of the new division was Ramcke's old brigade. In addition, the division received the 4th Battalion from the former Airborne Assault Regiment, the test battalion of the *XI. Flieger-Korps,* the 100th Special-Purpose *Luftwaffe* Battalion and *Fallschirmjäger-Regiment 2.* The division was formed in the Bretagne region of France and the division headquarters was located in Vannes and Auray.

After Ramcke's division was finished with its activation, the *XI. Flieger-Korps* had two complete airborne divisions available for the first time. At the end of June 1943, the German Armed Forces High Command designated the corps as its operational reserve. The corps headquarters was billeted in Nimes in France.

With a force of some 30,000 men, the airborne corps offered the high command its largest mobile reserve.

The question then arose how to employ the corps. On 1 June, *Generalfeldmarschall* von Rundstedt proposed that in case of an Allied landing along the Iberian Peninsula, the corps should be employed against the airheads and airfields of the Allied forces.

Similar recommendations followed on 23 June. This time it concerned countering any Allied invasion along the Mediterranean coast of France. All of those planning measures came to naught, when the Allies landed on Sicily on 9/10 July. The *XI. Flieger-Korps* was immediately alerted. *General der Flieger* Student recommended having the bulk of his two divisions jump into the middle of the Allied drop zones and landing zones to defeat the enemy from the inside. Student's recommendation, which might have succeeded, was turned down as being too bold a move. The high command vacillated and all of 10 July was spent with the two airborne divisions remaining on alert status in France. The old airborne saying that he who strikes first strikes best was not followed.

GERMAN PARATROOPERS ON SICILY

It was not until noon on 11 July that Student received orders to move the *1. Fallschirmjäger-Division* to Italy that afternoon. *Generalleutnant* Richard Heidrich, the division commander, flew with his battle staff to the headquarters of the Commander-in-Chief South at Frascati, near Rome.

A short while later, *Oberstleutnant* Heilmann's *FJR 3* started out from Avignon and Tarascon for Italy. The second lift consisted of the airborne machine-gun battalion and the division's airborne engineers. The third lift was *Oberst* Walther's *FJR 4* and the division's antitank battalion. The final lift was composed of *FJR 1* and the airborne artillery battalion.

When *FJR 3* approached the airfield at Rome to land, *Generalleutnant* Heidrich was already there. He greeted *Oberst* Heilmann with a powerful hand shake: "Good to see you, Heilmann. Despite the delay, I still think it's possible to throw the enemy back into the sea."

Heidrich then turned to the commander of the signals company, who had just landed with his men, and briefed him on the necessity of establishing a command and control apparatus on Sicily in the shortest time possible.

On the morning of 12 July, as the paratroopers of *FJR 3* were in the process of loading their weapons and equipment on the *He 111's*, an advance party was already flying to the island. It consisted of *Hauptmann* Stangenberg, an officer on the divisional staff, *Oberst i.G.* Beelitz, the operations officer at the headquarters of the Commander-in-Chief South, and *Hauptmann* Specht, the division's logistics officer.

While that *He 111* flew directly to Sicily, the *He 111's* of the paratroopers had to make an intermediate stop at Pompligiano near Naples for refueling. The refueling mission there was not without its problems. The day before, the airfield had been bombed and transformed into a wasteland. The refueling was delayed by hours and the regiment was unable to continue its flight to Sicily until the afternoon.

It was exactly 1815 hours, when the first jump horns sounded in the aircraft. *Oberstleutnant* Heilmann leapt out of the aircraft with determination and soon more than 1,400 parachutes could be seen deployed over the broad wheat fields at Catania. The regiment landed without enemy interference to the south of a line running from Stazione di Passo to Martino. Due to the heavy breeze that was blowing, there were some jump injuries. The regiment was able to jump so close together that Heilmann was able to assemble his regiment in the space of 45 minutes.

Heilmann ordered his men to head south to link up with the vehicles that were waiting for them.

They marched in the direction of Lentini and established contact there at 2000 hours with *Kampfgruppe Schmalz* of the "Hermann Göring" Division. *Oberst* Schmalz briefed the senior commanders of the paratroopers on the situation. That night, Heilmann had his men take up positions in a line running between Carlentini and the Mediterranean. The *II./FJR 3* was sent by Heilmann to Francofonte, where it was to close the gap between *Kampfgruppe Schmalz* and its parent division.

While all that was happening, the situation on the island had reached crisis proportions.

While the defensive fighting was raging in the sector of the three paratrooper battalions that had been inserted and *Kampfgruppe Schmalz*, the airborne division's machine-gun battalion had landed at Catania during the afternoon of 13 July. *Major* Schmid, the commander, immediately went to Schmalz's command post. At the same time, *Hauptmann* Laun led the battalion towards Primasole, where it rested in an orangetree orchard, taking up concealed positions from the air.

Also landing at the airfield at Catania was the division's antitank battalion. Two of the aircraft that had just landed fell victim to a bombing run by Flying Fortresses. The *Gigant* transporters were destroyed, along with all of the equipment and weapons they had on board, decisively weakening the division's antitank forces.

The division's signals company, under the command of *Oberleutnant* Fassel, was dispatched to safeguard Catania's harbor as soon as it landed, since the Italian garrison had disappeared.

THE BRITISH 1ST AIRBORNE BRIGADE AT THE PRIMASOLE BRIDGE

After the Allied landings on Sicily had succeeded, General Montgomery forced a breakthrough along the frontage of his XIII Corps at Lentini on 13 July. He headed into the plains at Catania. At the same time, he employed a British airborne force to force bridgeheads farther to the enemy's rear. This force was the 1st Airborne Brigade of Brigadier Lathbury.

The brigade received orders to take the bridge at Primasole and establish a large bridgehead on it northern side. At the same time, a commando detachment was to land west of Agnone and take the *Ponte dei Malati*. Both elements were to hold their bridges until the arrival of the British 50th Infantry Division.

Towards sundown on 13 July, 105 Dakota's headed out from six different airfields in Tunisia between Kairouan and Sousse. Towed by 19 Halifax and Stirling bombers, an additional 30 massive Horsa gliders also participated in this operation. The Horsa carried the heavy arms and equipment of the forces.

Several aircraft and gliders were out of the picture from the very start, three each of both. While inbound to the island, the aerial formations were mistaken for German bombers by Allied naval vessels and heavily engaged.

When the widely scattered formation reached the coastline of Sicily, German antiaircraft defenses opened fire. The Horsas, jammed to the gills with ammunition, exploded in brilliant flashes.

The pilots began dropping the parachutists with no regard to designated drop zones. The machines that were approaching Primasole started encountering fire from *Fallschirm-MG-Bataillon 1*, which had set up in the orange orchard that afternoon. One of the machine-gun platoons shot down three gliders. Another platoon succeeded in downing three transporters.

As a result, the operation had already lost 20 aircraft since it had started out. Another group of machines had been badly hit. The machines turned away and dropped their paratroopers wherever they happened to be at the time. The British brigade had suffered casualties amounting to 300 men. An additional 82 British paratroopers were found by the machine-gunners that night in the Primasole area and taken prisoner.

Despite all that, some 22% of the employed forces managed to land near the bridge. While those men headed for the bridge, the gliders with the equipment arrived. They headed for the bridge, where they landed, only to discover that Brigadier Lathbury only had one fifth of his original force.

The brigade's 2nd Battalion worked its way towards the river and reached it around 0400 hours. It linked up with a crash-landed Horsa there. The crew was busy trying to pull out the antitank guns and the jeep.

When the British forces reached the southern end of the bridge, there was firing on the northern end, where the 1st Battalion had jumped. The 1st Battalion was taking out the Italian forces guarding the bridge. Four German trucks that attempted to cross the bridge to the south were taken out and lit up the night skies from the northern bank. British sappers removed the wiring and then the demolition charges from the mounts, pilings and the spans. They threw everything into the river.

The 3rd Battalion had also landed north of the bridge and linked up with its sister battalion. Both formations dug in around the approaches to the bridge, while the 2nd Battalion on the southern end set up strongpoints on three hills. Despite all the setbacks, the British had taken the bridge.

It was not until 1000 on 14 July that German forces were first seen, and those were in the form of a few *Bf 109's*, which strafed the British positions. An individual German motorcycle messenger was engaged at the north end of the bridge. He turned around and headed back to Catania. The messenger had been sent to *FJR 3* by *Hauptmann* Stangenberg. It was only then that Stangenberg discovered what had happened at the bridge.

Stangenberg headed there immediately and gathered up some 20 paratroopers with him on the way. When he was within 400 meters of the bridge, he started to receive fire.

Stangenberg then took measures to isolate the bridge. A *Flak* battery went into position along the north at noon. Stangenberg then returned to Catania and contacted *Generalleutnant* Heidrich, who was headquartered in Frascati: "Reporting to the *Herr General*: Contact with *FJR 3* broken, because enemy airborne forces took the bridge over the Simeto River last night. I have blocked it off with 80 men and request release of the signals company, which is at the Catania harbor."

"Very well, Stangenberg. Get the company. Keep me informed on what is happening at the bridge."

Around 1500 hours, *Oberleutnant* Fassel's signals company arrived at the area of the bridge.

✠

At the same time that the British airborne forces descended on the bridge at Primasole, the British 3rd Commando of Lieutenant Colonel Slater headed for the *Ponte dei Malati*. The men jumped out of their assault craft when they touched land at Agnone. When the men were still at sea, they had been engaged by the *2./FJR 3* and a battery of Italian guns that was still in its positions. At Stazione Agnone, the commandos ran into the command post of the *3./FJR 3* of *Oberleutnant* Veth. Veth's men attacked immediately and drove the commandos back north. Despite that, Major Young succeeded in reaching the bridge with some 20 commandos around 0300 hours. When the commandos attempted to cross over the bridge to the southwest bank, they were taken under fire by a single German tank, which had moved forward from *Kampfgruppe Schmalz*. None of the commandos could get past the steel colossus.

When the German pressure became too strong during the morning of 14 July and the 50th Infantry Division was nowhere in sight, the commandos had to give up hope of taking the bridge. Lieutenant Colonel Slater divided his men into smaller groups and told them to cross the river to the east and make it back to their own lines.

Individual elements ran into the forces of *FJR 3* and were taken prisoner.

✠

When the main body of the British attack forces, which had been stopped at Carlentini, finally reached the bridge over the Simento the following day, it had also been abandoned by the airborne forces that had taken it. They had been too weak to establish an effective bridgehead on the south side of the bridge and, moreover, their ammunition was practically exhausted.

✠

On 14 July, the German airborne divisional engineers landed at the airfield at Catania. The battalion, minus its 2nd Company, was commanded by *Hauptmann* Adolff. The 1st Company was under the acting command of *Leutnant* Cords and the 2nd under *Oberleutnant* Matheus. The battalion immediately received orders to defend the crossings over the Simento. Adolff was able to successfully accomplish his mission with great aplomb and stopped the enemy from the north side of the river. Until the arrival of *FJR 4* under *Oberst* Walther, he held the bridge, which meant that he also defended Catania and the rear area as far as Messina, where there were hardly any German forces, since they had all been committed forward.

The 1st Company of *Leutnant* Cords had taken up positions on the northeast bank and dug in. From there they had held out against an attack by a British infantry battalion, which was supported by 40 armored vehicles and an artillery preparation of 90 minutes. When Cords was wounded, *Oberfeldwebel* Kaiser assumed acting command of the company. But he was also wounded—a round to the knee—and had to be evacuated.

In the sector of the 3rd Company, which had positioned itself on both sides of the road on the north bank, the paratroopers had two bunkers at their disposal.

Oberleutnant Matheus and eight volunteers went after an enemy element that had closed on the German positions. They were cut off and were taken prisoner, all wounded. Matheus later died of his wounds.

The aforementioned British armor also attacked in the sector of the 3rd Company, where it was engaged by a solitary 8.8-centimeter *Flak* used in a ground role. After eight British tanks were set alight, the *Flak* was knocked out with a direct hit. Once the *Flak* was knocked out, the bridge could no longer be held. The English infantry and tanks, supported by artillery, attempted to force the bridge. The airborne engineers had to pull back and moved 800 meters farther north and into the shallow depression of a dried-out riverbed, which became known as the "tank ditch". The company occupied a sector 600 meters in width.

Although the bridge had been abandoned, the British could not get across. On the afternoon of 16 July, *Hauptmann* Adolff had two bomb-laden trucks approach the bridge in an effort to blow it up. They were forced to turn back twice and half of the volunteer engineers were wounded.

Finally, some British forces were able to cross the bridge and advance as far as the "tank ditch", where they were stopped. In an immediate German counterattack, they were forced back to the bridge.

One day later, the German engineers attacked the bridge once again. Their initial effort was crowned with success, but the enemy's defensive fires kicked in and the attack came to a standstill. When *Hauptmann* Adolff again tried to blow up the bridge, he was so badly wounded in the process that he died a short while later.

After that difficult bloodletting, the engineers were happy to see the initial elements of *FJR 4* arrive to relieve them. *Major* Eggert's 1st Battalion took over the sector known as the "tank ditch".

In the meantime, a crisis situation had developed in the sector of *FJR 3*. *Kampfgruppe Schmalz*, to which the airborne regiment had been attached, had received orders to pull back to the Simento River line. The withdrawal was to take place over the bridge at Favotta, before the British closed down that avenue for good. All of the formations of the battle group confirmed the order to pull back, with the exception of *FJR 3*. During the night of 14/15 July, a messenger arrived at Schmalz's headquarters informing him that *Oberstleutnant* Heilmann wanted to hold his position a bit longer. *Oberst* Schmalz had the message sent several times to pull back, since otherwise the regiment was in danger of being encircled. *Oberstleutnant* Heilmann also received that radio traffic. But when *FJR 3* finally set out, it found that the British had already shot past it. The regiment's retreat route had been cut off.

On the morning of 15 July, *Oberst* Schmalz's forces reached the newly designated positions, with the exception of *FJR 3*. The following morning, it was joined by *FJR 4*, which was attached to him. It appeared, however, that the 800 men of *FJR 3* had fallen into enemy hands. But they showed up in the sector of *Kampfgruppe Schmalz* 48 hours later. Over the course of two night marches, it had snuck through the enemy's lines.

OTHER PARATROOPER OPERATIONS ON SICILY

On 20 July, *Kampfgruppe von Carnap* was formed. It consisted of a fortress battalion that was positioned in the village of Centuripe and the *I./FJR 3*, which was positioned immediately to the west. *Oberstleutnant* von Carnap was the adjutant of the *1. Fallschirmjäger-Division*. *Oberstleutnant* Heilmann also ordered his 2nd Battalion to von Carnap in support. Heilmann's remaining battalion, the 3rd, established positions in Regalbuto.

When the enemy launched his offensive in that sector on the night of 30/31 July, *Oberstleutnant* von Carnap was among the first to fall during the artillery preparation. An hour after the attack had begun, the enemy was already to the rear of the *1./FJR 3*, but he hesitated to attack Centuripe proper. By the time he decided to attack there, *Generalleutnant* Conrath, the commander of the *"Hermann Göring"* Division, to which the paratroopers of *FJR 3* in that sector also reported, had committed all of the airborne regiment.

That evening, the British 78th Infantry Division attacked Centuripe. It was turned back and suffered heavy losses. After a heavy bombing raid, which turned the mountain village into rubble and ash, the 36th Infantry Brigade of the British division took the lead in launching the second attack. *Hauptmann* Liebscher had removed his men from the village, however, and positioned them on the southern slope of the hill. As a result, his battalion had not suffered heavily from the aerial attack. He had to defend the entire night. It was not until the morning of 2 August that the enemy was able to enter Centuripe, but he was driven out again, when he was bombed by his own forces. Liebscher's men went back into the village.

Next, it was the turn of the 38th Infantry Brigade to attack. After the fighting had raged for three hours, *Oberstleutnant* Heilmann ordered his 3rd Battalion to pull back. In other sectors, Hielmann's men also held back the enemy. For instance, the attacks of the Canadian 3rd Brigade between Regalbuto and Centuripe was turned back by the 120 men of the 1st Battalion.

It was not until the evening of 2 August that the paratroopers were ordered back to the Ätna Position. *General der Panzertruppe* Hube, who had been entrusted with the defense of the island and to whom three divisions and the two airborne regiments reported, had decided to abandon it. *Oberstleutnant*

Heilmann and his men had set up defensive positions in Maletto, while *Kampfgruppe Walther* stood shoulder to shoulder with *Kampfgruppe Schmalz* on the east coast. Walther's paratroopers moved behind Taormina on 14 August. The *I./FJR 3* held out in Maletto until 12 August. Hube had established five defensive rings for the evacuation of the island. The last units to leave were the airborne forces on 16/17 August.

Allied planners had estimated that Sicily would be conquered quickly but the campaign turned out to be a frustrating one. Although heavily outnumbered, and largely abandoned by their Italian Allies, the Germans fought a bitter delaying action and it took over a month to capture the island. The remaining German and Italian troops, along with most of their heavy equipment, were successfully evacuated to the Italian mainland across the Straights of Messina.

Sicily had fallen; the next mission was the defense of the mainland.

PARATROOPER OPERATIONS ON THE ITALIAN MAINLAND:*FALLSCHIRMJÄGER-REGIMENT 1* AT TARENT

When the British 8th Army landed on European soil on 5 September, *Oberstleutnant* Heilmann's *FJR 3* was the first German formation to oppose it. On the evening of 10 September, the village of Battipaglia was taken back from the enemy. Without using any artillery preparation, it was the *I./FJR 3* that took it.

Up to then, events were occurring at a rapid pace in Italy. On the morning of 8 September, Allied forces had also landed at Pizzo. That evening they were also at Tarent. On the morning of 9 September, the main body of the Allied forces landed in the broad bay of Salerno. Brought onto land from 450 ships were 169,000 men and 20,000 vehicles. The force was commanded by General Harold Alexander, who was the Commander-in-Chief of the 15th Army Group.

At about the same time, the announcement was made that Italy was leaving the Axis. In addition to fighting the Allies, the Germans had to disarm the Italian forces as well. Once again, the operations of a single regiment—in this case, *FJR 1*—will be highlighted as illustrative of all. *Oberstleutnant* Schulz's *FJR 1* had originally been intended for employment on Sicily, but it was then held back on the mainland. The regiment was sent from the Naples area on 7 September

To Francaville, which is along the Brindisi–Tarent road. When Schulz and his men encountered a roadblock about 3 kilometers north of Tarent, he had his vehicle halt. He was held there by an Italian guard force. Even when Schulz requested to speak to the Italian commander, he was not allowed to pass. Via radio, Schulz asked *Generalleutnant* Heidrich whether he should break through using force. The general initially forbade any violent activity.

The next day, Schulz received the news that the Italians had changed sides. Because he had too few vehicles, he ordered his men to go to a nearby

Italian officer school and "procure" some. Schulz led the way in his staff car and arrived at the school that housed 800 Italian officer candidates.

Schulz had the officer candidates form up on the drill square and recalled the events in Africa and in Russia in a fiery speech that appealed to their sense of former comradeship. The talk was not without effect. More than 400 officer candidates requested to remain fighting with the Germans. The commander of the school, whom Schulz had wanted to see, had committed suicide in his office.

The Germans took the necessary vehicles, and no one stopped them. Now fully motorized, the regiment rolled on to Tarent. By the time they arrived there, the enemy had already landed. The fighting of the regiment against the landing force commenced. Gradually, all of the remaining divisional elements arrived in the area and, by the end of September, Heidrich had his entire division assembled there.

The German paratroopers put up extremely tough resistance at Tarent. The paratroopers pulled back, but only house-by-house and position-by-position. That was the start of the infamous "centimeter offensive", which inflicted heavy and bloody casualties on the enemy.

On 20 September, when *Oberstleutnant* Schulz headed to an area that had been penetrated by the enemy that morning—the enemy never attacked at night—his command car was strafed by low-flying fighter-bombers. Before he was able to get out of the vehicle, the fighter-bombers were already over him. Cannon and machine-gun rounds peppered the vehicle. The driver was killed immediately. Schulz's liaison officer was badly wounded, but the regimental commander emerged unscathed. He rallied his soldiers to the left and right of the enemy's point of penetration and pushed back the enemy forces, which included airborne personnel as well. After three hours of hard and uncompromising fighting, the enemy pulled back, defeated and decimated.

Two prisoners were then brought to the regimental commander. One of them was a captain, who introduced himself as Lord Brickleton. The British nobleman asked Schulz in broken German if he would be so kind as to let his unit know that he was still alive.

Schulz smiled as he heard the request and granted it. A few days later, in a sort of act of reciprocity, he received news that a German patrol, which had fallen into the hands of Italian partisans and had been freed by the British, was also in good health.

With the surprise landing of strong enemy forces on 21 and 22 September at Bari, the *1. Fallschirmjäger-Division* was once more involved in bitter defensive fighting. The regiment gradually had to pull back to behind the Ofanto River, 30 kilometers north of Bari. The fighting for Foggia lasted three days, before the important air base was lost. In Cerignola, Schulz's paratroopers participated in bitter street fighting with the enemy. The paratroopers fought under the arcades and along the drainage canals that lead to the sea. The enemy continued to advance, thanks to his superior numbers, and forced the paratroopers behind the Biferno River in the High Apennines.

✠

The fall of Rome also saw turbulent scenes, which will be described from the point of view of the airborne forces.

A NOTEWORTHY DISCUSSION

On 25 July 1943, Student was called late in the afternoon from the *Führer* headquarters and summoned to Rastenburg immediately. An hour later, the Commanding General was in his utility aircraft and flying to Rastenburg, where he landed five hours later.

Hitler received him immediately in his study, where there were only the two of them. They then went to the large briefing room. It was the same room in which the attempt on Hitler's life would be carried out nearly a year later. Student provided the author with a firsthand account:

"I have selected you and your paratroopers," Hitler explained, "for a very important mission. The *Duce* was removed from power today by the Italian king and taken into custody. That means that Italy will soon fall and go to the enemy camp.

"Student, I am asking you to go to Rome as soon as possible with all available airborne forces. I am holding you responsible for Rome being held. Otherwise, our forces on Sicily and in southern Italy will be cut off. You and your corps are being attached to the Commander-in-Chief South, *Feldmarschall* Kesselring. He has already been informed."

I was then briefed in detail. Hitler concluded in a raised voice: "One of your special missions is to find and liberate my friend Mussolini. He's going to be delivered by the Italians to the Americans."

Early on the morning of 26 July, I started for Rome. With me was *SS-Hauptsturmführer* Skorzeny, whom I had not met up to that point. During the night, he and an *SS* paratrooper detail had been attached to me for the execution of any missions of a police nature.

I reported to *Feldmarschall* Kesselring in Frascati.

He oriented me in more detail concerning the situation in Italy and asked me to stay there at his headquarters. I gladly accepted and enjoyed his tremendous hospitality until the middle of September, the conclusion of the fighting for Rome.

At the same time, airborne forces were being sent as rapidly as possible to Rome. Within 48 hours, 20,000 paratroopers landed at the *Pratica di Mare*, an airfield southwest of Rome. They took up billets in military facilities in the Pontine Swamps.

In Rome, Student attempted to find out Mussolini's location. He discovered that Mussolini had initially been taken to the island of Ponza. The police attaché in Rome at the time, *SS-Sturmbannführer* Kappler, confirmed the Italian dictator's presence on that island a short while later.

Student, who had received complete freedom of action from Hitler, started his preparation to free the imprisoned *Duce*. In the middle of those preparations, however, the news arrived that Mussolini had been taken to Maddalena.

Student was then ordered back to Rastenburg, where Hitler spoke privately to him. During the conversation, Student requested Hitler for permission to include Skorzeny in any search operations. It was Skorzeny who had located Mussolini in Maddalena.

The rescue operation's planning at high speed continued again, when Skorzeny reported to Student that Mussolini had also disappeared from Maddalena. Kappler's intelligence section had been given a tip that Mussolini was at the *Campo Imperatore* hotel in the mountains on the *Gran Sasso*. Student acted on his own at that point and sent his personal physician, *Dr.* Krutoff to Gran Sasso. The doctor returned and reported that the hotel had been closed over the past few days.

Then another event occurred that caused the rescue mission for Mussolini to move into the background: On 8 September, the Italian forces officially surrendered, five days after secret meetings in Cassible on Sicily between the Allies and General Castellano.

At the same time that the announcement was made, a powerful air strike was executed on Kesselring's headquarters at Frascati and von Richthofen's headquarters at Grottaferrata. Both command posts were destroyed, but thousands of Italian civilians also lost their lives.

During the afternoon of 8 September, *Major* Gericke's *II./FJR 6* received an unusual order. This was a follow-up to a conversation Gericke and Student had had at the end of July. At the time, Gericke's men were guarding the airfield at Foggia, when the Commanding General summoned the battalion commander to Frascati.

In July, Student had told Gericke that he had selected him "and his battalion for a special mission. It is top secret."

After a pause, Student continued: "We have to believe that the Italians will get out of the war, sooner or later, and join the Allies. It is imperative that the danger that could result for the German forces in Italy and even for Germany be averted. Therefore, you have the following mission:

"In case of an Italian capitulation you are to jump with your battalion on the Italian headquarters at *Monte Rotondo*, capture it and thus paralyze the entire command and control apparatus of the Italian Armed Forces. You are on your own for this mission. Support before the jump or during the fighting cannot be guaranteed, due to the necessity for secrecy."

Gericke went back to Foggia and started preparations. He studied the maps that had the location of the headquarters northeast of Rome marked on them. It was a 160-meter high hill that was packed full of concrete bunkers, dugouts, roadblocks and tank obstacles. Artillery pieces and antiaircraft guns were positioned all the way around the hill.

On his own initiative, Gericke flew in a Fieseler *Storch* from Frascati to the restricted area. He wanted to get a firsthand look. The *Storch* was greeted by a few rounds from antiaircraft guns. The pilot waved his wings as a sign that he understood and was turning away.

That was not enough for Gericke. He tried to get through to *Monte Rotondo* on the ground. He was able to get as far as the main roadblock, before he was stopped. Accompanied by an escort, however, he was allowed to move through the restricted area, which he studiously observed.

The plan was transformed to action on 8 September, when Gericke received orders to execute at 1830 hours on 8 September. At 0630 hours the following day, the battalion headed out in 52 *Ju 52's* to Rome and a jump operation on the Italian headquarters.

When the formation neared the mass of antiaircraft guns guarding *Monte Rotondo*, it started to receive fire. The first few aircraft turned away, hit. One blew up as the result of a direct hit. A portion of the battalion jumped at the wrong spot, and some squads landed as much as 4 kilometers from the objective.

Despite all that, the men who had landed on target stormed the redoubt. In bitter fighting, the paratroopers penetrated deeply into the Italian defensive network. Leading his men, Gericke attacked the fort in which he assumed the Italian command was located. The attackers received heavy fire from there, but they were able to advance, step-by-step. The fort was assaulted and Gericke and his men took 15 officers and 200 enlisted personnel prisoner.

The communications center was also taken. But General Roatta, the Italian Chief-of-Staff was not captured. He had sought his escape in the nick of time and was already waiting in Pescara for a flight to the Allies. By the end of the operation, Gericke and his men took 2,500 Italians prisoner, of which 250 were officers.

When Italian reinforcements arrived at *Monte Rotondo* in the afternoon, things became critical for *Major* Gericke. In fact, an Italian armored division was headed for his location from Rome. Gericke determined it was time to negotiate.

That afternoon, however, he discovered that Student had already sent an emissary to the Italians to allow his battalion to leave the *Monte Rotondo*. The Italians said he could do that on the morning of 10 September, while retaining all of his weapons.

Despite the assurances, the fighting continued until finally an Italian captain appeared and informed those fighting that a ceasefire had been arranged. It took until that afternoon for everything to crystallize, however. The battalion was allowed to leave, and it quickly linked up with German forces that were positioned around Rome, which were also involved in fighting in Rome's southern suburbs. They were forces of the *2. Fallschirmjäger-Division*.

THE FIGHTING FOR ROME

Starting on 26 July 1943, the forces of the *2. Fallschirmjäger-Division* started out for Italy from air bases at Istres and Avignon. Just from the air base at Istres alone, there were transport flights over the course of three days by 90 *Ju 52's*, 45 *He 111's*, 80 gliders, six *Gigant Me 323's* and a few *Go 242's*.

The *2. Fallschirmjäger-Division*, which was billeted in the Pontine Swamps outside of Rome had an on-the-ground strength of 13,000 men at the time. The *I./FJR 6* of *Hauptmann* Finzel and the *III./FJR 6* of *Major* Pelz were bivouacked in a grove of pines along the Tiber. Among the men of *FJR 6* was *Oberfeldwebel* Rudolf Harbig, a platoon leader in the *2./FJR 6*, who held the world record in the 800-meter run. Needless to say, he was always the winner in similar events whenever the regiment hosted sports competitions.

When the head of government of Italy, Marshal Badoglio, announced his country's capitulation at 1945 hours on 8 September on Radio Rome, that was the trigger for the Germans to issue codeword *"Achse"*—Axis—which was the signal to disarm the Italian armed forces.

A short while later, *Luftwaffe* reconnaissance assets identified a large formation of ships cruising to the south of Naples.

Major Mors, the commander of the Airborne Instruction Battalion, personally heard Badoglio's address and raced to Student's headquarters to report what he had heard. Student then immediately went to Kesselring, who gave the Commanding General complete freedom of movement in accomplishing what needed to be done.

Student ordered the *2. Fallschirmjäger-Division* to free itself from any constraints that the Italians had imposed upon it in recent weeks. The division then sent complete battalions to designated Italian military facilities and disarmed them early on 9 September.

Then orders were issued to march on Rome. In place of the division commander, *Generalleutnant* Ramcke, who was on temporary duty elsewhere, the division was led by *Oberstleutnant* Meder-Eggebrecht, assisted by the division operations officer, *Major* von der Heydte.[1]

At first light on 9 September, the battle groups of the division advanced in the direction of Rome. *Fallschirmjäger-Regiment 2* moved along both sides of the *Via Appia*, while *FJR 6*, augmented by the divisional artillery regiment and other divisional elements, moved along both sides of the *Via Ostiense* between Rome and Lido di Roma. The *I./FJR 7* (Airborne Instructional Battalion), which had been bivouacked at Lake Nemi, was engaged with Italian forces that morning. After a few sharp encounters, the battalion was able to disengage from the "Piacenza" Division.

---

1. *Major* Friedrich August von der Heydte, who had been taken out of Africa for admittance to the special hospital in Berlin-Dahlem for tropical diseases, was given the task of assuming the duties of division operations officer for the newly forming *2. Fallschirmjäger-Division* at the end of January 1943, after he had recovered. He started his new duties on 1 February and had participated in both the division's activation and its transfer to Italy.

The *3. Panzergrenadier-Division*, which had been attached to the airborne corps, advanced on Rome from Lago di Bolsena. By evening, it had fought a pathway through to the city.

Kesselring then had all of his forces stop after they had encircled Rome. He took pains to avoid fighting in the middle of the city, so as to protect valuable works of culture and art. Instead, he asked the Commanding General of the forces in Rome, Carboni, to lay down his arms on 9 September.

When there was no adequate response, the paratroopers moved forward. During the early-morning hours of 10 September, *Major* von der Heydte personally took command of a divisional battle group that consisted of six battalions. The mission, which had been personally given to him by Student, was: "Move into Rome from the sea. Break all resistance by the *Corps d'Armata di Roma.*"

When von der Heydte's *Kampfgruppe* reached a Roman suburb, it was greeted by fires from a Sardinian division. The German advance came to a standstill, and the airborne division's artillery was brought forward to engage the Italians.

Major Pelz's *III./FJR 6* also got stopped by a fortress-like building along its path. *Major* Pelz summoned *Hauptmann* Milch, the battery commander of the *4./Fallschirm-Artillerie-Regiment 2*, to discuss artillery support. *Major* von der Heydte also showed up at the same time in an armored car.

The building was engaged from a distance of 20 meters by two light infantry guns and blown to pieces. The armored car then took over the lead in the advance, the commander of the battle group sitting on top. He went from one attack group to the next. Wherever he appeared, the men renewed their efforts to advance. When *Hauptmann* Milch wanted to set up for the defense at the station for Radio Rome, von der Heydte told him to continue to advance into the city.

"I'll take the lead," von der Heydte called out to Milch. "Follow slowly with your battery . . . be prepared to engage at any time!" Following behind von der Heydte was an Army *Hauptmann* in a staff car. Milch followed him and provided the following firsthand account:

> The lead element drove into Rome peacefully. *Major* von der Heydte stopped at a marketplace and bought grapes, which we immediately ate. As we continued, we kept on seeing motorcycle messengers in Italian uniforms. Then we got to a tank obstacle. Since my *Kettenkrad* was the most maneuverable, I turned around and then formed the head of the column. I went ahead, followed by the staff car and the armored car. When we were not too far from the famous obelisks along the *Via Ostiense*, not far from the Coliseum, I saw tanks in a side street that were following our movement with their main guns. We were in a trap.
>
> In order to warn the vehicles following us, I fired at the closest tank with my rifle. A salvo from tank main guns was the answer. The

tanks rolled out, pursued the armored car, which was able to escape, and ran into my battery. The battery turned back all of the Italian attacks into the afternoon.

Despite those incidents, *Kampfgruppe von der Heydte* and the other airborne and Army formations were able to successfully complete the disarming of the Italian forces in the greater Rome area by 11 September. Towards the conclusion of the operation, *Major* von der Heydte had to be hospitalized again. He was conducting an aerial reconnaissance from a Fieseler *Storch* in the vicinity of Rome, when it crashed. Although the audacious officer survived, he was badly injured.

THE RESCUE OF THE *DUCE* FROM THE CAMPO IMPERATORE
On Sunday, 12 September, the raid to free the *Duce* from the enemy groups that were holding him prisoner could start. He was being held at the *Campo Imperatore* sanatorium on a plateau of the mountain mass of the *Gran Sasso*. The events of the recent past had forced the rescue operation into the background. But then the raid assumed increased importance again, and the situation allowed its execution. The area around the *Gran Sasso* was controlled by forces loyal to Bodaglio, and some 150 *Carabinieri* were guarding the former leader of Italy.

At 1300 hours, the engines of the Henschel tow aircraft came to life. The machines taxied out, pulled the gliders behind them and they were airborne. Once in the sky, the gliders dropped their landing gear.

A reconnaissance aircraft, piloted by *Hauptmann* Langguth, was in the lead. The gliders followed in one-minute intervals. The lead group consisted of two gliders with 18 paratroopers. *Oberleutnant* von Berlepsch, the commander of the *1./Fallschirm-Lehr-Bataillon*, which was the unit responsible for the raid, was in Glider No. 5. He wanted to land in the middle of the landing portion of the operation so as to quickly gather his company around him.

A Fieseler *Storch* under the command of *Hauptmann* Gerlach also took off. It was intended to take the freed Mussolini out of the area with it.

Flying due east, the aerial armada approached the 2,914-meter-high *Gran Sasso*. The *Campo Imperatore* was located at about the 2,000-meter mark. In the third glider, which was piloted by *Leutnant* Meier-Wehner, was *SS-Hauptsturmführer* Skorzeny and the *Carabinieri* general, Soletti, whose role it was to hold the guard force in check and order it to lay down its arms. In addition, there were two other SS officers—*SS-Untersturmführer* Schwerdt and *SS-Untersturmführer* Warger—as well as five *Waffen-SS* noncommissioned officers on the glider.

Glider No. 4 carried Skorzeny's adjutant, *SS-Untersturmführer* Radl, *SS-Untersturmführer* Menzel and seven other *Waffen-SS* enlisted personnel. In all, there were 16 soldiers of the *Waffen-SS* who participated in the mission. All of the remaining gliders had men from von Berlepsch's company. The remaining gliders also carried heavy weapons, in case Mussolini's guards put up any type of stiff resistance.

Once on the ground, *SS-Hauptsturmführer* Skorzeny was to be in charge. A second operation, conducted at the valley station, was conducted by *Major* Mors, the commander of the airborne instructional battalion.

Overall command of the operation rested with *General der Flieger* Student.

✠

During the night of 11–12 September, the men of the companies of the instructional battalion—minus the 1st Company, which was part of the actual *Gran Sasso* operation—left their bivouac area at the Mondragone Cloister in trucks for the 300-kilometer trek to the valley station of the mountain railway that led up the *Gran Sasso* and to the sanatorium. Their mission was to secure the station and prevent any Badoglio forces from reinforcing the guards at the hotel.

They reached the valley station around noon. At 1400 hours, the air guards that *Major* Mors had posted saw specks in the sky. *Oberjäger* Kirschner reported: "*Herr Major*, the gliders are coming!"

✠

After the 12 gliders and their tow aircraft had formed up, they headed due east. The cruising altitude was 3,500 meters. It was an experience that remained indelibly etched in the memory of Skorzeny. After the war, he wrote:

I held the detailed map in my hands, which Radl and I had marked based on the photos taken by *Hauptmann* Langguth on 8 September. I remembered the words of *General* Student (who had issued his last directives for the execution of the rescue operation that morning on the airfield at Pratica de Mare): "I am convinced that all of you will fulfill your duty . . ."

Then *Leutnant* Meier-Wehner (the commander of the glider pilots) reported to me that the pilot of our towing aircraft had reported that the lead aircraft piloted by Langguth and Gliders No. 1 and 2 were no longer in sight. Later on, I discovered that these aircraft had simply turned around and head back to Pratica di Mare. That meant that my assault group and Radl's no longer had our backs covered and I would have to land first, if I still wanted to carry out the operation. I also didn't know that two gliders behind me were missing. I called out to Meier-Wehner: "We'll take the lead!"

With my paratrooper knife I cut two openings in the glider's skin, so that I could orient myself to a certain extent and give the two pilots instructions.

Finally, I saw the town of Aquila in the Abruzzi Mountains, then, somewhat farther, Mors's column on the serpentine to the valley station. It had just passed Assergi. They were punctual. On the ground, everything was going to plan! It was almost H-Hour . . .

The hotel appeared below us. "Release the cable!" *Leutnant* Meier-Wehner ordered. Shortly afterwards, we were executing a turn over the plateau. I saw that the supposedly flat pasture, on which we were supposed to glide in, was just a short, steep meadow that was covered with rocks. I called out immediately: "Crash landing . . . as close to the hotel as possible!"

Despite the braking parachute, our glider landed at much too fast a speed, making a few bounces and then, practically completely destroyed, stopped 15 meters from the corner of the hotel.

I jumped out and ran, weapon in my fist, as fast as I could to the hotel. My seven comrades from the *Waffen-SS* and *Leutnant* Meier-Wehner followed me. A guard stared at me, startled. I saw a door to the right, forced my way in and kicked the chair out from under the radio operator, who was sitting on it. He flew to the ground. A hit on the radio with my submachine-gun, and the apparatus was destroyed.

Since the room had no other doors that led into the interior of the hotel, we raced back outside and along the front of the hotel to find an entry way. But there was none. Only a terrace at the end of the wall. I climbed up over the wall on the shoulders of *SS-Scharführer* Himmel. Another effort and I was on the front side. I continued running and suddenly glimpsed the striking features of Mussolini in a window.

"*Duce*, get away from the window!" I yelled, as loudly as I could.

There were two machine-guns in position at the main entrance. We kicked them over and forced back the Italian crews. Behind me, a roar: "*Mani in alto!*—Hands up!"

I slammed into the *Carabinieri*, who were jammed around the entrance and fought my way through them. I had seen the *Duce* on the second floor, to the right. A stairwell led up. I ran up it. To the right, a hallway. The second door! The *Duce* was there, along with two officers and a person in civilian dress. I put all three of them up against the wall. *SS-Untersturmführer* Schwerdt pushed them out to the hallway. *SS-Unterscharführer* Holzer and *SS-Unterscharführer* Benzer appeared at the window. The two had climbed up on the lightning rod. Everything took place in the space of four minutes. Not a shot had been fired.

Through the open window, I saw Radl and his section come running up. Their glider had landed in front of the hotel. I called out to Radl: "Everything's fine here! Safeguard below!"

A short while later, when Radl finally also came into the hotel, Skorzeny went back to the room where Mussolini and *SS-Untersturmführer* Schwerdt were.

"*Duce*, the *Führer* gave me orders to liberate you!" Skorzeny reported to the dictator.

Mussolini gave him both hands, hugged him and replied: ""I knew my friend Adolf Hitler would not leave me in the lurch!"

In the meantime, *Oberleutnant* von Berlepsch had surrounded the entire complex with his paratroopers. Skorzeny had him disarm all the Italians.

The "civilian", who was in the room with Mussolini, turned out to be General Cueli, who had been directed to deliver Mussolini to the Allies that afternoon.

In the course of landing, 10 men had been injured. They were treated by *Dr.* Brunner and Italian medics.

In the meantime, Mors's battalion had reached the valley station and taken the station house after a short firefight. After the surrounding area had been secured, *Major* Mors and 20 paratroopers climbed into the gondolas and rode to the mountain station. At the transfer point, the Italian guards, who still knew nothing of what had happened, were taken prisoner. Mors and his men took the final stretch up to the hotel. When *Major* Mors climbed out of the gondola, *Oberleutnant* von Berlepsch raced over to him and reported: "Operation executed! No complications! The *Duce* has been freed!"

The only thing left was to take the *Duce* to Rome. There were three planned options. One of them had the *Duce* taken to the airfield at Aquila di Abruzzi, where three *He 111's* would land after paratroopers had successfully taken the airfield at 1600 hours. Communications had been broken with the *XI. Flieger-Korps*, however, so there was no way to ascertain whether the three *He 111's* were headed for that airport. That ruled out option one.

The second option was to take the *Duce* down to the valley, where a Fieseler *Storch* had landed. But the pilot there reported that he had damaged his landing gear while landing and it was no longer possible to take off.

That left the third option: The Fieseler *Storch* that flew along with the group, which was flown by Student's personal pilot, *Hauptmann* Gerlach, would land on the plateau and take the *Duce* onboard. To do that, however, all of the men had to construct an impromptu landing strip. That they did and, after a green pyrotechnic had been fired, the aircraft landed safely.[2]

Skorzeny insisted on flying with the *Duce*. *Hauptmann* Gerlach was concerned that the aircraft had too short a runway for such a heavy payload. But Skorzeny would not relent and he fell back on an order that the *Führer* had personally given him. Gerlach had no choice but to attempt the dangerous take-off.

Skorzeny later wrote:

If I had let Mussolini fly away alone with Gerlach and then he crashed

---

2. In several accounts it has been speculated that the dramatic and dangerous rescue flight by *Storch* was intended primarily for propaganda purposes. A much safer, and more mundane, method of transporting Mussolini would have been by the motor vehicles that were stationed a little farther down the mountain.

with the *Duce*, then I would have had no other choice but to have put a bullet in my head. They would have said that I didn't want to risk the dangerous takeoff with Mussolini and Gerlach.

That may have well been the case, but it should also be noted that the additional weight of such a big man as Skorzeny significantly increased the danger of a crash as opposed to just Gerlach and Mussolini by themselves. Apparently, Skorzeny was thinking of saving his own head more at the moment than that of Mussolini. Regardless, it demonstrated a remarkable courage to go on the aircraft.

In the end, *Hauptmann* Gerlach gave the green light. The aircraft headed down the much-too-short landing strip. It had a tailwind, but it was also sloping downwards towards the valley. The *Storch* continued to gain ground speed and approached the precipice. When it left the solid ground, it dove and seemed to sink like a stone. But, in the end, Gerlach had obtained so much airspeed that he was able to catch the aircraft and get it under control.

An hour later, the aircraft landed at Pratica de Mare, right next to an *He 111*, which then took the *Duce* to Germany to his friend, Adolf Hitler, whom he could thank personally.

Hauptmann Melzer was there to greet the *Duce* on behalf of Student and to congratulate Skorzeny and Gerlach. Otto Skorzeny accompanied Mussolini to Germany.

The paratroopers who had remained behind on the *Gran Sasso* destroyed the stockpiles of ammunition that were there. The instrument panels of the gliders were removed and then what remained burned. Two hours later they left the mountain top with their prisoners. They went down to the valley station, where they bivouacked with their battalion.

A unique airborne mission had been executed and come to a good end.

FROM COASTAL PROTECTION TO OPERATIONS ON ELBA

After the capitulation of the Italian Armed Forces and the disarming of the divisions of the former allies, the *XI. Flieger-Korps* was entrusted with coastal defense duties along a stretch of the Mediterranean running 200 kilometers from Civitacecchia and Gaeta. Additional Allied landings were expected in that area.

One paratrooper battalion was employed to "retrieve" approximately 15,000 English prisoners-of-war, who had broken out of camps between Ancona and Pescara and intended to make their way south—armed with Italian weapons—to link up with the Allied forces that had landed there. That mission was quickly accomplished. An additional 3,000 English prisoners, who had been released by the Italians at Sulmona were also rounded up over the next five days.

On 17 September, the division started *Unternehmen "Goldfasan"*—"Golden Pheasant"—which was a jump operation on the island of Elba, which was still being held by Italian forces.

The battle groups participating in the operation were the *I./Panzergrenadier-Regiment 200* of the *90. Panzergrenadier-Division* and the reinforced *III./FJR 7* of the *2. Fallschirmjäger-Division.*

There were 7,000 Italian soldiers garrisoned on Elba. Some of them manned heavy gun batteries that were in the position to seriously interfere with German logistics traffic at sea. Moreover, an island chain that was still under Italian control was a tempting target for the Allies, which practically begged to be taken.

The transfer negotiations that were conducted between General Giraldi, the island's commander, and the German emissaries yielded no results. Giraldi was determined to defend the island against any German attack.

The negotiations on 15 September formed the prelude to the taking of the island. On 16 September, it was subjected to aerial attack. That same afternoon, while General Giraldi was still under the influence of the bombing raids, he announced that he was ready to negotiate again and, in the process, offered his immediate capitulation. As he was doing that, however, the assault forces were already underway; Siebel ferries were taking to sea from Livorno with the mechanized infantry battalion. It was too late to call off the attack.

Early on the morning of 17 September, *Major* Hübner's 600 paratroopers could see the Italian soldiers fleeing the city of Portoferraio as they approached. The jump horn sounded and the paratroopers jumped into the southwestern area of the Bay of Portoferraio around 0830 hours.

Even before the paratroopers could ditch their chutes, many of which had been caught up in the vines of a vineyard, the Italians came running up to them unarmed, hands raised, wanting to surrender. Not a single shot was fired.

The mechanized infantry forces had a similar encounter as they landed at Portoferraio on their ferries. The Italians surrendered immediately.

In the end, the operations on Elba were more like a training mission than anything else, although there were a number of jump injuries, as was always the case in those situations.

On 18 September, the paratroopers left Elba and returned to the west coast of Italy in the Ostia–Pratica de Mare area.

LEROS, THE MALTA OF THE AEGEAN

In Greece, where there were also Italian forces garrisoned, their disarming also took place relatively quickly. It was only on the Dodecanese Islands that the Italians took sides with Bodoglio. The German Army High Command issued directives to *Generalleutnant* Friedrich-Wilhelm Müller, the commander of the *22. Luftlande-Division* to take control of those islands. Once again, the division, which had participated in air-landed operations with the airborne forces in Holland, was to fight shoulder-to-shoulder with paratrooper formations.

One of the main strongpoints of the Italians, which was soon occupied by English forces as well, was the island of Leros. In the end, there were some 2,300 English and 5,350 Italian forces arrayed against the Germans. In order to cross the waterways to the islands, the *1./Küstenjäger-Abteilung "Brandenburg"* (*Hauptmann* Kuhlmann) and *Pionier-Landungs-Kompanie 780* (*Oberleutnant* Bunte) were attached to Müller's forces.[3]

The latter two elements had to transport the German forces between and among the islands of the Dodecanese. With the presence of medium and heavy naval squadrons of the Royal Navy, that could be a dangerous undertaking, as was shown in the encounters that took place again and again.

The island of Kos was the first one to be assaulted by the "Brandenburgers". The airfield at Antimacchia was taken by the *1./Jäger-Regiment "Brandenburg"*, when it was brought in by *Ju 52's*. Like many of the "Brandenburger" formations, it had been trained in airborne operations. By 4 October, Kos was in German hands. That was followed by Kalymnos. On 8 October, everything was ready for the assault on Leros.

The attack on the island started early on the morning of 12 November. In addition to the landing craft and assault boats of the seaborne formations, a battalion of the *11. Luftwaffen-Feld-Division*[4] also participated. The airborne portion of the operation was to be conducted by the *I./FJR 2* and the *15. (Fallschirmjäger)/Regiment "Brandenburg"*.

Supported by *Stukas* and fighter-bombers, the attack started at 0600 hours. While the ground forces steered towards the island, the paratroopers flew in at first light.

The 470 paratroopers of *Hauptmann* Kühne had been transported from the Ferrara airfield to Tattoi, near Athens. There they practiced for the operation based on aerial photographs. It was there that Kühne also discovered that he was being augmented by the "Brandenburgers". The company commander, *Oberleutnant* Oschatz, arrived a short while later and was thoroughly briefed on the planning.

When the 40 aircraft were just outside the drop zone, they were ordered back by radio to Athens. The ground forces had not succeeded in landing. After three attempts, which the enemy had spoiled, the western force had to return to Kalymnos.

The second attempt was launched at 1000 hours. The 40 machines formed up and headed west for the three-hour flight to Leros, which they reached, approaching from the west, at 1300 hours.

When the force got close to the island, it received fire from Italian and English antiaircraft weapons. The fires were intense, since the aircraft, which were flying through the mountains, were at roughly the same altitude as the defenders. Despite that, the pathfinders, the battalion and the

---

3. Translator's Note: The 1st Company of the "Brandenburg" Coastal Raiding Battalion and the 780th Engineer Landing Company.

4. Translator's Notes: The *Luftwaffe* Field Divisions were formed out of excess ground personnel. They were employed in ground operations. Towards the end of the war, the *Luftwaffe* also transferred large numbers of ground personnel directly into the Army and the *Waffen-SS* as well.

"Brandenburgers" were able to jump into the designated drop zone between the bays of Gourna and Alinda, that is, the narrow portion of the island.

Despite extremely heavy fires from the enemy, *Hauptmann* Kühne was able to assemble his companies and give them their initial missions. The northern portion of the island was screened by the 1st Company of *Oberleutnant* Haase. His mission was to prevent the enemy from breaking through to the south. *Oberleutnant* Fellner's 2nd Company, as well as *Oberleutnant* Möller-Astheimer's 4th Company, moved out to attack *Monte Racchi*. *Oberleutnant* Raabe screened in the direction of the town of Leros and the Bay of Alinda.

Oschatz's "Brandenburger" company was to be dropped later. It had received directives to drop on the Racchi ridgelines. For that reason, *Hauptmann* Kühne stressed the need to watch out for German uniforms during the assault on the mountain.

The paratroopers moved by leaps and bounds in the rocky terrain. *Oberleutnant* Möller-Astheimer led his company through a narrow defile that was overgrown with vegetation up the mountain. When it received fire, the company took cover and returned it. *Oberjäger* Franzrahe crawled forward with the company headquarters section until he had reached the enemy machinegun nest and took it out with hand grenades. The company then continued its assault up the hill.

Farther to the left, the 2nd Company had reached the crest line. A while later, both of the companies assaulted across the ridge line and took the mountain. "Where are the 'Brandenburgers', *Herr Oberleutnant?*" one of the platoon leaders inquired.

"They have to be out there somewhere, since they jumped as planned . . . be careful!"

✠

The jump horn had sounded for *Oberleutnant* Oschatz and his men. Oschatz nodded to *Leutnant* Hörl, who was to be the first one to jump. The officer flung himself through the door and sailed through the air. The jolt from the chute's deployment hit hard, but he then found himself floating down towards the island. He started receiving fire. Off to the right, he saw other men jumping from a *Ju 52*. Up ahead, another aircraft, which had just started its approach, was caught up in a burst of fire from antiaircraft weapons. Flames shot out of the engines and a wing started to come off. At that moment, as the machine began to falter, the men inside started to jump.

Leutnant Hörl saw the ground racing towards him. He pulled up his legs, initiated his parachute landing fall, bounced against the rocks off a cliff and lost consciousness for a moment. The pain from the hard blows he had sustained reawakened him. He released his chute, collected himself and saw several men running towards him. All of them were limping, and a man was crying for a medic off to the right. He had probably broken his foot in that terrible, jutted terrain.

In all, nearly a third of the company sustained bad jump injuries. Enemy mortar fire then started to concentrate on the assembling men. Machine-guns opened up with rapid bursts and forced them to the ground. Shells tore open the cliffs and sent rocks and glowing bits of shrapnel through the air.

A platoon from the coastal raider company worked its way forward to the "Brandenburgers", who were fixed in their positions. While the fighting of the elements of the 22. *Luftlande-Division* and the "Brandenburger" coastal raiders raged, the men of Oschatz's company tried to extricate themselves from the enemy fires.

In the meantime, the paratroopers of *Hauptmann* Kühne had finished clearing the *Monte Racchi* and prepared for farther operations. At first light on 13 November, they attacked again.

Raabe's company, which was screening in the direction of Leros, had a pleasant surprise in the morning, when German soldiers suddenly appeared on a neighboring ridge line. They were soldiers from *Hauptmann* Aschoff's *II./Infanterie-Regiment 16*, that had been put ashore at first light, crossed the ridge line of Hill 192 and then linked up with the paratroopers. When *Hauptmann* Kühne received a report by radio that these two elements had linked up, he breathed a sigh of relief. He ordered his main body to advance on *Monte Meraviglia*. If they could take that hill, the battle for the island would be decided.

The 2nd and 4th Companies were suddenly stopped by enemy fire. The men dug in. They had only gotten as far as the western slope of *Monte Meraviglia*.

The fighting started against English combat patrols. British destroyers—particularly the *Echo* and the *Belvoir*—opened fire and engaged the German positions from the sea.

At first light on 14 November, the British attacked the western slope of *Monte Meraviglia*. They first encountered the paratroopers of the 4th Company. English forces attacking from the northeast ran into the 1st Company. Raabe's 5th Company was almost overrun before elements of a battalion from the 22. *Luftlande-Division* came to the rescue by attacking the enemy in the flank. The English repeated their attacks twice.

On that 14 November, however, the heavy weapons of *Infanterie-Regiment 16* finally made it over on ferries to Leros. Their support substantially increased the combat power of the German forces already on the island.

When the attacks of the British against the German positions abated, *Hauptmann* Kühne decided to launch an immediate counterattack against the *Monte Meraviglia*. Once again, the 2nd and 4th Companies moved out to attack.

They moved uphill as it started to turn dark. They advanced, meter-by-meter, up the hill. It looked as if the enemy had pulled back. Then, all at once, the paratroopers received fire from some three dozen rifle and machine-gun barrels. The attack had failed, before it had even properly begun.

Kühne ordered his men back to the line of departure.

✠

During the night of 14–15 November, the British destroyer *Echo* succeeded in landing 250 soldiers and their equipment at Portolago to reinforce the island's defenders. Another group landed that evening from Samos, being ferried over in motor-torpedo boats and launches.

At first light on 15 November, the paratroopers were positioned along the broad expanse of *Monte Racchi,* some 100 meters below the crown of the adjacent *Monte Meraviglia.* That day, they succeeded in establishing firm contact with the other battle groups on the island. In a conference among the commanders, it was stated by *Major* von Saldern from the 22. *Luftlande-Division* that they would have to launch another attack the next day. *General* Müller was sending in another battalion from Kalymnos, which would be brought over by torpedo boats after sundown.

At noon on the decisive day of battle, *Stukas* attacked *Monte Meraviglia* four times. When they transformed the terrain into a fire-breathing hell, the British attempted to abandon their positions, but could not break out.

During the aerial attacks, the paratroopers regrouped for their own attack.

When the additional battalion arrived and started approaching *Monte Meraviglia,* the paratroopers on the far side of the mountain joined in. The German forces attempted to take the mountain from three sides. The newly arrived German forces got as far as the main enemy bunker, when *Hauptmann* Froböse was wounded. *Oberleutnant* Max Wandrey assumed acting command of the battalion and tried assaulting the east side of the mountain one more time. He took 20 volunteers with him.

While the paratroopers fixed the enemy in place from the other side, Wandrey and his men assaulted up the mountain. Upon encountering enemy obstacles they blew a clear path with demolitions, entered the bunker and reached the casemate with the British headquarters.

When a green pyrotechnic climbed skyward into the afternoon skies, *Hauptmann* Kühne had his men attacked again. Three companies charged, as well as one third of Oschatz's company.

On that side of the mountain, however, the bunkers and dugouts were still spewing lances of flame. Despite that, the men continued to attack. They knew that their assault would help split apart the enemy force and help their other comrades in the process.

The fighting on *Monte Meraviglia* reached an intensity and bitterness that had never been seen before in the Aegean. "Brandenburgers", paratroopers and regular German infantry alike assaulted the high ground. Step-by-step, they gained ground in the rocky terrain and against heavy enemy counterfires.

Oberleutnant Wandrey, in the midst of the English forces on the hilltop, won out. His men tossed hand grenades and blew open steel bunker doors. All at once, the firing around them fell silent. They crawled farther forward, blew open a side passage and advanced through a narrow tunnel into the mountain itself. Once there, they took out a concrete cupola and its crew. Finally, they were in some sort of interior open area. As they set about to open the large iron door, a man came out, who was waving a white flag. He was followed by a group of officers. It was General Tilney, the island commander, and the Italian governor general of the island, Admiral Mascherpa. They surrendered at exactly 1700 hours.

BACK IN RUSSIA: THE 2. *FALLSCHIRMJÄGER-DIVISION* ON THE WAY TO THE SOVIET UNION

Even before *Hauptmann* Kühne's battalion had finished its operations on Leros, *Generalmajor* Barenthin, who was commanding the 2. *Fallschirmjäger-Division* during Ramcke's medical leave, and *Oberst i. G.* Trettner, the Chief-of-Staff of the *XI. Flieger-Korps*, had discussed returning the battalion to the division, which had been moved to the Shitomir area of the Eastern Front in November.

The elements of the battalion that had not jumped and all of the battalion trains were already on their way to the Soviet Union and the main body fought on Leros. The movement order for the division had come from the German Armed Forces High Command on 8 November. The movement started two days later at the railway station at Chiusi, 120 kilometers north of Rome.

Part of the same order also dictated that not all of the division was to move to the Eastern Front. It was to leave behind four battalions—a regimental equivalent—and a company from *Fallschirm-Pionier-Bataillon 2*. These elements were to form the personnel cadre for the formation of the two new airborne divisions, the 3rd and the 4th. The 2. *Fallschirmjäger-Division* was promised personnel replacements for those personnel left behind.

While all of this was happening, another battalion of the division—the *III./FJR 6* of *Major* Pelz—was given a special mission during those turbulent days of November. Kesselring ordered it moved immediately to the area of the mountain road running from Venafro to St. Pietro Infine, 10 kilometers south of *Monte Cassino*, where it intersected with the *Via Casilina*. The Allies had started an offensive there on 18 October, which was directed against the German's *Richard* Line, that highly regarded field position located in front of what would later become the front around *Monte Cassino*. That position blocked the Allied route to Rome. It was directed to be held until the final defensive line—the *Gustav* Line—could be constructed outside of Rome.

Moving rapidly by truck, the battalion reached the city of Cassino after a few hours. From there, the march was continued on foot, since the roads were already under Allied artillery fire.

The paratroopers relieved the mechanized infantry of *Panzergrenadier-Regiment 8* of the 3. *Panzergrenadier-Division* there. Bitter close-in fighting commenced immediately and lasted for the next few days, as the two U.S. battalions around *Monte Cesima* attacked. Still defending there was also the *9./Panzergrenadier-Regiment 8*.

In the fighting over the next few days, the paratroopers faced forces from three different U.S. divisions, the 3rd, 34th and 45th Infantry. Despite the intense fires received from U.S. artillery, the enemy was denied a breakthrough. Penetrations were sealed off and eliminated by means of immediate counterattacks. Pelz's battalion fought in the front lines until 17 November. When the Americans stopped their attacks, the battalion was pulled out of the line. After a few days of rest, it was given screening missions until 15 December.

When the U.S. forces succeeded in crossing the Sangro River and gained ground—joined by British divisions on 7 December—the battalion was sent to Canosa. On 16 December, it launched a counterattack from Arielli, supported by 16 tanks from the *II./Panzer-Regiment 26* of the *26. Panzer-Division.* After taking some ground, the attack was stopped in the vicinity of the cemetery at Orsogna. At first light the next day, New Zealand forces answered with a counterattack. That signaled the end of any farther efforts by the Germans to advance in that sector. In the course of the fighting, the tank battalion lost six vehicles and *Major* Pelz was killed. The paratroopers had to pull back to their lines of departure.

The next attempt to break through by the Allies in that sector was on 24 December. After a heavy artillery preparation, the positions of the paratroopers at Arielli were attacked. The Germans were able to seal off a penetration and the main line of resistance restored. That round of fighting signaled the end of combat operations along the Sangro for those paratroopers.

At the end of December, the battalion was pulled from the front and moved to France, where it became part of the *3. Fallschirmjäger-Division* of *Generalmajor* Schimpf.

OPERATIONS ALONG THE INGUL—RETREAT TO KISCHINEW

It was 17 November 1943, when *Major* Mors, the new operations officer of the division, reported the arrival of the first elements of the *2. Fallschirmjäger-Division* to the *4. Panzer-Armee* of *Generaloberst* Hoth.

By the end of November, the entire division, minus the elements previously discussed, was employed in the southern sector of the Eastern Front. Initially, it was the German Army High Command's operational reserve. *Oberstleutnant* Kroh held acting command of the division, since *Generalleutnant* Ramcke was still ill.

The division command post was at Shitomir. The last formation of the division to arrive—the *I./FJR 6* of *Hauptmann* Finzel—reported on 28 November.

The division conducted its first attack two days later through a vermin-infested stretch of woods. An enemy attack on 3 December against the positions of the *II./FJR 5*, was turned back in an exemplary performance by *Major* Rolschewski's men. While sealing off the penetration, a handful of men of the *7./FJR 5* under *Oberleutnant* Richter threw back the enemy.

The division then participated in *Operation "Advent"*, an offensive operation conducted by the *4. Panzer-Armee* from the Shitomir area towards Radomyschl. It started its attack on the second day of the offensive by moving out from the area around Garboroff, supported by an armored group under the command of *SS-Hauptsturmführer* Burfeind and consisting of four *Tigers*, three *Panthers* and four *Panzer IV's*. The main effort of the attack was conducted by *Hauptmann* Finzel's *I./FJR 6*. It had to struggle through thick wooded terrain, from which it also received small-arms fire. In the dramatic fighting that ensued, the *SS* commander was badly wounded. *Hauptmann* Finzel had a bullet lodged in his lower arm, but he remained with his paratroopers. Under cover of darkness, the battalion pulled back from its all-round defensive position to its original lines of departure.

Several elements of the division continued to participate in the offensive, but the division itself was pulled out of the line on 9 December and moved to the area around Kirowograd. The Russians had succeeded in achieving a deep penetration there.

By then, the division was under the acting command of *Generalmajor* Wilke. It was airlifted to Kirowograd via *Ju 52's*, with only the *I./FJR 6* having to march there. Up to Christmas Eve, the Red Army had not been able to force a decision. Then, on 24 December, the 1st Ukrainian Front launched an offensive along the Kiev-Shitomir road. This was followed by a general Soviet offensive on 5 January, which moved from the area of Snamenka north past Kirowograd. At the same time, a southern pincer moved out of the Werschina-Kamenka area to the south and past Kirowograd. Obviously, the effort was to bag the city.

The *2. Fallschirmjäger-Division*, south of Kirowograd, was hit by the full weight of Russian armor and the five rifle divisions that followed. All of the battalions were forced to fight on their own against the all-engulfing flood of enemy tanks and personnel carriers. Soviet tanks with mounted infantry reached the command post of the *III./FJR 2*, but *Hauptmann* Tannert was able to ward them off. In close combat, two tanks were destroyed. The effort by the enemy to take Nowo Andrejewka failed.

The fighting on Hill 191.1 under *Leutnant* Flemming and what remained of the *7./FJR 5* was a tribute to self-sacrifice. One after the other of the men were wounded or killed. Flemming was badly wounded. His last radio transmission: "We are still holding but with very few men left."

Major Rolschewski attempted to bring relief forces forward, but it proved impossible to break the iron ring of Soviet armor.

Just in the sector of the airborne division alone the Soviets committed 500 tanks. The division's antitank battalion, which only had 10 guns, was able to knock out 34 Soviet tanks. Seven of the kills were registered by the gun crew of *Gefreiter* Hirsch; five from *Oberjäger* Herz. Nine tanks were taken out by paratroopers with close-combat means.

In Nowo Andrejewka, *Oberstleutnant* Kroh, the Commander of *FJR 2*, was a tower of strength in the fighting. *Hauptmann* Tannert was able to fight his way through to him with his 60 remaining paratroopers. Also arriving at the regiment's location were the remnants of *Hauptmann* Gerstner's *Fallschirm-Pionier-Bataillon 2.*

When it appeared the village was about to be completely encircled by the Soviets, Kroh had his forces pull back to the southwest. By doing so, he was also able to protect the open left flank of *FJR 7.*

The *II./FJR 2* held out at Hill 159.9. The tried and true soldiers under *Leutnant* Lepkowski of the 5th Company stood fast against several Soviet tank attacks. Lepkowski's men numbered only 45, but they were able to withstand all of the Soviet attempts to dislodge them.

The division was able to hold its sector until 8 January 1944. When the enemy charged Hill 159.9 again that day, he lost another four tanks, The division had succeeded in reinforcing Lepkowski with a few antitank guns and elements of the 4th Company of the divisional engineers. When the enemy finally called off his attacks that evening, the division had lost in killed, wounded and missing a total of 20 officers and 745 noncommissioned officers and enlisted personnel up to that point. But it had held its sector. The division was later praised by *Luftflotte 4* for its destruction of some 150 enemy tanks. Even Hermann Göring remembered his paratroopers and sent a telegram to the division on 5 February in which he gave his complete praise to the "death-defying assault soldiers".

A deceptive calm reigned over that sector of the front for the next few weeks. On 6 February, a movement order was sent to the division by the *LII. Armee-Korps.* It was directed that the division be employed in the operations to relieve the two encircled army corps west of Tscherkassy.

But the movement took so long that the division was never employed there. Instead, the formation was redirected to Ukrainka. *Generalleutnant* Ramcke finally rejoined the division there, after having successfully recovered from his debilitating illness.

On 23 February, the division was attached to the *XXXXVII. Panzer-Korps.* It received orders to relieve the *11. Panzer-Division* east and west of the Jekaterinopol-Swenigorodka road and both sides of the Gniloy-Tikitsch River.

During the night of 2/3 March, prisoner statements led to the conclusion that a new attack was imminent in the sector. Next morning, the Red Army attacked with a battalion in the sector of the *II./FJR 7.* Large assault detachments attempted to penetrate through the lines. The sector of the *I./FJR 6* around Olchowez was also attacked, and the enemy succeeded in penetrating there. The penetration was later sealed off and eliminated by means of an immediate counterattack by the men of the *4./FJR 6.*

The next night, the Red Army men moved in closer to the paratroopers. A short while later, after 45 minutes of artillery preparation, the Soviet offensive started, which again fell with its full weight on the airborne division. The attack, which was nurtured and sustained over the next few days by the introduction of new elements, forced the division to abandon Gussakowo. In general, however, the division was able to hold its other positions until 8 March. Then a general withdrawal followed, which was hotly pursued by Soviet formations supported by armor. The division concentrated in the area around Nowo Archangelsk by order of the *8. Armee.* The new area of operations around Ssinjucha was reached on 13 March after a foot march through mountains of mud. The division set up its command post in Trojanka.

When the Red Army broke through there on 16 March, Ramcke needed to pull his men back to the Kuzaja defile. The next day, Ramcke received orders to fly to Germany to the Cologne-Wahn training area and make preparations for the reconstitution of his division there. *Oberstleutnant* Kroh assumed acting command of the division again.

The *2. Fallschirmjäger-Division* conducted a fighting delay as part of the general withdrawal movements in the southern sector of the Eastern Front. In the Kochanowka area, the division once again succeeded in thwarting all efforts of the Soviets to outflank it, before it was pulled back to Schibka by order of the *LII. Armee-Korps.* It arrived there on 3 April. The division had shrunk to just 17 officers and 514 noncommissioned officers and enlisted personnel. It should also be mentioned that the division only had a trench strength of 2,468 men when the Soviet offensive started on 5 March.

Kampfgruppe 2. Fallschirmjäger-Division[5] was attached to the *320. Infanterie-Division* in the Minizkoje sector. The small force conducted a determined local counterattack there and succeeded in ejecting the enemy from Karmanowo.

When it was ordered on 6 April to pull all of the formations of the *6. Armee* back across the Dnestr, the divisional battle group crossed at Delacheu. On 20 April, the division received personnel replacements, 640 recently trained recruits who reported to the command post of *Oberst* Kroh. They had just come from training at Quedlinburg and were under the leadership of *Oberleutnant* Backhaus.

The final operations of the division in the Soviet Union were as part of *Operation "Bollwerk"*, the elimination of Soviet bridgeheads along the bend in the Dnjestr. To that end, Kroh's men were attached to the *3. Panzer-Division.*

Kampfgruppe Kroh broke through the Soviet positions at 0200 hours on 10 May. The battle group reached Pugoceni and captured 35 antitank guns, 8 artillery pieces and 12 heavy machine-guns there. Supported by tanks from the *3. Panzer-Division,* the battle group was able to hold the positions and move out the following night to eliminate the bridgehead. In a dramatic struggle, the battle group was able to force the enemy across the river. The German Armed Forces Daily Report of 12 May announced the following:

> In the course of the elimination of the enemy bridgehead on the lower Dnjestr that was reported yesterday, the forces reporting to *General der Infanterie* Buschenhagen defeated seven enemy rifle divisions, as well as elements of an artillery and antiaircraft division.

The division received orders on 12 May to be pulled out of the line. What remained of it concentrated in the Cimiseni vicinity. The companies had

5. A *Kampfgruppe* consists of the remaining combat elements of a depleted division that will usually be reconstituted at a later date.

trench strengths ranging from 6 to 12 men. They were loaded up at the train station at Kischinew. On 20 May, the paratroopers of the *2. Fallschirmjäger-Division* left the Soviet Union for ever.

THE END IN ITALY: ANZIO-NETTUNO—OPERATIONS OF THE *4. FALLSCHIRMJÄGER-DIVISION*

In October 1943, the *4. Fallschirmjäger-Division* was established in Perugia, with *Oberst i. G.* Trettner being the first commander. Trettner was an old hand and had been on the Student's staff in the corps headquarters. He had participated in almost all of the airborne planning since the very beginning. He received instructions on 18 January 1944 to establish an alert battalion within each of the airborne regiments established for the division—the 10th, 11th and 12th. The mission was to establish a powerful reaction force in case of Allied landings behind the Cassino front. Trettner entrusted *Major* Gericke with the command of that ready force within the division.

With the landing of Allied forces on the beaches at Anzio and Nettuno during the morning of 22 January, *Operation "Richard"* went into effect.

Kampfgruppe Gericke was immediately sent to the sector where the Allies had landed and committed. Initially, it marched to Aprilia. But the enemy spent time consolidating instead of advancing with all of the forces that had landed. He apparently wanted to wait for the entire initial wave of the invasion force to come ashore.

Later on, Churchill wrote: "I had hoped at the time to put a wild cat ashore. But all that we had at Anzio-Nettuno was a stranded whale."[6]

The way from Anzio-Nettuno to Rome was open for General Lucas, the Commanding General of the U.S. VI Corps. In 14 days, he brought ashore 18,000 vehicles, 380 tanks and 70,000 men.

That occasioned another very biting remark from Churchill: "We must have had a damned high number of surplus drivers there. Apparently, the enemy had more soldiers that we did."

On 22 January, all German forces in Rome were alerted and—in an effort to assure unity of command—attached to *Kampfgruppe Gericke.*

By noon of that day, Gericke had all threatened roads that led to the Italian interior blocked. Weak U.S. forces, consisting of assault detachments and patrols, were driven back. By 26 January, all of the *4. Fallschirmjäger-Division* had been inserted into the front. Up to that point, the enemy had not undertaken the slightest effort to advance inland. After the *3. Panzergrenadier-Division* had also arrived in sector, *Generaloberst* von Mackensen, the Commander-in-Chief of *Heeresgruppe C,* gave orders to counterattack.

Kampfgruppe Gericke, supported by two regiments of the *65. Infanterie-Division,* which had also just arrived, advanced in the direction of Carroceto.

---

6. Translator's Note: Reverse-translated into English from the German without access to the original English source quotation. The same is true of the quotation that follows.

Those German forces got as far as the base of Hill 80 and the outskirts of the rail station there.

General der Flieger Schlemm, the Commanding General of the newly formed *I. Fallschirm-Korps*, ordered an attack on the hill. The attack started on 12 February. *Major* Gericke had *Major* Kleye's battalion swing out to the north to hit the enemy's positions in the flank. The attack succeeded, but the bitter fighting also claimed the life of Kleye. *Oberleutnant* Weiß assaulted the group of buildings around the rail station with his company of 60 men, cleared them and then entered the station building itself. There, 180 Scots surrendered after a bitter struggle. The enemy then attacked with tanks and *Oberleutnant* Weiß found himself with only 12 paratroopers left defending the building.

As Shermans approached, they were engaged with close-combat means and destroyed. The train station and Hill 80 remained in German hands. When Kleye's battalion was finally pulled from the line, it only had 6 officers and 259 noncommissioned officers and enlisted personnel left. The battalion had suffered casualties of 4 officers and 278 soldiers killed and wounded. After that, the fighting subsided.

A follow-on attack on 16 February to collapse the Allied beachhead advanced 2 kilometers deep along a width of 4 kilometers. But an Allied air attack stopped the German attack wedge at that point. The attack was repeated two later and again advanced, that time pushing the Allied forces back to the area of their beachhead on the first day.

General Mark Clark, the U.S. Army Commander-in-Chief in the Italian Theater, later wrote in his memoirs: "We were pushed back to a line behind which there was only sea. Every blow that Mackensen delivered to us the next day would hit us on the chin."[7]

But *Generalfeldmarschall* Kesselring was forced to call off the attack 12 kilometers outside of Anzio. His attacks so far had cost too many casualties, and the Germans had no idea how battered the Allied force was.

Another attack, which was ordered by Hitler for 29 February, bogged down during the afternoon of 1 March. The enemy-occupied Hill 17 was able to hold against the attack by the tanks of the *26. Panzer-Division*. Fighter-bombers and other close-air-support aircraft helped tip the scales, and the Allied counterattack during the night of 1–2 March pushed the Germans back once and for all. *General der Kavallerie* Westphal, Kesselring's Chief-of-Staff, later wrote: "Our forces were no longer sufficient. We were no longer capable of attacking."

General Truscott, who had been placed in command of the forces in the beachhead, had his command advance on 23 May. *Major* Timm's *FJR 12* was able to turn back the initial assault on both sides of Velletri. It was not until the night of 30–31 May that the Allies finally succeeded in breaking through in the sector of the *LXXXVI. Panzer-Korps* in the area of *Monte Artemisio*. As a result, the Allies were to the rear of the airborne forces. The front of the *14.*

---

7. Translator's Note: Reverse-translated passage.

Armee collapsed. The Allies then stormed with all their weight and fury across the Alban Mountains. Their objective was Rome, which was reached on 4 June by the U.S. 88th Infantry Division.

Trettner's *4. Fallschirmjäger-Division* was employed as a rearguard and was able to brake the Allied advance so effectively that all German formations were able to pull back in an orderly fashion and save all of their heavy equipment. The last ones to leave the "Eternal City" were the paratroopers. According to author Eric Linclater: "Even more convincingly than at *Monte Cassino*, the Germans in the Anzio-Nettuno beachhead demonstrated their thorough mastery of military operations."[8]

THE FIGHTING FOR MONTE CASSINO

After the employment of *Major* Pelz's *III./FJR 6* outside of *Monte Cassino*, the first battle of the same name started on 17 January 1944. It was there that Verdun was resurrected for the Second World War. General Clark wrote the following in his memoirs: "The fighting for Cassino was the most casualty-heavy, painful and perhaps most tragic of the entire Italian Campaign."

The U.S. 34th Infantry Division had almost taken the mountain with the world-famous abbey atop it, when *Generalleutnant* Richard Heidrich arrived with the first elements of his *1. Fallschirmjäger-Division* and decisively turned back the enemy. Heidrich had his men set up in the cliff. His regiments defied attack after attack by the enemy. He saw his own main role in directing the artillery fight. On more than one occasion, he came down with artillery fires at the decisive moment, just as the Allies thought they had taken the mountain.

Coming from the frying pan of Anzio-Nettuno and into the fire for the first battle was *Kampfgruppe Schulz*, consisting of *FJR 1*, augmented by *Major* Schmidt's *Fallschirm-Pionier-Bataillon 1* and the *3./FJR 3*. *Oberst* Schulz and his men defended the mountain above and in front of the *Via Casilina*. The men never entered the abbey, which was strictly off limits to them. When the enemy, for certain reasons, dropped leaflets in which it was claimed that German soldiers had occupied the abbey, Schulz had a Morse code message sent in plain text to the Allies, in which he claimed the assertion was an outright lie. He also immediately notified his division commander, who also confirmed Schulz's report.

When the soldiers of the 34th Infantry Division succeeded in taking the village of Cairo on 30 January and then, 48 hours later, were positioned north of the *Via Casilina*, the high point of the struggle started for Schulz and his men. In a bitter struggle, *Major* Kratzert and his *III./FJR 3* retook Calvarien Mountain. The city of Cassino proper was defended by *Grenadier-Regiment 211* of the *71. Infanterie-Division*.

When the enemy attacked with both the 34th and the 36th Infantry Divisions on 11 February, he was turned back. The U.S. II Corps was badly

---

8. Translator's Note: Reverse-translated passage.

battered. Although that signaled the end of the battle for the time being, there would be three more before the Germans were finally ejected from the mountain.

On the morning of 15 February, 142 "Flying Fortresses" took off from various airfields around Foggia. They reached *Monte Cassino* around 1000 hours and dropped 353 tons of bombs. They were followed by 47 B 25's and 40 B 26's, which dropped another 100 tons of bombs on the cloister and completely destroyed it.

Schulz and his men experienced that gruesome and completely senseless bombing from their positions on the slopes and cliff caves above and in front of the *Via Casilina*. The paratroopers did not suffer any losses, because they were not in the beaten path of the bombs. Only the civilian populace and the monks of the abbey were forced to endure that punishment.[9]

On 17 February, Schulz and his men took the monks and the civilians to safety. Then he ordered his soldiers to take up positions in the ruins of the cloister, which had been transformed into ideal defensive positions by the bombardment.

During the Allied operational pause that followed, Heidrich was able to regain all of his divisional elements and employ them in the defense of the Cassino sector.

✠

For the Second Battle of Cassino, it was up to the New Zealanders to pull the chestnuts out of the fire. Replacing *Oberst* Schulz in the defensive positions was *Oberst* Heilmann's *FJR 3*.

An aerial bombardment of the city of Cassino signaled the start of the second battle on 15 March. In all, 600 bombers dropped their payloads. The city was transformed into smoldering ruins. The ferocity of the attacks against the land and people of a current ally came as somewhat of a surprise, although everything was allowed by the Hague Conventions, since the enemy was defending from the area.

The *II./FJR 3* defended the city proper, while the 1st Battalion of the regiment dug in at the abbey. Arrayed around the mountain were the 1st and 4th Regiments of Heidrich's division.

After the last bomber turned away, the Germans were subjected to an artillery preparation from 750 guns. *Hauptmann* Foltin, whose *II./FJR 3* had lost some 200 soldiers as a result of the air attack on the city, then had to defend against 400 approaching armored vehicles, some of which penetrated into the middle of the city. But the armored vehicles were then thwarted by obstacles that their colleagues from the air had created. Separated from the tanks, the Allied infantry advanced, only to be turned back in close combat with Foltin's men.

_____

9. All the contents of the abbey, including priceless relics and artworks, were removed several weeks earlier for safekeeping. Every item was returned after the war.

That night, the Indian 4th Infantry Division attacked. It succeeded in taking *Rocca Janule* and then assaulting farther in the direction of the abbey. By the morning of 16 March, the Gurkas had reached Hill 435 and were some 400 meters behind the defenders at *Monte Cassino.* At that point, the *I./FJR 4* launched an immediate counterattack, stopping the Indians and pushing them back.

The New Zealand division was entrusted with taking the abbey were able to take two-thirds of it. The paratroopers could not be dislodged from the remaining pockets of resistance, however. It was *Major* Böhmler's men of the *I./FJR 4,* who defended there. During the early-morning hours of 17 March, Böhmler had an assault detachment attack the Indians on Hill 435. The assault detachment completely surprised them. In a well-aimed blow, they dislodged the Commonwealth forces from the hill top. The Indians launched an immediate counterattack. Using their 10 to 1 advantage in men, they pushed the German paratroopers back off. Some 30 paratroops against an entire Gurka battalion!

Left completely to its own devices—communications with both the regiment and the division had been lost—Böhmler's battalion held the mountain. When relief forces in the form of the *III./Panzergrenadier-Regiment 115* of the *15. Panzergrenadier-Division* arrived the following day, Böhmler and his men attacked the *Roca Janule,* which had been taken by the Indians and New Zealanders the previous day.

The attack, which suffered from a lack of forces, did not succeed. *Oberleutnant* Böhlein's *2./FJR 4* was able to enter the enemy's main line of resistance, but he was thrown back, and the entire attack stalled.

The Allied attack had been stopped for a second time. From London, Churchill once again asked what was going on. He was unable to understand why General Alexander continued to hammer *Monte Cassino* instead of hitting the Germans in the flank and finally marching into Rome. A reporter for *Stars & Stripes* indignantly wrote: "The advance, after all, can't be drawn out like this due to a handful of paratroopers."[10]

None of that changed one basic fact: That was, indeed, what was happening. Heidrich skillfully employed his divisions and each *Kampfgruppe* had an experienced commander who knew how to hold up the enemy.

At the end of March, the burnt-out *1. Fallschirmjäger-Division* was pulled out of the line. It was intended to put it in a rest position for a week. But that did not occur, since there were not enough forces. The division enjoyed only three days of rest before it was sent forward again. *Oberst* Walther's *FJR 4* went to the city of Cassino and the abbey. The division's machine-gun battalion was attached to the regiment in support.

Oberst Heilmann and his *FJR 3* went to the mountains and occupied positions on Calvarien Mountain, the *Colle S. Angelo* and the *Monte Caira.* *Kampfgruppe Ruffin* was attached to Heilmann's forces on the *Monte Caira.* The latter battle group was composed of *Gebirgsjäger-Regiment 100* of the *5.*

10. Translator's Note: Reverse-translated passage.

Gebirgs-Division and *Hochgebirgs-Bataillon 4.*[11]

Schulz's regiment became the division reserve and was held in the rear. While all of this was going on, the *5. Fallschirmjäger-Division* was also being formed and all three regiments of Heidrich's division had to reassigned their 3rd Battalion to serve as personnel cadre for the new division. As a result, the division was even weaker than before when the Third Battle of Cassino started.

✠

One of the decisive sources of help for the beleaguered paratroopers in the previous two rounds of fighting was *Oberstleutnant* Andrae and his *Werfer-Regiment 71*[12], who helped stop the attacks of the Allied forces, especially those of the New Zealanders and the Indians, by massive salvoes from his rocket launchers. Heidrich employed Andrae's forces at the defensive focal points.

✠

At the conclusion of the fighting after the second battle, the wounded were evacuated under the Red Cross flag. The New Zealanders recovered their wounded as well, and both sides respected each other's wounded recovery details. One time, however, the flag was not respected and a stretcher-bearer party was taken prisoner so as to provide information to the enemy's intelligence services. The German airborne engineers in the city of Cassino formed an assault detachment and attacked a building where they had observed New Zealand guards. It turned out that they were Maoris, who fled the building in wild flight after being attacked by the demolition and shaped charges and *Panzerfäuste.*[13]

In the nights that followed, several combat raids were conducted by the airborne engineers. The enemy also dispatched patrols, and there were frequent short, sharp firefights between combatants as they encountered one another in the ruins of the city. The paratroopers had barricaded themselves in the *Hotel Continental.* A Maori battalion, which was positioned in the former botanical gardens, attacked the hotel from there. The Maoris were turned back each time they attacked. The handful of paratroopers were able to hold their ground. One of the indefatigable patrol leaders was *Feldwebel* Walter Werner, who always succeeded in ejecting the enemy from his defensive sector. For his actions, he was later awarded the Knight's Cross on 9 June.

On 26 March, a few days after the end of the second battle, Heidrich issued a division order-of-the-day in which he singled out the headquarters of the *II./FJR 3* for praise in combating a numerically superior enemy. Also

---

11. Translator's Note: 4th Alpine Battalion (High Altitude).

12. Translator's Note: 71st Rocket Launcher Regiment.

13. Translator's Note: The *Panzerfaust* was a handheld rocket-propelled grenade with very limited range but which was highly effective against armor due to its shaped-charge warhead. It was the precursor of the world-famous RPG 7.

singled out was the *1./Fallschirm-Pionier-Bataillon 1* of *Leutnant* Cords, which had participated in numerous immediate counterattacks and combat patrols. The focal point of the praise was expressed this way:

There was practically no combat patrol in Cassino in which flamethrower sections, demolition parties or elements with bundled charges from the *1./Fallchirmjäger-Pionier-Bataillon 1* did not participate . . .

I wish to extend special recognition to the company for its heroic operations and for its exemplary performance of duty.

/signed/ Heidrich
Generalleutnant and Division Commander

THE THIRD BATTLE OF CASSINO

On 11 May 1944, the Third Battle of Cassino was ushered in with a massive artillery preparation coming from more than 2,000 guns that started firing at 2300 hours, when the BBC of London announced the time. From the upper Rapido Valley to the coast, the lances of flame penetrated into the night at the same time.

Once again, *FJR 3* was in the center of the action. *Major* Böhmler's *I./FJR 3* defended Hill 593, Calvarien Mountain. Böhmler was badly wounded in the knee and had to be evacuated. Heidrich had the wounded men evacuated to the rear in armored personnel carriers. That was part of the maxim he himself had created for his division: "*Kameradschaft!—Können!—Korpsgeist!*"[14]

All of the attacks of the Polish II Corps were turned back. The Polish Carpathian light infantry, a brave force, fresh and rested, was unable to overwhelm the paratroopers holding out in the ruins, who were far inferior to them in numbers. The *3./FJR 3* fought against the Polish 2nd Armoured brigade. The *1./FJR 3* was overrun by the Carpathian light infantry several times. But the men rallied each time and took back the hill. But then the enemy appeared to have established himself permanently. The reserves of the *I.* and *II./FJR 3* attacked the hill four times and were turned back each time.

During the evening of 12 May, *Oberfeldwebel* Karl Schmidt with his patrol from the *14./FJR 3* tried one more time. With a handful of comrades, he stormed up the hill, tangled with the enemy and ejected him from his foxholes and trenches. Karl Schmidt wrested control of the hill back for the Germans and earned himself the German Cross in Gold in the process.

General Alexander was forced to pull the Polish II Corps back to its line of departure.

The fighting, however, continued to 17 May. Calvarien Mountain and the abbey remained in German hands. On the morning of 18 May both were abandoned without a fight. The French Expeditionary Corps, with a Moroccan and an Algerian division, had succeeded in advancing through the Acrunian

---

14. Translator's Note: "Comradeship! —Ability!—*Esprit de Corps!*"

Mountains and reaching the Itri-Pico Road. As a result, strong forces were located 40 kilometers north of the Cassino Front and the paratroopers were about two-thirds surrounded. The advance by French General Juin forced the withdrawal of the German airborne forces at *Monte Cassino.*

The battle groups pulled back, their rearguards keeping the enemy at bay. Their first stop was Piedmonte.

Heidrich then assumed command of the *I. Fallschirm-Korps* on 31 October 1944 and was promoted to *General der Fallschirmtruppe* on the same day. *Oberst* Karl-Lothar Schulz was given command of the *1. Fallschirmjäger-Division* on 18 November 1944 and promoted to *Generalmajor* two months later. Schulz would continue to lead the division in Italy until the end of the war. The division pulled back, step-by-step, and reached the Adria south of Bologna in August.

TO THE BITTER END

On 10 September 1944, the U.S. 5th Army started its major offensive, with the objective of capturing Bologna. It was already looking as though Bologna had been lost, when the paratroopers showed up on the slopes outside the city. The enemy was defeated in a series of smaller actions, and the American offensive was called off on 27 September.

While the two divisions of the corps—the 1st and 4th—continued to fight in Italy, the *3. Fallschirmjäger-Division,* the *5. Fallschirmjäger-Division* and *FJR 6* (*Major* von der Heydte) were committed to the fighting in Normandy when the Allies landed there. The fighting there will be covered in the next chapter.

The *I. Fallschirm-Korps* fought in the Romagna area during the fall fighting. Heidrich, who was eventually promoted to *General der Fallschirmtruppe,* was given exceptionally tough missions. The fighting withdrawal across both the Reno and Panaro Rivers stand in testimony to his skilled combat leadership. The *1. Fallschirmjäger-Division* continued to hold around Bologna.

Under *Generalmajor* Trettner, the *4. Fallschirmjäger-Division* fought at Florence and in the Rimini area. Once that division reached the Bologna area, Heidrich had all of his corps assembled in the same area of operations. When the retreat north had to be initiated from there in April 1945, the formations of the corps discovered to their chagrin that there were no crossings over the Po River and nothing had been done to prepare for the crossing.

In the meantime, the *278. Infanterie-Division* of *Generalleutnant* Harry Hoppe had also been attached to the corps. During the morning of 23 April 1945, Heidrich summoned all of his division commanders to his command post and briefed them on the depressing situation:

> Gentlemen, nothing has been done for our divisions crossing the Po. I must therefore issue the following orders:
>
> 1. The *I. Fallschirm-Korps* crosses the Po at Felonica during the night

of 23/24 April and prevents the crossing of pursuing enemy forces from the north bank.

2. To screen the crossing, the *278.Infanterie-Division* forms a bridgehead along the railway line south of Felonica and assumes responsibility for the corps' right flank on the boundary with the *14. Armee* with the initial forces that cross.

3. All remaining vehicles are to be destroyed and primarily combat-capable forces to be taken across the river. Ambulances with wounded have priority over all other vehicles. Vehicle tires are to be dismounted for non-swimmers.

Nobody knew how much the general had struggled within himself to issue this order. The crossing was initiated. Many soldiers who attempted to swim were drowned.

The retreat that followed has remained etched in the memories of all who participated like a nightmare. Ambushed again and again by partisan bands, many paratroopers were killed as the end was so near. On 2 May, the war in that theater ended as the result of a separate capitulation. Heidrich issued a last order-of-the-day to his paratroopers:

> To the very end, we have done our duty and do not feel defeated. Keep you airborne spirit. Even if we have to separate temporarily, we still remain a community. Everyone of you must know that the darkest hour of our people demands manly virtue. Remember our fallen comrades who died for us.

The formations of the corps that were taken prisoner were sent to camps in Trentino. They were then sent to camps at Ghedi, with way stations at Rovereto and Verona. From there, the paratroopers were scattered to the four winds.[15]

---

15. *General der Fallschirmtruppe* Heidrich was released from captivity as a gravely ill man in 1947. On 22 December 1947, he died in the hospital at Hamburg-Bergedorf. His paratroopers—some of them travelling more than 100 kilometers by foot in winter—gave him the last honors on 27 December 1947.

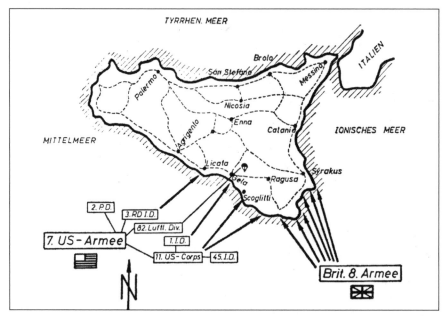

The Allied assault on Sicily—Operation Husky—began on 10 July 1943.

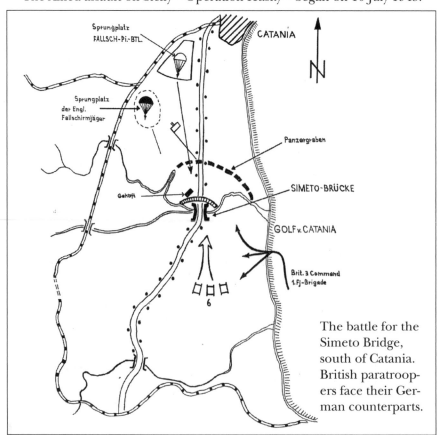

The battle for the Simeto Bridge, south of Catania. British paratroopers face their German counterparts.

Oberstleutnant Heil-
mann on Sicily.

Fallschirmjäger-Regiment 3 succeeded in breaking through.
Oberstleutnant Heilmann speaks to his men.

The fighting around Rome on 10 September 1943. Paratroopers enter the Eternal City.

The way to the city center, past two destroyed Italian M15/42 tanks.

Il Duce has been freed. To the left in the picture is *Oberleutnant* Berlepsch. Behind Mussolini is Otto Skorzeny.

General der Flieger Kurt Student on the roof of the Campo Imperatore. Next to him is *Stabsarzt* Dr. Krutoff.

Generalleutnant Heidrich with *Oberst* Heilmann (camouflage jacket) at Cassino.

Paratrooper engineers undertake an assault at Cassino. The incredible devastation of the town is evident.

The destroyed monastery at Monte Cassino, where *Bataillon Böhmler* defended.

Karl-Lothar Schulz, the defender of Monte Cassino, during the first battle.

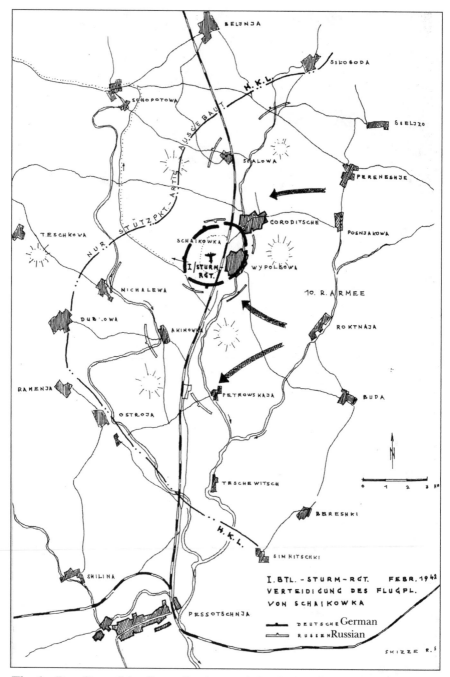

The 1st Battalion of the Storm-Regiment defends the airfield of Schaikowka, February 1942.

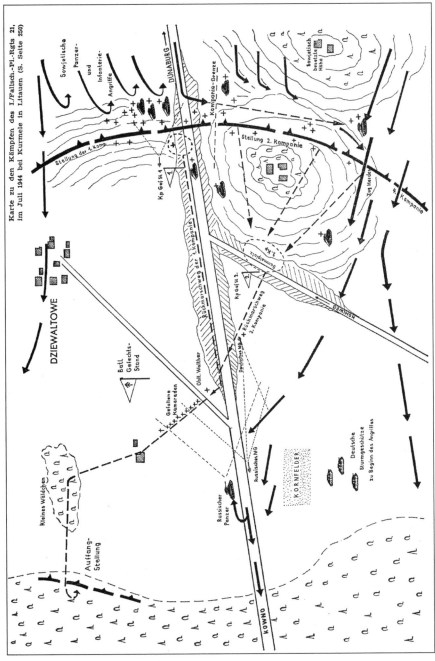

Map of the battles of *I./Fallschirm-Pioneer- Regiment 21* (Airborne Engineer Regiment 21) in July 1944 around Kurmele in Lithuania.

1. The town of Cassino.
2. Castle Mountain and the ruins of the castle.
3. Monastary Mountain and the Monastary at the summit.
4. Cassino station.

5. The Rapido River.
6. The railway line from Naples.
7. The Rome-Naples highway.
8. Allied attack to outflank Cassino.
9. German counterattack in the northern sector.

10. Unsuccessful Allied attacks on both mountains.
11. Attacks against the German paratroop positions south of Cassino.
12. German counterattacks.
13. May 17th, 1944 the retreat begins.

14. Rearguard actions covering the German withdrawal from the mountains.
15. Allied artillery firestorm against Castle Mountain.

CHAPTER 9

The End in the West

FALLSCHIRMJÄGER-REGIMENT 6 IN NORMANDY

At the beginning of June 1944, *Major* von der Heydte's *FJR 6* moved to Normandy, with the regimental command post located in Carentan. On the evening of 5 June, *General der Fallschirmtruppe* Student made a surprise visit to the headquarters. *Major* von der Heydte was not there; he had just left to reconnoiter in another sector. At this point, Student was the Commander-in-Chief of the German's airborne field army, with headquarters in Nancy. A second airborne corps had been formed—the *II. Fallschirm-Korps* of *General der Fallschirmtruppe* Meindl—and it had been positioned in France to defend against possible Allied invasions. The corps consisted of the *3.* and the *5. Fallschirmjäger-Division.*[1]

When Student showed up at von der Heydte's headquarters, only a liaison officer was there. The field-army commander shared dinner with the troops and then addressed them. As he parted, he said two words: "Be alert!"

His words proved prophetic. That night, a massing of naval vessels, aircraft, arms and equipment, the likes of which had never been seen before, gathered along and over the French coast. It signaled the start of a week's worth of uninterrupted fighting for the German paratroopers.

Allied paratroopers landed in among the strongpoints of *FJR 6.* *Oberfeldwebel* Pelz took 1 major, 2 captains, 1 lieutenant and 73 enlisted personnel prisoner when he searched the area around his positions when the alert was sounded. During the early-morning hours of 6 June, von der Heydte drove to Carentan to interrogate the prisoners. They were assigned to the 101st Airborne Division, from the 501st Parachute Infantry Regiment. He reported to the intelligence section of the *LXXXVI. Armee-Korps* that he believed the invasion was on.

At 0900 hours, the regimental commander was at St. Côme du Monts, 15 kilometers inland, and saw the coast through his binoculars. He observed a gigantic flotilla at sea, which was firing on Utah Beach.

---

1. Meindl's corps had started to be formed in December 1943 in the area east of Melun, near Paris. The personnel collection point for the corps saw trainloads of volunteers arrive daily for their new assignment, although they had been given an expedited basic and specialized training in Germany and elsewhere. (Schools were located at Wittstock, Salzwedel, Kraljewo, Serbia and Dreux, the latter near Paris.) The cadres were formed from personnel reassigned from the *1. Fallschirmjäger-Division,* as well as residual elements of the *Hauptmann* Göttsche's *Luftlande-Lehr-Abteilung.*

Von der Heydte attempted to reach the coast by attacking through St. Marie du Mont and Turqueville. The *I./FJR 6* succeeded in getting through St. Marie du Mont. The *II./FJR 6*, which had been directed to turn at Turqueville and advance across the embankment through the flood area, was stopped by heavy enemy fires from St. Mère Eglise. *Hauptmann* Mager, the battalion commander, submitted a report immediately, whereupon von der Heydte ordered him not to pivot but instead attack and take St. Mère Eglise, which otherwise would be a constant danger to the flanks. The subsequent attack bogged down, and the battalion sustained heavy casualties. Later that morning, it set up defensive positions along the limits of its earlier advance. The *I./FJR 6* also dug in, and the regiment formed a blocking position on the "entryway to the Cotentin Peninsula". The regiment defended a sector 20 kilometers wide and 15 kilometers deep!

The enemy concentrating in front of the regiment grew stronger daily. Elements of the German regiment were encircled and had to be relieved by means of rapidly conducted immediate counterattacks. When U.S. tanks approached the regimental command post, von der Heydte had only a bicycle platoon and the headquarters clerks at his disposal. *Hauptfeldwebel* Bräu assembled the men and then positioned them in outposts. When the tanks had closed upon the command post, they were engaged by the paratroopers with demolitions and destroyed.

The paratroopers were then surrounded. They had to wade through marshland, swim across rivers and fight with small-arms to escape. The Americans seemed to outnumber them a hundred to one. *Major* von der Heydte, whose arm was in a sling due to bruised nerves, continued to lead his men despite the intense pain. His compassion and caring for his soldiers extended down to the very last man.

On the evening of 8 June, the regiment had to pull back to the eastern and northern outskirts of Carentan. It established a blocking position on *Route National 13*, between the two U.S. bridgeheads that were forming. Carentan was bitterly contested. The paratroopers were able to turn back every attack, until they were almost out of ammunition. The 101st Airborne Division was battered. But when a handful of men from the 1st Battalion made it back to the regimental command post, they reported that they were all that was left of the 700-man battalion.

On 10 June, von der Heydte was asked to surrender. When the U.S. emissary left, the *Ju 52's* arrived with the requested rations and ammunition. The air-dropped canisters were recovered successfully by von der Heydte's men.

At the outskirts of Carentan and at the new command post at Pommenauque, it was the last time that paratroopers fought one another. *Leutnant* Brunnklaus made a name for himself there as a small-unit commander; he was able to achieve great success defensively and turned back the enemy several times. In the end, he was killed during an enemy assault.

On 11 June 1944, the German Armed Forces Daily Report announced:

During the difficult fighting in the enemy beachhead and the elimination of the enemy paratrooper and air-landed forces that were dropped in the rear area, *Fallschirmjäger-Regiment 6* of *Major* von der Heydte distinguished itself tremendously.

At 1700 hours on 11 June, von der Heydte had to order the evacuation of Carentan and pulled his regiment back to prepared positions. In one final effort, the paratroopers advanced as far as the *Hotel du Commerce* and the rail station. But they had to abandon that last bridgehead for good the following day.

Through 27 July, von der Heydte and his regiment defended along both sides of the road from Carentan to Perier. The regiment succeeded in launching a surprise attack during the period. Twenty men on bicycles, with a tank in support, ambushed a U.S. infantry battalion. They took 13 officers and 600 enlisted personnel prisoner.

After the breakthrough of U.S. forces at St. Lô, von der Heydte's men fought with a *Waffen-SS* division, breaking out of the encirclement at Coutances and making their way south, reaching the positions of the *353. Infanterie-Division* at Garray on 30 July. By doing so, von der Heydte had spared his men enemy captivity.

On 12 August, the regiment was pulled out of the line after a final operation northwest of Vire. In all, 3,000 officers and men were no longer there. They had been killed, wounded or taken prisoner. The regiment was moved to Güstrow, reconstituted and then sent into the area of northern Belgium and southern Holland, to be employed as a fire brigade for the field-army group there.

OPERATIONS OF *FALLSCHIRMJÄGER-REGIMENT 9*

Fallschirmjäger-Regiment 9 of the *3. Fallschirmjäger-Division* was moved to the hills around the *Mont d'Arree* at the beginning of May. The alert was sounded there by hand-cranked sirens at 0100 hours on 6 June. Towards 0800 hours, orders were received from the division ordering the regiment to move its 1st Battalion (*Major* Alpers), along with two companies from *FJR 8* and a medical unit, to the landing areas in Normandy. At first light the next day, the battle group reached the village of Romangne.

On the next day, Campeaux was reached. That morning, the paratroopers heard the following German Armed Forces Daily Report announcement:

While large-scale defensive fighting rages on the Eastern Front, the Allied air and sea landing took place during the morning of 6 June 1944. The *II. Fallschirmjäger-Korps* of *General* Meindl, with the *3. And 5. Fallschirmjäger-Division*, is fighting there along side other infantry divisions and the *Waffen-SS*.

Kampfgruppe Alpers was not employed until 12 June. On that day, the paratroopers received their first taste of the massive Allied artillery power. When the Americans penetrated the line of the 3rd Company with a platoon, the *1./FJR 9* of *Oberleutnant* Moser was committed to seal off the penetration. The advancing company was received by a veritable hail of bullets. Two wounded men approached him. One, *Leutnant* Schröder, had only been wounded in the arm. He was supporting the badly wounded 3rd Company commander, *Oberleutnant* Schlöhmann. The battle group's mortars registered on the enemy positions and took them out, one after the other. The penetration was then sealed off in a determined attack and cleared up. When changing positions along the front, several paratroopers were wounded by snipers.

At the end of the first day of operations, *Kampfgruppe Alpers* had lost 58 soldiers, 11 of them killed. There were no more large-scale Allied attacks through 15 June. But a strong artillery preparation started at 0500 hours on 16 June, which lasted two hours. The fires were then shifted to the rear, and the U.S. assault groups moved out. They approached to within 10 meters of the positions of the *1./FJR 9*. It appeared that the Americans would succeed in breaking through there. At the last second, however, two engineer squads with flamethrowers appeared. Their streams of flames landed squarely among the advancing groups of Americans, who scattered screaming and rolling on the ground. It was a terrible image, and the garish cries of the burning men even surpassed the racket of the attacking fighter-bombers, which fired their rockets and strafed the German positions.

The U.S. attack was turned back. However, the *1./FJR 9* had lost 32 men. The *2./FJR 9* came away somewhat better. It had only 29 dead and wounded. The 3rd Company lost 24 men. During the fighting, *Leutnant* Horst Ansorge knocked out two enemy tanks with the *Ofenrohr* [2] and *Panzerfäuste*. When he attempted to reload his *Ofenrohr*, a U.S. tank started firing at him. The main-gun round landed in a pile of rocks in front of the officer and exploded. He was wounded in the shoulder. Despite that, he continued to lead the fight of his men, even though he was on a stretcher. After the immediate danger had passed, he was evacuated to the rear.

The *4./FJR 9* suffered "only" 13 wounded and dead.

When the attack launched at 1100 hours was turned back, the battle group clerk tallied the losses: 28 dead, 71 wounded 1 prisoner and 2 missing. In all there were 102 men on the list.

The U.S. attack was repeated on 20 June. The paratroopers were in an equally difficult situation again, but the enemy did not press his attack as hard as he had the first time. At the end, there were 38 dead and wounded. *Generallieutnant* Schimpf, the divisional commander, appeared at Alpers' command post after the attack and congratulated him on his great defensive effort. He told the field-grade officer to listen to the German Armed Forces Daily report that evening:

---

2. Translator's Note: The *Ofenrohr* (stovepipe) was the German equivalent of the U.S. bazooka, firing an 8.8-centimeter rocket-propelled grenade with a hollow-charge warhead.

After an immediate counterattack northeast of St. Lô, the [enemy's] penetration from the previous day was cleared up. The *3. Fallschirmjäger-Division* of *Generalleutnant* Schimpf distinguished itself in particular in those operations.

THE *II. FALLSCHIRM-KORPS*

The headquarters of the *XIII. Flieger-Korps* was redesignated and reorganized as the *II. Fallschirm-Korps* at the end of 1943, with *General der Fallschirmtruppe* Meindl named as the first Commanding General after the reorganization. His Chief of Staff was *Oberstleutnant i.G.* Ernst Blauensteiner, a future Knight's Cross recipient.

The corps reported logistically to the headquarters of the *1. Fallschirm-Armee* until the beginning of May 1944. It reported tactically to the Commander-in-Chief West.

On 12 May, the corps assumed command of the *3.* and *5. Fallschirmjäger-Division* in the Bretagne region, where it then reported to the *7. Armee*. Its command post was located about 120 kilometers east of Brest.

As a reserve for the western theater, the corps received a directive to "form and train the corps troops and continue the supervisory, training and command and control functions over the attached *3.* and *5. Fallschirmjäger-Division* and conclude them as soon as possible."

The corps troops consisted of:

Korps-Aufklärungs-Abteilung 12
Korps-Nachrichten-Abteilung 12
Sturmgeschütz-Brigade 12
Corps logistics command
Corp medical group
Fallschirmjäger- Ausbildungs- und Ersatz-Regiment 12[3]

Commanding the *3. Fallschirmjäger-Division* was *Generalleutnant* Richard Schimpf (Knight's Cross on 6 October 1944). *Generalleutnant* Wilke commanded the sister division. The former division had 100% of its authorized personnel and equipment, whereas the latter had only 80%.

The *Korps-Flak-Regiment 12* and the *Korps-Artillerie-Regiment 12* were formed in Germany but never served with the corps, considerably diminishing its combat power.

The Commanding General directed that the focal point of training be "light infantry training in the field in the defense." To that end, he was proven right in the upcoming fighting in Normandy.

At the start of the Allied invasion on 6 June, the training for the *3. Fallschirmjäger-Division* and *Korps-Aufklärungs-Abteilung 12* was considered completed. In contrast, the *5. Fallschirmjäger-Division* had only started training at the platoon level.

---

3. Translator's Note: 12th Assault Gun Brigade and 12th Airborne Training and Replacement Regiment.

As a result of the increasing destruction of the railway network in France, as well as the "road hunts" that started in the middle of May by enemy fighter-bombers, there were considerable logistical difficulties. Despite that, morale was good among the corps' formations.

During the morning of 6 June, the corps received orders from the *7. Armee* to move to the area of St. Lô in Normandy. The corps troops and the *3. Fallschirmjäger-Division* moved out. The *5. Fallschirmjäger-Division* and the corps replacement battalion remained in their garrison for the time being, while the *2. Fallschirmjäger-Division* of *Generalleutnant* Ramcke moved in to take its place.

THE FIGHTING IN NORMANDY

In the first few days and weeks of fighting in Normandy, it appeared that a new "Stalingrad" was developing, this time in the west. The enemy's numerical superiority was overwhelming. The Germans could not face their opponents with numbers that were even approximately close.

No less than 30 infantry divisions and 5 airborne divisions had headed out from Great Britain to the French coastline. They were safeguarded by a vast number of fighters and fighter-bombers. At the start of the invasion, the fighter-bombers and bomber formations increasingly attacked the road networks, on which the German armored formations were attempting to make their way to the front. Some of the armored formations had to road march more than 150 kilometers to reach their assigned sectors, in which to they were supposed to "throw the enemy back into the sea."

It would exceed the scope of this book to describe the enemy landings and the initial fighting on the different beachheads. Suffice it to say: The largest armada of all time was positioned off the coast of France on 6 June 1944 and for the next two days:

> There were 7 battleships, 2 monitors, 24 cruisers, 123 destroyers, 360 torpedo boats 1,073 smaller naval vessels and 1,700 landing craft in the Western Naval Task Force; in all, there were 2,426 vessels in the Eastern Task Force. The total number of military vessels numbered 5,358. By means of auxiliary and transport ships, the number of vehicles initially brought ashore was 6,480.

After the initial tug-of-war that ensued as to whether the actual Allied invasion was taking place—and some of the most absurd theories imaginable were pursued—the *II. Fallschirm-Korps* was finally attached to the *LXXXIV. Armee-Korps* on 11 June! *General der Fallschirmtruppe* Meindl immediately had all available forces move into the designated sector east of the Dives River as far as Tilly.

The command and control elements of *General der Panzertruppen Freiherr*[4] Geyr von Schweppenburg's *7. Armee*, which was responsible for the sector the airborne corps was entering, were severely disrupted by an enemy air attack

---

4. Translator's Note: Baron (nobility).

302

conducted against Caen on 9 June. Although the Commander-in-Chief was unscathed, his Chief of Staff and 17 other officers were killed. The field army remained without a command and control apparatus for some time, and it was not until 30 June that a replacement headquarters was able to go forward and reassume full command in the sector from the mouth of the Orne to the Vire. Consequently, Meindl and his forces were often without a direct chain-of-command above; they also saw themselves fighting not only U.S. forces, but also those of the Commonwealth.

The aforementioned *LXXXIV. Armee-Korps* assumed command and control of the field army's sector and was expanded into a field-army detachment for the purpose. The airborne corps reported to it as well as the *77. Infanterie-Division*, the *275. Infanterie-Division* and a number of other smaller formations.

The field-army detachment had its work cut out for it. A day after assuming command of the sector, the U.S. forces launched their attack against the bulwark of that sector, St. Lô. Initially, the elements of the *3. Fallschirmjäger-Division* could not be broken. Several enemy penetrations were sealed off and eliminated in close-quarters fighting.

On 12 June, the third Commanding General of the *LXXXIV. Armee-Korps*, *General der Artillerie* Erich Marcks, was killed when a salvo from a fighter-bomber attack split open his skull. He was replaced by *Generalleutnant* von Choltitz. Despite the string of horrendous bad luck for the Germans in this sector, they were able to hold the line until 10 July with virtually no loss of terrain. According to *Generalleutnant* Fritz Bayerlein, the commander of the *Panzer-Lehr-Division*, which was also employed in the sector, the holding of the main line of resistance was "largely the incontestable service of the *II. Fallschirm-Korps*."

It was the service in particular of the *3. Fallschirmjäger-Division*, which blocked the path of the U.S. V Corps in its advance from the Bois de Verigny area towards St. Lô. The Americans were attempting to unhinge that bulwark of the defense by an outflanking maneuver from the east.

In preparations of its attack, the corps requested and received bomber support, which dropped an unprecedented number of bombs in the entire sector of the German airborne corps. Despite the punishing preparation, the Americans were only able to advance about 1.5 kilometers.

Deserving of special mention during that fighting were the *II./FJR 9* and the *I./FJR 5*, which held firm in the face of all assaults. Between the two battalions, 19 enemy tanks were destroyed in close combat. In the end, the British had to advance to help out their Allies in the fight. They were able to force the breakthrough, but it cost them 1,000 dead.

It was during that fighting that a future Knight's Cross recipient made a name for himself. It was *Oberfeldwebel* Grünewald, who had left his staff position in the corps headquarters to volunteer for the corps' assault-gun brigade. Walter Faber, a war correspondent, captured the operations of the remarkable assault-gun commander for posterity:

We were in the assembly area and listened to the order to attack. Next to me was my comrade, *Oberfeldwebel* Grünewald, who also appeared aglow with the desire to do something. He can barely wait to get into his steel crate, move out against the enemy and stop him.

He had already received his Iron Cross, First Class after his third engagement.

The orders were issued, and when we went to the platoon leader's gun, the crews were already there.

"Gun refueled and uploaded," his assistant platoon leader reported. Grünewald greeted the comrades of the three guns that had been attached to his platoon.

He grinned conspiratorially at the members of his crew.

"Let's mount up for the fracas!"

They mounted their guns and I took my place with my camera next to the gun commander.

"Move out!" *Leutnant* Deutsch's voice could be heard through the intercom.

They left the patch of woods, in which they had taken up concealed positions from the fighter-bombers, and rattled not to the asphalt road, which would allow them to get to the area of operations more quickly.

From the far side of the road, we could already hear the report of the guns from the 1st Platoon. Fighter-bombers appeared, but Grünewald did not pay any attention to them. It was imperative to get to the area of operations as quickly as possible—and start the engagement.

The first artillery rounds impacted. At first seemingly arbitrarily, then closer and closer. By giving it the gas and then slowing down to a snail's pace, the driver—Leipold—attempted to escape the barrage.

Then, all of a sudden, the dull thuds of main guns firing. Limbs from the trees along the *Chausee* had been ripped off.

"Prepare to engage!" the gun commander ordered.

"Vehicle ready . . . gun loaded and safety on!"

Off to the right, the rail line came into view.

"That's where the infantry are," Grünewald said.

"Half right . . . 800 meters . . . enemy tanks!" Grünewald informed his men.

Everyone was ready to fire. Grünewald counted a line of Shermans through his binoculars. To the left and right of them, two tank destroyers emerged from the thick vegetation.

"Guns two and three: Flank right. Gun four: Off to the left somewhat. Everyone else: Follow me!"

Georg Grünewald, called "Sepp" by his comrades, rolled rapidly towards the Shermans that were the most advanced.

"1 o'clock . . . 800!" he barked to his gunner.

"Identified!" the gunner replied.

"Firing halt . . . fire, when ready!"

The vehicle stopped abruptly. There was a small correction on the part of the gunner and then the first 7.5-centimeter round whipped out towards the enemy. The round grazed the enemy tank and ricocheted.

Another correction and the second round left the barrel. It immobilized the targeted vehicle. Behind it, infantry dove for concealment behind the tank.

"1100 . . . left . . . next to the barn!" the gun commander guided the gunner.

"Identified!"

The loader had already placed the next round in the breech. It slammed shut and, seconds later, the gun recoiled. One second after that, the next enemy tank took a direct hit. The tanks that followed had their infantry dismount into the uncertainty of the vegetation.

The two assault guns off to the right engaged a group of Shermans that had advanced off to the side. After knocking out three, the rest pulled back. They disappeared farther to the right behind the railroad embankment.

The firefight devolved into individual engagements, which ended victoriously for the assault gun crews each time. Then the assault gun to the left of Grünewald was immobilized when it was hit in the engine compartment. The men dismounted from the steel crate and threw themselves to the ground.

Another assault gun was immobilized when one of its tracks was shot off.

The battlefield was covered with gunpowder smoke and thick fumes. When the Allied artillery started registering on the area after the last of the Shermans had pulled back, *Oberfeldwebel* Grünewald ordered a change of position. The fight was not over, however. Grünewald still had eight rounds ready and an additional one already in the gun tube for use against any enemy forces.

The gun turned slightly to the right, while Grünewald observed ahead.

"One of them's being towed away . . . 2 o'clock . . . quick!"

They rolled toward the prime mover that had hooked up to the immobilized Sherman. The first round set the prime mover alight; the second one put an end to the Sherman for good.

A hard blow on the right against the sideskirt caught the driver's attention. He reacted and turned away. He rolled forward into a corn field at full speed and waltzed down the tall shoots, creating a broad cut through the field.

"Five rounds left, *Herr Oberfeld!*" the loader reported. When the gun got to the far side of the field and broke out of the corn, two more enemy tanks were sighted. They formed a portion of a tank wedge, whose other side was hanging farther back to the rear. "Damn! There's six of them!" the driver called out. Grünewald's fire command was drowned out by the ear-deafening racket of their rations box on the rear deck being shot off. Then there was another ear-deafening blow to the front slope. Shrapnel whistled above the gun. Grünewald was hit by shrapnel in the left arm.

When I attempted to dress his wound, Grünewald dismissed me. He fired the last three antitank rounds and then the high-explosive ones against infantry targets, forcing the enemy to pull back even faster.

Only then did Grünewald give orders to pull back.

That evening, *Leutnant* Deutsch turned in Grünewald's fifth through fourteenth "kills".

General Meindl summoned "Sepp" Grünewald to him during the evening of the next day and gave him a portrait with a heartfelt dedication.

On 29 October 1944, Georg Grünewald became the first assault-gun man of the airborne corps to receive the Knight's Cross.

THE FIGHTING AT ST. LÔ

On 20 July 1944, the day the most famous attempt was made on Hitler's life, the headquarters of the *II. Fallschirm-Korps* was located in Torigny. The orders of the day remained unchanged: Defend! It was proving increasingly impossible to hold out against a numerically vastly superior force with seemingly endless supplies of equipment. The enemy attacked on 26 July and continued his attacks the next day. The U.S. 1st Army wanted to break through. The U.S. forces were able to take an important hill. It was retaken by the Germans and the position occupied by the remnants of the *5. Fallschirmjäger-Division* of *Generalleutnant* Wilke. The division had been battered considerably by several bombing raids conducted against it over the previous few days.

The 27th of July saw another attack by bombers of immense proportions. The terrain north of the St. Lô–Periers–Lessay road was bombed in an area 5 kilometers wide by 2.5 kilometers deep in the sector of the *Panzer Lehr Division*. The entire area was transformed into a wasteland. Then Allied tanks assaulted along a narrow frontage to force a breakthrough. As they were attacking, they were covered by approximately 450 fighter-bombers, which attacked anything and everything that still moved. *Generalleutnant* Bayerlein's division was so badly battered that it had to be pulled out of the line, when the commander reported it was no longer capable of combat operations.

The *II. Fallschirm-Korps* fought for three days in that area and *Generalleutnant* Meindl had to commit his last reserve, *FJR 15*, into the mix. If the enemy succeeded in pivoting to the north and west from the area around Camisy, then the front of the entire field army would collapse.

At the crossroads of Le Mesnil–Herman, *Korps-Aufklärungs-Abteilung 12* set up defensive positions. It was thanks to that battalion that the entire headquarters of the *352. Infanterie-Division* was saved from being eliminated.

Fortunately for the paratroopers and infantry defending there, the *2. Panzer-Division* was able to link up with them in time and funnel them back to the east. At the same time, what was left of the *Panzer Lehr Division* and elements of the *352. Infanterie-Division* covered the open left flank of the *LXXXIV. Armee-Korps.*

Masses of U.S. tanks suddenly advanced southwest from attack positions at Hamby. They were identified as heading for the coastline at Coutances. That meant there would probably be another attack on Avranches.

Thirty U.S. tanks were knocked out, but it appeared the enemy would again encircle the beleaguered forces. It was thanks to *Generalleutnant* Mahlmann's *353. Infanterie-Division* that the gap could be held open. The 52-year-old division commander assaulted at the head of his men.

When crossing points over the Sienne were reached on 29 July, there were only 400 soldiers left in both the *243.* and *353. Infanterie-Division. General der Artillerie* von Choltitz was reassigned to a position of greater authority, and he was replaced by *Generalleutnant* Elfeldt in command of the corps. The "Green Line", which ran from Percy–south bank of the Sienne–Brehal, could be held on 29 July. The position was overrun the next day by the U.S. 4th Armored Division after an artillery preparation. A single assault-gun brigade and the *353. Infanterie-Division* were unable to slow down the overwhelming enemy force and had to pull back to Villedieu during the night of 30–31 July.

In the Marigny area, the paratroopers of *Major* Noster's *FJR 14* dug in. The fighting grew increasingly desperate as the Allies started to close the noose. Efforts to mount a vigorous aggressive defense seemed doomed to failure due to the lack of resources.

On one of those days, *General* Meindl, who was returning to his command post after a briefing at higher headquarters, was attacked no less than 30 times by fighter-bombers. It took him four hours to move a short distance. The air attacks had become so bad that the doors were removed on many vehicles to facilitate a speedy exit when attacked form the air.

When *General* Meindl finally arrived at his command post that day, he was met by the son of *Generalfeldmarschall* von Kluge, *Major* von Kluge, who relayed a message from his father to continue to hold.

Meindl told the field-grade officer: "Please inform your father exactly what I am telling you now: We have reached the point where Normandy can no longer be held, because our forces are defeated and exhausted."

THE II. FALLSCHIRM-KORPS IN THE FALAISE POCKET

After the enemy broke through at Avranches, it was imperative for the German forces to pull back as quickly as possible to escape encirclement. It was hoped that the *II. Fallschirm-Korps* could push the enemy back to the Vire by means of a counterattack on Torigny, but no one seriously counted on the effort to be successful. In spite of everything, the attack succeeded! That was due in large measure to the employment of heavy *Flak* batteries, which had been brought forward quickly and which effectively supported the airborne forces. It was possible to hold the town of Vire against the enemy to the north and northeast. On 9 August, the *3. Fallschirmjäger-Division* was able to seal off and contain an enemy penetration in the sector of the *363. Infanterie-Division.*

On 11 August, the regiments of the division, which were employed as the corps rearguard, succeeded in knocking out 32 enemy tanks, most of them with demolitions. But none of these superhuman efforts could prevent the enemy from closing the circle with strong forces at Trum on 18 August.

From that point forward, the enemy fired artillery constantly into the pocket. Despite the constant pounding, the paratroopers were able to hold their positions. The majority of the vehicles that had been brought into the pocket were destroyed by artillery and fires from the air; any immobilized vehicles were blown up prior to the breakout attempts. The accomplishments of the airborne forces of the *II. Fallschirm-Korps* are reflected in a letter Meindl later sent home concerning the breakout:

> Our paratroops and some *SS* forces couldn't believe it when I called out to them from the enemy side and dressed them down because they were not conducting the attack properly. How was it possible they were attacking the way they were over the open plain!
>
> We needed to crawl for long stretches and exploit every bit of cover if we wanted to get through. The enemy forces on the high ground and the artillery fire that drummed down on us from three sides gave us the most worries.
>
> Swinging out far to the flank, I reached a pond at 0930 hours that was on the side of the road. I found our Commander-in-Chief there, *SS-Oberstgruppenführer* Paul Hausser.
>
> We were then faced with our most difficult task: The dominant high ground just east of Cordehard, which was occupied by a lot of enemy tanks. I had to initiate the attack there, only 200 meters in front of us.
>
> Moving out to the north, we tried to envelop the enemy. By evening, we were in his rear; despite the heat and our thirst, we had succeeded. I then sent the paratroopers and the *SS* north to attack. I was able to start it with one and a half battalions of paratroopers, four tanks, two assault guns and our artillery, which was without ammunition.
>
> We went through the ditches, covered by the hedges, and through patches of woods. Suddenly, the enemy opened fire on us. An artillery round that landed next to a machine-gun nest killed and wounded a

number of my magnificent paratroopers. *General* Schimpf[5] was also wounded.

All of a sudden, two enemy tanks a few meters uphill from us were on fire. They had been taken out by two volunteers with *Panzerfäuste*. And, once again, on the hill, the signal flames of destruction shot skyward from additional enemy tanks. Capitalizing on this multiple blow to the enemy, our paratroopers assaulted with a battle cry. We took more than 30 prisoners and only two tanks succeeded in escaping. The neighboring hill was also evacuated by the enemy, because, *Oberstleutnant* Blauensteiner, my Chief-of-Staff, was attacking from the south.

Our opponents turned out to be from the Polish division. Hard men and brave fighters.

But there were still 20 enemy tanks in front of us. They were attacked by surprise by a battalion from the *2. SS-Panzer-Division "Das Reich"* and 18 of them were eliminated. Another *Waffen-SS* battalion and our paratroopers also attacked the enemy forces somewhat farther back and were able to keep the gap open.

The evacuation of our wounded could start at 1900 hours. Among them was *Generalleutnant* Schimpf.

We continued to hold open the gap and Army elements streamed through to freedom, escaping the pocket and captivity. After that, I moved the command post to Coudehard.

At 0030 hours the next morning, the *SS* rearguards reported that no one else was coming and that everyone had closed up to within a few kilometers of us.

I went to the acting regimental commander of *FJR 8* through the burning village of Coudehard and ordered him to assemble his forces without making a sound and march off to the east on the road. The machine-guns and *Panzerfäuste* were to be ready to be used.

We took off. One man after the other, not speaking a word, heading east. All of the wounded were taken in vehicle that had been made serviceable.

A breakout point had been created and, at 1400 hours, the battle groups of *Oberst* Liebach, *Oberstleutnant* Blauensteiner and *Oberst* Mahrle had arrived. The *3. Fallschirmjäger-Division* had gotten through with all of the men it still had alive.

During that period of fighting in Normandy, the men of the *II. Fallschirm-Korps* accounted for 606 enemy armored vehicles in close combat. In addition, 76 aircraft had been shot down with small-arms or troop machine-guns.

The 21st of August 1944 forever remained an unforgettable day for *General der Fallschirmtruppe* Meindl. It was the day he got out of the pocket with all of his men.

---

5. Once Schimpf was wounded, Meindl personally assumed command of the division, in addition to his responsibilities as the Commanding General.

It was not until 28 August, however, that the General was able to get all of his airborne formations that were with other formations back. They no longer had any heavy weapons. They had been in almost constant combat since 12 June without being relieved and always at the hot spots of the front.

The corps was then ordered to the area around Nancy for reconstitution. But the order was rescinded by a field army commander-in-chief, with the result that the paratroopers were once again employed as rearguards for the *5.* and *7. Armee* on 2 and 3 September. On 20 September 1944, Meindl wrote scathingly:

> Why were the other formations no longer fighting, due to cowardice? As a result, my corps had to move out to be the last sacrifice in France. And since everything was streaming to the rear, my *3. Fallschirmjäger-Division* was outflanked on 4 September at Mons and ended up, to a large extent, in captivity. Only a few succeeded in getting away.

Written on 20 September 1944.

Eugen Meindl
General der Fallschirmtruppe

For their self-sacrificing sense of duty, which also cost the lives of many paratroopers, Meindl was awarded the Oak Leaves to the Knight's Cross of the Iron Cross. The commanders of the breakout groups, *Oberstleutnant* Blauensteiner and *Major* Stephani, who was killed in the effort, were awarded the Knight's Cross.

From 6 June until the end of August, *Heeresgruppe B* in Normandy lost 400,000 dead, wounded and captured. The number of prisoners was around 200,000.

Two German field armies had ceased to exist.

In weapons, the field-army group lost 1,300 armored vehicles, 500 assault guns, 1,3000 artillery pieces and antitank guns and some 20,000 trucks and staff cars.

OPERATIONS AROUND NIJMEGEN: OVERVIEW

At the end of August, after the Allies had achieved a breakthrough, the headquarters of Montgomery's 21st Army Group vowed to continue the pursuit "to the last breath of rider and steed through Northern France and Belgium."[6]

The intent succeeded and by 4 September, Antwerp was occupied by the Allies. However, crucially, the approaches to the huge port were still in German hands. From the North Sea as far as Maastricht, there was a huge gap in the German main line of Resistance.

---

6. Translator's Note: Reverse-translated.

Generaloberst Student was in his headquarters in Berlin-Wannsee overseeing the formation of new airborne formations, when he received a directive from *Generaloberst* Jodl: "Assemble all available airborne forces and establish a new defensive front along the Albert Canal. The front is to be held under all circumstances."

The telephone and telegraph lines ran hot, as the senior officer of the airborne force assembled all available forces in the designated staging area. In terms of actual airborne formations, there was not too much—*FJR 6* and the *I./FJR 2* (*Major* Finzel)—but the *719.* and *176. Infanterie-Division* also augmented the *1. Fallschirmjäger-Armee,* which was a field army in name only. The designated defensive sector was occupied. Within the space of 24 hours, there were 32 battalions positioned along the canal for a distance of 120 kilometers. In addition, there were a few weak artillery batteries and some platoons of *Flak.*

Student's formations were allocated to *Generalfeldmarschall* Walter Model's *Heeresgruppe B.* By the middle of September, the situation stabilized somewhat. That was primarily due to differences of opinion among the senior Allied commanders, however.

While General Eisenhower wanted to attack the "Siegfried Line" along a broad front and force it all at once, Montgomery strove for the main effort to be placed with his 21st Army Group. In his memoirs, Montgomery later wrote that he wanted to avoid a long winter campaign with its corresponding disadvantageous consequences for England. His plan was to advance with strong armored forces to the north at Arnhem and cross the Rhine there, turning east into the area around Münster and then take the Ruhr area. His plan gained favor and was approved.

To take the route to Arnhem, he needed airborne assets to take key towns and transportation nodal points. To that end, he was given operational control of the U.S. 101st and 82nd Airborne Division, as well as the British 1st Parachute Division. The main ground force was the British XXX Corps, which was to advance across the Albert Canal through Son and head towards Arnhem, building a corridor along the way. The British XII Corps would follow, screening to the west with the British VIII Corps to the East.

The operation was to go down in history books as Operation "Market Garden". The drop zones of the Allied airborne forces and the axis of attack of the main body divided Student's forces into two halves. Forces from the 101st Airborne Division landed right next to Student's headquarters.

THE *II. FALLSCHIRMJÄGER-KORPS* IN ACTION
When Operation "Market Garden" started, the *II. Fallschirm-Korps* was positioned in the area east of Cologne, where it was being reconstituted. Corps troops were there, as well as the *3.* and *5. Fallschirmjäger-Division.* Initially, only 10% of the authorized strength of those formations was there. Missing were some 30,000 experienced paratroopers, who had been killed, wounded or captured in the preceding fighting.

The corps had no artillery at its disposal, and even the lift capacity for the corps' heavy weapons and equipment was too small for what little remained. It was in that situation that orders arrived from Model's *Heeresgruppe B* on 18 September that the corps was to immediately move with all available personnel to the Kleve area and eliminate the air-landed forces between the Meuse and the Rhine. *General der Fallschirmtruppe* Meindl attempted to make clear to the Commander-in-Chief that his "corps" consisted of about 700 combatants. Model's response was clear: He had to attack!

The 700 men were sent to the front on the available lift capacity. Whatever else that could be gathered up would follow by train.

Meindl went with his headquarters to the headquarters of the *406. Infanterie-Division* in Rindern. There he found the division commander, *General der Kavallerie* Kurt Feldt, whose formation was fighting air-landed forces north of the *Reichswald*. The *406. Infanterie-Division* was also a division in name only, and it consisted of only remnants of the original division and *ad hoc* elements that had been hastily attached to it.

On 19 September, all forces in the immediate area were subordinated to Meindl. The total number of forces Meindl could commit against the enemy was 3,400 men, 6 tanks, 3 armored cars and a few *Flak*. He also had 130 heavy and light machine-guns and 24 mortars.

It should be stated, however, that the attack of Meindl's pitifully small force was conducted with such force and surprise that the U.S. forces were completely nonplussed.

For instance, *Major* Becker's *FJR 5* and attached elements attacked early on the morning of 19 September and took the hill south of Bergendal by surprise. Becker then received reinforcements from *Kampfgruppe Fürstenberg* and the attack was continued with considerable élan. By the afternoon of that day, all of the ground that had been taken by the U.S. paratroopers was retaken by the Germans. That area, which had been intended for the landing of some 450 gliders, appeared to have been lost.

When everything hung in the balance, the calls for help were heard by the U.S. command. The forces that had been intended to take the bridge at Nijmegen were pulled back and committed against the German force. The German paratroopers then found themselves attacked not only from the front but also along their right flank and had to pull back.

On the morning of the next day, the armored elements of the British XXX Corps succeeded in linking up with the Americans at Grave. That meant that it would almost be impossible to reduce and eliminate the Allied bridgehead at Nijmegen, even though the German command had been doing its utmost starting on the evening of 19 September to accomplish just that.

At 0630 hours on 20 September, three German battle groups attempted to wrest back control of the bridge: *Kampfgruppe Becker, Greschick* and *Herrmann*.

Initially, the attack made rapid progress. Then daylight broke and fighter-bombers raced over the battlefield, strafing everything that moved without a single German fighter answering in return. *Kampfgruppe Becker* was hit by heavy defensive fires just outside of Wyler. Some houses were taken, but the German paratroopers were being hit hard by fires from "Devil's Mountain", which dominated the terrain.

An assault detachment was sent to the flank to approach the ridgeline from the blind angle. It advanced as far as the four machine-gun nests that were posted along its route, and it sustained heavy casualties.

Kampfgruppe Hermann advanced as far as Mook. After three hours of street and house-to-house fighting, the village was taken. When the enemy advanced with three columns of tanks a few hours later and systematically blew apart the village, the Germans there also had to pull back.

Kampfgruppe Greschick, which was committed in the center of the sector, got as far as Groesbeek. It also had to take that village house-by-house. It suffered heavy losses in the street fighting. Despite that, it put the U.S. forces there in a precarious position. The Germans were able to overrun the barricades in the road and, supported by four tanks, continue to advance. It was not until the evening and the Americans brought up more reinforcements that the Germans were also forced back, returning to their original points of departure.

The German attack on Nijmegen collapsed for good.

✠

That afternoon, U.S. forces crossed the Waal in assault boats and were able to take the road bridge, with the result that by that evening the first tanks of the Guards Armoured Division were headed across to the north.

When Hitler discovered that the bridge had been taken by the attackers, he contacted the headquarters of *Heeresgruppe B* and asked Model directly why the bridge had not been blown up. Model replied that he intended to retake the bridge by means of an attack by the *II. Fallschirm-Korps*. That seemed to satisfy the *Führer*.

After having some time to mull things over, Hitler directly intervened again and ordered that "the enemy forces in the Arnhem, Nijmegen, Mook and Groesbeek areas be eliminated as quickly as possible." Farthermore, the gap in the front north of Eindhoven was to be closed by means of a concentric attack.

It was directed that the *II. Fallschirm-Korps* be prepared to conduct those attacks on 26 September. *Panzer-Brigade 108* and a separate heavy antitank battalion were immediately attached to the corps for that purpose.

The next day, the *Führer* order was refined by stating that the main effort of the attack was to lie between the Waal and the Meuse and that the Nijmegen–Grave road had to be taken.

More reinforcements flowed into the airborne corps for that purpose. Among them was the *Pionier-Lehr-Bataillon*,[7] which had been trained in fighting in urbanized areas.

---

7. Translator's Note: Engineer Battalion (Instructional).

THE ATTACK ROLLS!

Early in the morning of 28 September, the attack force moved out with the *II. Fallschirm-Korps* at its head. It was supported by flamethrowers, armor and occasional *Luftwaffe* sorties. The U.S. 82nd Airborne Division suffered heavy losses, particularly from the air. Both of the bridges at Nijmegen were damaged, but not destroyed, by a bombing raid from a group of *He 111's*.

The area around Erlekom was reached, after having lost five tanks. It was there that the German attack came to a standstill, after already having taken considerable casualties.

New German fighter-bomber attacks during the night caused the middle span of the railway bridge at Nijmegen to collapse. The road bridge was also badly damaged.

At Den Heuvel, mechanized infantry, tanks, assault guns and flamethrower elements attacked the American front and forced it back 500 meters. The German penetration was sealed off and cleared up later in the morning when additional British reserve armored forces showed up and launched an immediate counterattack.

A last bitter attempt by the paratroopers, supported by all available infantry formations, took place during the night of 1–2 October under a moonlit sky and after a short artillery preparation. Leading that time was *Fallschirm-Aufklärungs-Abteilung 12*. By first light, it had taken the outskirts of Groesbeek. But all of the sacrifice was for naught, when reserve armor forces showed up in the morning and eliminated the German gains by means of three groups of tanks.

At 1745 hours on 2 October, the Commander-in-Chief of the *1. Fallschirm-Armee* submitted the following report to the German Army High Command:

> Attack operation of the *II. Fallschirm-Korps* did not succeed. Strong enemy air superiority during the day. Training of the forces in the field too poor for nighttime operations.

The German front firmed up along a line running Erlekom–Wyler–Den Heuvel–Riethorst–Middelaar and the *II. Fallschirm-Korps* received orders from the *1. Fallschirm-Armee* to go over to the defense. The paratroopers had practically no heavy weapons left.

When the enemy started to clear gaps in his own minefields and concentrations of armor were observed near Groesbeek during the night of 6–7 October, the airborne corps reported that an attack was probably imminent.

The assumption proved correct, when bombers came in at 1345 hours and covered the entire area with an avalanche of fire, which was caused by some 100,000 fire bombs. The main part of the payloads was dropped over Emmerich; within half an hour, the entire city was engulfed in flames.

At about the same time, a second massed formation of bombers attacked the logistics nodal point of Kleve. As the records of the Royal Air Force noted, 1,700 tons of high-explosive bombs and 1,000 tons of fire bombs were dropped

314   JUMP INTO HELL

on Kleve alone. Emmerich, by contrast received "only" 650 tons of high explosive and 1,280 tons of fire bombs (100,000 individual bombs). Among the bombs dropped were 2,000-pounders. The amount of tonnage dropped that day in that sector was the equivalent of 2,350 *V2* attacks on England, a number that was never reached. A total of 691 bombers were employed in these raids, which were flown on special request.

NEW AREAS OF OPERATION FOR THE *II. FALLSCHIRM-KORPS*

At the end of November 1944, the airborne corps was relieved in sector by the *LXXXVI. Armee-Korps* and moved to the Roermond-Venlo area. The *7. Fallschirmjäger-Division,* which was fighting there, and the *8. Fallschirmjäger-Division,* which was still being formed but located near the front in case of emergency, were attached to the corps for operations.

The corps moved its command post in the middle of December from Vorst to St. Hubert. At the end of December, the *7. Fallschirmjäger-Division* was relieved by the *190. Infanterie-Division* and moved to the Straßberg area for a planned counterattack that never materialized.

In the meantime, *Fallschirm-Sturmgeschütz-Brigade 12* had been reequipped and started to conduct training at the unit level. The brigade was attached to the *1. Fallschirm-Armee* and moved to the Elmpt Woods.

The *7. Fallschirmjäger-Division* was returned to the corps command and control, but when it arrived, it was committed in the sector of the *LXXXVI. Armee-Korps.*

Let us now return to operations by other airborne formations in Normandy.

THE *2. FALLSCHIRMJÄGER-DIVISION* IN NORMANDY

After the return of the *2. Fallschirmjäger-Division* from Russia to Cologne-Wahn, *Generalleutnant* Ramcke and his operations officer, *Major* Herbert Schmidt, attempted to get the battered division, which had also been tasked to release personnel for the formation of other new elements, back on its feet again.

When the invasion started, Ramcke waited every day for the orders to move out. He did not receive a call until 11 June, however. It was from Nancy and the operations officer of the *1. Fallschirm-Armee.* "*Herr General,* the Commander-in-Chief requests you report here tomorrow morning at the headquarters in Nancy."

"Thank you, I will fly out when I can," Ramcke replied.

The operations officer cleared his throat: "*Herr General,* the usage of aircraft is forbidden in light of the danger posed by fighter-bombers.

Ramcke confirmed that he would go by road. Ramcke soon had thoughts racing through his read. The Allies had initiated their invasion on 6 June. The plan of *General der Fallschirmtruppe* Student to attack with airborne forces had been rejected, even though it stood to have good chances of success. Student had long recommended having the 1st and 4th Divisions returned from Italy and the 2nd from Russia to be prepared to launch an immediate counterblow on the Western Front and to jump into the middle of the enemy forces that were landing.

Early on the morning of 12 June, Ramcke went with a liaison officer and some other personnel from his headquarters to Nancy.

"I'm glad you made it here in one piece!" Student said, greeting him.

"I'm eager to hear what my new mission is, *Herr General!*" Ramcke replied.

"Your division will move immediately to the Bretagne to continue its reconstitution. At the same time, you have the mission of protecting the fortress of Brest from enemy air landings. You will get more instructions from the *XXV. Armee-Korps* in Pontivy. The first trains will be leaving Cologne-Wahn tomorrow. I want you to go to the Bretagne tomorrow and coordinate the billeting of your forces with the corps quartermaster there."

As was Student's manner, he had already arranged for a number of things.

✠

On 16 June, Ramcke met with the Commanding General, *Generalleutnant* von Choltitz and discussed the tactical employment of the division around Brest. The same day, he took quarters in Landevisiau, a small town on the Elorne, which emptied into the roads of Brest. Three days later, he moved to Lampaul. That placed the division headquarters 25 kilometers from Brest.

After personally reconnoitering the terrain, Ramcke positioned *FJR 2* in the Chateaulin area, the *FJR 7* around Zizun and the divisional engineers in Douarnenez Bay. After the coming days, during which the elements of the division arrived and continued their training, incidents of sabotage increased. In the sector of *FJR 7*, three medical personnel were ambushed, murdered and plundered by partisans, even though they were wearing Red Cross armbands. Their naked, mutilated bodies were found in a roadside ditch. The perpetrators were found and executed, as was the right granted to combatants under the laws of war. It was the son and nephew of a farmer named Cavaloc. Cavaloc himself could not be proven of having done anything and, based on advocacy advanced by *Hauptmann* Kamitschek, he was released.

At the beginning of July, Ramcke summoned all of the mayors, pastors and teachers of the region to a meeting in Landevisiau. More than 200 men gathered. He explained to them that he had to punish each act of sabotage in accordance with the law of war and that such acts did not affect the combat power of the German Armed Forces, no matter what one otherwise may have been led to believe. He appealed to the reason of those assembled and asked them to exert a moderating influence on the *Maquisards*; then they had nothing at all to fear from his division.

Although things calmed down a bit, 50 paratroopers were ambushed and killed between 29 July and 12 August. More than 200 were wounded and 100 soldiers were never heard from again.

At the end of July, *Oberst* Kroh's *FJR 2* and *Oberstleutnant* Pietzonka's *FJR 7* were attacked by strong U.S. armored forces, which were attempting to break through to Brest after the offensive at Avranches had succeeded.

Ramcke led the defensive fighting of his division from the high ground around Comana. He was always able to employ his antitank guns at the right place and the right time in the most endangered sectors. The ordinary paratrooper had to combat the assaulting enemy tanks with either the *Panzerfaust* or the *Ofenrohr*. One *Gefreiter* knocked out two enemy tanks in as many minutes. Ramcke personally presented him with the Iron Cross, First Class on the battlefield.

For three days, the Americans attempted to storm *Monts d'Arree*. Then they were exhausted. There were 32 knocked-out enemy tanks scattered across the terrain. Because the defensive success was primarily due to *Oberstleutnant* Pietzonka and his men, he was awarded the Knight's Cross on 5 September 1944.

Ramcke then received orders from Student to pull back into Brest proper. That order arrived at the last second, since U.S. forces of General Middleton's corps had advanced as far as Lesneven. From there, it was only 22 kilometers to Brest. They advanced without a fight as far as Guipavas, because the *2. Fallschirmjäger-Division* was not yet in position. On 8 August, a U.S. negotiating party asked the commander of Brest, *Oberst* von Mosel, to surrender. He turned down the request.

One day later, Ramcke's lead elements reached the outskirts of Brest and started to prepare to defend. On 12 August, the German Armed Forces High Command designated Ramcke as the local area commander for all of the forces in the fortress of Brest.

That same day, the city shook under a mighty aerial assault. Ramcke, concerned about the civilian populace, succeeded in contacting Middleton's VIII Corps to arrange a ceasefire for their evacuation. It was to take place on four successive days for 0800 to 1100 hours. During that time, the civilians were transported on trucks out of the city along four "open" egress routes. Those incapable of being transported for health reasons were moved into the underground chambers of the hospitals.

Brest had become an encircled fortress. Ramcke established his command post on the Crozon Peninsula. Ramcke then sent an emissary to Middleton. The German officer presented Middleton with a map on which all of the hospitals of the city were marked and asked that they be spared. He also asked that the Le Fret hospital complex near Cape Espagnol be declared a neutral zone. The U.S. prisoners would be taken there, so that nothing else could happen to them. Ramcke had done his best to protect those who were incapable of defending themselves, perhaps more so than any other fortress commander in the history of warfare.

On 26 August, the Americans opened their assault on the fortress with a strong artillery preparation which primarily fell in the sector of the *I.FJR 7*. As a result, the division operations officer, *Oberstleutnant* Moeller, and the intelligence officer, *Hauptmann Dr.* Hoven, concluded the focal point of the ground attack on Brest would be at Gousenou.

Ramcke went to the threatened position with *Hauptmann* Kamitschek, driven there by his long-time driver, Dietinger. *Major* Hamer, the battalion commander, was already waiting for them.

When they reached the forward observation post, they could already see the advancing enemy tanks through the scissors scope. Hamer explained to Ramcke that he had placed experienced paratroopers in the forward-most position. They were to allow the tanks to roll over them before engaging them with *Panzerfäuste* and demolitions.

Hamer had already positioned his immediate counterattack force and held back some heavy weapons in reserve.

The division commander was satisfied with the preparations. His men were used to making decisions on their own.

When the lead elements of the enemy infantry forces moved out after the artillery fires had been shifted to the German rear, the paratroopers were ready. The tanks rolled out and overran the initial positions. Hamer raised is flare pistol and fired the designated signal.

With a single hammer blow, the previously quiet defensive weapons sprang into life. Muzzle flashes could be seen form 8.8-centimeter *Flak*, 7.5-centimeter antitank guns, field guns and airborne small-arms. The first few tanks were hit head on by that salvo and were immobilized or knocked out. One of them blew asunder after its ammunition went up. Another one sent up thick plumes of smoke. From a third, wounded tankers could be seen dismounting. The half-tracks that followed were likewise shot up with *Panzerfäuste* from the men in the front lines.

In that wild clash, Hamer ordered his counterattack force to move out. The men of that group landed in the flank of the enemy's attacking force. It was a fight the likes of which had never happened in the Bretagne before and hopefully never again. The enemy lost momentum, came to a standstill and then fled in panic. Hamer's battalion took more than 500 prisoners.

Just before that defensive success occurred, an incident took place that will be presented here because it demonstrates the peculiar paratrooper élan. The incident took place behind enemy lines and in the midst of the *Maquisards*.

An *Obergefreiter*, who had been taken prisoner by the *Maquisards* along with other elements of the *II./FJR 2*, was released to bring an ultimatum back to Brest. He reported to *Oberst* Kroh that 100 additional comrades were being held in a school in the village of Braspart. They were being tortured every day, and it was only a matter of time before they were all killed. The Germans had only 48 hours to evacuate Brest to prevent that from happening.

Oberst Kroh summoned *Major* Ewald, the acting command of the 2nd

Battalion. He asked him who would be a candidate to free the paratroopers. Only one name came to his mind: "Lepkowski, *Herr Oberst!*"

✠

Leutnant Lepkowski was summoned to the command post. Ramcke was present when Lepkowski arrived. Kroh asked them to the situation map and started: "It's like this, Lepkowski . . . approximately 130 paratroopers of Becker's battalion have fallen into the hands of the *Maquisards*. One of them made it back today. He reported that the *Maquisards* informed him that they would be shot if we did not leave Brest within 48 hours!"

"We need to get them out of there, *Herr Oberst!*" That was Lepkowski's immediate response.

"We were hoping you would volunteer, Lepkowski. The prisoners are in Braspart, a village 60 kilometers behind the lines. That means that for you to get there, you need to go through the enemy lines. You need to go through these villages . . . " The commander paused, pointing to the localities, before continuing, ". . . in order to reach Braspart. No easy task. Especially since you'll probably have to go back though the same villages after the raid, and they have all been alerted."

"I accept the mission, *Herr Oberst!*"

"Good . . . then get ready. I want you to start at 2400 hours. Pick 40 paratroopers—volunteers! I'll get the vehicles and weapons ready for you. The division will launch a feint at another location to divert the attention of the Americans"

✠

When the fortress artillery opened up, the engines of the trucks, armored car and 2-centimeter self-propelled *Flak* roared to life. At the front of the column was *Leutnant* Lepkowski in the armored car. When the hands on his watch struck midnight, he gave the order to move out.

The most remarkable raid in the entire history of the German airborne corps had started.

Initially, the vehicles moved out through the vegetated terrain, which was covered with shell craters. The engine noises from his vehicles were drowned out by the sounds of firing and impacting artillery.

When the column reached a roadblock, it was held up by two guards with submachine-guns.

"Step on it!" Lepkowski ordered. "Fire!"

The armored car picked up the pace. A burst of fire rattled from its machine-gun, sending the two surprised outpost sentries scurrying for cover. The obstacle was easily bypassed, and the column continued on at high speed.

The first of several villages appeared in the distance. Partisans from the *Les Diables Bleus* organization were positioned at its outskirts. An antitank gun opened fired, when the German markings on the armored car were identified. The 2-centimeter *Flak*, which was right behind the armored car, blew apart the antitank gun as the vehicles moved forward. When the group reached the city hall, Lepkowski called a halt. He jumped off the armored car and assaulted the building with his headquarters section. The telephone boxes were smashed and the wires cuts. Three *Maquisards*, who were caught by surprise, were captured. Once Lepkowski was sure no alarm could be sounded from the village, he mounted up again and took off.

He bypassed the next two villages, just in case they had been notified of the German patrol anyway. When the group got to the fourth village, it saw a tank obstacle. Luckily, it was not covered, and the men were soon able to fashion a passageway through it. The column rolled on. The 40 men of Lepkowski's company were sitting nervously in their trucks, weapons at the ready. At a moment's notice they were prepared to dismount and fight their way forward to free their imprisoned comrades, who had been marked for death.

"There's Braspart, *Herr Leutnant!*" *Obergefreiter* Müschenborn called out to Lepkowski. Müschenborn was an experienced hand from the fighting in Russia.

"We'll stay on the vehicles until we reach the school. The two trucks will be stationed at the front and rear entrances. The armored car will position itself off to the right and a little farther back. The twin *Flak* will cover the main door!" Lepkowski's orders were short and to the point.

A few seconds later, they reached the large marketplace. The school had to be close by. Then they saw it in the moonlight. The vehicles moved to their designated positions.

A few figures approached them and addressed them in French. "Germans!" The surprised outcry echoed through the nighttime alleyways. A few seconds later, a machine-gun opened fire, followed by the bark of the automatic cannon. The 2-centimeter on the armored car replied in kind and soon took out the French heavy weapon. The enemy machine-gun fire ended abruptly.

"Follow me!"

The hand-picked paratroopers followed Lepkowski and stormed into the schoolhouse. They ran through the dark hallways; doors were flung open. *Maquisards* were startled awake. They surrendered and were chased out to the market place. More than 40 men were taken prisoner, but not a trace of the German paratroopers could be found.

Finally, they discovered from a small boy that the paratroopers had been taken to the small school on the far side of the village.

The rescuers ran in that direction. They started to receive rifle fire from the windows and the cellar openings. They fired with their submachine-guns on the run and silenced the partisans.

"Don't stop!" Lepkowski shouted, spurring his men on.

Then they saw the second schoolhouse. They ran inside. After a short firefight, the partisans there also surrendered.

The group's vehicles, brought up by Müschenborn, appeared. The men stormed into the large basement of the building, shooting off the lock on the door. The German prisoners then streamed outside into freedom. They embraced Lepkowski when they recognized who the leader of the group was. Lepkowski, who had an eagle's beak for a nose, was not too hard to identify.

In all, there were 113 Germans freed. They looked terrible, dressed only in trousers and shirts, the signs of mistreatment tangible on their faces and bodies. All of their personal belongings, as well as their boots, had been pilfered. They had not been in the hands of regular French forces; it was the work of fired-up partisans.

"Don't waste any time!" Lepkowski barked. 'We need to clear out of here!" As soon as the last man had been accounted for, they mounted their vehicles and took off at high speed. The first two villages were passed without a fight. French civilians, who were outside by chance, greeted the men enthusiastically, thinking they were Americans. By the time they realized their mistake, it was too late: The vehicles had already sped past.

A new obstacle had been established in the third village, however. Lepkowski's men jumped down from the trucks and drove away the enemy with bursts from their machine-guns. They knocked down the barrier, using the armored car, and fought their way through.

One of the truck drivers was driving with only one hand. The other one had been shattered by a rifle round. He had a handkerchief applied as a dressing and was able to make it all the way back through to Brest.

When *Leutnant* Lepkowski stood in front of *General* Ramcke and rendered his report, Ramcke was visibly moved. He approached Lepkowski, removed his *Leutnant* shoulder boards and replaced them with those of an *Oberleutnant*.[8]

✠

Despite local success enjoyed by men such as Lepkowski and Hamer, the ring around Brest grew ever tighter. The Americans succeeded in taking Hill

---

8. In the further fighting in and around Brest, *Oberleutnant* Lepkowski continued to distinguish himself. When he conducted an immediate counterattack against a section of American flamethrowers, he succeeded in sealing off the group and eliminating it. On another immediate counterattack at night, Lepkowski and his men assaulted a complex of ruins occupied by U.S. forces that was between the two front lines. He then went on to the suburb of St. Pierre. There he and his men were greeted by a wall of fire, which forced them back. In the process, Lepkowski was badly wounded. A section of men was sent out to find him. The group found him unconscious and assumed he was dead. They carried him back to the main clearing station, where he was placed among the other dead.

Oberstabsarzt Dr. Marquard, who knew Lepkowski from Russia, took another look at the "dead" man and determined he was alive. The young officer remained unconscious for five days. When he awoke, he was in U.S. captivity. It was later determined that a small piece of shrapnel was lodged in the left front chamber of his heart. He was operated on in the U.S. and returned to Germany in September 1945.

103 along the western outskirts of Brest, but they were stopped at Guipavas on 4 and 6 September by *Hauptmann* Becker and his men. Two days later, the Americans attacked again and succeeded in breaking through Becker's sector and rolling up the adjacent engineer battalion. Becker and *Hauptmann* Kamitschek were taken prisoner, along with a number of their soldiers.

Despite all that, the division held out against the Americans, who outnumbered it four-to-one.

The paratroopers were forced back into their final main line of resistance in the fortress. On 13 September, a U.S. emissary arrived with correspondence from General Middleton, asking that the General and his division surrender honorably. Ramcke declined.

On 14 and 15 September, the U.S. forces continued their attacks. By the evening of the next day, St. Pierre was almost lost. Ramcke ordered the fighting in the city to cease and his forces to pull back to the Crozon Peninsula. On 18 September, the division's artillery fired their remaining rounds on St. Pierre before being blown up. The city of Brest was surrendered by *Generalmajor* von Mosel that same day. Ramcke continued to fight on Crozon, however.

The last fighting was on the Espagnol Peninsula. The last 170 paratroopers—men of *Major* Mehler's airborne signals battalion—fought along a blocking position. The Americans fired artillery on the position for three days. The infantry attacked. They were thrown back twice, but they succeeded the third time when supported by tanks.

Oberstleutnant Moeller, the operations officer, destroyed all of the important documents. *Hauptmann Dr.* Hoven burned the classified materials. When the enemy stopped firing in front of the division command post, Ramcke went outside. He was greeted by an American general, who saluted. Ramcke returned the salute and said: "I am *General* Ramcke!"

"I am happy to see you in one piece, general. Your command post is the last element to fight in the entire area of the fortress. Consider yourself as my prisoner. You were a terrific opponent!"

The fighting for Brest was over and the majority of the *2. Fallschirmjäger-Division* went into captivity.

THE LAST JUMP IN THE WEST

After the *II. Fallschirm-Korps* transitioned to the defense on 3 October 1944, the fighting in the Arnhem, Nijmegen, Mook and Groesbeek areas of Holland was over.

With the withdrawal of *FJR 6*, which had still been fighting Canadian forces in the Scheldt Estuary, the last German forces left the area around Woendsdrecht on 16 October. The Germans knocked out more than 250 enemy armored vehicles in that area.

The operations of the airborne forces weren't over quite yet, however. There was still one more large-scale airborne operation in the west to be conducted, in addition to the ground fighting, which continued to the bitter end. That operation was to be launched during the Ardennes offensive, better known among English speakers as the Battle of the Bulge.

On 9 December, *Oberstleutnant* von der Heydte received orders from *Generaloberst* Student to be prepared to conduct an airborne operation with a strong airborne battle group in support of an upcoming large-scale German offensive.

Within 48 hours, von der Heydte reported he had assembled his force. The battle group was formed up at Camp Senne on 11 December. The battle group conducted training for several days, before von der Heydte was summoned to the headquarters of *Generalfeldmarschall* Model on 15 December, where he received his top-secret special mission. He was informed that his force would be employed to open and hold bottlenecks for the *6. SS-Panzer-Armee*. Von der Heydte's men were attached for tactical purposes to the *SS* field army for the operation.

Early on the morning of 16 December, the offensive was launched. Participating on the ground were also the *3.* and *5. Fallschirmjäger-Division*. Under the acting command of *Oberst* Heilmann, the *5. Fallschirmjäger-Division* wrested a crossing point over the Clerf from the enemy and then advanced in the direction of Wiltz. By 22 December, it had reached the area around Vaux lez Rosières, 15 kilometers west of Bastogne, after sharp fighting, where it then became involved in the attempt to take the bitterly contested city. As the tide turned against the Germans after Christmas, it was thanks to Heilmann's skilled leadership that the division was able to escape encirclement and he was promoted to *Generalmajor* on 3 January 1945.

The *3. Fallschirmjäger-Division* fought alongside elements of the *6. SS-Panzer-Armee*. It suffered heavy losses, even though it did not participate extensively in the initial successes of the operation because it had been employed at the wrong location.

That leaves the discussion of the last airborne operation in the west by von der Heydte's men.

The enemy had sent strong reinforcements from the north towards the area of Elsenborn. The route of those forces and their crossing through the Schnee Eifel region were to be blocked by the paratroopers.

Just before midnight on 16 December, 1,200 paratroopers took off for the area of operations, 75 kilometers behind enemy lines. Von der Heydte later told the author about this operation:

> I was firmly convinced that in that type of operation the commander had to be the first one to jump. Not so much to make a good impression, but rather to get a first impression on the ground of the terrain and the enemy situation and to assemble the forces that followed.

When the lead aircraft arrived over the drop zone and the jump horn sounded, the *Oberstleutnant* was the first one out the door. Von der Heydte:

> The scene at the drop zone was eerily beautiful. Above me, like

lightning bugs, were the position markers of the aircraft and, whipping up towards me from below were the tracers of the light American antiaircraft weapons. Beyond the black trees, like the fingers of a hand, were the probing beams of the searchlights. Then impact. The roll forwards worked; I unhooked. Initially, I was alone. I ran to the designated fork in the road that was a collection point. On the road, I encountered the first of my soldiers. There were only a few—far too few. There were also only a few at the collection point. What had happened to the rest?

To my horror, I had seen a few of my comrades as burning torches shortly after the jump. Nevertheless, that did not explain why so many were missing. As I later found out, the jump was a disaster. The first batch of paratroopers had been signaled to jump <u>over Bonn</u> by the pilots. Others followed in short intervals, with the result that only a portion of my battle group reached the drop zone.

As morning arrived, I had a total of 250 men assembled. That was a little more than one fifth of the force. We pulled back from the fork in the road into the woods and formed and all-round defense. The radio equipment was damaged and did not work, with the result that we could not establish contact with our own forces. I had no way at all of forwarding the most important results of our reconnaissance.

When we retrieved additional information the next day and the following days, including even corps orders for the U.S. XVIII Corps we could not do the slightest thing with it. Men who volunteered to take the information to our lines, which were more than 50 kilometers away, did not get through.

When the small group pulled back through the woods to the northeast on the afternoon of the second day, it ran into a group of 150 paratroopers, who were under the command of *Oberleutnant* Kaiser, a war correspondent, who was the senior man present. That group had been dropped too soon, as well. Von der Heydte's battle group then had a total strength of nearly 400 men. The rumor went around that the pilots had been "yellow in the face of the enemy's fires".

There were a few small skirmishes with the enemy, and the group took some casualties in wounded and dead. On the fourth day, von der Heydte decided to try to make it back to the German lines to the east. When the group ran into strong U.S. outposts on 21 December, which succeeded in thwarting von der Heydte's initial intent, he then decided to disband the force and have small groups attempt to get through, which had a better chance of success.

On 24 December, however, he and the small group he was with were captured by U.S. forces.

The special operation in the Ardennes had failed. Von der Heydte: "Despite that, one has to admire the courage of the men who volunteered for this dangerous jump as if it were no big deal."

THE ALLIES BREAK THROUGH ALONG THE RHINE

General der Fallschirmtruppe Alfred Schlemm was awakened from his sleep early on 8 February 1945 by the sounds of artillery fire. The dull roar of an artillery barrage, which carried across the Rhine from the west, reached the headquarters of the *1. Fallschirm-Armee* in Dinxperlo on the Dutch-German border near Bocholt.

Schlemm immediately headed towards the front in a *Kübelwagen*. It was not long before his initial gut instincts were being confirmed: The Allies had started the expected big offense in the *Reichswald* west of Kleve. One of his liaison officers stated he thought it was all part of a deception plan. But Schlemm discounted that. He knew this was a big push on the part of the Allies.

Aerial reconnaissance reports had noted enemy movements in the area of Eindhoven that were directed towards Nijmwegen, which meant, by extension, towards the *Reichswald*, where Schlemm's forces were. On-the-ground patrols confirmed the reports.

On 8 February 1945, the frontage of the *1. Fallschirm-Armee* extended in the north from the Rhine at Millingen, though Kronenburg to the Meuse at Gennep. From there, it traced along the Meuse to Venlo as far as Roermond, where the Roer emptied into the Meuse. There the airborne field army had a boundary with the *15. Armee*. The *25. Armee* was north of the airborne soldiers.

Based on the situation and patrol reports, Schlemm reported to *Generaloberst* Blaskowitz's *Heeresgruppe H* that afternoon after returning form the front that the Allied offensive in the *Reichswald* had commenced, starting in the sector of the *84. Infanterie-Division*. At the same time, Schlemm reported that he had alerted his immediate reserve, the *7. Fallschirmjäger-Division*, had it loaded on trucks and transported towards Gennap from the area east of Venlo. It was the general's intent to hold up the enemy advance through an immediate counterattack by that division.

But the field army group did not share his estimate of the situation. It dismissed Schlemm's report, believing that the attack in the airborne sector was only a part of the whole and the second attack, with a main effort focused on Venlo, could commence at any time. To that end, the field-army group overruled Schlemm and ordered the *7. Fallschirmjäger-Division* to return to its billeting area around Venlo.

The field army group could support its countering viewpoint by pointing out that the prisoners taken during the afternoon of 8 February had only come from two Canadian divisions. That unmistakably indicated that the remaining divisions had not been committed and that they would be employed at Venlo. That was the immediate reason that the field-army group advanced.

In fact, there were other reasons, and they could be traced back to 2 February when all of the commanders of the northern front along the Rhine were assembled at the headquarters of the Commander-in-Chief West, *Generalfeldmarschall* von Rundstedt. *Generaloberst* Blaskowitz had briefed at the time that he expected the attack of the British and Canadian field army at Venlo. There, he stated, it was possible for the British and Commonwealth forces to be supported by the Americans, since the American advance across the Roer in the direction of Cologne could be expected any day.

Schlemm, on the other hand, had represented the viewpoint that the enemy would attack along the *Reichswald*, so as to advance on Wesel via Kleve. That attack would be advantageous for the Allies, in that they would then not have to force a crossing over the Meuse, which was at flood stage. Farthermore, they would avoid the *Westwall*, which ran parallel to the Meuse from Goch-Geldern to Aachen, by doing so. If their attack succeeded, they could then roll up the entire front from the north.

Generalfeldmarschall von Rundstedt sided with *Generaloberst* Blaskowitz during the discussion. For that reason, the reserves were not weighted to the north on 8 February, as Schlemm had requested. Instead they were in the southern part of the field army's area of operations. The *7. Fallschirmjäger-Division* was to remain in the Venlo area, as previously described, and the *XXXXVIII. Panzer-Korps*, consisting of the *15. Panzergrenadier-Division* and the *116. Panzer-Division*, was in the Viersen–Kempen area.

Schlemm was faced with a difficult decision the afternoon of 8 February. Should he follow an unmistakable order or should he act on his own initiative? The general decided on a compromise. He ordered the division to stay where it was—halfway to where he had originally wanted it—and not back to Venlo. The division remained in the Kevelaer area for the time being.

By the next day, it was obvious that the enemy was committing all of his forces to the game. Prisoners were taken from five Canadian and British divisions. Schlemm reported the new information and asked for the release of the *7. Fallschirmjäger-Division*. This time, the field army group consented, and the forces continued their march to the battlefield.

On the Allied side, the Canadian 1st Army of General Crerar was employed against the *Reichswald*. That field army had elements of the British 2nd Army attached to it, consisting of the XXX Corps of General Horrocks. In all, there were five infantry divisions, 3 tank brigades and 11 special regiments that had already been committed. They had received a directive to advance through the *Reichswald* as rapidly as possible and continue on to Wesel. In conjunction with the U.S. Operation "Grenade", which was the offensive to be launched by the 9th Army on 10 February across the Roer and in the direction of Cologne-Neuß, the German forces west of the Rhine were to be caught in a large-scale pincers movement and eliminated.

As the Canadians attacked along the northern edge of the *Reichswald* and reached the western outskirts of Kleve at 1645 hours on 10 February, the U.S. forces had not yet initiated their offensive. Although General Simpson, the Commander-in-Chief of the 9th Army, had taken the last remaining reservoirs along the Roer, he then found himself on the west bank of that long contested river and came to the realization that there could be no thought of crossing the river in his sector.

The river was at flood stage. By opening the Urft Valley barrier, *Generalfeldmarschall* Model had created an impassable water obstacle along the lower run of the Roer. Simpson reported that it would not be possible to cross the river for at least another two weeks. In the meantime, an offensive effort across the Roer would be senseless.

That meant that the Canadian 1st Army and its supporting British forces would have to carry on the offensive on their own.

The *84. Infanterie-Division* fought in the middle of the *Reichswald* with everything it had. It had held out against the combined attack of eight enemy divisions—an attack preceded by a barrage lasting several hours—on 8 February. It fought on its own for 48 hours in a futile struggle. The soldiers had to pull back, step-by-step. They mined the lanes through the woods and both of the main roads leading through it. Despite that heroic stand, the breakthrough to Kleve could not be prevented. The enemy still needed another day to take the city proper, which was done on 11 February.

Schlemm was up front with the forces that had been attached to him. He skillfully directed the defensive effort, which was made easier by the rugged and wooded terrain.

In the three days of fighting for the *Reichswald, Generaloberst* Blaskowitz succeeded in getting the release of the *XXXXVII. Panzer-Korps* from the Commander-in-Chief West. The two divisions rolled into the area of operations, followed by the *7.* and *8. Fallschirmjäger-Division*. The offensive momentum of the enemy began to abate. *Korps Straube*, with the *180.* and *190. Infanterie-Division*, defended farther south along the Meuse around and south of Gennep. The enemy attempted to get some breathing room for his bogged-down forces in the *Reichswald* and to its east, by launching a secondary attack across the Meuse. But *General* Straube directed his defensive efforts with a calm and sovereign air. His two divisions fought bravely and accomplished their mission.

The men of the two airborne divisions, under the command of *General der Fallschirmtruppe* Meindl's *II. Fallschirm-Korps* also fought and performed well, even though one of the divisions had had to give up a large number of personnel for von der Heydte's ill-fated operations in the Ardennes in December.

None other than Field Marshal Montgomery later wrote: "No enemy formations had put up such bitter resistance in the course of the entire war as the paratroopers fighting for the Rhineland."[9]

Schlemm had moved his field-army headquarters from Dinxperlo to Xanten on 8 February. He wanted to be as close as possible to the front, in order to be able to personally reach the frontline commanders in the main defensive areas. On 13 February, he moved his headquarters to Rheinberg, since the building up of the southern front started to take precedence. Schlemm received unambiguous orders from the *Führer* headquarters that the bridgehead in the south had to be held under all circumstances. In order

---

9. Translator's Note: Reverse-translated.

to do that, Schlemm pulled the *15. Panzergrenadier-Division*, the *84. Infanterie-Division* and the *Panzer Lehr Division*, which had also bee attached to him, out of the line in the north. All three of those divisions had been battered, however, and each barely had the strength of a regiment.

In the area around Goch, the fighting continued with unabated harshness. On 14 February, the Allies reached the left bank of the Rhine at Emmerich. The Germans had pulled their lines back to Üdem-Keppeln. Facing the Allies there was primarily the *7. Fallschirmjäger-Division* and a security battalion.

Nobody on the Allied side doubted that the 500 tanks of the XXX Corps would break through in the first assault and simply smash the few opposing forces there into the ground. The corps direction of attack was the Kalkar–Xanten road. The German forces had just been stripped of almost all of the armor support they had had, since the greater threat was perceived to be south.

The 500 tanks of Horrocks's corps rolled out on 22 February. In the lead was General Adair's Guards Armoured Division. They wanted to take the area that was of vital importance as a rear area for the British crossing of the Rhine. The British were not yet familiar with the "Death Hill of Keppeln" yet. They still had no idea what a fearful fight a handful of paratroopers and assault guns would deliver them. Over the next several days, however, the "Death Hill" would become the greatest tank graveyard in history, at least as far as the density of the sector is concerned. For two days, the British were turned back, whenever they appeared.

By the evening of 25 February, the British 3rd and 51st Infantry Divisions had reached and taken Üdem. Although they had made gains there, the paratroopers were still holding out on their hill at Keppeln. On the morning of 26 February, the III Corps moved out again. In the uncertain light of early morning and signal pyrotechnics, the defenders thought the tanks must be the 100 armored vehicles that the chain-of-command had promised as reinforcements. But then *Unteroffizier* Steinke recognized the familiar outline of a Churchill. The enemy had employed a trick and painted German crosses on his turrets.

The fighting started anew. Once again, the tank armada was stopped.

Once it was daybreak, 200 Lancasters flew in and bombed "Death Hill" in order to soften it up for another assault. That was followed by a broad smokescreen that blew towards the hill. Distributed by hundreds of generators, the smoke hid the advancing tanks of the XXX Corps.

Once again, the paratroopers engaged the tanks. Man versus machine—a struggle that was carried out with unbelievable intensity. The sound of *Panzerfäuste* being fired could be heard in the artificial fog. Main guns roared and coaxial machine-guns rattled. The hill at Keppeln went into the history books as one of the largest sites of tank destruction in history. And it wasn't tank-versus-tank, it was tank-versus-man!

One man, one tank—that was roughly how it turned out. When the tank avalanche had finished rolling past and the dead had to be buried, there were 276 German soldiers and 54 civilians. The British left behind 320 smoking tank wrecks.

In the face of those numbers and sheer overwhelming superiority in numbers, the *1. Fallschirm-Armee* had to pull back, step-by-step. During the evening of 27 February, the mayor of Kalkar surrendered the city to a British Major, whose battle group had reached the city just as German military forces were evacuating it.

✠

The Canadian 1st Army, which had taken Kleve on 13 February, moved out on Emmerich. On 14 February, it took the dikes across from the city. The small bridgehead of a company from *Sicherungs-Bataillon 1031* held the left bank of the Rhine. At the last minute, it was reinforced by an airborne company. Artillery fire commenced and both of the companies defended the bridgehead with all the means at their disposal. The Germans could not count on any relief, since the river, which was at flood stage, had already covered the Rhine promenade at Emmerich.

But the high waters also restricted the enemy's courses of action. The Canadian 5th Armoured Division could not be employed, since the two elevated roads—the only ones that could be used—were densely mined. The meadowlands were out of the question for armored vehicles.

From their elevated positions on the dikes and hills, the paratroopers and militiamen turned back the first Canadian attack, which was conducted by battle groups from the Canadian 2nd and 3rd Infantry Divisions. The Germans then launched an immediate counterattack. The German advance came as such a complete surprise to the Canadians that they pulled back to the outskirts of Warbeyen 3 kilometers away. The Canadian infantry regained its composure, however, and then succeeded in clearing the mines along the road at least as far as Warbeyen. In the evening, a concentration of tanks from the 5th Armoured and the Polish 2nd Armoured Division advanced on Warbeyen. The fighting lasted an hour until the last farmstead was taken. Most of the paratroopers, who had conducted the immediate counterattack, were either killed or taken prisoner. Only a few succeeded in disengaging from the enemy and working their way back to German lines through Grieth and Reeserschanz.

The Canadians then bogged down outside of Emmerich. It was not until the XXX Corps was able to advance farther in the area of Keppeln and Üdem that General Crerar ordered his II Corps to move from north to south. One after the other, Grieth, Wissel, Wisselward and Hönnepel fell. The few forces of the *1. Fallschirm-Armee* were pinned in from two sides. It had to pull back slowly. The only thing that would have meant the airborne field army could have completely escaped from the threat of encirclement would have been a withdrawal across the Rhine, but that was categorically forbidden by the Armed Forces High Command. It went so far that orders were issued to the field armies in the west on 1 March that not a single staff officer could cross the Rhine to the east without express orders from the Armed Forces High Command! The presence of staff officers was thought to increase the power to resist on the part of the forces in the field!

On 28 February, the XXX Corps reached Marienbaum, Appeldorn, Niedermörmter and Ward, which fell over the next two days. The Allied tank avalanche came to a halt at Xanten. A paratrooper regiment set up 300 meters to the east of the city at *Haus Erpath*. The airborne soldiers were later joined by elements of the *Panzer Lehr Division*, which was pulling back to the northeast. The paratroopers and tankers gave it their all. The fighting around *Haus Erpath* lasted for days.

It took until 8 March before the city fell.

In the sector of the *1. Fallschirm-Armee* there were no fewer than nine bridges over the Rhine. According to *General der Fallschirmtruppe* Schlemm:

I was responsible for nine bridges over the Rhine. If I only allowed one of them to fall into Allied hands, a catastrophe could follow. The simplest thing would have been to blow them up immediately. But that was not possible, since there were still large quantities of industrial materials and livestock that had been driven from the areas of combat operations that had to be evacuated across the Rhine. I designated a decisive engineer officer as the bridge site commander for each of the bridges. He prepared them for demolition and had to remain in constant radio contact with me. In spite of that, things did not go smoothly. The last formations of the *15. Armee* streamed into the bridgehead from the south, and they frequently countermanded my orders, referring to directives form *Feldmarschall* Model.

When I radioed the order to blow up the road bridge at Homberg early on the morning of 3 March, an *Oberst* from forces belonging to the *15. Armee* tried to prevent the bridge site commander from blowing it up. It was not until I threatened that gentleman with personally shooting him in half an hour that the demolition could be carried out. If someone wanted to wait until the enemy had closed to within firing distance of the bridge, then the demolition cables could easily be shot up. I had large field-police details sent to the remaining bridge commanders, with the result that all of [the remaining] bridges could be destroyed at the right time.

On 2 March, the Americans attacked from Neuß in the direction of Krefeld. Since the headquarters of the *1. Fallschirm-Armee* was of the opinion that the enemy would bypass Neuß on both sides so as to avoid a costly street fight, *General* Schlemm accepted the recommendation of the local party headquarters to have its police and party forces defend the southern outskirts of the city. The regular forces would then be freed to defend on the flanks, where the main enemy thrust was expected.

When *General* Schlemm arrived in Neuß just before the anticipated start of combat operations, he was aghast to discover that a formation of Hitler Youth—around 200 boys and teenagers—were also employed in the city's defensive line. He ordered them out of the line immediately.

But before they could be pulled out, the American attack started. Contrary to the defensive planning assumption, the Americans did not attempt to bypass the city. Instead, they headed straight for it, approaching the southern outskirts. While the police officers and party functionaries left their positions, the Hitler Youth stayed and fought. In the fires of the approaching American tanks, the small group was practically wiped out. What remained went into captivity.

Thanks to the Allies' huge pool of resources and forces, it would have been very easy for them to reach the western bank of the Rhine at Wesel on 3 or 4 March. Instead, they broke any and all types of resistance by means of artillery barrages that lasted for hours and the use of flamethrower tanks before they continued their advance.

Despite the slow pace of the American attack, the German position on the west side of the Rhine became more precarious with each passing day. When *General* Schlemm proposed to send burnt-out forces to the east back to establish a new defensive line there, he was turned down out of hand. It was only through decisive personal action on the part of the Commander-in-Chief of the airborne field army that he could save one of his officers from being hanged. After 21 days of continuous combat, the officer crossed over to the east bank after he had lost the last man in his unit. He was taken prisoner there and due to be executed.

It was not until *Generaloberst* von Blaskowitz, the Commander-in-Chief of the field-army group was personally convinced that the rear-area services of both the *15. Armee* and the *1. Fallschirm-Armee* were getting in each other's way in the bridgehead that shrunk daily that Schlemm was able to at least send his logistics forces across the river.

Despite all of the prohibitions, Schlemm also attempted to clandestinely establish an outpost line along the east bank of the river. *Generaloberst* Student attempted to help, however he could. He sent replacement airborne formations under *Generalmajor* Barenthin to the Rhine.

The German forces were pushed back through Moers to Rheinberg. From the observation post he had established on the *Bönninghardt*, Schlemm was able to observe the enemy launch his tank attacks. He saw flamethrower tanks set positions alight and then allow the burning soldiers to run back across the open meadows as human torches.

Schlemm had heavy *Flak* elements withdrawn from air defense duties and inserted into the southwestern sector of his bridgehead to help establish a deeply echeloned antitank defense.

On 6 March, the English took Schlemm's observation post on the *Bönninghardt*. The bridgehead west of the Rhine had shrunk to an area 15 kilometers wide by 12 kilometers deep. The enemy fired into the small area constantly, and the casualties were correspondingly horrific.

Schlemm reported to the field-army group that that bridgehead needed to be evacuated immediately, if there was to be any chance at all of defending from the east bank.

Once again, it was pointed out to Schlemm that Hitler had ordered a defense west of the river at all costs. Schlemm then requested the German Army High Command send an officer to his bridgehead, so that he could form a personal impression of the situation.

On 7 March, an *Oberstleutnant* from the General Staff arrived at Schlemm's headquarters. Schlemm afforded the officer an opportunity to spend an exciting day in the bridgehead. That evening, the visiting officer reported back to the High Command, and Schlemm was given permission a short while later to evacuate to the east bank.

It was then imperative, of course, to carefully prepare the crossing under enemy pressure. During the night of 8–9 March, all of the artillery was taken across the river.

The next night, the paratroopers and the other formations of the field army crossed the Rhine to the east. The train of men seemed almost endless. It was 0400 hours, when Schlemm gave the order to blow the bridges at 0600 hours. But there were still thousands of soldiers on the west bank. The engineer officer in charge of the bridge site delayed execution of the order for an hour. But then, he could wait no longer. He gave the critical order.

At exactly 0710 hours, four of the charges that had been placed went up with a huge crack. The railway bridge of Wesel lifted up from its pilings and then collapsed into the river in several pieces.

Along with the bridge were several groups of men who disregarded the warnings at the last minute and tried to cross. They were still grouped on the west bank. They opened fire on the German engineers who had taken away their last chance to escape. Just in the Büderich area alone, some 3,000 soldiers marched into Allied captivity. The German Armed Forces High Command Daily Report of 11 March 1945:

> In order to use the better defensive lines on the east bank of the Rhine, our forces evacuated the left-hand side of the Rhine in the Wesel Bridgehead in a deliberate and disciplined manner.

The east bank of the Rhine then became a combat zone. The *7. Fallschirmjäger-Division* set up for defense from Haffen through Diersford to Bislich. The *8. Fallschirmjäger-Division* took up a defensive sector in the area around Rees, where the field army's command post was also established. They were adjoined north of Rees by some *Volkssturm* elements.

THE FINAL FIGHTING OF THE 2. *FALLSCHIRMJÄGER-DIVISION* IN THE RUHR POCKET

Although we have been concentrating on the fighting of the *7.* and *8. Fallschirmjäger-Division* in the fighting along the Rhine, the *2. Fallschirmjäger-Division* was also employed there. It engaged the Canadian forces of General Crerar and was also pushed back to the Rhine. After it crossed, it established defensive positions from Duisburg as far as Kaiserswerth, where it was attached to the *LXIII. Armee-Korps* of *Heeresgruppe B.* Although it was granted a short respite, it was not enough time to replace losses sustained in either men or materiel. Replacements arrived, but they were only a fraction of what had been requested.

The main reason for the respite was an operational pause on the part of the Allies. The Western Allies regrouped and prepared to cross the Rhine and advance into Germany. The initial plan was to encircle all of the German forces defending in the Ruhr area. In order to maximize the ground offensive, numerous bombing raids were conducted against important transportation nodal points. As always, there were unintended consequences, since the havoc wrought later impeded the Allied advance as well.

Starting on 20 March, the Allies intensified their air strikes against the German defensive positions on the far side of the river and the hinterland. Garrisons and billeting areas were also struck and the approach marches of forces considerably disrupted.

THE STORM BREAKS

During the evening of 23 March 1945, the 21st Army Group of Field Marshal Montgomery launched its offensive after a strong artillery preparation. The men moved out against minimal defensive fires to their assault craft, which were staged along the shoreline.

The Allied engineers had brought no less than 250,000 tons of ammunition, rations and bridging equipment to well-camouflaged staging areas near the river.

The Canadian 1st Army and the British 2nd Army moved out from positions from Wesel to Rees to force the river. The U.S. 9th Army, which had also been allocated to the field-army group, moved out from Rheinberg, south of Wesel.

These operations were supported by a surprise parachute and air-landed operation, which started early on 24 March. It was to be the last combat jump and landing of the war for the affected Allied formations. No less than 1,500 gliders landed in the fields near Lackhausen, while the paratroopers jumped before and after the glider landings between Wesel and Haminkeln and Lokkum und Meerhog.

The thin German lines were overrun and, by the evening of 24 March, the Allied forces were already 10 kilometers east of the Rhine. From that point, the British and Canadian forces turned to the north and northeast, while the U.S. forces headed south, southeast and east.

The *2. Fallschirmjäger-Division* was alerted in its rest positions in the areas around Duisburg, Mühlheim and Kaiserswerth and sent north. The enemy had advanced east from the Lippe River and the Rhine-Herne Canal. The Allied advance occurred so rapidly that the German airborne division could not be committed as such. Instead, its individual battalions and regiments were committed as a "fire brigade" into the fight.

Fallschirmjäger-Regiment 7 was the first element to have contact with the enemy with its lead forces. That was in the Holten-Sterkraden area. The headquarters of the regiment set up in the underground chambers of the *Ruhrchemie* firm in Holten. At the same time, *FJR 23* started arriving from Mühlheim-Saarn. *Fallschirmjäger-Regiment 2* arrived in sector from Düsseldorf-Mündelheim and Duisburg. There were delaying actions in the greater Duisburg area. The enemy pressure increased north of the Rhine-Herne Canal. Thanks to his tanks and artillery and the fighter-bombers that pounced on anything that moved in the provisional German defensive positions, there was no stopping him.

On Easter Sunday, *Oberst i.G.* Vorwerck assumed command of *FJR 2*. He employed his formation in the defense of the inner city of Gelsenkirchen, after arriving there from Bottrop. The paratroopers took up positions along the Rhine-Herne Canal. The regimental command post was set up in the shower area for the *Wilhelmine Viktoria* mine.

When a group of foreign workers started plundering a supply depot for the local civilian populace, a company moved into the middle of the looters and dispersed them with warning shots. The paratroopers also succeeded in stopping the senseless destruction, which had been ordered by the local party leadership, from taking place.

In order to prevent the city of Gelsenkirchen from being completely destroyed by enemy artillery and fighter-bombers, the city was surrendered on 9 April. The Americans entered the city without a fight the next day.

✠

One battalion from *FJR 23* of the division defended Castrop-Rauxel from 2 to 9 April. It was able to put up a stubborn defense. As indicated by the amount of time the area was held.

Over the next few days, more and more cities of the Ruhr were lost to the Americans: Essen, Mühlheim and Witten.

By then, the Ruhr Pocket had been about two-thirds formed, with all of the German forces being compressed into an ever-smaller area. The *2. Fallschirmjäger-Division*—that is, what was left of it—conducted its final fighting at Langenberg, Volmarstein and Ratingen. During the evening of 15 April, the remaining combat weaponry was destroyed in anticipation of the surrender that was to take place the next day. The division command post in the *"Kleine Kuh" Gasthaus* in Niedersprockhövel sent its final report to the field army and checked out. A short while later, the headquarters was overrun by American tanks. The division had seen its last fight.

In less than a month, so would all of its sister formations as well, both in the East and the West.

The notorious hedgerow country of Normandy—ideal defensive terrain that the Germans exploited to the full against overwhelming numerical superiority.

Defensive positions at Bohars, near Brest.

Hans Kroh had acting command of the *2.
Fallschirmjäger-Division* at Brest (seen here as a
general officer in the *Bundeswehr*).

Erich Lepkowski freed captured comrades at
Braspart by means of an ambush.

Generalfeldmarchall Rommel with the Commanding General of the *II. Fallschirm-Korps, Generalleutnant* Meidl, in Normandy.

English paratroopers taken prisoner by German paratroopers on 17 September 1944 at Arnhem.

Generaloberst Student reviews the few paratroopers of *Kampfgruppe von der Heydte* who made it back after the disastrous drop in the Ardennes.

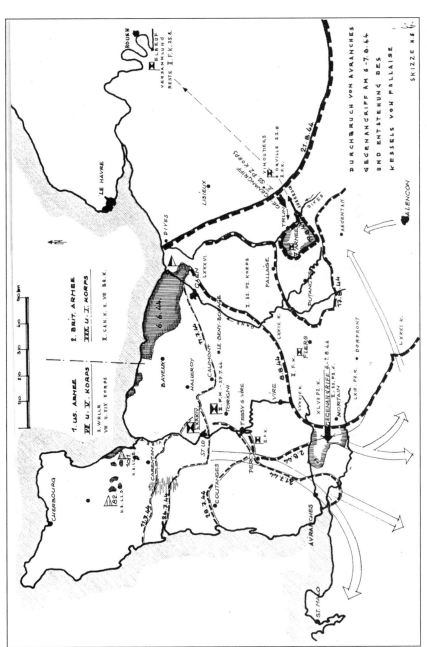

U.S. forces break through at Avranches; the German counterattack at Mortain from 6 to 7 August 1944; the escape from the Falaise Pocket.

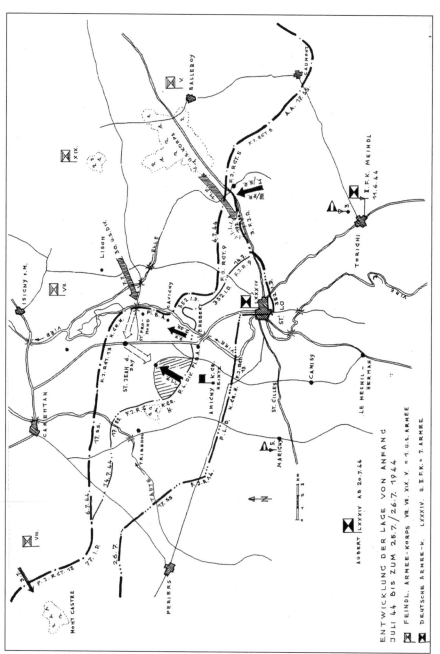

Development of the situation in Normandy around St. Lô in July 1944 until 25–26 July 1944.

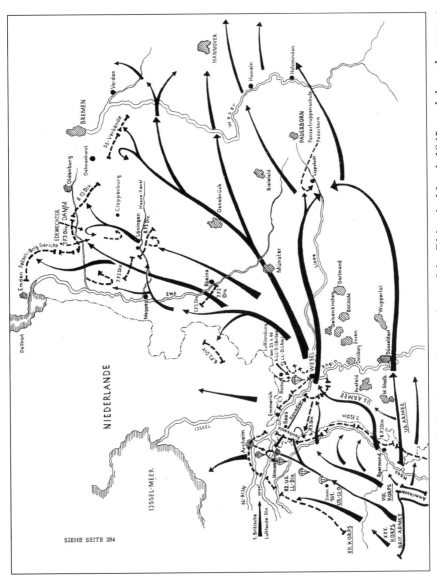

Allied advances in the Netherlands; the crossings of the Rhine in March 1945; and the subsequent advances into Germany.

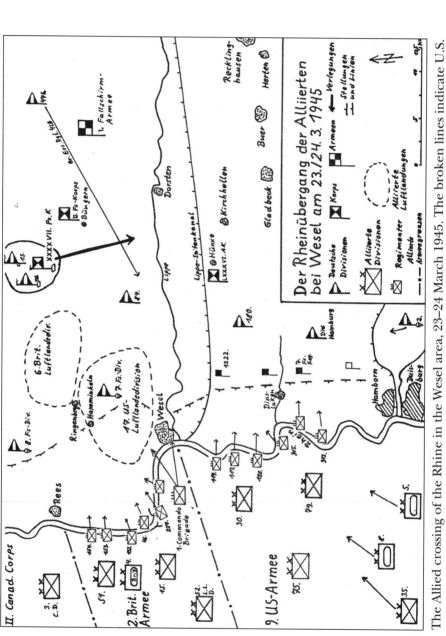

The Allied crossing of the Rhine in the Wesel area, 23–24 March 1945. The broken lines indicate U.S. and British paratroop and glider troop landings. These airborne operations were massive in scope and far surpassed the German operations on Crete.

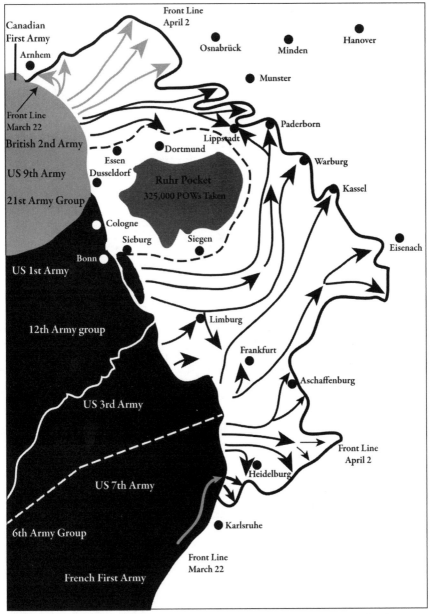

Allied offensive operations after the Rhine crossing, leading to the formation of the "Ruhr Pocket" in April 1945.

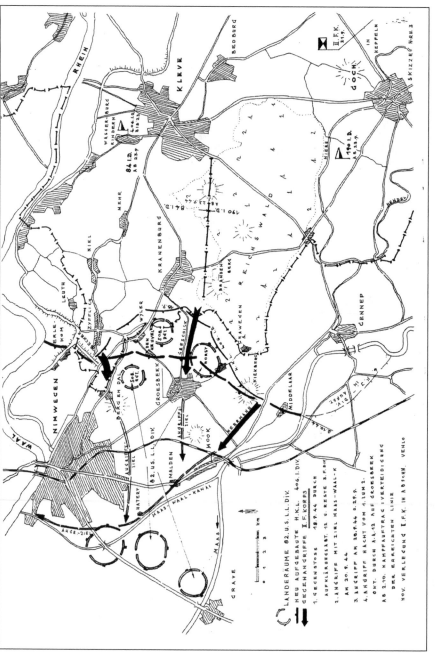

The combat area west of the Rhine; Kleve-Goch-Kalkar-Uedem; the *II Fallschirmjäger-Korps* counterattacks the U.S. 82nd Airborne Division.

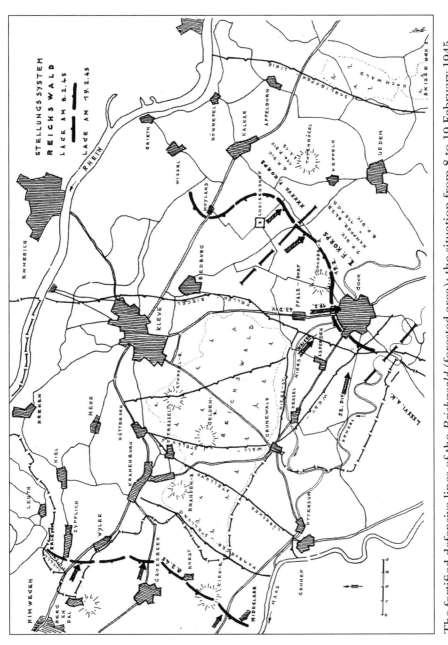

The fortified defensive lines of the *Reichswald* (forested area); the situation from 8 to 19 February 1945.

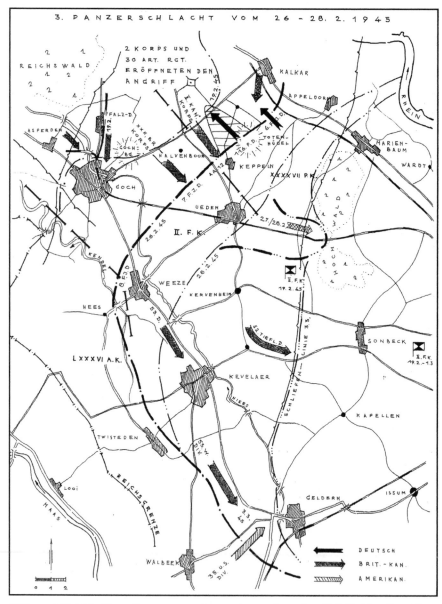

U.S. and British-Canadian armored assaults against the *II Fallschirmjäger-Korps* defense lines from 26 to 28 February 1945.

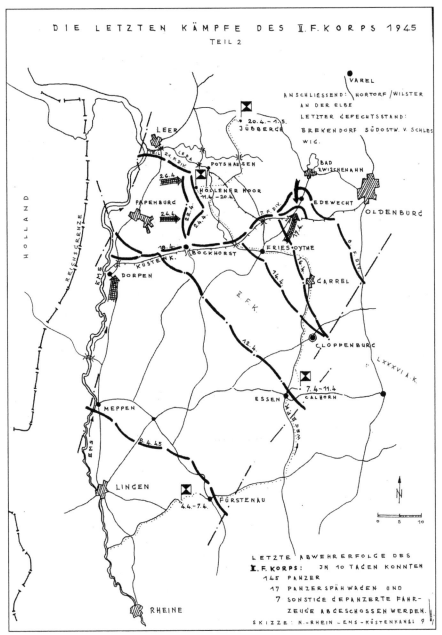

The last battles of the *II Fallschirmjäger-Korps* in April 1945.

Rank Comparisons

U.S. ARMY	BRITISH ARMY	GERMAN ARMY
Enlisted Men		
Private	Private	*Schütze*
Private First Class	Private 1st Class	*Oberschütze*
Corporal	Lance Corporal	*Gefreiter*
Senior Corporal	Corporal	*Obergefreiter*
Staff Corporal		*Stabsgefreiter*
Noncommissioned Officers		
Sergeant	Sergeant	*Unteroffizier*
	Staff Sergeant	*Unterfeldwebel*
Staff Sergeant	Technical Sergeant	*Feldwebel*
Sergeant First Class	Master Sergeant	*Oberfeldwebel*
Master Sergeant	Sergeant Major	*Hauptfeldwebel*
Sergeant Major		*Stabsfeldwebel*
Officers		
Second Lieutenant	Second Lieutenant	*Leutnant*
First Lieutenant	First Lieutenant	*Oberleutnant*
Captain	Captain	*Hauptman*
Major	Major	*Major*
Lieutenant Colonel	Lieutenant Colonel	*Oberst Leutnant*
Colonel	Colonel	*Oberst*
Brigadier General	Brigadier General	*Generalmajor*
Major General	Major General	*Generalleutnant*
Lieutenant General	Lieutenant General	*General der Fallschirmjäger, etc.*
General	General	*Generaloberst*
General of the Army	Field Marshal	*Feldmarschall*

Select Bibliography

PRIMARY SOURCES

Arent, Ernst. *Aus dem Leben meines Bruders.* Unpublished manuscript: 1963.

Arent, Peter. Letters after the fighting. Unpublished: 1941-1943

Barnikol, Dr. H.A. *Kriegserlebnisse in Tunesien.* Unpublished manuscript: ?

Benz, Heinrich. *Das Fallschirmjäger-Regiment 5 in Tunesien.* Unpublished manuscript: 1965.

Böhmler, Rudolf. *General Ludwig Heilmann.* Unpublished manuscript: 1964.

———. *General Richard Heidrich.* Unpublished manuscript: 1964.

Gasteyer, Peter. *Mein Zugführer Peter Arent.* Unpublished manuscript: ?

Genz, Alfred. After-action Reports. Date unknown.

Gericke, Walter. *Sprungeinsatz Monte Rotundo,* Unpublished manuscript: ?

———. Gefechtsbericht des FJR 11. Unpublished manuscript: ?

———. *Im Landekopf Anzio-Nettuno.* Unpublished manuscript: ?

Hambuch, Rudolf. *Einsätze des FJR 5 in Tunesien.* Unpublished manuscript: ?

Heilmann, Ludwig. *Fallschirmjäger auf Sizilien.* Unpublished manuscript: ?

von der Heydte, Prof. Dr. Friedrich-August. After-Action Reports and Orders-of-the-Day. Date unknown.

———. *Der Fehler in der Rechnung Cotentin.* Unpublished manuscript: ?

Jensen, Hans. After-action report of the 1st Platoon of the *1./FJR 5.* Date unknown.

Kerutt, Helmut. After-action reports, sketches and orders. Date unknown.

Knoche, Wilhelm. Contribution to the history of *FJR 5.* Unpublished manuscript: date unknown.

———. *The Wiborgskaja Bridgehead.* Unpublished manuscript: date unknown

Langemeyer, Dr. Carl. *Die Männer mit den blauen Spiegeln.* Unpublished manuscript: ?

Lepkowski, Erich. After-action reports from Korinth, Crete, the Mius Front, Kirowograd and Brest. Date unknown.

Nehm, Heinz. *Zwei Einsätze in Tunesien.* Unpublished manuscript: ?

Nehring, Walther K. Die erste *Phase der Kämpfe in Tunesien.* Unpublished manuscript: ?

Neumann, Dr. Heinrich. *Der Kretaeinsatz des Luftlande-Sturmregiments.* Unpublished manuscript: ?

Ramcke, Bernhard Hermann. Personal information provided to the author. Unpublished manuscript: ?

Ringel, Julius. Personal information provided to the author. Unpublished manuscript: ?

Sauer, Paul. Combat reports of *Kompanie Sauer* in Tunisia. Date unknown.

———. *Kampfgruppe Sauer im Einsatz.* Unpublished manuscript: ?

Schirmer, Gerhard. After-action reports of *FJR 16.* Date unknown.

Schmalz, Wilhelm. *Kampf der Brigade Schmalz auf Sizilien.* Unpublished manuscript: ?

———. *Kampf bei Salerno.* Unpublished manuscript: ?

Schacht, Gerhard. *Die Kämpfge der Gruppe Walther in Südholland.* Unpublished manuscript: ?

Schäfer, Heinrich. *Auf der Kaktus-Farm.* Unpublished manuscript: ?

Schulz, Karl-Lothar. After-action report from Heraklion. Date unknown.

———. Personal information provided to the author. Unpublished manuscript: ?

Schuster, Erich. *Von der Versuchsabteilung zum Sturmregiment.* Unpublished manuscript: ?

———. *Stoßtrupps in Tunesien.* Unpublished manuscript: ?

Student, Kurt. *Memoirs.* Unpublished manuscript: ?

Teusen, Hans. After-action reports and personal information. Unknown date.

Trettner, Heinz. *Werdegang und soldatischer Einsatz als Fallschirmjäger.* Manuscript presented to the author: ?

Volz, Heinz. *Fallschirmjäger-Regiment von Hoffmann.* Unpublished manuscript: ?

Zimmermann, Horst. *Mein Einsatz mit dem II./FJR 5 in Tunesien.* Publication status unknown: ?

SECONDARY SOURCES

Alman, Karl. *Sprung in die Hölle.* Rastatt (Germany): ?, 1964.

Barré, Georges. *Tunisie, 1942-1943.* Paris: ?, 1950.

Bernig, Heinrich. *Hölle Alamein.* Balve (Germany): ?, 1960.

———. *Angriffsziel Festung Europa.* Balve (Germany): ?, 1960.

Benz, Heinrich. *"Unser Peter Arent".* Unknown periodical: 1965.

Bischhaus, Erwin. *"Korinth und Kreta".* Unknown periodical: 1962.

Böhmler, Rudolf. *Monte Cassino.* Darmstadt: ?, 1955.

———. *Fallschirmjäger.* Bad Nauheim: ?, 1960.

Bourgeon, Charles. *Les Carillons sans joie.* Paris: ?, 1959.

Buchner, Alex. *Der deutsche Griechenlandfeldzug.* Heidelberg: ?, 1958.

———. *Schwere Tage bei Rethymnon.* Unknown periodical: 1960.

———. *Gebirgsjäger an allen Fronten.* Hannover: ?, 1954.

Bräuer, Bruno. *Unser Oberst Schulz.* Unknown periodical: 1944.

Bradley, Omar. *A Soldier's Story.* New York: ?, 1964.

Carell, Paul. *Sie kommen.* Oldenburg: ?, 1960.

Cunningham, Admiral. *A Sailor's Odyssey.* London: ?, 1951.

Divine, A. *Road to Tunis.* ?: ?, 1944.

Dobiasch, Sepp and A.H. Farrar-Hockley. *Kurt Student, General der Fallschirmjäger.* Munich: ?, 1983.

Fleckner, Major ?. *Gebirgsjäger auf Kreta.* Berlin: ?, 1942.

Eisenhower, Dwight D. *Kreuzzug in Europa.* Amsterdam: ?, 1948.

Gavin, James M. *Airborne Warfare.* Washington, D.C.: ?, 1947.

Gericke, Walter. *Da gibt es kein zurück.* Münster: ?, 1955.

———. *Fallschirmjäger hier und da.* Berlin: ?, 1941.

Grabler, Josef. *Eine Armee flog durch die Luft.* Unknown periodical: 1955.

Heilmann, Ludwig. *Chania.* Unknown periodical: 1941.

———. *Monte Cassino.* Unknown periodical: 1944.

Heilmann, Grete. *Mein Mann Ludwig Heilmann.* Unpublished manuscript: ?

von der Heydte, Prof. Dr. Friedrich-August. *Daedalus Returned.* London: ?, 1958.

Kurowski, Franz. *Der Kampf um Kreta.* Herford: ?, 1965.

———. *Das Tor zur Festung Europa.* Neckargemünd: ?, 1966.

———. *Brückenkopf Tunesien.* Herford: ?, 1967.

———. *"Fallschirmjäger in Rußland"* (*Parts I-IV*). ?: *Der deutsche Fallschirmjäger,* 1966–1967.

———. *Ihr Stadion ist der Himmel.* Bochum: ?, 1971.

———. *Das Buch der Fallschirmspringer.* Göttingen: ?, 1973.

Madjalany, Fred. *Monte Cassino.* Munich: ?, 1958.

Milch, Werner. *Unser Einmarsch in Rom.* Unknown periodical: ?

Montgomery, Field Marshal Bernard Law. *Memoirs.* London: ?, 1966.

Ramcke, Bernhard Hermann. *Vom Schiffsjungen zum Fallschirmjägergeneral.* Berlin: ?, 1943.

———. *Fallschirmjäger damals und danach.* Frankfurt am Main: ?, 1951.

Rechenberg, Hans. *Stunde der Bewährung: Kreta.* Berlin: ?, 1941.

Richter, R. Peter. *Im Großkampfraum Normandie und Brest.* Unknown periodical: ?

Ringel, Julius. *Hurra die Gams.* Graz (Austria): ?, ?

Robinett, Paul McDonald. *Armor Command.* Washington, D.C.: ?, 1958.

Schubert, Erich. *Erinnerungen an Oberst Bräuer.* Unknown periodical: ?

Schacht, Gerhard. *Eben Emael—10. Mai 1940.* Unknown periodical: ?

Schulz, Karl-Lothar. *So nahmen wir Waalhaven.* Unknown periodical: ?

Seemen, Gerhard von. *Die Ritterkreuzträger 1939–1945.* Friedberg: Podzun-Pallas-Verlag, 1976.

Spencer, John Hall. *Battle for Crete.* London: ?, 1962.

Strassl, Ernst E. *Die Nacht von Galatas.* Berlin: ?, 1941.

Stephanides, Theodore. *Climax in Crete.* London: ?, 1950.

Student, Kurt. *So sahen wir die Kreter.* Unknown periodical: ?

———. *Der Kampf um Rom.* Unknown periodical: ?

———. *Arnhem—Letzter deutscher Erfolg.* Unknown periodical: ?

———. *Die Kapitulation.* Unknown periodical: ?

———. *Die Wahrheit über die Fallschirmtruppe.* Unknown periodical: ?

Winterstein, Martin and Hans Jacobs. *General Meindl und seine Fallschirmjäger.* Braunschweig: ?, ?

Witzig, Rudolf. *Die Einnahme von Eben Emael.* Unknown periodical: 1940.

Acknowledgments

M y special thanks to all former soldiers of the *Fallschirmtruppe*, regardless of rank, who selflessly helped the author to write this book.

In addition, I wish to thank those institutions that have been providing me material for many years: *Zentralbibliothek der Bundeswehr*, *Bundesarchiv/ Militärgeschichtliches Forschungsamt*, *Stadt- und Landesbibliothek Dortmund*, *Verband der ehemaligen Angehörigen der Fallschirmtruppe*, *Bund deutscher Fallschirmjäger e.V.* I would especially like to thank Lieutenant Colonel Brongers, Lieutenant Colonel Leiderdorp and Mr. S.A. Beekman, who provided the Dutch materials, without which I would not have been able to write about the fighting for Fortress Holland and the Palace at Den Haag.

Index